Developing Writers: A Dia

MW00717710

TITLES OF RELATED INTEREST

College Writing Basics: A Progressive Approach, Third Edition,
Thomas E. Tyner (1993)

Composing Through Reading, Second Edition,
Peter Elias Sotiriou (1994)

*Critial Thinking and Writing: A Developing Writer's Guide
with Readings,* Kristan Cavina (1995)

Developing Writers: A Dialogic Approach, Second Edition,
Pamela Gay (1995)

Inside Writing: A Writer's Workbook, Form A, Second Edition,
William Salomone, Stephen McDonald, and Mark Edelstein (1993)

Inside Writing: A Writer's Workbook, Form B, Second Edition,
William Salomone, Stephen McDonald, and Mark Edelstein (1994)

The Language of Learning: Vocabulary for College Success,
Second Edition, Jane N. Hopper and JoAnn Carter-Wells (1994)

Making Connections Through Reading and Writing,
Maria Valeri-Gold and Mary P. Deming (1994)

Patterns and Themes: A Basic English Reader,
Judy R. Rogers and Glenn C. Rogers (1993)

Right Words, Right Places, Scott Rice (1993)

Texts and Contexts: A Contemporary Approach to College Writing,
Second Editions, William S. Robinson and Stephanie Tucker (1995)

Variations: A Rhetoric and Reader for College Writing,
Judy R. Rogers and Glenn C. Rogers (1991)

Writing as a Life-Long Skill, Sanford Kaye (1994)

*Writing Paragraphs and Essays: Integrating Reading, Writing,
and Grammar Skills,* Second Edition, Joy Wingersky, Jan Boerner,
and Diana Holguin-Balogh (1995)

Writing Voyage: A Process Approach to Basic Writing,
Fourth Edition, Thomas E. Tyner (1994)

Writing with Writers, Thomas E. Tyner (1995)

Developing Writers:
A Dialogic Approach

Second Edition

Pamela Gay

Binghamton University, State University of New York

Wadsworth Publishing Company

I(T)P™ **An International Thomson Publishing Company**

Belmont • Albany • Bonn • Boston • Cincinnati • Detroit • London • Madrid • Melbourne
Mexico City • New York • Paris • San Francisco • Singapore • Tokyo • Toronto • Washington

English Editor: Angela Gantner Wrahtz
Assistant Editor: Lisa Timbrell
Editorial Assistant: Kate Peltier
Production : Johnstone Associates
Designer: Leigh McLellan
Print Buyer: Barbara Britton
Copy Editor: Judith Johnstone
Cover Design: Harry Voigt
Cover Art: Carl Heldt, "Echo Canyon," oil on canvas
Compositor: G & S Typesetters
Printer: Arcata Graphics / Fairfield

COPYRIGHT © 1995 by Wadsworth Publishing Company
A Division of International Thomson Publishing Inc.

I(T)P   The ITP logo is a trademark under license.

Printed in the United States of America
  2 3 4 5 6 7 8 9 10—01 00 99 98 97 96 95

For more information, contact Wadsworth Publishing Company:

Wadsworth Publishing Company
10 Davis Drive
Belmont, California 94002, USA

International Thomson Publishing Europe
Berkshire House 168-173
High Holborn
London, WC1V 7AA, England

Thomas Nelson Australia
102 Dodds Street
South Melbourne 3205
Victoria, Australia

Nelson Canada
1120 Birchmount Road
Scarborough, Ontario
Canada M1K 5G4

International Thomson Editores
Campos Eliseos 385, Piso 7
Col. Polanco
11560 México D.F. México

International Thomson Publishing GmbH
Königswinterer Strasse 418
53227 Bonn, Germany

International Thomson Publishing Asia
221 Henderson Road
#05-10 Henderson Building
Singapore 0315

International Thomson Publishing Japan
Hirakawacho Kyowa Building, 3F
2-2-1 Hirakawacho
Chiyoda-ku, Tokyo 102, Japan

All rights reserved. No part of this work covered by the copyright hereon may be reproduced or used in any form or by any means—graphic, electronic, or mechanical, including photocopying, recording, taping, or information storage and retrieval systems—without the written permission of the publisher.

Library of Congress Cataloging-in-Publication Data

Gay, Pamela.
    Developing writers: a dialogic approach / Pamela Gay. — 2nd ed.
      p.   cm
    Includes bibliographical references and index.
    ISBN 0-534-24510-2
    1. English language—Rhetoric.   2. College readers.   I. Title.
PE1408.G358   1995
808'.042—dc20   94-31068
                                                         CIP

This book is printed on acid-free recycled paper.

Developing writers will grow. . . if they are able to write for people who care about language, people who are willing to sit with them and help them as they struggle to write about difficult things.

Mike Rose, Lives on the Boundary

for all the students who have taught me
& for struggling writers everywhere
& for my "only daughter," Angela, a musician

Brief Contents

Contents

Chapter 4   Going to College: Educational Histories   101

Part III   Writing Projects: Becoming Educated/Defining, Analyzing, & Arguing   183

Chapter 5   Becoming Educated   185

Chapter 6   **Reading the News: Questioning
the Word & the World   235**

Appendix   Guidelines for Editing Your Own Writing   351

Preface for Teachers

How can we help our students develop their writing abilities? We can create an environment that enables them to see themselves as writers, and we can provide opportunities for them to be writers—to be writers at work.

Students who use this book are treated as writers. Instead of being victims of their writing backgrounds, they play an active role in their own development by first locating themselves historically as writers. What kind of writing have they done? How has their writing been received? What kinds of problems do they have in writing and editing? From this perspective they can then begin to think about the kind of movement or progress that they would like to make by the end of the course.

What do writers do? They work on writing projects over time. Developing writers need to spend time with each writing project, rather than writing on one topic one week and on another the next. They typically do not engage in the full struggle to articulate their ideas that is necessary to produce an effective piece of writing. Nor do they carry on the necessary conversations with others and with themselves. Sometimes counterproductive voices, based on misconceptions about the nature of writing and how writers work, hinder their development. By having developing writers work on projects and engage in dialogue, this book helps make this struggle a more productive one.

Writers begin each project by writing about what they already know, and then they proceed from there, through reading, talking, listening, reseeing, and rewriting. They keep searching and examining, looking from one angle, then another, and then still another, reconsidering, re-viewing, recreating, and then taking what poet Robert Frost calls "a momentary stay against confusion" in the ongoing conversation. All interpretations are subject to revision or replacement as writers continue to think and rethink and learn. This dialogic approach to writing is dynamic, based not only on students' current interactions with texts and with other students but also on all they've already heard, felt, seen, and read.

Students are invited to try out various perspectives as they work toward a way of looking at or understanding an experience, event, or problem. Dialogue with texts and with other students helps them to think critically and to move naturally back and forth between private and public forums until they are ready to "go public" with the explorations and tentative conclusions they have expressed in writing. Finally, students are guided to reread their writing critically—that is, to have a dialogue with or to question their own texts as they try to anticipate readers' responses to their writing.

Project activities help students write richer texts. This approach encourages them to take increasing responsibility for the development of their writing abilities, a responsibility they will have to assume to a greater extent as they move across the curriculum. This work is exciting because it engages students in their own learning (to write): they write to learn. And learning is what going to college is all about.

The book is divided into three parts and an appendix. Part One gives students some background for working on writing projects. Chapter 1 focuses on the role of attitude in the development of writing abilities. Students examine their writing histories and their misconceptions about the nature of writing and set goals for developing their writing abilities. Chapter 2 helps students understand writing as a way of reading or interpreting the world. They are asked to look, and look again, at objects and to compare their observations and ways of looking. Finally, they are introduced to a method of active reading that shows them how to have a dialogue (reflective conversation) with a text.

In Part Two ("Representing Ourselves: Writing Our Histories"), students are asked to do two writing projects that draw on their own lives. Chapter 3 ("Recollections & Reflections") emphasizes personal histories. It includes published critical reflections by authors from various cultures and ends with guidelines for writing-workshop activities designed to help students write about their own recollections and reflections. Chapter 4 ("Going to College") emphasizes educational histories. Students explore what it means to them to go to college. The readings included help them to place their stories in a larger social context and to reflect more critically on what it means to get an education.

Part Three ("Becoming Educated: Defining, Analyzing, & Arguing") emphasizes definition and analysis and asks students to position themselves or argue for a reading or way of looking. In Chapter 5 ("Becoming Educated"), students explore what it means to become an educated person. How do others define *educated?* What are some issues related to getting an education? Students also have the option of exploring formal and informal education, education and cultural dislocation, women and education, and enrollment issues in education. This chapter can follow Chapter 4 on educational histories or can be used separately. Chapter 6 ("Reading the News") encourages students to question the word and the world. Students carefully examine newspaper articles about events and issues and learn to read critically—finally writing their own analyses and viewpoints. Chapter 7 ("Ethnic Identification") asks students to reflect critically on the problems of ethnic identification in the United States of the 1990s. A specific identification problem is used for collaborative research and as a starting point for individual exploration.

The book ends with an appendix that offers specific guidelines to help students edit their own writing systematically, and practice in getting them used to a system. This resource is, of course, intended for reference and use throughout the writing projects. Systematic editing needs to be introduced early in a course, and students need to practice editing regularly so that they are in a position to edit their final drafts with some degree of success at the end of each project.

Two writing projects are suitable for a semester-long course, with the "Developing Writers" project framing the course. Students could develop project portfolios that include different kinds of writing as well as the end-project writing and a letter/essay about their development as writers mid-course and at the end. This book may be used in one course, or in a sequence of courses, and can be adapted according to the needs and interests of a classroom community. (See suggestions in the Instructor's Edition.)

I would like to thank the reviewers of the first edition for their enthusiastic support: Peter Adams, Essex Community College; Jeannie Campanelli, American River College; Marcia Dickson, The Ohio State University, Marion; Suellyn Duffy, The Ohio State University; Robert Howell, University of North Carolina, Chapel Hill; Geoffrey Sirc, University of Minnesota; Jeff Sommers, Miami University; Lizabeth Wilson, University of Illinois at Urbana-Champaign; Frances Zak, State University of New York, Stony Brook.

I also want to thank these manuscript reviewers of the second edition: Joanne McGurk, Mercyhurst College; Norma L. Gaskey, Jefferson Community College; Peter Dorman, Central Virginia Community College; Susan McCall, American River College; Stella Gildemeister, Palo Alto College; Caroline Stern, Ferris State University; Michael A. Miller, Longview Community College; and Theresa Grupico, Monmouth College.

I want to thank all the students at Binghamton University (State University of New York) who gave me permission to use their work and whom I have cited by name in this text. I'd like to acknowledge the Educational Opportunity Program that made "going to college" possible for some of these students. Deborah Folaron, of the Translation Research and Instruction Program, kindly checked the Spanish portions of this text. I'd also like to thank graduate teaching assistants who tried out some of this new material and gave me suggestions.

I especially want to thank Sharon Fellows for talking with me about new writing projects from the perspective of a classroom "teacher at work" and for her work on the Instructor's Edition.

Wadsworth provided a fine book "producer" in Judy Johnstone, who was meticulous, caring, and energetic about this book project.

And, again, I'm grateful for my editor Angie Gantner's continuing support and her belief that I have a contribution to make.

Finally, in this edition I hope I have moved closer to Ann Berthoff's response to the personal/academic "killer" dichotomy: "The way to bridge the gap between personal and academic writing is never to separate them in the first place."

Pamela Gay

Part I

Introduction to the Writing Projects

Writing is learned by writing, by reading, and by perceiving oneself as a writer.
Frank Smith

1 Developing Your Writing Ability

Writing is something writers are always learning to do.

Mina Shaughnessy

I talk to myself. That's what writers do. We carry on a constant dialogue between language and hands and images, one or another of our identities trying desperately to get in a word, an image, a sound.

Gloria Anzuldúa
Making Face, Making Soul

Being a Writer

Writers usually work on a piece of writing over some period of time. Each piece of writing is, in a sense, a project. Writers go about their work in various ways, but all writers engage in the process of searching and re-searching to make meaning or to arrive at what they want to say. The movement is to and fro, back and forth, like dialogue. Writing is a social activity, even when a writer sits alone writing.

In a sense, a writer is never writing alone. Writers talk over ideas with themselves, one self to another. Frequently, they engage in dialogue not only with themselves but also with the texts they are reading. They may talk with others about their ideas or ask for a response to their writing. Writers look and look again, trying out various ways of looking, finally creating a text or piece of writing that draws on all they've seen, heard, felt, and read. A writing project is completed through reading, writing, thinking, talking, and listening, and then through more writing and rewriting. This interactive process—this extended conversation or dialogue—I describe as "dialogic."

The writing projects included in this book will engage you in this dialogic process. Each project includes an end-project or final piece of writing toward which you work all along. Some additional or project-related writing opportunities are also included. Each project begins where you are and encourages you to push your thinking and writing further. You will learn to:

1. observe closely and critically.
2. reflect, interpret, and analyze.
3. read your own writing critically; that is, talk with yourself about your writing so that you can begin to imagine reader responses.
4. work collaboratively with other writers so that they can learn to resee their writing.

3

5. go through the full struggle of writing and thinking, finally presenting the product of your process.

This is exciting work. The ways of writing, thinking, and knowing that you will learn through this dialogic process will help you both learn to write and write to learn your way across the curriculum.

The "Developing Writer" Assessment Project

As you move through the college curriculum, you will need to take increasing responsibility for the development of your writing abilities. This ongoing project will help you begin to take charge of your writing. To maximize your development in this course, it would be helpful for you from the start to assess your strengths and weaknesses as a writer, to look at your story or past as a writer, and to set some goals. The following activities will help you begin to think about yourself as a writer.

Seeing Yourself as a Writer

Take out a piece of notebook paper now and write an informal response to this question: How do you see yourself as a writer? If you are writing with a word processor, create a new file (perhaps entitled "Self Writer"); or, if you have access to electronic mail, write and send your response electronically. Whatever your writing tool or medium, do not worry about grammar, punctuation, spelling, or organization when you do this writing. Write person-to-person or, better still, writer-to-writer to your writing instructor. Your writing will not be read aloud but will be read by your instructor, who is interested in what you have to say.

Read the following excerpts from responses written by other developing writers:

"I'm not sure if I am a good writer or a bad writer."

"I would like to think of myself as a writer who hasn't come into age yet."

"I've never enjoyed writing."

"I can't seem to produce a good quality of writing."

"I'm just an OK writer."

"I can't get started."

"I'm a confused writer."

"The path from my mind to my hand is filled with pitfalls, potholes, and loopholes."

"I feel uncomfortable, like a worm in a puddle."

"I've never really thought of myself as a writer."

Then read this complete (unedited) response:

Edgar Allen Poe, Emily Dickinson, Mark Twain, and Patti Fervan. Somehow that doesn't quite fit. When one thinks of a writer one thinks of the great minds of the era although in fact all of us are writers. My main drawback as a writer is the fact that I was never truly educated in this aspect of English. Somewhere along the way I missed the grammar, punct. and language skills and simply sharpened my mathematic skills. To see me writing is to see a pile of books and papers with an occasional grunt and groan floating from the middle.

Patti Fervan

Edgar Allan Poe, Emily Dickinson, Mark Twain, and Patti Fervan. Somehow that doesn't quite fit. When one thinks of a writer one thinks of the great minds of the era although in fact all of us are writers. My main drawback as a writer is the fact that I was never truly educated in this aspect of English. Somewhere along the way I missed the grammar, punct. and language skills and simply sharpened my mathematic skills. To see me writing is to see a pile of books and papers with an occasional grunt and groan floating from the middle.

Patti Fervan

What do these writers have in common? What do you have in common with them? How do you differ in your attitude?

Writing a Time Line & a Writing History

What kind of writing have you been doing and how much? What's the last writing you did and when? To answer these questions, make a *time line* of your writing. What have you written most recently? A letter? A list? Directions? An application? An essay exam? What kind of nonschool writing do you do, if any? Think back to high school, if you are a recent graduate. What kind of writing did you do during your senior year? As you go further back in time, you'll need to trigger your memory. Thinking of a teacher's name or a particular subject or some event that occurred in a specific grade may help you tap your memories, especially those of your elementary school years.

Look at one college student's (Bernard's) writing time line, and then read the beginning of his writing history.

Bernard's Writing Time Line

Most recent writing: A writing sample placement test on the question: Should athletes receive special treatment when fulfilling academic requirements?

Nonschool writing: Letters to friends and relatives who live in different states. My last letter was to my grandmother about a week ago, but normally I write when I miss someone.

School writing:
College—I wrote a paper in geology for extra credit.

12th grade—I wrote a term paper on Martin Luther King, Jr. and another one on Jackie Robinson.

11th grade—I didn't write any papers. I did reading assignments.

10th grade—I wrote an essay about my parents.

Bernard's Writing History

When writing was first introduced to me, I had to learn what all kids learn—the fundamentals of basic grammar. I was like everybody else learning to write. First, I had to learn the difference between a capital letter and a lowercase letter. Once I was able to master the letters, then came the hard part. I had to form those letters into words and transform those words into sentences. I was soon completing elementary schooling. I felt I was ready to take my writing skills to a higher level. Throughout my junior high school days, I would write without any serious purpose. Writing was something I did only when it was assigned for me to do so. I can recall back in the tenth grade I had to write an essay about my parents. I remember that essay . . . .

Review your notes and then write about your writing history—your story as a writer. Label it "My Writing History" and begin writing. Then get into a small discussion group and exchange stories about your writing backgrounds. You'll be meeting in small groups during the writing projects and talking about your ongoing work; talking about your writing backgrounds is a good starting point for the work ahead.

Examining Misconceptions About Writing

What misconceptions do you have about the way experienced writers work and about the nature of writing? Review the following lists of common misconceptions and the accompanying revised beliefs ("The Truth").

Common Misconceptions About Experienced Writers	*"The Truth"*
Good writers do not struggle.	All writers struggle; writing is work.
Good writers know "The Way" to write.	Good writers know the way they write. There are many ways of writing.
Good writers know what they want to say before they write.	Good writers often write to learn what they want to say.
Good writers write perfect copy the first time.	Good writers usually rewrite many times.

Common Misconceptions About the Nature of Writing	*"The Truth"*
Writing is an ordered, step-by-step process.	Writing is a to-and-fro process.
Writing involves directly transferring thoughts from the mind to paper.	Writing is a complex process. Thoughts don't automatically transfer.
Writing is an individual act; writers work alone.	Writing is a social act in the sense that writers draw on everything they have read, seen, heard, or known.

Make some notes about your own misconceptions or erroneous beliefs about how writers work and the nature of writing. Write down any misconceptions you would like to discuss or any questions you have. Discuss these misconceptions and "truths" in class and then write about your discussion.

What did you talk about? What misconceptions did other students have? Relate the discussion back to yourself as a writer, to your writing process, and to your understanding of the nature of writing.

Monitoring Your Writing Progress

Keep a "Developing Writer" project file and add to it as you progress through this course and work on various projects. Place your start-of-the-course writing about yourself as a writer, your writing about the nature of writing, and your writing history in this file. Throughout the process of working on a writing project, continue to write about yourself as a writer. What problems did you have writing a particular piece? What worked well? Periodically—perhaps at the end of a writing project or chapter—stop and assess your writing performances and progress and then set new goals. How do you see yourself as a writer in the middle of this course? If you are writing in other courses, assess your writing performances in them, too. When you make notes about your development as a writer, cite specific examples from your own writing. Continue this assessment throughout the course, finally ending with an essay about your development as a writer. Look back at what you wrote at the start of this course. How have you progressed or changed as a writer? What are your strengths? How could you improve? What are your goals now?

2 Reading & Writing the World & the Word

[A]ll human beings read the world: we all make sense of our experience, construing and constructing and representing it by means of language.

Ann Berthoff's reading of Paulo Freire's "pedagogy of knowing"

You're the only person in the gene-pool with your possible set of experiences, perceptions, pleasures, tortures, difficulties in getting the work done. Those things are unique, and if you fail to write those down in the best possible way and leave them for us, we'll never have them.

William Matthews

Some people (literary and visual artists and philosophers, for example) spend considerable energy trying to make meaning or interpret (or read) what they see. But all of us try to make some sense of our lives. We observe, reflect, and interpret. We look and then reflect on our looking. We see through our self-selective lenses. What we see (or don't see) depends upon who is doing the viewing.

Each one of us is different; no two of us ever have the same experience. If each of us observed the "same" event, we would record it differently: it would not be exactly the same event. We each have different readings or understandings of events. In everyday conversation, we may hear (or say), "Oh, I didn't see it that way at all. I thought . . ." In writing, we often record our readings or renderings of an event; we offer our perspective or our expertise. It's important that we record some of our experiences and interpretations: our stories, our compositions.

Take and make your own notes now. (For an explanation of note*taking* and note*making,* see pp. 18–19.) Copy the quotation in the margin by Dorothea Brande. (Copying a sentence or even a whole paragraph slows you down, makes you pay attention, and helps you make meaning. Meaning is not something you find; you create meaning through your own interactions or dialogue with the text you are reading.)

What meaning do you make of the sentence you just copied? What do you think this writer is saying? Begin by writing, "I think she's saying that . . ." Talk with others about what you wrote and about reading (and writing) the world.

It is well to understand as early as possible in one's writing life that there is just one contribution which every one of us can make; we can give into the common pool of experience some comprehension of the world as it looks to each of us.

Dorothea Brande,
Becoming a Writer

Looking (Really Looking)

"Shall I say 'nothing happened today?' " asked Virginia Woolf in the beginning of a diary entry (1915). "It wouldn't be true," she was quick to add. She decided to "talk" about a "vague kind of discomfort caused by the eccentric character of the new servant Maud." How did Woolf come to think of Maud as eccentric? "When one speaks to her," Woolf wrote, "she stops dead and looks at the ceiling. She bursts into the room, 'just to see if you are there.' "

The day is rather like a leafless tree: there are all sorts of colors in it if you look closely.

The Diary of Virginia Woolf, 1915

She "never stays long in any place" and "puts down plates with a start." Woolf, trying to make sense of Maud's behavior, speculates that she "lives in dread of something." Woolf moved from observation to reflection and a possible interpretation or reading that she might later reread. She talks with herself about Maud through writing.

Looking (really looking) goes beyond simply taking in or receiving what you see. Critical reflection requires you to participate in the viewing by engaging in an inner dialogue or conversation that we call thinking—to think and think again, reviewing until you can position yourself, holding firm your vision (or version) at least for the moment. (The "moment" might be a deadline.) The "text" you read could be anything in your world, from a character like Maud to a book of words.

In the next section, you'll practice sharpening your powers of observation and recording your readings, first of a natural object and then of a painting. Even though we read or interpret things differently because of who we are—because of our unique experiences—we can also read from different viewpoints. We can read as an artist, a scientist, a philosopher, a sociologist, or a feminist, for example. And, of course, not all artists, scientists (and so on down the list) would "read" alike. You'll get some practice changing points of view here, enough to introduce you to the concept. Finally, you'll be introduced to an active reading method I call "Reader's Dialogue" that you'll be asked to use in the writing projects that follow. With some practice you'll come to read (and write) "the word" as you already do the world.

Reading a Natural Object

Scientific Viewing & Writing

Looking: Making First Observations

It is very difficult to observe and describe accurately even simple phenomena.

W. I. B. Beveridge

Observation is not passively watching but is an active mental process.

W. I. B. Beveridge

Study a natural object (a flower, leaf, weed, or fruit) in class. A common daisy will serve as the object (or subject) of study here, but you could make a substitution according to what is available in your area or of interest to your particular group. (I have used black-eyed Susans and Valencia oranges, for example.) Select a daisy for observation, and study it. Instead of taking a quick look at the daisy and taking notes immediately, look and look again without writing. Take time to see. Observe its size, weight, shape, texture, color, smell, and perhaps its taste.

Comparing Observations with Others

Read your description to another observer in your class. You may want to work with a partner. (For random pairing, count off by the total number of students in class divided by two. For example, if you have eighteen students in your class, count to nine and repeat. Then the Ones can be partners, the Twos partners, and so on, until nine groups of two are formed.)

Read your description aloud while your partner holds or looks at the subject of your observation. Ask your observation partner for comments: Is any information missing? Could your description be more accurate? If so, how? Then have your partner take the lead and repeat the activity.

Next, place your flower and your partner's side by side and compare them: How are they alike? How are they different? Did you count the petals in each case? Does each flower have the same number? Did you estimate the length of the petals, the diameter of the center, the height of the stem? Are the centers similar? Is one flatter than the other? How would you distinguish between the two? Take more notes.

Looking Again: Scientific Viewing

Scientific observation of objects calls for the closest possible scrutiny, if necessary with the aid of a lens.

W.I.B. Beveridge

Now look at your flower through a magnifying glass. Take more notes. Look at your partner's flower again and then look at your flower yet again. Take still more notes.

Collaborative Re-Viewing

Powers of observation can be developed by cultivating the habit of watching things with an active, enquiring mind.

W.I.B. Beveridge

Join another pair of observers and talk about the differences you found and how the four flowers might be distinguished. Perhaps look at all four through a magnifying glass. Take more notes. Read what one writer wrote after reviewing a flower.

Writer at Work: Kelly-Ann Chung

This flower has thirty-eight whitish-yellow petals that surround the core of the flower. Each petal is approximately a quarter of an inch long and a little less wide. Each petal consists of stemlike veins running along its center. At their base, they are pointed and make tiny holes in the core. The petals also have shades of green at their base.

The core, which is approximately one-half of an inch across, consists of tiny yellow-green grains that come together to form the circular shape of the core. On the outer part of the core the seedlike grains tend to be high and they stick out and have a yellow shade. On the inner part, these grains are shorter and have a lighter yellow shade.

Underneath the petals there is a green section enclosing the base of the petals, which resembles tiny green petals that are not yet mature.

The stem is about 15 cm long and 2 mm wide. It has different shades of green and yellow. The stem has veins that go down the length of the stem. It also has four leaves and each leaf is unique. And just like the petals, each leaf has veins running along its middle. They have a peculiar shape. They have approximately four thornlike projections on either side; and as we go down the stem, the leaves get larger and longer.

Revising

Outside class, rewrite your description to improve accuracy and clarity. Work from your notes.

Optional Research & Writing

1. You could review the parts of a typical flower, using a biology textbook, encyclopedia, or other resource. Use scientific terms when possible. For example, instead of writing about the flower's center or "core," use the proper scientific term. Does your flower have a corolla? Are the sepals and petals identical? Is your flower a representative (typical) flower: does it have all the parts? When you rewrite your description, include the names of the parts and comment briefly about how the flower you observed is like or unlike the typical flower. You may also want to comment on the function of a part. Cite the source you used. Then briefly compare your revised description with your original description. Cite specific examples (of your use of language, for example) to illustrate the differences.

2. You could also research the flower's story. What is its place in the plant kingdom? Look up the scientific classification of the flower you observed. What is the scientific name of this flower? In what family does this flower belong? What is the "proper name" of the composite family? How many other flowers belong to this family? What are the names of some of them? Name some other kinds of daisies. Draw a partial family tree if you like. What does the scientific name of this flower mean? Does it go by any other common names? Each month is associated with a particular flower; for what month is the daisy the "flower of the month"? Find out what you can about different attitudes toward the daisy. How do some farmers, for example, view the daisy? Write a brief report of your findings, citing your source or sources.

Creative Viewing & Writing

Still—in a way—
nobody sees a
flower—really—
it is so small—
we haven't time—
and to see takes time
like to have a friend
takes time.

Georgia O'Keeffe

Georgia O'Keeffe wanted people to notice flowers. She knew that if she painted the flower exactly as she saw it, no one would see what she saw because she would "paint it small like the flower is small." So she said to herself: "I'll paint it big and they will be surprised into taking time to look at it—"[1]

Stop now and, if possible, look at her painting *Jimson Weed* in *One Hundred Flowers*. Then read what O'Keeffe wrote about this weed, which has a beautiful flower:

> The first Jimson weed I saw was blooming between the first two steps of a ladder at Puye Pueblo. I have had it growing near my house in Abiquiu for many years and I have painted it many times. It is a beautiful white trumpet flower with strong veins that hold the flower open and grow longer than the round part of the flower—twisting as they grow off beyond it. In the tropics where the plant grows almost to the size of a small tree these ribs sometimes curl an inch and a half beyond the flowers and the blossoms droop instead of looking

1. "About Myself," 1939, in *One Hundred Flowers*, Nicholas Callaway (ed.). New York: Knopf, 1989.

out at you. Some of them are a pale green in the center—some a pale Mars violet. The Jimson weed blooms in the cool of the evening—one moonlit night at the Ranch I counted one hundred and twenty-five flowers. The flowers die in the heat of the day. Don Juan speaks of uses the Yaqui Indians make of the Jimson weed that almost make one afraid. When I found that they are poisonous, I dug them up but in Abiquiu a few keep on growing persistently. Now when I think of the delicate fragrance of the flowers, I almost feel the coolness and sweetness of evening.

This paragraph appeared opposite her painting of a Jimson weed. How would you describe her writing here? What kind of language does she use to describe this flower? To what extent is she objective? Subjective? Cite words, phrases, or lines from her text. Would her writing here be appropriate in a biology class? Is this writing effective as a commentary accompanying her view (her painting) of the Jimson weed?

Now look at the flower you observed from another point of view. Instead of recording information objectively, as a scientist would, look at the flower subjectively. Let the flower become your flower and use it as a starting point for some creative writing. What are your impressions of this flower? What are your associations? What do you see in (or, to borrow from artist Judy Chicago, "through") the flower? You could work with a metaphor: My flower looks like. . . . One student (Kelly-Ann Chung) thought about how her flower must feel (like "a lonely child"):

When I look at my flower, I see a lonely child who has been separated from the world. And this child has needs. This child has the need to be clothed, the need to be fed, the need to have companionship, and the need to be loved.

For as long as this child is alone, there will be the need. For it won't be too long before he'll outgrow his clothes, he'll get hungry, he'll find the need for company, and he'll have the need to be loved.

For this child is a lovely child. He is an example of beauty, of peace, of joy. He is like a golden child. He is given to this world to help us see, to help us care, and to help us love.

Another student (Ricardo Sewell) wrote a poem in which his flower was like a high-rise office building competing in the sky with other buildings.

Begin writing about your flower and see where the writing leads you. See if an image comes to mind, or some comparison or some idea or a poem. If you like, read your writing to your small group and perhaps share one or two creative viewpoints with the whole class.

Optional Research & Writing

Look at other impressions of flowers by Georgia O'Keeffe. For example, see her *Jack-in-the-Pulpit* in six (magnified) parts in her book *One Hundred Flowers* (1989).

Compare two studies of the "same" flower by two different painters. You could compare, for example, Georgia O'Keeffe's representation of flowers with Charles Demuth's flower studies. If you are observing a daisy, compare Demuth's *Daisies* (1918) and *African Daisies* (1925) with O'Keeffe's *Yellow Hickory Leaves with Daisy* (1928).

It may be interesting to compare Vincent van Gogh's and Claude Monet's different views of the sunflower, which is in the same family as the daisy. See also Georgia O'Keeffe's *Sunflower, New Mexico, II* (1935). There are many possibilities. Make a trip to a fine arts library or to the art section of any library and look through some art books.

Reading a Painting

Look at the photograph of an untitled painting by developing writer and painter Martin Molina (Plate 1, opposite page 172).

Viewing

Study the painting for five minutes. Observe carefully. When the time is up, close your book.

Recording Your Observations

What did you notice? What do you remember? What comes to mind? Make a list of what you observed. Do not write a reaction or give your impressions; just list what you saw (colors, shapes, objects, and so on).

Re-Viewing & Comparing Observations

Look at the painting again. Review your notes. What did you miss? Did you distort anything? Compare your list with lists made by other observers. Look more closely now at the painting and take more notes. Write a brief comparison of your viewing and re-viewing experience.

Interpreting What You See

What title would you give this painting? What do you make of it? What do you think this painting is about? How do you read this painting?

Write about the title you gave this painting. Use some of your notes (the "facts" of the painting) to show your readers how you arrived at this title or came to view the painting in this particular way. How do the notes you took connect with your impression of the painting?

Sharing Your Reading (Interpretation) with Others

Share your reading (impression or interpretation) of Martin Molina's painting with other observers in your class. Are the readings similar? Did almost everyone who viewed this painting have the same view, or were there a variety of readings? Are some readings better than others, or are they all equally valid? What makes for a good reading or rendering of this visual event?

Readers at Work

Figure 2.1 shows one student's associations with Martin's painting and the title she suggested. To get started, this writer tried writing down and stringing together words she associated with the painting. Instead of making a "shopping list," she used a more visual form (sometimes called a *cluster, map,* or *web*). She then wrote quickly, trying to come up with a title, and shared her reading in class.

"Talking about the painting made me see more than my eyes could see," one student commented after listening to several different ways of looking at Martin's painting. In this excerpt, a student (Cynthia Tsui) begins to explain her reading of Martin's painting.

I would give Martin's painting the title "The New Frontier." When I saw his painting, the first thing that I felt was a strong sense of a new beginning. The colors that dominated the painting's background are yellow and other yellow-based colors such as orange and brown. These colors suggested to me that it was the time of sunrise. The yellow object located at the top-right corner of the painting represents the sun that is giving this space the burst of brightness and energy.

Everything in this painting suggests advancement . . .

Another student (Lisette E. Andrades) wrote a letter to the painter.

Dear Mr. Molina:

I just recently saw your painting in class and I find it quite interesting. I was wondering if this is your first painting. If not, do all your paintings look similar to this one, concerning space? When I was looking at your painting I imagined what the painting was saying. At first it confused me to see so many different objects, but as I kept on looking I figured out what this painting could mean.

To me this painting was focused on space because I saw stars, circles, the sun, etc. I noticed an erupted hole located on the top left-hand corner of this painting. And through this hole I saw another small circle that looked distant. I concluded this to be Earth. There was also a white, oval-shaped object coming towards the erupted hole. I concluded this to be a missile.

I pictured this painting to be dealing with Earth shooting a missile to another planet in the sky and this is what caused the hole to erupt. And within this erupted hole is what this planet contains inside. I was able to see what was inside of this planet. You may or may not see what I am trying

Figure 2.1

Martin's painting really reaches into my mind and pulls out a memory I had of my art class in my senior year in high school. I had an art teacher named Mrs. M. She was great. I loved being in her class. She was different from other teachers I had in art. She would teach a lesson and let you develop your own ideas. And she taught a few lessons on abstraction. Martin's painting reminded me of those lessons. His painting is abstract. When I saw his painting, I wanted to go back and start painting again. I would call Martin's painting "Abstraction."   (Julie) Ping Hung Leung

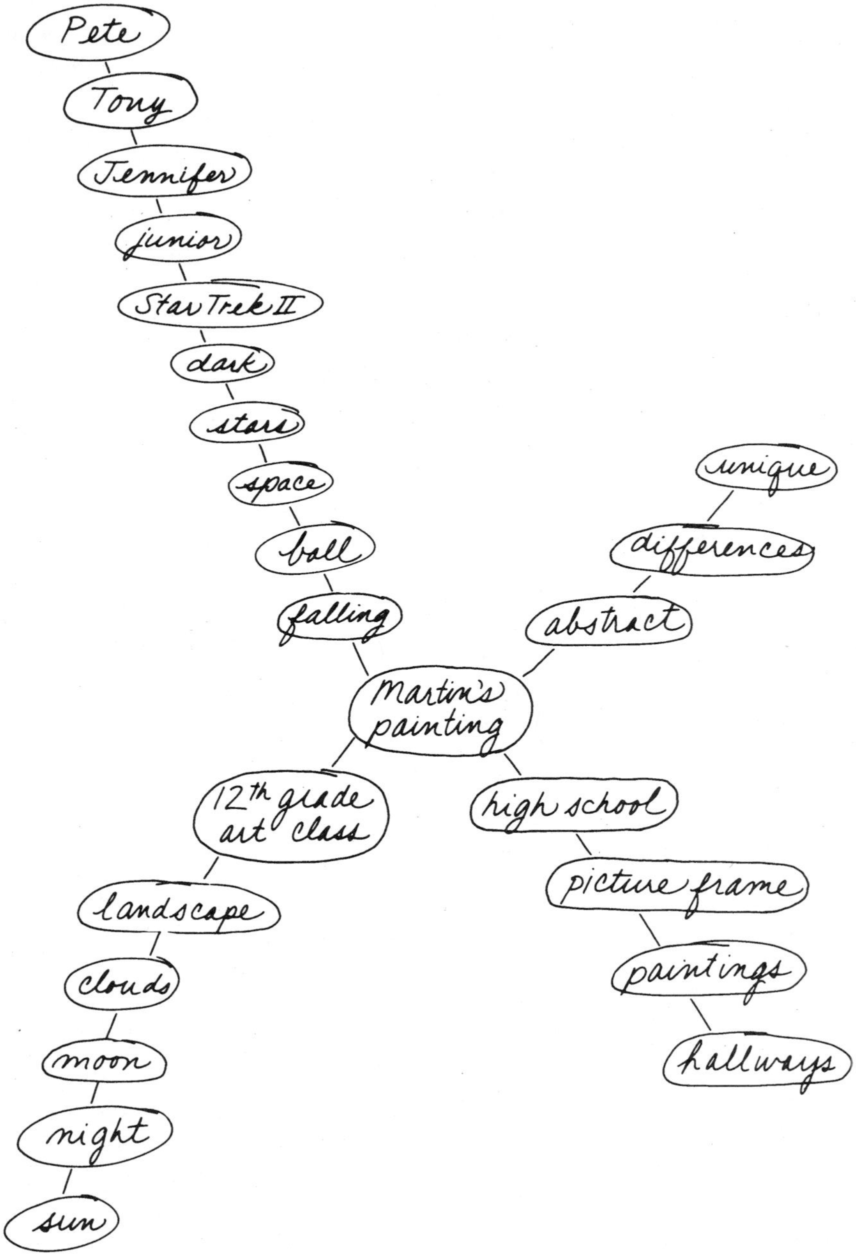

Pete
Tony
Jennifer
junior
Star Trek II
dark
stars
space
ball
falling
Martin's painting
unique
differences
abstract
high school
picture frame
paintings
hallways
12th grade art class
landscape
clouds
moon
night
sun

to say. You may also not agree with me, but this is what I concluded this untitled painting to be saying. I was, though, curious to know what all those triangle-shaped figures meant. It looked like some kind of dimension that if you stepped into it, it would take you to another world.

Lisette E. Andrade

Reading & Reflecting

Each writing project in this textbook includes a number of project-related readings. Why read? Why not go directly to the end-project writing and write and revise? The readings will help you become engaged in a writing project and move you toward what you finally decide to write about. Some of the writing based on your reading can also stand alone. Besides offering different perspectives or ways of reading the world, the readings also suggest various ways you can frame or shape your own writing: There is more than one way to write a memoir or essay. You will be asked to read each reading selection in a writing project twice and to take and make notes during your second reading. This section introduces the concept of active reading and a method I call "Reader's Dialogue." Guidelines for rereading and making Reader's Dialogue notebook entries also follow each reading selection in a writing project.

Active Reading

Have you ever read something but couldn't remember what you read? You read the words and could say you did the reading assignment, but you hoped no one would ask you to talk or write about what you read. What happened while you were reading? Little activity happened! You read passively rather than actively. In other words, you did not engage or involve yourself in the reading process; you did not give the text a critical reading. When you just go through the motions of reading, you give a "readerless" reading just as a writer produces "writerless" writing by going through the motions of writing, stringing one word after another without being engaged in the writing/thinking process.

Sometimes a passive reading is desirable. Sometimes you don't want to think while you are reading. You just want to read words, letting in an image or phrase here and there. This is a kind of relaxed reading, not work, and it may serve as a break from the kind of critical reading you are asked to do in school. Passive reading is like watching TV. But for college work, you need to develop and use your critical reading ability—you need to be a reader alive.

Here are three advantages to active reading:

1. Paying attention to the way an effective piece of writing turned out—paying attention to a writer's beginning, to the shape of a text, to the sounds and rhythm, and to the movement (the dance) of words—will help you discover the range of possibilities for creating a piece of writing, will help you make decisions as a writer, and will encourage you to try different ways of writing (or perhaps even create a new way).

2. Learning to read actively—to be a questioning, reflective reader—will help you become both an effective reviewer or reader of writing produced by members of your writing community and a better, more critical reader of your own writing.

3. Active reading may also get you started thinking about an idea you want to pursue.

 ## Reader's Dialogue

Having a dialogue or conversation with the text you are reading will get you into the act of reading; it will enable you to become an active reader. Reader's dialogue is a method of recording your active reading process.

How to Have a Dialogue with a Text

Ideas come out of the dialogue we sustain with others and with ourselves.

Mina Shaughnessy

Fold a sheet of looseleaf paper in half or, if you want more room, use two sheets of paper side by side. For large projects, you may want to use facing pages in a separate notebook. If you are writing with a word processor, you may be able to split the screen in two. Whatever you use—sheets of paper, a notebook, or a word processor—make double entries concerning your reading (see Figure 2.2).

After you have taken some notes on the right side (perhaps a page of notes or notes on a section of the reading), stop, read over the notes you took, reflect, and make notes: What meaning do you make of what you read? When you are note*making* and find yourself writing and wanting to continue, go to

Figure 2.2

NOTE*MAKING*	NOTE*TAKING*
Use the left side (of the page or screen for note*making*—making notes about your notes: summaries, reactions, impressions, associations triggered by your reading, critical reflections, interpretations (of a quotation you noted, for example), and questions.	Use the right side for note*taking*—observational notes, fragments, lists, images, direct quotations.

another full page or computer screen and keep writing; then return to the reading and take and make more notes.

When you copied the quotation by Dorothea Brande earlier, you were doing a form of *notetaking* (copying a direct quotation). Then, when you wrote what you thought she was saying—when you paraphrased or put the quotation in your own words—you were doing a kind of *notemaking.*

Learn about and perhaps experiment with different kinds of notetaking and notemaking. Notetaking can include writing down direct quotations, words, fragments, lists, definitions, explanations, and other information. Perhaps bring to class some recent lecture or reading notes you took for another class. What kind of notes did you take? Try making some notes from a section of the notes you took. What kind of notemaking is appropriate for these notes? If your notes came from a biology lecture, for example, how can notemaking help you learn? Try summarizing part of your notes and perhaps raising a question. What confuses you? What might you need to look up in a book? Your notemaking should vary according to your purpose. Good notemaking will enhance your learning in all disciplines.

Suggestions for Further Reading

Ormsby, Eric. 1990. "Conch Shell," *The New Yorker,* January 15, 44–45.

Scudder, Samuel H. 1990. "Take This Fish and Look at It," *The Critical Eye,* Sally H. Taylor (ed.). Orlando, FL: Holt, Rinehart & Winston.

Part II

Writing Projects: Representing Ourselves— Writing Our Histories

Writing is not apart from living. Writing is a kind of double living. The writer experiences everything twice. Once in reality and once more in that mirror which waits always before or behind him [or her].

Catherine Drinker Bowen

3 Recollections & Reflections: Stories from Our Lives

A story is, first of all, a composition, a construct. It is a way of ordering, shaping, interpreting events. Stories do not happen "out there"; we shape stories as a means of representing the world to ourselves and to others. In this sense, all narratives are fictions; there is no one true story.

Judith Summerfield and
Geoffrey Summerfield, *Texts & Contexts*

During the course of this writing project you will read the published recollections and reflections of many writers, all of whom compose their stories and frame their experiences in different ways. And you will learn to have a dialogue with the writing (the writer/the text) you are reading. You will be asked to look at an event from various points of view and to compare and contrast experiences. Finally, you will have an opportunity to tell a story—to write imaginatively and critically about an event or events in your own life. The work of some developing writers at various points in their composing processes is also included. You can end this project with your own recollections and reflections, or you can continue by reading one or more published works that you can use as springboards for additional writing. Some suggestions for further reading are included at the end of this chapter.

Why "Recollections & Reflections"? This project requires you to move beyond telling what happened. You will be asked to interpret what happened—not by writing an analysis, but through what you choose to tell and how you shape your recollections. This project is a good starting point for understanding the project method and the dialogic approach. Writing-workshop guidelines are provided to assist you with your end-project writing.

Although you should not try to generate ideas and edit for mechanical and grammatical problems at the same time, strive to develop editing skills so that you will be able to edit writing that you plan to submit for evaluation. It is important to practice editing regularly during a project and throughout a course. See the appendix, "Guidelines for Editing Your Own Writing," to develop an editing plan.

Consider compiling a writing project portfolio of varied writings—sample notebook entries, both critical and creative, for example—as well as drafts of your end-project writing. Perhaps as a class you can decide what work to include in a project portfolio. How can you represent your development as a writer? You could include your problems as a writer as well as your successes. How have you progressed? What do you need or want to work on? You could write a letter-essay to your instructor about portfolio selection and specifically about your development as a writer and editor. This self-evaluation could be part of a collaborative evaluation process between you and your writing teacher-consultant.

My Name

Sandra Cisneros

Told in a series of vignettes, Sandra Cisneros' The House on Mango Street *is the story of Esperanza Cordero, "a young girl growing up in the Hispanic quarter of Chicago." In this brief selection, Esperanza tells her story of her name.*

In English my name means hope. In Spanish it means too many letters. It means sadness, it means waiting. It is like the number nine. A muddy color. It is the Mexican records my father plays on Sunday mornings when he is shaving, songs like sobbing. 1

It was my great-grandmother's name and now it is mine. She was a horse woman too, born like me in the Chinese year of the horse—which is supposed to be bad luck if you're born female—but I think this is a Chinese lie because the Chinese, like the Mexicans, don't like their women strong. 2

My great-grandmother. I would've liked to have known her, a wild horse of a woman, so wild she wouldn't marry. Until my great-grandfather threw a sack over her head and carried her off. Just like that, as if she were a fancy chandelier. That's the way he did it. 3

And the story goes she never forgave him. She looked out the window her whole life, the way so many women sit their sadness on an elbow. I wonder if she made the best with what she got or was she sorry because she couldn't be all the things she wanted to be. Esperanza. I have inherited her name, but I don't want to inherit her place by the window. 4

At school they say my name funny as if the syllables were made out of tin and hurt the roof of your mouth. But in Spanish my name is made out of a softer something, like silver, not quite as thick as sister's name—Magdalena—which is uglier than mine. Magdalena who at least can come home and become Nenny. But I am always Esperanza. 5

I would like to baptize myself under a new name, a name more like the real me, the one nobody sees. Esperanza as Lisandra or Maritza or Zeze the X. Yes. Something like Zeze the X will do. 6

From *The House on Mango Street.* Copyright © 1984 by Sandra Cisneros. Published by Vintage Books, a division of Random House, Inc., New York, and published in hardcover by Alfred A. Knopf in 1994.

Writing & Discussion Activity

Tell your story of your name. Write "My Name" at the top of a piece of paper or on your computer screen and begin writing. What do you know about your name or how you came to be named? What memories do you have about your name? If you could change your name, what name would you choose and why? Write quickly and informally, as if this were a journal or notebook entry or "first thoughts."

After writing about your name, introduce yourself to someone you don't know in your class or to a classmate you know but who doesn't know your naming story or stories. If you want to change the classroom setting and add a little formality, stand up and shake hands with your new (or renewed) acquaintance. Read what you have written. Listen to what your classmate has written. Then introduce each other by name (and a story) to the rest of the class.

Read and discuss bell hooks' story of her name, a family naming story by Elizabeth Stone, and "The Waterbug Story" by Barbara Kingsolver. Perhaps add some other naming stories. See "Suggestions for Further Reading" at the end of the chapter.

Writing about your name is one way to begin the process of recollecting. You may want to leave this writing "as is" or you may want to use it as a basis for your own "Recollections & Reflections." Leave this writing for now and try other ways of tapping your memory, eventually choosing from several different starts.

to gloria, who is she: on using a pseudonym

bell hooks

bell hooks grew up in "an 'old school' Southern black world where children were meant to be seen and not heard" and "talking back" was punished with silence. Writing autobiographical narrative helped her look at her past from a different perspective, "not as singular isolated events but as part of a continuum." In this selection from Talking Back *(1989), bell hooks, who writes under a pseudonym, looks back on the "Gloria" of her childhood and explains how claiming a new name (and identity) empowered her.*

. . . bell hooks is a name that comes from family. It is the name of my great- 1 grandmother on my mother's side. In the beginning, I took this name because I was publishing a small book of poems in a community where someone else had the same given name. It was then mostly a practical choice—one I could easily make because I had not been attached to the name "Gloria." It had always seemed a name that was not me, evoking much that I am not. As I grew older, I began to associate this name with frivolity and dizziness (as in the stereotype of the dumb blonde, often named Gloria). Even though I am sometimes dizzy and quite frivolous, I was afraid then that this name would take me over, become my identity before I could make it what I wanted it to be. I welcomed the chance to choose and use another name.

I chose the name bell hooks because it was a family name, because it had 2 a strong sound. Throughout childhood, this name was used to speak to the memory of a strong woman, a woman who spoke her mind. Then in the seg-regated world of our black community—a strong woman was someone able to make her own way in this world, a woman who possessed traits often as-sociated only with men—she would kill for family and honor—she would do whatever was necessary to survive—she would be true to her word. Claiming this name was a way to link my voice to an ancestral legacy of woman speaking—of woman power. When I first used this name with po-etry, no one ever questioned this use of a pseudonym, perhaps because the realm of imaginative writing is deemed more private than social.

. . . Through the use of the name bell hooks I was able to claim an iden- 3 tity that affirmed for me my right to speech. Gloria as I had constructed her was meant to lead a monastic, spiritual life or a solitary reclusive writer's life; she was not to be a writer of feminist books. Again it is important to remem-ber that I was nineteen when I began this writing. Bell hooks could write feminist books and have a voice. And it seems to me quite fitting that this was a good old-fashioned 19th century name. Black female intellectual tra-ditions were strong during that century. Women like Anna Cooper, Frances Ellen Harper, and Mary Church Terrell were giving expression to the radical vision of black women concerned with politics, with struggles for liberation. It was fitting and appropriate for me to draw strength and courage from an unknown 19th century black woman whose legacy of strong and serious speech was carried on in oral history, was remembered. Bell hooks as I came to know her through this sharing of family history, as I dreamed and in-vented her, became a symbol of what I could become, all that my parents had hoped little Gloria would never be. Gloria was to have been a sweet southern girl, quiet, obedient, pleasing. She was not to have that wild streak that characterized women on my mother's side. Indeed it seemed my mother Rosa Bell was proud that she had learned to control her wild and cre-ative impulses, that she would obey and conform.

Choosing this name as a pseudonym was a rebellious gesture. It was part 4 of a strategy of empowerment, enabling me to surrender Gloria, give her back to those who had created her, so that I could make and find my own voice, my identity.

bell hooks, from *Talking Back: Thinking Feminist, Thinking Black,* South End Press, Boston, 1989. Reprinted by permission of South End Press.

Family Stories: "And Her Name Was Annunziata"

Elizabeth Stone

Elizabeth Stone, associate professor of English and media studies at Fordham University's College at Lincoln Center, New York City, tells this naming story in her book Black Sheep and Kissing Cousins: How Our Family Stories Shape Us *(1988).*

In the beginning, as far back in my family as anyone could go, was my great-grandmother, and her name was Annunziata. In the next generation, it would be my grandmother's first name. In the generation after that, in its anglicized form, Nancy, it would be my aunt's first name and my mother's middle name, and in the generation after that, my sister's middle name as well. I never met that first Annunziata, but my mother often told me a family story about her which, as a child, I knew as well as I knew the story of Cinderella and loved better.

Annunziata was the daughter of a rich landowner in Messina, Sicily [Italy], so the story went, and she fell in love with the town postman, a poor but talented man, able to play any musical instrument he laid eyes on. Her father heard about this romance and forbade them to see each other. So in the middle of one night—and then came the line I always waited for with a thrill of pleasure—she ran off with him in her shift.

I didn't know what a shift was and didn't want my settled version of the story disrupted by any new information. I loved the scene as I saw it: in the background was a house with a telltale ladder leaning against the second-story window. In the foreground was my great-grandmother, like some pre-Raphaelite maiden, dressed in a garment white and diaphanous and flowing, holding her hand of her beloved as she ran through a field at dawn, toward her future, toward me.

As a child, I was on very close terms with that story. I loved and admired my family—my grandmother especially—and as I saw it, her mother had been the start of us all. I never thought about any of my other great-grandparents or who they were. My grandfather, my mother's father, had died long before I was born; so I didn't think about him in any way that would bring him or his parents to life for me. As for my father, his parents had come from Austria, but he wasn't close to them, so I certainly wasn't. Nothing to build on there.

As a further refinement, I have to add that I paid absolutely no attention to the framed picture of my great-grandmother hanging over my grandmother's bed. That was just an old woman who, despite the fact that she happened to look like Sitting Bull, was of no interest to me. It was years before I realized that the person in the frame and the one in the story were the same. For me, it was always the stories that held the spirit and meaning of our family.

The first appeal of that story, then, was that it seemed to be the story of our genesis as a family. But there was a second appeal as well, and it was that my great-grandmother was everything I would have made her if I were inventing her. She was spunky, dazzlingly defiant, and I was sure, beautiful. Later, when I understood more about class and money, I admired her for having chosen my poor but talented great-grandfather in the first place. She was principled and egalitarian, someone I wanted to be like, hoped maybe I already was a little like, and most important, felt I *could* be like. She wasn't distant like a film star or imaginary like a fairy-tale heroine. She was real. And she was my relative.

Other family stories stayed with me, too. Some were old and ancestral but some were new, about my mother's generation or mine. none was elaborately plotted; some relied only on a well-developed scene—like the one in which my great-grandfather and his half-dozen sons were playing music after dinner in the courtyard as people came "from miles around" to listen. And still other were simply characterizations of people—"you had one ancestor who was a court musician" or "you had another ancestor who was an aide to Garibaldi." These qualified as stories in the way haiku qualify as poems. Almost any bit of lore about a family member, living or dead, qualifies as a family story—as long as it's significant, as long as it has worked its way into the family canon to be told and retold.

These stories last not because they're entertaining, though they may be; they last because in ways large and small they matter. They provide the family with esteem because they often show family members in an attractive light or define the family in a flattering way. They also give messages and instructions; they offer blueprints and ideals; they issue warnings and prohibitions. And when they no longer serve, they disappear. 8

From *Black Sheep and Kissing Cousins* by Elizabeth Stone. Copyright © 1988 by Elizabeth Stone. Reprinted by permission of Times Books, a division of Random House, Inc.

The Waterbug Story

Barbara Kingsolver

All the stories in Homeland *are bound by the power of place and the compelling ties of love and family history. In* Homeland, *a child accepts the impossible responsibility of remembering her Cherokee great-grandmother's dying culture. "Great Mam," as she was called, belonged to the Bird Clan, one of the fugitive bands of Cherokee who resisted capture. In these excerpts, the child asks Great Mam to tell her the story of "Waterbug," the name she called her great-grandaughter. Barbara Kingsolver has also written* The Bean Trees *and* Pigs in Heaven.

My name is Gloria St. Clair, but like most people I've been called many things. My maiden name was Murray. My grown children have at one time or another hailed me by nearly anything pronounceable. When I was a child myself, my great-grandmother called me by the odd name of Waterbug. I asked her many times why this was, until she said once, to quiet me, "I'll tell you that story." 1

We were on the front-porch swing, in summer, in darkness. I waited while she drew tobacco smoke in and out of her mouth, but she said nothing. "Well," I said. 2

Moonlight caught the fronts of her steel-framed spectacles and she looked at me from her invisible place in the dark. "I said I'd tell you that story. I didn't say I would tell it right now." 3

· · · · ·

"I see you, Waterbug," said Great Mam in the darkness, though what she probably meant was that she heard me. All I could see was the glow of her pipe bowl moving above the porch swing. 4

"Tell me the waterbug story tonight," I said, settling onto the swing. The 5 fireflies were blinking on and off in the black air above the front yard.

"No, I won't," she said. The orange glow moved to her lap, and faded 6 from bright to dim. "I'll tell you another time."

. . . . .

Before there was a world, there was only the sea, and the high, bright sky 7 arched above it like an overturned bowl.

For as many years as anyone can imagine, the people in the stars looked 8 down at the ocean's glittering face without giving a thought to what it was, or what might lie beneath it. They had their own concerns. But as more time passed, as is natural, they began to grow curious. Eventually it was the waterbug who volunteered to go exploring. She flew down and landed on top of the water, which was beautiful, but not firm as it had appeared. She skated in every direction but could not find a place to stop and rest, so she dived underneath.

She was gone for days and the star people thought she must have 9 drowned, but she hadn't. When she joyfully broked the surface again she had the answer: on the bottom of the sea, there was mud. She had brought a piece of it back with her, and she held up her sodden bit of proof to the bright light.

There, before the crowd of skeptical star eyes, the ball of mud began to 10 grow, and dry up, and grow some more, and out of it came all the voices and life that now dwell on this island that is the earth. The star people fastened it to the sky with four long grape vines so it wouldn't be lost again.

From *Homeland and Other Stories* by Barbara Kingsolver. Copyright © 1989 by Barbara Kingsolver. Reprinted by permission of HarperCollins Publishers, Inc.

Getting Started Writing About Memories

Perhaps writing about your name got you started on recollections for reflection. You can return to this writing later. Try various ways of tapping your memory before deciding what you want to work on. Make many writing attempts. Writers often go through many starts before they settle on what to write about. Perhaps you will decide to work with the first memory that came to your mind. Perhaps not. As you read, talk, write, and reflect, you'll come to see various ways of framing your story. Look ahead and keep end-project writing possibilities in mind, but take time to tap your memory and let memories unfold. Write. Stop. Listen! Reflect. Then try another way of tapping your memory. Read other "Recollections & Reflections." Slowly allow your writing to take shape.

If you are used to being assigned a topic and writing a first-and-only draft or even writing a couple of drafts of your first attempt, this "project" method may seem confusing or annoying at first. Inexperienced writers often bring their writing to a close too early. Take time to write your way into your story. Think of yourself as a member of a community of writers working on stories

Memory mutates the past. It is our happy human frailty to romanticize older days. However, the more distant the past, the more sharply it seems to come back into focus, however distorted the lens of recall.

Maxine Kumin

from your lives. Think of yourself as a participant in a process of recollecting and reflecting.

Before you read the published "Recollections & Reflections" included in this project, begin thinking about your own memories. Try these ways of getting started: free association, listing, and freewriting.

Free Association

Try writing your associations with childhood memories. Place "childhood memories" in a circle in the center of a piece of paper. Then draw a short line out and write a word or phrase that comes to mind (see Figure 3.1). Continue stringing together your associations, as in Figure 3.2. When you have gone as far as you can, return to the center and begin another string, which might look like Figure 3.3.

When words begin clustering together and you find you have something you want to write about, stop and write. Or stop after five or ten minutes, review your associations, and then write. You may find that you want to write from all the associations or from one or two strings of associations. Or you may want to choose to write about one string just to see what you write.

When some students try free association for the first time, they immediately like this way of getting started on a piece of writing. For them associations come easily, and they find that before they know it they have plenty to write about. Some writers find that free association sparks creativity and works well for writing stories and poems. Others do not feel comfortable brainstorming in this way. There is no one way to write or to get started writ-

Figure 3.1

Figure 3.2

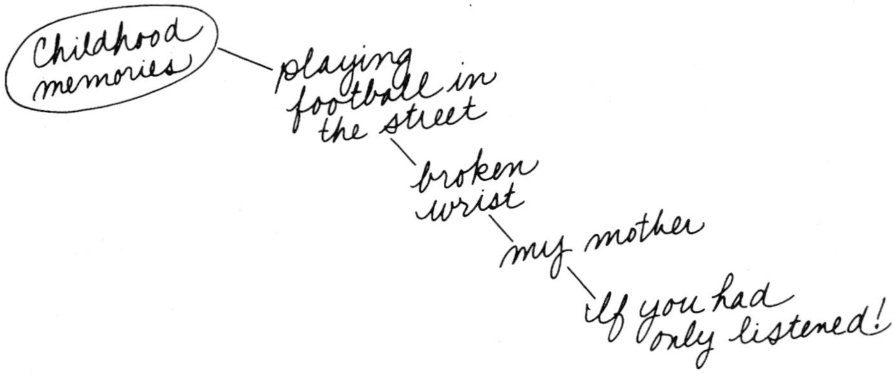

Figure 3.3

ing, and what works well for one writer or one kind of writing may not work well for another. This approach may take some practice if you are a highly anxious writer, and it may be worth doing as a limbering-up exercise.

Listing

List-making is one of the simplest, most direct methods of increasing one's conceptual ability. People often compile lists as memory aids (shopping lists, "do" lists). However, lists are less frequently used as thinking aids. List-making is surprisingly powerful, as it utilizes the compulsive side of most of us in a way which makes us into extremely productive conceptualizers.

Jane Adams

Sometimes when you cannot get started writing, working with a list helps. When thinking about your childhood or early adolescent years, try listing ages and see what memories come to mind. Or you might try listing grades in school and memories. Consider Margaret's use of listing to stimulate her recollections of childhood.

Writer at Work: Margaret Blacknall-Baurs

Childhood Memories
    New York City
    circus
    Alvin Ailey's dance company
    the Temptations at Apollo Theater
    West Virginia
    Pa.
    St. Croix
    St. Thomas
    Puerto Rico
    talent shows

Childhood Memories

I was born in Harlem the third child of four children. Mom was taking me to the Ringling Brothers and Barnum and Bailey's circus since the age of three. When I got older, I saw the Alvin Ailey Dance Company at Lincoln

Center. When the Temptations were a hit in the 1970s, I saw them at the Apollo on 125th Street. My dad came by once in a while to take us to visit his side of the family in Harrisburg, Pa. As a teenager, I was always in talent shows. My dream was to become a rhythm-and-blues singer. At the age of fourteen, we moved to St. Croix, Virgin Islands. While living there, I went to St. Thomas for carnival and Puerto Rico for a four-day vacation. . . .

Freewriting

You may also uncover a memory through the act of writing freely (freewriting). When you wrote quickly about your name, you were freewriting with your name as a focal point. Now put "Memories" at the top of a piece of paper or a computer screen and try writing whatever comes to mind. Do not censor your writing by telling yourself, "This isn't important. This isn't interesting." Keep writing. Write for about ten minutes or fill a couple of pages. If you like, try writing about a specific memory. Free yourself to write. If you hear a voice telling you to correct grammar or punctuation, tell your internal critic to come back later. For now, go with the flow of your memories. Listing and rewriting helped Viki Levitt tell stories from her life.

Writer at Work: Viki Levitt

In certain favourable moods, memories— what one has forgotten—come to the top. Now if this is so, is it not possible—I often wonder—that things we have felt with great intensity have an existence independent of our minds; are in fact still in existence? And if so, will it not be possible, in time, that some device will be invented by which we can tap them?

Virginia Woolf

Mountain lion, shooting stars, meteor shower, northern lights, Hawk Hill, St. Lawrence River, Azure Mountain, Wasatch Front, columbine, lupine—why do I list these things? I'm looking for my story. When my life begins perhaps; it wasn't really when I was born in Colorado, but that's one story. It may be that part of my story needs to have a sense of place. I've lived in Potsdam for more than twenty years but don't know its place deeply.

I am more grounded in Utah in the Wasatch Mountains where I lived for only six years. That's where home is when I go "home" to visit. I ride up Little Cottonwood Canyon feeling enfolded by the glacier-formed walls.

Last summer on the road, caught in the headlights of the car in front of me was a mountain lion. We all stopped, a line of cars headlighting the lion's stately measured walk from the lower canyon across the pavement and up the steep bank on the other side. I had never seen a mountain lion before. They don't roam the roadsides the way deer and porcupines and raccoons seem to do each summer.

After we left the mountain lion, we sat on the deck of the lodge and watched the meteor showers. I'd never seen a shooting star before either.

My daughter kept asking if I'd wished on them as they fell. Wishes were being granted without my asking that night.

This quickwriting (5–10 minutes) then led her to the following recollection from her childhood:

I grew up on a farm near Boulder. We had cattle—Guernseys, a little land for corn, and pasture, a little less money than the townies seemed to have. I remember cottonwood trees along the creek and one locust tree near the yard. If we had fireflies, I never saw them. Fireflies flew into my experience when I was an Army wife at Ft. Leonard Wood, Missouri, and again later when they competed with Fourth of July fireworks over Norwood Pond, and my friend's children caught them in jars. I didn't know much about natural things in spite of the farm—my mind was on Hans Brinker and Little Women and, later, sappy stuff by Lloyd Douglas, which the high school librarian said wasted my good mind.

As an experiment, my father planted birdsfoot trefoil [a wildflower] in the pasture, but I never knew its delicate yellow flower until last summer when someone named it for me in the clumps of yellow blossoms growing in the cracked concrete curbs around Maxcy Hall [Potsdam College]. Did the cattle eat the flowers from my sight? I never saw those yellow flowers on the farm.

I did not, and do not, know the land, my homeland, my home land the way the storyteller knows. I am only now becoming comfortable in the land—I am a long way from old Betonie.[1]

---

1. "Old Betonie" is a reference to Leslie Marmon Silko's *Storyteller*. Viki Levitt did this writing in preparation for a discussion at a workshop led by Jamie Hutchinson of the Bard Institute of Writing and Thinking. She teaches writing and literature at SUNY College of Technology (Canton, New York) and basic writing at Potsdam College (Potsdam, New York).

Writer at Work: Suna Savlaski

Suna could not get started writing: "My childhood seems so long ago. I don't know. I'm not sure about what was significant either." She finally began writing about the summers of her childhood:

I remember my summers as long as I know myself. My mother used to send me to my grandfather's country house after the schools closed. I had two choices, either to go to the summer house with them or to the country house (to my grandfather's). I always wanted to go to the country because I was in love with the country life. . . .

Writing About Getting Started Writing

I always have trouble getting started. I just don't know how to begin.

Patti Fervan

To know how to begin . . . is the great art.

Jacques Barzun

After you have tried several ways of getting started writing about memories, write about your process. Did you get started easily? Did you prefer writing from free associations, freewriting, or working from a list? What worked best for you? If you had difficulty writing, what blocked you?

Listening to the following writers talk about getting started may help you get started.

Will: Well, I didn't know what to select. Should I write about the time a fire started and I ran? Should I write about playing basketball or the time I went to the hospital?

Clarisse: Nothing significant happened. There were adventures and misadventures.

Ricardo: There are so many memories I don't know where to begin.

Suna: I tried to find a period that has significance. . . . The good part of putting down whatever I remember is that I remember more.

Erikka: I found myself wanting to write about a recent memory. I told myself not to and then I decided, 'Why Not?'

Your understanding of significance will grow as you read recollections and reflections by other writers and continue to take and make notes. At this time you are trying to trigger your memory and explore some possibilities; in the end, you may write about a different memory or about the same memory in a different way.

Writer Virginia Woolf decided to take a brief break one morning from some writing she was doing (a biography) and sketch some of her own memories. About getting started, she wrote:

> There are several difficulties. In the first place, the enormous number of things I can remember; in the second, the number of different ways in which memoirs can be written. As a great memoir reader, I know many different ways. But if I begin to go through them and to analyse them and their merits and faults, the mornings—I cannot take more than two or three at most—will be gone. So without stopping to choose my way, in the sure and certain knowledge that it will find itself—or if not it will not matter—I begin: the first memory.

In the following excerpt, which picks up where the previous excerpt left off, Virginia Woolf begins with her first memory as it came to her mind in the moment of writing, a way of getting started referred to earlier as "freewriting." She always revised her writing many times before it was published. The memoirs from which the excerpt was taken were not intended for publication; they were published after her death.[1]

> This was of red and purple flowers on a black ground—my mother's dress; and she was sitting either in a train or in an omnibus, and I was on her lap.

---

1. Woolf, V. "A Sketch of the Past," in *Moments of Being,* J. Schulkind (ed.). New York: Harcourt Brace Jovanovich, 1985, pp. 64–65. Copyright © 1976 Quentin Bell and Angelica Garrett. Reprinted by permission of the publisher.

I therefore saw the flowers she was wearing very close; and can still see purple and red and blue, I think, against the black; they must have been anemones, I suppose. Perhaps we were going to St Ives; more probably, for from the light it must have been evening, we were coming back to London. But it is more convenient artistically to suppose that we were going to St Ives, for that will lead to my other memory, which also seems to be my first memory, and in fact it is the most important of all my memories. If life has a base that it stands upon, if it is a bowl that one fills and fills and fills—then my bowl without a doubt stands upon this memory. It is of lying half asleep, half awake, in bed in the nursery at St Ives. It is of hearing the waves breaking, one, two, one, two, and sending a splash of water over the beach; and then breaking, one, two, one, two, behind a yellow blind. It is of hearing the blind draw its little acorn across the floor as the wind blew the blind out. It is of lying and hearing this splash and seeing this light, and feeling, it is almost impossible that I should be here; of feeling the purest ecstasy I can conceive.

Woolf gave significance to the color of the flowers on her mother's dress and the sound of waves, what she called her "colour-and-sound memories."

Experiment. Try remembering (or imagining) things from your childhood—images, colors, sounds, smells, tastes, objects. Try writing about a memory that does not seem particularly significant and see where your writing takes you.

One only remembers what is exceptional. And there seems to be no reason why one thing is exceptional and another not. Why have I forgotten so many things that must have been, one would have thought, more memorable than what I do remember?

Virginia Woolf

Talking About Memories

After you have written about some memories, perhaps from different periods of your life, review your writing to decide what memories you want to talk about to other writers at work.

In a small group of perhaps three to five people, talk about one or two of your memories and listen to those of others. Also talk about the ease or difficulty of this kind of writing and your process. Leave a few minutes at the end to list the memories others talked about and any new ideas or directions that come to mind.

Developing a Writing Project

Place your writing and notes in a file folder labeled "Recollections & Reflections Writing Project." Include notes you make after listening to responses to your writing in your small group or whole class or after a writing consultation. This work is part of your writing/thinking process. As you move through this project, periodically review your folder, and then write about your development on this project and where you seem to be heading.

Writer at Work: Darlene Ford

Darlene knew immediately that she wanted to focus on a particular place. Whenever she thought of her childhood, Prospect Park came to mind. She began clustering her associations around Prospect Park (see Figure 3.4). When

Figure 3.4

Darlene felt ready to write, she stopped clustering and began writing, using "Prospect Park" as a working title.

Prospect Park

I was looking through a photo album and saw the picture of me in front of some camels. I was about five. I was wearing a red hat and red shoes and a blue jacket and white stockings. I was so scared I would be eaten by alligators. There weren't any alligators. I see camels in the picture. This is a favorite memory that may seem funny. . . .

Darlene continued writing and then read to her group what she wrote. Will, a member of her writing group, begins the following session of dialogue by relating what he heard Darlene say. Summarizing or telling other writers your account of their writing is one way to help them get started. The writer is present to say yes or no and to clarify or elaborate. Notice that in this writing group Darlene's writing triggered Will to recall more of his own memories. What kind of a role does Susan play in this dialogue?

Will: You wrote about going to a park when you were a child, about five, and how you liked to go on the merry-go-round and see the animals. You liked to ride a certain pony.

Susan: Yes, but she wrote about fear, too. She was afraid of the animals in cages. I want to ask you about that picture in your album. Did you expect to see alligators?

Darlene: Yes, I remembered that all the time that my picture was being taken, I thought alligators were behind me and they would eat me. It was funny to look now and see camels. There weren't any alligators at all.

Will: I remember a dream I had when I was little. A big lion opened his mouth and I almost fell in, but I woke up just in time.

Susan: Your mother wouldn't let you get too close to the animals?

Darlene: I felt happy all dressed up in those red shoes and that red hat and that little blue jacket. I loved my mother to take me to the park. I used to tug on her, "I want to go there. Over there."

Will: I used to go to a park, too, right near where I lived. Now it's all closed off. It's a shelter for the homeless. It's supposed to be temporary, but it's been there for two years now. You could tell about an afternoon at Prospect Park and tell how it was for you then as a little girl.

Susan: You could begin your writing with you browsing through the album of pictures from your childhood and stopping at this picture. And you could end with your mother taking the picture and you telling about your fear.

Will: Yes, don't mention the camels until the end.

Darlene: I might try that. I'm starting to remember more and more now. The park was just one memory I wrote down, but as soon as I wrote the words, I knew I wanted to write about it. That picture is my favorite picture. It's funny how I was sure there were alligators. We may publish these in class. Do you think anyone will be interested? Do you think it's too—?

Susan: We all have our own pictures we remember.

Will: If you write it so we can picture you . . .

Darlene made notes, based on her group's responses, and placed them in her "Recollections & Reflections Writing Project" folder. When she's ready to continue writing, she can refer to her notes to get restarted. Try making your own notes for continuing writing after a writing group session or a writing consultation. It's also helpful to make notes about what you want to work on next after you've reached the end of your writing time and have to stop. Part of what's difficult about continuing the process of writing is remembering where you left off and where you were headed the last time you wrote.

If you stay in the same writing group throughout a writing project, as Darlene, Will, and Susan did, you'll come to know how different group members respond and what they have to offer as critical readers of your writing. You may look to one group member for a certain kind of help. For example, in Darlene's writing group, Susan typically asked for clarification and also was good at offering possible directions a piece of writing might take. Eventually, once you've become accustomed to getting responses to your writing, you may anticipate reader response during your writing process: "I'd better clarify this. Susan will ask about it," Darlene might come to say to herself before trying out her writing in her group. Good writers anticipate reader response, at least to some extent, and most writers try out their writing on various selected readers. Sometimes writers just want someone to listen, and other times they may want someone to read their writing for a specific purpose. To help members of your writing group become better writers, you'll need to develop your critical reading ability, too.

Reading & Reflecting on the Experiences of Others

In this section you'll read some recollections and reflections by both published and developing writers. These readings will help you think about what you might write and will also show you different ways of framing or composing your experiences. When you "write your writing," you'll find it helpful to have read a variety of recollections and reflections. See "Suggestions for Further Reading" at the end of this chapter if you would like to explore more possibilities.

Project-related writing includes Reader's Dialogue (notetaking and notemaking), role-playing, and recollecting and comparing and contrasting experiences. Just as you will read recollections and reflections by others, reading enough selections to see the possibilities and the differences, you may also want to select certain project-related writing activities. You may not want to try role-playing in writing, for example, after reading every selection. You could try role-playing after the first reading and perhaps rewrite later or select another one, making this kind of writing one of the pieces you submit for evaluation. You may want to try moving from story to essay. (See the suggestions following writings by Alice Walker, Richard Rodriguez, and Russell Baker.) You could try an essay—or more than one—and perhaps choose one to submit for evaluation.

The reading and project-related writing can help you:

1. trigger your own memories.
2. compare and contrast experiences and points of view.
3. see a range of possibilities for framing your experiences.
4. understand recollections and reflections as reading or interpreting events in your life.
5. think about "stories" as compositions.

Stop now and read once through the following reading by Alice Walker. She uses a series of stories to tell her story. Do not take notes during this first reading. After you have read it, take and make your own notes, using the guidelines for notetaking and notemaking that follow the reading.

Beauty: When the Other Dancer Is the Self

Alice Walker

In her first collection of nonfiction, In Search of Our Mothers' Gardens, *Alice Walker speaks out as an African-American woman, writer, mother, and feminist (or* womanist, *as she would say). In this memoir, the final essay in this collection, she tells of her scarring childhood "accident" and her daughter's healing words.*

It is a bright summer day in 1947. My father, a fat, funny man with beautiful eyes and a subversive wit, is trying to decide which of his eight children he will take with him to the county fair. My mother, of course, will not go. She is knocked out from getting most of us ready: I hold my neck stiff against the pressure of her knuckles as she hastily completes the braiding and then beribboning of my hair. 1

My father is the driver for the rich old white lady up the road. Her name is Miss Mey. She owns all the land for miles around, as well as the house in which we live. All I remember about her is that she once offered to pay my mother thirty-five cents for cleaning her house, raking up piles of her magnolia leaves, and washing her family's clothes, and that my mother—she of no money, eight children, and a chronic earache—refused it. But I do not think of this in 1947. I am two and a half years old. I want to go everywhere my daddy goes. I am excited at the prospect of riding in a car. Someone has told me fairs are fun. That there is room in the car for only three of us doesn't faze me at all. Whirling happily in my starchy frock, showing off my biscuit-polished patent-leather shoes and lavender socks, tossing my head in 2

Walker

a way that makes my ribbons bounce, I stand, hands on hips, before my father. "Take me, Daddy," I say with assurance; "I'm the prettiest!"

Later, it does not surprise me to find myself in Miss Mey's shiny black car, 3
sharing the back seat with the other lucky ones. Does not surprise me that I
thoroughly enjoy the fair. At home that night I tell the unlucky ones all I
can remember about the merry-go-round, the man who eats live chickens,
and the teddy bears, until they say: that's enough, baby Alice. Shut up now,
and go to sleep.

It is Easter Sunday, 1950. I am dressed in a green, flocked, scalloped-hem 4
dress (handmade by my adoring sister, Ruth) that has its own smooth satin
petticoat and tiny hot-pink roses tucked into each scallop. My shoes, new T-
strap patent leather, again highly biscuit-polished. I am six years old and
have learned one of the longest Easter speeches to be heard that day, totally
unlike the speech I said when I was two: "Easter lilies/pure and white/blos-
som in/the morning light." When I rise to give my speech I do so on a great
wave of love and pride and expectation. People in the church stop rustling
their new crinolines. They seem to hold their breath. I can tell they admire
my dress, but it is my spirit, bordering on sassiness (womanishness), they secretly applaud.

"That girl's a little *mess*," they whisper to each other, pleased. 5

Naturally I say my speech without stammer or pause, unlike those who 6
stutter, stammer, or, worst of all, forget. This is before the word "beautiful"
exists in people's vocabulary, but "Oh, isn't she the *cutest* thing!" frequently
floats my way. "And got so much sense!" they gratefully add . . . for which
thoughtful addition I thank them to this day.

It was great fun being cute. But then, one day, it ended. 7

I am eight years old and a tomboy. I have a cowboy hat, cowboy boots, 8
checkered shirt and pants, all red. My playmates are my brothers, two and
four years older than I. Their colors are black and green, the only difference
in the way we are dressed. On Saturday nights we all to go the picture show,
even my mother; Westerns are her favorite kind of movie. Back home, "on
the ranch," we pretend we are Tom Mix, Hopalong Cassidy, Lash LaRue (we've
even named one of our dogs Lash LaRue); we chase each other for hours
rustling cattle, being outlaws, delivering damsels from distress. Then my parents decide to buy my brothers guns. These are not "real" guns. They shoot
"BBs," copper pellets my brothers say will kill birds. Because I am a girl, I do
not get a gun. Instantly I am relegated to the position of Indian. Now there
appears a great distance between us. They shoot and shoot at everything
with their new guns. I try to keep up with my bow and arrows.

One day while I am standing on top of our makeshift "garage"—pieces of 9
tin nailed across some poles—holding my bow and arrow and looking out
toward the fields, I feel an incredible blow in my right eye. I look down just
in time to see my brother lower his gun.

Both brothers rush to my side. My eye stings, and I cover it with my hand. 10
"If you tell," they say, "we will get a whipping. You don't want that to hap-

pen, do you?" I do not. "Here is a piece of wire," says the older brother, picking it up from the roof; "say you stepped on one end of it and the other flew up and hit you." The pain is beginning to start. "Yes," I say. "Yes, I will say that is what happened." If I do not say this is what happened, I know my brothers will find ways to make me wish I had. But now I will say anything that gets me to my mother.

Confronted by our parents we stick to the lie agreed upon. They place me 11 on a bench on the porch and I close my left eye while they examine the right. There is a tree growing from underneath the porch that climbs past the railing to the roof. It is the last thing my right eye sees. I watch as its trunk, its branches, and then its leaves are blotted out by the rising blood.

I am in shock. First there is intense fever, which my father tries to break 12 using lily leaves bound around my head. Then there are chills: my mother tries to get me to eat soup. Eventually, I do not know how, my parents learn what has happened. A week after the "accident" they take me to see a doctor. "Why did you wait so long to come?" he asks, looking into my eye and shaking his head. "Eyes are sympathetic," he says. "If one is blind, the other will likely become blind too."

This comment of the doctor's terrifies me. But it is really how I look that 13 bothers me most. Where the BB pellet struck there is a glob of whitish scar tissue, a hideous cataract, on my eye. Now when I stare at people—a favorite pastime, up to now—they will stare back. Not at the "cute" little girl, but at her scar. For six years I do not stare at anyone, because I do not raise my head.

Years later, in the throes of a mid-life crisis, I ask my mother and sister 14 whether I changed after the "accident." "No," they say, puzzled. "What do you mean?"

What do I mean? 15

I am eight, and, for the first time, doing poorly in school, where I have 16 been something of a whiz since I was four. We have just moved to the place where the "accident" occurred. We do not know any of the people around us because this is a different county. The only time I see the friends I knew is when we go back to our old church. The new school is the former state penitentiary. It is a large stone building, cold and drafty, crammed to overflowing with boisterous, ill-disciplined children. On the third floor there is a huge circular imprint of some partition that has been torn out.

"What used to be here?" I ask a sullen girl next to me on our way past it 17 to lunch.

"The electric chair," says she. 18

At night I have nightmares about the electric chair, and about all the 19 people reputedly "fried" in it. I am afraid of the school, where all the students seem to be budding criminals.

"What's the matter with your eye?" they ask, critically. 20

When I don't answer (I cannot decide whether it was an "accident" or 21 not), they shove me, insist on a fight.

My brother, the one who created the story about the wire, comes to my 22 rescue. But then brags so much about "protecting" me, I become sick.

After months of torture at the school, my parents decide to send me back 23 to our old community, to my old school. I live with my grandparents and the teacher they board. But there is no room for Phoebe, my cat. By the time my grandparents decide there *is* room, and I ask for my cat, she cannot be found. Miss Yarborough, the boarding teacher, takes me under her wing, and begins to teach me to play the piano. But soon she marries an African—a "prince," she says—and is whisked away to his continent.

At my old school there is at least one teacher who loves me. She is the teacher who "knew me before I was born" and bought my first baby clothes. It is she who makes life bearable. It is her presence that finally helps me turn on the one child at school who continually calls me "one-eyed bitch." One day I simply grab him by his coat and beat him until I am satisfied. It is my teacher who tells me my mother is ill. 24

My mother is lying in bed in the middle of the day, something I have never seen. She is in too much pain to speak. She has an abscess in her ear. I stand looking down on her, knowing that if she dies, I cannot live. She is being treated with warm oils and hot bricks held against her cheek. Finally a doctor comes. But I must go back to my grandparents' house. The weeks pass but I am hardly aware of it. All I know is that my mother might die, my father is not so jolly, my brothers still have their guns, and I am the one sent away from home. 25

"You did not change," they say. 26
Did I imagine the anguish of never looking up? 27

I am twelve. When relatives come to visit I hide in my room. My cousin Brenda, just my age, whose father works in the post office and whose mother is a nurse, comes to find me. "Hello," she says. And then she asks, looking at my recent school picture, which I did not want taken, and on which the "glob," as I think of it, is clearly visible, "You still can't see out of that eye?" 28

"No," I say, and flop back on the bed over my book. 29

That night, as I do almost every night, I abuse my eye. I rant and rave at it, in front of the mirror. I plead with it to clear up before morning. I tell it I hate and despise it. I do not pray for sight. I pray for beauty. 30

"You did not change," they say. 31

I am fourteen and baby-sitting for my brother Bill, who lives in Boston. He is my favorite brother and there is a strong bond between us. Understanding my feelings of shame and ugliness he and his wife take me to a local hospital, where the "glob" is removed by a doctor named O. Henry. There is still a small bluish crater where the scar tissue was, but the ugly white stuff is gone. Almost immediately I become a different person from the girl who does not raise her head. Or so I think. Now that I've raised my head I win the boyfriend of my dreams. Now that I've raised my head I have plenty of friends. Now that I've raised my head classwork comes from my lips as faultlessly as Easter speeches did, and I leave high school as valedictorian, most popular student, and *queen,* hardly believing my luck. Ironically, the girl who was voted most beautiful in our class (and was) was later shot twice through the chest by a male companion, using a "real" gun, while she was pregnant. But that's another story in itself. Or is it? 32

"You did not change," they say. 33

It is now thirty years since the "accident." A beautiful journalist comes to   34
visit and to interview me. She is going to write a cover story for her magazine that focuses on my latest book. "Decide how you want to look on the
cover," she says. "Glamorous, or whatever."

Never mind "glamorous," it is the "whatever" that I hear. Suddenly all I   35
can think of is whether I will get enough sleep the night before the photog-
raphy session: if I don't, my eye will be tired and wander, as blind eyes will.

At night in bed with my lover I think up reasons why I should not appear   36
on the cover of a magazine. "My meanest critics will say I've sold out," I say.
"My family will now realize I write scandalous books."

"But what's the real reason you don't want to do this?" he asks.   37

"Because in all probability," I say in a rush, "my eye won't be straight."   38

"It will be straight enough," he says. Then, "Besides, I thought you'd   39
made your peace with that."

And I suddenly remember that I have.   40

I remember: 41

I am talking to my brother Jimmy, asking if he remembers anything un-   42
usual about the day I was shot. He does not know I consider that day the last
time my father, with his sweet home remedy of cool lily leaves, chose me,
and that I suffered and raged inside because of this. "Well," he says, "all I remember is standing by the side of the highway with Daddy, trying to flag
down a car. A white man stopped, but when Daddy said he needed somebody to take his little girl to the doctor, he drove off."

I remember: 43

I am in the desert for the first time. I fall totally in love with it. I am so over-   44
whelmed by its beauty, I confront for the first time, consciously, the meaning
of the doctor's words years ago: "Eyes are sympathetic. If one is blind, the other
will likely become blind too." I realize I have dashed about the world madly,
looking at this, looking at that, storing up images against the fading of the
light. *But I might have missed seeing the desert!* The shock of that possibility—
and gratitude for over twenty-five years of sight—sends me literally to my
knees. Poem after poem comes—which is perhaps how poets pray.

ON SIGHT   45

I am so thankful I have seen   46
The Desert
And the creatures in the desert
And the desert Itself.

The desert has its own moon   47
Which I have seen
With my own eye.
There is no flag on it.

Trees of the desert have arms   48
All of which are always up
That is because the moon is up
The sun is up
Also the sky

Walker

The stars
Clouds
None with flags.

If there were *flags, I doubt*   49
the trees would point.
Would you?

But mostly, I remember this: 50

I am twenty-seven, and my baby daughter is almost three. Since her birth   51
I have worried about her discovery that her mother's eyes are different from
other people's. Will she be embarrassed? I think. What will she say? Every day
she watches a television program called "Big Blue Marble." It begins with a
picture of the earth as it appears from the moon. It is bluish, a little battered-
looking, but full of light, with whitish clouds swirling around it. Every time
I see it I weep with love, as if it is a picture of Grandma's house. One day
when I am putting Rebecca down for her nap, she suddenly focuses on my
eye. Something inside me cringes, gets ready to try to protect myself. All
children are cruel about physical differences, I know from experience, and
that they don't always mean to be is another matter. I assume Rebecca will
be the same.

But no-o-o-o. She studies my face intently as we stand, her inside and me   52
outside her crib. She even holds my face maternally between her dimpled little hands. Then, looking every bit as serious and lawyerlike as her father, she
says, as if it may just possibly have slipped my attention: "Mommy, there's a
world in your eye." (As in, "Don't be alarmed, or do anything crazy.") And
then, gently, but with great interest: "Mommy, where did you *get* that world
in your eye?"

For the most part, the pain left then. (So what, if my brothers grew up to   53
buy even more powerful pellet guns for their sons and to carry real guns
themselves. So what, if a young "Morehouse man" once nearly fell off the
steps of Trevor Arnett Library because he thought my eyes were blue.) Crying and laughing I ran to the bathroom, while Rebecca mumbled and sang
herself off to sleep. Yes indeed, I realized, looking into the mirror. There *was*
a world in my eye. And I saw that it was possible to love it: that in fact, for
all it had taught me of shame and anger and inner vision, I *did* love it. Even
to see it drifting out of orbit in boredom, or rolling up out of fatigue, not to
mention floating back at attention in excitement (bearing witness, a friend
has called it), deeply suitable to my personality, and even characteristic of me.

That night I dream I am dancing to Stevie Wonder's song "Always" (the   54
name of the song is really "As," but I hear it as "Always"). As I dance, whirling and joyous, happier than I've ever been in my life, another bright-faced
dancer joins me. We dance and kiss each other and hold each other through
the night. The other dancer has obviously come through all right, as I have
done. She is beautiful, whole and free. And she is also me.

From *In Search of Our Mothers' Gardens* by Alice Walker. Copyright © 1983 by Alice Walker.
Reprinted by permission of Harcourt Brace and Company.

Reader's Dialogue: Making & Sharing Connections

What associations does your reading bring to mind? Because you will be writing about recollections for this writing project, writing about your associations is appropriate for notemaking. For this project, your primary purpose is not to analyze the readings but both to use the readings to reflect on your own experience and to learn about different possibilities for shaping or forming your own writing. For some other kinds of writing, however, writing about your associations may be inappropriate; analysis may be more appropriate. You can keep a Reader's Dialogue notebook for different purposes in different disciplines or even within the same discipline.

Reread Alice Walker's "Beauty: When the Other Dance Is the Self" and take and make your own notes. To help you get started, read an excerpt from the beginning of one reader's reading of the opening passage (see Figure 3.5).

Continue rereading, taking and making more notes. You may want to continue taking notes about Alice at different ages (at six, eight, twelve, fourteen, twenty-seven, and thirty-eight). Then compare the notes you made on a particular section of the reading with notes several other readers made. (See "Developing Writers at Work" at the end of this chapter for an example of how one writer's—Ricardo Sewell's—notebook entry led to a first draft.) Try recalling an event from your childhood, even some memory that may not seem very eventful, and see where your writing leads you.

Figure 3.5

NOTEMAKING	NOTETAKING
I thought at first the story was going to be told from a child's view. But then I see Alice is looking back. I like the way she begins. I do see the child's view and then her view years later. I'm glad her mother refused that work. Alice is daddy's girl here. Only years later does she see her mother, her strength and pride.	Summer of 1947 1 of 8 children Miss Mey (rich old white lady landowner) offered 35 cents to Alice's mother for cleaning house and raking leaves and washing clothes. Her mother—no money, 8 children, sick—refused. "But I do not think of this in 1947. I am two and a half years old. I want to go everywhere my daddy goes."

Optional Writing Opportunities

Changing Points of View: Acting Through Writing

In many courses you take across the college curriculum, you will be asked to examine different points of view and to demonstrate your understanding, frequently through writing. How can you come to understand someone else's point of view or "reading"? Role-playing or acting out a point of view can help improve your understanding.

1. Try assuming a point of view of one of the characters Alice Walker presents in her writing. Read the following list of suggestions for role-playing and select one to try out. Write a monologue (or more than one, if you like) using the first-person point of view ("I"). Imagine you are Alice's father, mother, brother, or Alice herself at different times in her life. Do not recollect and reflect here, but rather write about the event *as if it were happening now*. Use the present tense.

   a. Write the opening scene from Alice's father's point of view. What is going through your mind on this bright summer morning in 1947?

   b. Write the opening scene from Alice's mother's view. Role-play Alice's mother and write down your thoughts while you are braiding Alice's hair.

   c. Describe the "accident," as it is happening, from Alice's point of view at age eight. Your two brothers (ages ten and twelve) are outside playing cowboys. Wearing your cowboy outfit and carrying a bow and arrow, you step outside to join them. Write a monologue of what you are thinking as you go outside to play and climb up on the "garage" and look out. Continue writing your thoughts immediately following the blow to your right eye.

   d. Write about the "accident" from the point of view of the brother who shot the BB gun. The accident has just happened.

   e. You are Alice at age six. Write what is going through your mind before, during, and after your Easter speech in church. Begin with your walking into church and sitting down to wait your turn.

   f. Almost every night, Alice abused her eye: "I rant and rave at it, in front of the mirror. I plead with it to clear up before morning. I tell it I hate and despise it. I do not pray for sight. I pray for beauty." Pretend you are Alice at age twelve. Write a monologue in which you talk to your eye while you are standing in front of the mirror. Rant and rave, plead, talk to this eye you so despise.

   g. Imagine this is the first time Alice has been back to school since the "accident." The children have gone out for recess after lunch. Several ask Alice, "What is the matter with your eye?" Everyone stares at her (at least she feels they do), and some make fun of her. Assume Alice's point of view and write what you are thinking about during this scene with your classmates.

   h. You are Alice at age twenty-seven. You have just tucked your daughter Rebecca, who is almost three, into bed for the night. Write an entry Alice might have written in her journal about her anxiety over her daughter's discovery that her mother has a "physical difference."

This assignment may *seem* easy, but it's likely to be quite difficult. Why? To make your monologue believable, you must first study the character closely. Go back and reread, carefully placing the character in context. Think about the character's past experiences and possible motives. Consider how the character sounds. What kind of language would be appropriate? You will need to create some distance between yourself and the character so that the character doesn't sound like you. To be successful with this writing, in other words, you'll need to change your point of view.

2. Try writing about an event in your own childhood from your viewpoint at that time. Write in the voice of yourself as a child during the time of this event. You might also try writing about the "same" event from another person's (a relative's or friend's perhaps) point of view, or from your own point of view later in life.

Writing Reflections

After you have written from one or more points of view, write about this particular writing experience. Did you enjoy role-playing? Did you find it difficult? Were you surprised by what you wrote? What did you learn? Read your writing to other writers for their responses and then discuss your reflections on this writing experience.

Before & After: Looking & Looking Again

Using your notes as a guide, write about Alice's view of herself before and after the "accident," and then describe her re-view of herself as an adult. End by writing about the meaning you make (your reading or interpretation) of the author's choice of "Beauty: When the Other Dancer Is the Self" as the title of this memoir.

I Remember . . .

Richard Rodriguez

In Hunger of Memory, *Richard Rodriguez traces his experience growing up in different cultures: the Mexican-immigrant culture of his home, the American culture into which he was born, and the academic culture (the world of school). He did not learn to speak English until he went to school. In this selection, he recalls his first day of school and explores language, cultural, and class differences.*

I remember to start with that day in Sacramento—a California now nearly 1 thirty years past—when I first entered a classroom, able to understand some fifty stray English words.

The third of four children, I had been preceded to a neighborhood Roman 2 Catholic school by an older brother and sister. But neither of them had revealed very much about their classroom experiences. Each afternoon they returned, as they left in the morning, always together, speaking in Spanish as they climbed the five steps of the porch. And their mysterious books, wrapped in shopping-bag paper, remained on the table next to the door, closed firmly behind them.

An accident of geography sent me to a school where all my classmates 3 were white, many the children of doctors and lawyers and business executives. All my classmates certainly must have been uneasy on that first day of school—as most children are uneasy—to find themselves apart from their families in the first institution of their lives. But I was astonished.

The nun said, in a friendly but oddly impersonal voice, "Boys and girls, 4 this is Richard Rodriguez." (I heard her sound out: *Rich-heard Road-ree-guess.*) It was the first time I had heard anyone name me in English. "Richard," the nun repeated more slowly, writing my name down in her black leather book. Quickly I turned to see my mother's face dissolve in a watery blur behind the pebbled glass door.

Many years later there is something called bilingual education—a scheme 5 proposed in the late 1960s by Hispanic-American social activists, later endorsed by a congressional vote. It is a program that seeks to permit non-English-speaking children, many from lower-class homes, to use their family language as the language of school. (Such is the goal its supporters announce.) I hear them and am forced to say no: It is not possible for a child—any child—ever to use his family's language in school. Not to understand this is to misunderstand the public uses of schooling and to trivialize the nature of intimate life—a family's "language."

Memory teaches me what I know of these matters; the boy reminds the 6 adult. I was a bilingual child, a certain kind—socially disadvantaged—the son of working-class parents, both Mexican immigrants.

In the early years of my boyhood, my parents coped very well in America. 7 My father had steady work. My mother managed at home. They were nobody's victims. Optimism and ambition led them to a house (our home) many blocks from the Mexican south side of town. We lived among *gringos* and only a block from the biggest, whitest houses. It never occurred to my parents that they couldn't live wherever they chose. Nor was the Sacramento of the fifties bent on teaching them a contrary lesson. My mother and father were more annoyed than intimidated by those two or three neighbors who tried initially to make us unwelcome. ("Keep your brats away from my sidewalk!") But despite all they achieved, perhaps because they had so much to achieve, any deep feeling of ease, the confidence of "belonging" in public, was withheld from them both. They regarded the people at work, the faces in the crowds, as very distant from us. They were the others, *los gringos*. That term was interchangeable in their speech with another, even more telling, *los americanos*.

I grew up in a house where the only regular guests were my relations. For 8 one day, enormous families of relatives would visit and there would be so many people that the noise and the bodies would spill out to the backyard and front porch. Then, for weeks, no one came by. (It was usually a salesman who rang the doorbell.) Our house stood apart. A gaudy yellow in a row of white bungalows. We were the people with the noisy dog. The people who raised pigeons and chickens. We were the foreigners on the block. A few neighbors smiled and waved. We waved back. But no one in the family knew the names of the old couple who lived next door; until I was seven years old, I did not know the names of the kids who lived across the street.

In public, my father and mother spoke a hesitant, accented, not always 9 grammatical English. And they would have to strain—their bodies tense—to catch the sense of what was rapidly said by *los gringos*. At home they spoke Spanish. The language of their Mexican past sounded in counterpoint to the English of public society. The words would come quickly, with ease. Conveyed through those sounds was the pleasing, soothing, consoling reminder of being at home.

During those years when I was first conscious of hearing, my mother 10 and father addressed me only in Spanish; in Spanish I learned to reply. By contrast, English (*inglés*), rarely heard in the house, was the language I came to associate with *gringos*. I learned my first words of English overhearing my parents speak to strangers. At five years of age, I knew just enough English for my mother to trust me on errands to stores one block away. No more.

I was a listening child, careful to hear the very different sounds of 11 Spanish and English. Wide-eyed with hearing, I'd listen to sounds more than words. First, there were English (*gringo*) sounds. So many words were still unknown that when the butcher or the lady at the drugstore said something to me, exotic polysyllabic sounds would bloom in the midst of their sentences. Often the speech of people in public seemed to me very loud, booming with confidence. The man behind the counter would literally ask, "What can I do for you?" But by being so firm and so clear, the sound of his voice said that he was a *gringo;* he belonged in public society.

I would also hear then the high nasal notes of middle-class American 12 speech. The air stirred with sound. Sometimes, even now, when I have been traveling abroad for several weeks, I will hear what I heard as a boy. In hotel lobbies or airports, in Turkey or Brazil, some Americans will pass, and suddenly I will hear it again—the high sound of American voices. For a few seconds I will hear it with pleasure, for it is now the sound of *my* society—a reminder of home. But inevitably—already on the flight headed for home—the sound fades with repetition. I will be unable to hear it anymore.

When I was a boy, things were different. The accent of *los gringos* was 13 never pleasing nor was it hard to hear. Crowds at Safeway or at bus stops would be noisy with sound. And I would be forced to edge away from the chirping chatter above me.

I was unable to hear my own sounds, but I knew very well that I spoke 14 English poorly. My words could not stretch far enough to form complete thoughts. And the words I did speak I didn't know well enough to make into distinct sounds. (Listeners would usually lower their heads, better to hear what I was trying to say.) But it was one thing for *me* to speak English with difficulty. It was more troubling for me to hear my parents speak in public: their high-whining vowels and guttural consonants; their sentences that got stuck with "eh" and "ah" sounds; the confused syntax; the hesitant rhythm of sounds so different from the way *gringos* spoke. I'd notice, moreover, that my parents' voices were softer than those of *gringos* we'd meet.

Rodriguez

I am tempted now to say that none of this mattered. In adulthood I am 15 embarrassed by childhood fears. And, in a way, it didn't matter very much that my parents could not speak English with ease. Their linguistic difficulties had no serious consequences. My mother and father made themselves understood at the county hospital clinic and at government offices. And yet, in another way, it mattered very much—it was unsettling to hear my parents struggle with English. Hearing them, I'd grow nervous, my clutching trust in their protection and power weakened.

There were many times like the night at a brightly lit gasoline station (a 16 blaring white memory) when I stood uneasily, hearing my father. He was talking to a teenaged attendant. I do not recall what they were saying, but I cannot forget the sounds my father made as he spoke. At one point his words slid together to form one word—sounds as confused as the threads of blue and green oil in the puddle next to my shoes. His voice rushed through what he had left to say. And, toward the end, reached falsetto notes, appealing to his listener's understanding. I looked away to the lights of passing automobiles. I tried not to hear anymore. But I heard only too well the calm, easy tones in the attendant's reply. Shortly afterward, walking toward home with my father, I shivered when he put his hand on my shoulder. The very first chance that I got, I evaded his grasp and ran on ahead into the dark, skipping with feigned boyish exuberance.

But then there was Spanish. *Español:* my family's language. *Español:* the 17 language that seemed to me a private language. I'd hear strangers on the radio and in the Mexican Catholic church across town speaking in Spanish, but I couldn't really believe that Spanish was a public language, like English. Spanish speakers, rather, seemed related to me, for I sensed that we shared— through our language—the experience of feeling apart from *los gringos.* It was thus a ghetto Spanish that I heard and I spoke. Like those whose lives are bound by a barrio, I was reminded by Spanish of my separateness from *los otros, los gringos* in power. But more intensely than for most barrio children—because I did not live in a barrio—Spanish seemed to me the language of home. (Most days it was only at home that I'd hear it.) It became the language of joyful return.

A family member would say something to me and I would feel myself 18 specially recognized. My parents would say something to me and I would feel embraced by the sounds of their words. Those sounds said: *I am speaking with ease in Spanish. I am addressing you in words I never use with* los gringos. *I recognize you as someone special, close, like no one outside. You belong with us. In the family.*

(Ricardo.) 19

At the age of five, six, well past the time when most other children no 20 longer easily notice the difference between sounds uttered at home and words spoken in public, I had a different experience. I lived in a world magically compounded of sounds. I remained a child longer than most; I lingered too long, poised at the edge of language—often frightened by the sounds of *los gringos,* delighted by the sounds of Spanish at home. I shared with my family a language that was startlingly different from that used in the great city around us.

For me there were none of the gradations between public and private so- 21
ciety so normal to a maturing child. Outside the house was public society;
inside the house was private. Just opening or closing the screen door behind
me was an important experience. I'd rarely leave home all alone or without
reluctance. Walking down the sidewalk, under the canopy of tall trees, I'd
warily notice the—suddenly—silent neighborhood kids who stood warily
watching me. Nervously, I'd arrive at the grocery store to hear there the
sounds of the *gringo*—foreign to me—reminding me that in this world so
big, I was a foreigner. But then I'd return. Walking back toward our house,
climbing the steps from the sidewalk, when the front door was open in summer, I'd hear voices beyond the screen door talking in Spanish. For a second
or two, I'd stay, linger there, listening. Smiling, I'd hear my mother call out,
saying in Spanish (words): "Is that you, Richard?" All the while her sounds
would assure me: *You are home now; come closer; inside. With us.*

"*Sí,*" I'd reply. 22

Once more inside the house I would resume (assume) my place in the 23
family. The sounds would dim, grow harder to hear. Once more at home, I
would grow less aware of that fact. It required, however, no more than the
blurt of the doorbell to alert me to listen to sounds all over again. The house
would turn instantly still while my mother went to the door. I'd hear her hard
English sounds. I'd wait to hear her voice return to soft-sounding Spanish,
which assured me, as surely as did the clicking tongue of the lock on the
door, that the stranger was gone.

Plainly, it is not healthy to hear such sounds so often. It is not healthy to 24
distinguish public words from private sounds so easily. I remained cloistered
by sounds, timid and shy in public, too dependent on voices at home. And
yet it needs to be emphasized: I was an extremely happy child at home. I remember many nights when my father would come back from work, and I'd
hear him call out to my mother in Spanish, sounding relieved. In Spanish,
he'd sound light and free notes he never could manage in English. Some
nights I'd jump up just at hearing his voice. With *mis hermanos* I would come
running into the room where he was with my mother. Our laughing (so
deep was the pleasure!) became screaming. Like others who know the pain
of public alienation, we transformed the knowledge of our public separateness and made it consoling—the reminder of intimacy. Excited, we joined
our voices in a celebration of sounds. *We are speaking now the way we never
speak out in public. We are alone—together,* voices sounded, surrounded to tell
me. Some nights, no one seemed willing to loosen the hold sounds had on
us. At dinner, we invented new words. (Ours sounded Spanish, but made
sense only to us.) We pieced together new words by taking, say, an English
verb and giving it Spanish endings. My mother's instructions at bedtime
would be lacquered with mock-urgent tones. Or a word like *sí* would become,
in several notes, able to convey added measures of feeling. Tongues explored
the edges of words, especially the fat vowels. And we happily sounded that
military drum roll, the twirling roar of the Spanish *r*. Family language: my
family's sounds. The voices of my parents and sisters and brother. Their voices
insisting: *You belong here. We are family members. Related. Special to one another.
Listen!* Voices singing and sighing, rising, straining, then surging, teeming

Rodriguez

with pleasure that burst syllables into fragments of laughter. At times it seemed there was steady quiet only when, from another room, the rustling whispers of my parents faded and I moved closer to sleep.

From *Hunger of Memory* by Richard Rodriguez. Copyright © 1981 by Richard Rodriguez. Reprinted by permission of David R. Godine, Publisher, Boston.

Reader's Dialogue: Making & Sharing Connections

1. Use the comparison frame in Figure 3.6 to take notes about what set Richard apart from others around him. What differences in types of housing and occupation signify differences in class?

2. Include in your note*taking* these two quotations:

> It is not possible for a child—any child—ever to use his family's language in school.
> Just opening or closing the screen door behind me was an important experience.

What meaning do you make of these quotations? What is your reading or interpretation? Respond in the note*making* side of your reader's dialogue notebook opposite the quotations you have copied.

3. Talk, perhaps in a whole-class group, about the notes you made and your personal connections or experiences with regard to cultural and language differences at home and at school.

Optional Writing Opportunities

Changing Points of View: Acting Through Writing

1. Imagine you are one of Richard's classmates or a *gringo* or Richard at a particular time in his life. Consider the suggestions in the following list. Write

Figure 3.6

Point of Comparison	Richard	Others
1. Race	Mexican–American	Anglo/Euro (White)
2. Language	English– Public, School	Spanish– Private, Family
3. Class		

a monologue (or more than one) using the first person point of view ("I") and the present tense. Do not recollect and reflect here. Write about your thoughts as if you are thinking from someone else's point of view. What is going through your mind in these situations? Let your readers in.

a. You are one of Richard's first-grade classmates and have just returned home from school. Your mother asks you how the first day went, and you tell her about Richard.

b. You are one of the *gringos* living in one of the big, white houses in the Sacramento, California, neighborhood where the young Richard lives with his family. Richard and his brother have just walked by your house. You see the parents across the street and shout, "Keep your brats away from my sidewalk!" Use this line to begin an exchange between this neighbor and another about the Rodriguez family.

c. Assume Richard's point of view as a child. You have gone to the gas station with your father, who struggled to speak English with the station's teenaged attendant. You are a "listening child." Narrate the scene between your father and the attendant from your point of view. Tell about what is going through your mind and how you escape. Use the first-person point of view and get the reader to listen as you tell what's going through your mind.

d. "I was an extremely happy child at home," writes Richard Rodriguez, looking back. Describe a happy time at home from Richard's point of view. You are in your room when you hear your father come home from work and call to your mother. You come downstairs for dinner.

2. Assume a point of view in your life as a child. Recollect some event or interaction that relates to school or illustrates language or class differences. Write as you might have spoken then. If English is your second language, perhaps write in your first language and then write a translation.

First Day at School: Remembering Through Writing

Write a brief account of your first day of school or a first day in a new school. Look back. Recollect. If possible, ask someone (a brother, sister, parent, other relative, or friend) who might remember some details. Even if you are having difficulty remembering some things, you probably remember the name and location of the school, the teacher, and the kinds of students there. Begin perhaps with a list and then write. Rely more on your imagination than on your memory to recreate your impressions of that first day. Or write about another "First Day."

Developing Your Writing Project

Review your "Recollections & Reflections Writing Project" folder and write about the writing you have done so far. What have the readings and group talk caused you to recollect and reflect on?

Growing Up

Russell Baker

Russell Baker's boyhood in the mountains of Virginia and the Depression-stricken neighborhoods of northern New Jersey is chronicled in his memoir Growing Up, *which won him a second Pulitzer Prize. In this selection, he writes about when he began his career in journalism (at age eight) and his struggle with his mother's idea of work.*

I began working in journalism when I was eight years old. It was my mother's idea. She wanted me to "make something" of myself and, after a level-headed appraisal of my strengths, decided I had better start young if I was to have any chance of keeping up with the competition. 1

The flaw in my character which she had already spotted was lack of "gumption." My idea of a perfect afternoon was lying in front of the radio rereading my favorite Big Little Book, *Dick Tracy Meets Stooge Viller.* My mother despised inactivity. Seeing me having a good time in repose, she was powerless to hide her disgust. "You've got no more gumption than a bump on a log," she said. "Get out in the kitchen and help Doris do those dirty dishes." 2

My sister Doris, though two years younger than I, had enough gumption for a dozen people. She positively enjoyed washing dishes, making beds, and cleaning the house. When she was only seven she could carry a piece of short-weighted cheese back to the A&P, threaten the manager with legal action, and come back triumphantly with the full quarter-pound we'd paid for and a few ounces extra thrown in for forgiveness. Doris could have made something of herself if she hadn't been a girl. Because of this defect, however, the best she could hope for was a career as a nurse or schoolteacher, the only work that capable females were considered up to in those days. 3

This must have saddened my mother, this twist of fate that had allocated all the gumption to the daughter and left her with a son who was content with Dick Tracy and Stooge Viller. If disappointed, though, she wasted no energy on self-pity. She would make me make something of myself whether I wanted to or not. "The Lord helps those who help themselves," she said. That was the way her mind worked. 4

She was realistic about the difficulty. Having sized up the material the Lord had given her to mold, she didn't overestimate what she could do with it. She didn't insist that I grow up to be President of the United States. 5

Fifty years ago parents still asked boys if they wanted to grow up to be President, and asked it not jokingly but seriously. Many parents who were hardly more than paupers still believed their sons could do it. Abraham Lincoln had done it. We were only sixty-five years from Lincoln. Many a grandfather who walked among us could remember Lincoln's time. Men of grandfatherly age were the worst for asking if you wanted to grow up to be President. A surprising number of little boys said yes and meant it. 6

I was asked many times myself. No, I would say, I didn't want to grow up 7
to be President. My mother was present during one of these interrogations.
An elderly uncle, having posed the usual question and exposed my lack of
interest in the Presidency, asked, "Well, what *do* you want to be when you
growup?"

I loved to pick through trash piles and collect empty bottles, tin cans 8
with pretty labels, and discarded magazines. The most desirable job on earth
sprang instantly to mind. "I want to be a garbage man," I said.

My uncle smiled, but my mother had seen the first distressing evidence 9
of a bump budding on a log. "Have a little gumption, Russell," she said. Her
calling me Russell was a signal of unhappiness. When she approved of me I
was always "Buddy."

When I turned eight years old she decided that the job of starting me on 10
the road toward making something of myself could no longer be safely de-
layed. "Buddy," she said one day, "I want you to come home right after school
this afternoon. Somebody's coming and I want you to meet him."

When I burst in that afternoon she was in conference in the parlor with 11
an executive of the Curtis Publishing Company. She introduced me. He bent
low from the waist and shook my hand. Was it true as my mother had told
him, he asked, that I longed for the opportunity to conquer the world of
business?

My mother replied that I was blessed with a rare determination to make 12
something of myself.

"That's right," I whispered. 13

"But have you got the grit, the character, the never-say-quit spirit it takes 14
to succeed in business?"

My mother said I certainly did. 15

"That's right," I said. 16

He eyed me silently for a long pause, as though weighing whether I could 17
be trusted to keep his confidence, then spoke man-to-man. Before taking a
crucial step, he said, he wanted to advise me that working for the Curtis
Publishing Company placed enormous responsibility on a young man. It was
one of the great companies of America. Perhaps the greatest publishing house
in the world. I had heard, no doubt, of the *Saturday Evening Post?*

Heard of it? My mother said that everyone in our house had heard of the 18
Saturday Evening Post and that I, in fact, read it with religious devotion.

Then doubtless, he said, we were also familiar with those two monthly 19
pillars of the magazine world, the *Ladies Home Journal* and the *Country
Gentleman.*

Indeed we were familiar with them, said my mother. 20

Representing the *Saturday Evening Post* was one of the weightiest honors 21
that could be bestowed in the world of business, he said. He was personally
proud of being a part of that great corporation.

My mother said he had every right to be. 22

Again he studied me as though debating whether I was worthy of a 23
knighthood. Finally: "Are you trustworthy?"

My mother said I was the soul of honesty. 24

"That's right," I said. 25

Baker

The caller smiled for the first time. He told me I was a lucky young man. 26
He admired my spunk. Too many young men thought life was all play.
Those young men would not go far in this world. Only a young man willing
to work and save and keep his face washed and his hair neatly combed could
hope to come out on top in a world such as ours. Did I truly and sincerely
believe that I was such a young man?

"He certainly does," said my mother. 27

"That's right," I said. 28

He said he had been so impressed by what he had seen of me that he was 29
going to make me a representative of the Curtis Publishing Company. On
the following Tuesday, he said, thirty freshly printed copies of the *Saturday
Evening Post* would be delivered at our door. I would place these magazines,
still damp with the ink of the presses, in a handsome canvas bag, sling it
over my shoulder, and set forth through the streets to bring the best in journalism, fiction, and cartoons to the American public.

He had brought the canvas bag with him. He presented it with reverence 30
fit for a chasuble. He showed me how to drape the sling over my left shoulder and across the chest so that the pouch lay easily accessible to my right
hand, allowing the best in journalism, fiction, and cartoons to be swiftly extracted and sold to a citizenry whose happiness and security depended upon
us soldiers of the free press.

The following Tuesday I raced home from school, put the canvas bag over 31
my shoulder, dumped the magazines in, and, tilting to the left to balance
their weight on my right hip, embarked on the highway of journalism.

We lived in Belleville, New Jersey, a commuter town at the northern 32
fringe of Newark. It was 1932, the bleakest year of the Depression. My father
had died two years before, leaving us with a few pieces of Sears, Roebuck furniture and not much else, and my mother had taken Doris and me to live
with one of her younger brothers. This was my Uncle Allen. Uncle Allen had
made something of himself by 1932. As salesman for a soft-drink bottler in
Newark, he had an income of $30 a week; wore pearl-gray spats, detachable
collars, and a three-piece suit; was happily married; and took in threadbare
relatives.

With my load of magazines I headed toward Belleville Avenue. That's 33
where the people were. There were two filling stations at the intersection
with Union Avenue, as well as an A&P, a fruit stand, a bakery, a barber shop,
Zuccarelli's drugstore, and a diner shaped like a railroad car. For several hours
I made myself highly visible, shifting positions now and then from corner to
corner, from shop window to shop window, to make sure everyone could see
the heavy black lettering on the canvas bag that said *The Saturday Evening
Post*. When the angle of the light indicated it was suppertime, I walked back
to the house.

"How many did you sell, Buddy?" my mother asked. 34

"None." 35

"Where did you go?" 36

"The corner of Belleville and Union Avenues." 37

"What did you do?" 38

"Stood on the corner waiting for somebody to buy a *Saturday Evening Post*." 39

"You just stood there?"   40

"Didn't sell a single one."   41

"For God's sake, Russell!"   42

Uncle Allen intervened. "I've been thinking about it for some time," he   43
said, "and I've about decided to take the *Post* regularly. Put me down as a regular customer." I handed him a magazine and he paid me a nickel. It was the
first nickel I earned.

Afterwards my mother instructed me in salesmanship. I would have to   44
ring doorbells, address adults with charming self-confidence, and break down
resistance with a sales talk pointing out that no one, no matter how poor,
could afford to be without the *Saturday Evening Post* in the home.

I told my mother I'd changed my mind about wanting to succeed in the   45
magazine business.

"If you think I'm going to raise a good-for-nothing," she replied, "you've   46
got another think coming." She told me to hit the streets with the canvas
bag and start ringing doorbells the instant school was out next day. When I
objected that I didn't feel any aptitude for salesmanship, she asked how I'd
like to lend her my leather belt so she could whack some sense into me. I
bowed to superior will and entered journalism with a heavy heart.

My mother and I had fought this battle almost as long as I could remem-   47
ber. It probably started even before memory began, when I was a country child in northern Virginia and my mother, dissatisfied with my father's
plain workman's life, determined that I would not grow up like him and his
people, with calluses on their hands, overalls on their backs, and fourth-
grade educations in their heads. She had fancier ideas of life's possibilities.
Introducing me to the *Saturday Evening Post,* she was trying to wean me as
early as possible from my father's world where men left with their lunch
pails at sunup, worked with their hands until the grime ate into the pores,
and died with a few sticks of mail-order furniture as their legacy. In my
mother's vision of the better life there were desks and white collars, well-
pressed suits, evenings of reading and lively talk, and perhaps—if a man
were very, very lucky and hit the jackpot, really made something important
of himself—perhaps there might be a fantastic salary of $5,000 a year to
support a big house and a Buick with a rumble seat and a vacation in
Atlantic City.

And so I set forth with my sack of magazines. I was afraid of the dogs that   48
snarled behind the doors of potential buyers. I was timid about ringing the
doorbells of strangers, relieved when no one came to the door, and scared
when someone did. Despite my mother's instructions, I could not deliver an
engaging sales pitch. When a door opened I simply asked, "Want to buy a
Saturday Evening Post?" In Belleville few persons did. It was a town of 30,000
people, and most weeks I rang a fair majority of its doorbells. But I rarely
sold my thirty copies. Some weeks I canvassed the entire town for six days
and still had four or five unsold magazines on Monday evening; then I
dreaded the coming of Tuesday morning, when a batch of thirty fresh *Saturday Evening Posts* was due at the front door.

"Better get out there and sell the rest of those magazines tonight," my   49
mother would say.

I usually posted myself then at a busy intersection where a traffic light 50
controlled commuter flow from Newark. When the light turned red I stood
on the curb and shouted my sales pitch at the motorists.

"Want to buy a *Saturday Evening Post?*" 51

One rainy night when car windows were sealed against me I came back 52
soaked and with not a single sale to report. My mother beckoned to Doris.

"Go back down there with Buddy and show him how to sell these maga- 53
zines," she said.

Brimming with zest, Doris, who was then seven years old, returned with 54
me to the corner. She took a magazine from the bag, and when the light
turned red she strode to the nearest car and banged her small fist against the
closed window. The driver probably got startled at what he took to be a mid-
get assaulting his car, lowered the window to stare, and Doris thrust a *Saturday Evening Post* at him.

"You need this magazine," she piped, "and it only costs a nickel." 55

Her salesmanship was irresistible. Before the light changed half a dozen 56
times she disposed of the entire batch. I didn't feel humiliated. To the contrary. I was so happy I decided to give her a treat. Leading her to the veg-
etable store on Belleville Avenue, I bought three apples, which cost a nickel,
and gave her one.

"You shouldn't waste money," she said. 57

"Eat your apple." I bit into mine. 58

"You shouldn't eat before supper," she said. "It'll spoil your appetite." 59

Back at the house that evening, she dutifully reported me for wasting a 60
nickel. Instead of a scolding, I was rewarded with a pat on the back for having the good sense to buy fruit instead of candy. My mother reached into her
bottomless supply of maxims and told Doris, "An apple a day keeps the doctor away."

By the time I was ten I had learned all my mother's maxims by heart. 61
Asking to stay up past normal bedtime, I knew that a refusal would be explained with, "Early to bed and early to rise, makes a man healthy, wealthy,
and wise." If I whimpered about having to get up early in the morning, I
could depend on her to say, "The early bird gets the worm."

The one I most despised was, "If at first you don't succeed, try, try again." 62
This was the battle cry with which she constantly sent me back into the
hopeless struggle whenever I moaned that I had rung every doorbell in town
and knew there wasn't a single potential buyer left in Belleville that week.
After listening to my explanation, she handed me the canvas bag and said,
"If at first you don't succeed . . ."

Three years in that job, which I would gladly have quit after the first day 63
except for her insistence, produced at least one valuable result. My mother
finally concluded that I would never make something of myself by pursuing
a life in business and started considering careers that demanded less competitive zeal.

One evening when I was eleven I brought home a short "composition" 64
on my summer vacation which the teacher had graded with an A. Reading it
with her own schoolteacher's eye, my mother agreed that it was top-drawer
seventh grade prose and complimented me. Nothing more was said about it

immediately, but a new idea had taken life in her mind. Halfway through supper she suddenly interrupted the conversation.

"Buddy," she said, "maybe you could be a writer."   65

I clasped the idea to my heart. I had never met a writer, had shown no   66
previous urge to write, and hadn't a notion how to become a writer, but I loved stories and thought that making up stories must surely be almost as much fun as reading them. Best of all, though, and what really gladdened my heart, was the ease of the writer's life. Writers did not have to trudge through the town peddling from canvas bags, defending themselves against angry dogs, being rejected by surly strangers. Writers did not have to ring doorbells. So far as I could make out, what writers did couldn't even be classified as work.

I was enchanted. Writers didn't have to have any gumption at all. I did   67
not dare tell anybody for fear of being laughed at in the schoolyard, but secretly I decided that what I'd like to be when I grew up was a writer.[1]

From *Growing Up* by Russell Baker. Copyright © 1982 by Russell Baker. Reprinted by permission of Congdon & Weed, Chicago.
l. Russell Baker grew up to be a writer for *The New York Times*. He has covered the White House, Congress, and national politics and has writen a column called "Observer" since 1962. He is also the host for "Masterpiece Theatre" on PBS.

Reader's Dialogue: Making & Sharing Connections

Read the beginning of one reader's notes in Figure 3.7. Stop and make your own connections. Do you remember being asked what you wanted to be when you grew up, or wondering about this yourself? What were some of your responses? Write about your memories on the note-making side. Then continue notetaking and notemaking. End your Reader's Dialogue notebook entry for this selection by copying this quotation: "So far as I could make out, what writers did couldn't even be classified as work. I was enchanted. Writers didn't have to have any gumption at all." Do you agree with this view of writers and writing?

Discuss your notemaking and your own stories with other writers in your class. Has anyone ever tried to push you in a direction contrary to your interests? Do you know anyone who pursued a career or went in a particular direction to please others? Do you recall your parents comparing you to others (brothers, sisters, other relations, or other children) or having certain expectations regarding your future? Did you ever compare yourself to others concerning what you wanted to be or the way you wanted to be when you grew up?

Optional Writing Opportunities

Changing Points of View: Acting Through Writing

1. Write a monologue from Russell's mother's point of view. It is 1932, the bleakest year of the Depression. Your husband died two years ago and you

Figure 3.7

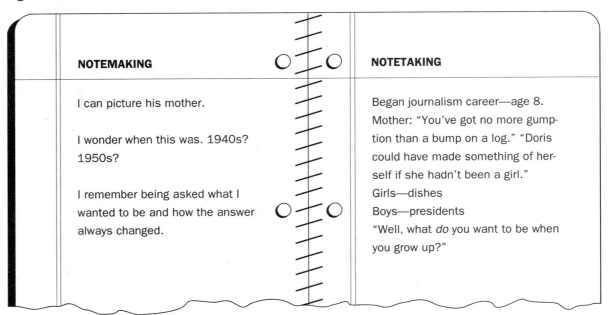

NOTEMAKING	NOTETAKING
I can picture his mother.	Began journalism career—age 8.
	Mother: "You've got no more gump-
I wonder when this was. 1940s?	tion than a bump on a log." "Doris
1950s?	could have made something of her-
	self if she hadn't been a girl."
I remember being asked what I	Girls—dishes
wanted to be and how the answer	Boys—presidents
always changed.	"Well, what *do* you want to be when
	you grow up?"

and your two children are living with Uncle Allen, who has "made something of himself." Russell has just turned eight years old. You are sitting in your favorite chair late in the evening, thinking about your son's future.

2. Russell has decided to tell his mother he does not want to be a magazine salesman. His mother objects to his quitting. Write a dialogue of a scene between Russell and his mother.

Writing Topic: Two Lives at Age Eight

1. Based on the information provided in Russell Baker's "Growing Up," write a description of his background and situation in 1932. Use these questions to guide your rereading and rethinking: What was life like in the 1930s? Where was Russell Baker living at this time? Why did he move? What is his family history? Why was his mother dissatisfied with her husband's world? How did Uncle Allen's life contrast with Baker's father's? What was his mother's vision of a better life, and what did she want for her son? Begin your summary with "In 1932, Russell Baker was eight years old."

2. Then think about your life at age eight. What was the year? Describe your background in terms of the times, your family history and cultural background, and your expectations with regard to your future. Begin your summary in the same way you began writing about Baker: "In [date], I was eight years old."

3. Finally, write about your reflections, including similarities and differences between Russell Baker's life and times and yours.

Autobiography is a very personal story telling—a unique recounting of events not so much as they have happened but as we remember and invent them.

bell hooks

Further Reading: More Recollections & Reflections

In the pages that follow you will be reading some additional selections from writers who reveal unique perspectives on their own life experiences. Readings include:

- "Annie John" by Jamaica Kincaid
- "The Seam of the Snail" by Cynthia Ozick
- "Fish Cheeks" by Amy Tan
- "The Language We Know" by Simon Ortiz
- "Growing Up Game" by Brenda Peterson
- "My Daughter Smokes" by Alice Walker

Annie John

Jamaica Kincaid

Born in St. John's, Antigua, an island in the Caribbean, Jamaica Kincaid now lives in Vermont. Her stories have appeared in The New Yorker *and other magazines, and some are published in a collection called* At the Bottom of the River *(1984). She is also the author of* Lucy *(1990). This selection from an earlier novel,* Annie John *(1983), is about Annie's first day at school.*

After peeping over my shoulder left and right, I sat down in my seat and 1 wondered what would become of me. There were twenty of us in my class, and we were seated at desks arranged five in a row, four rows deep. I was at a desk in the third row, and this made me even more miserable. I hated to be seated so far away from the teacher, because I was sure I would miss something she said. But, even worse, if I was out of my teacher's sight all the time, how could she see my industriousness and quickness at learning things? And, besides, only dunces were seated so far to the rear, and I could not bear to be thought a dunce. I was now staring at the back of a shrubby-haired girl seated in the front row—the seat I most coveted, since it was directly in front of the teacher's desk. At that moment, the girl twisted herself around, stared at me, and said, "You are Annie John? We hear you are very bright." It was a good thing Miss Nelson walked in right then, for how would it have appeared if I had replied, "Yes, that is completely true"—the very thing that was on the tip of my tongue.

As soon as Miss Nelson walked in, we came to order and stood up stiffly 2 at our desks. She said to us, "Good morning, class," half in a way that someone must have told her was the proper way to speak to us and half in a jocular way, as if we secretly amused her. We replied, "Good morning, Miss," in unison and in a respectful way, at the same time making a barely visible curtsy, also in unison. When she had seated herself at her desk, she said to us, "You may sit now," and we did. She opened the roll book, and as she called out our names each of us answered, "Present, Miss." As she called out our names, she kept her head bent over the book, but when she called out my name and I answered with the customary response she looked up and smiled at me and said, "Welcome, Annie." Everyone, of course, then turned and looked at me. I was sure it was because they could hear the loud racket my heart was making in my chest.

It was the first day of a new term, Miss Nelson said, so we would not be 3 attending to any of our usual subjects; instead, we were to spend the morning in contemplation and reflection and writing something she described as an "autobiographical essay." In the afternoon, we would read aloud to each other our autobiographical essays. (I knew quite well about "autobiography" and "essay," but reflection and contemplation! A day at school spent in such a way! Of course, in most books all the good people were always contemplating and reflecting before they did anything. Perhaps in her mind's eye she could see our futures and, against all prediction, we turned out to be good people.) On hearing this, a huge sigh went up from the girls. Half the sighs were in happiness at the thought of sitting and gazing off into clear space, the other half in unhappiness at the misdeeds that would have to go unaccomplished. I joined the happy half, because I knew it would please Miss Nelson, and, my own selfish interest aside, I liked so much the way she wore her ironed hair and her long-sleeved blouse and box-pleated skirt that I wanted to please her.

The morning was uneventful enough: a girl spilled ink from her inkwell 4 all over her uniform; a girl broke her pen nib and then made a big to-do about replacing it; girls twisted and turned in their seats and pinched each other's bottoms; girls passed notes to each other. All this Miss Nelson must have seen and heard, but she didn't say anything—only kept reading her book: an elaborately illustrated edition of *The Tempest,* as later, passing by her desk, I saw. Midway in the morning, we were told to go out and stretch our legs and breathe some fresh air for a few minutes; when we returned, we were given glasses of cold lemonade and a slice of bun to refresh us.

As soon as the sun stood in the middle of the sky, we were sent home for 5 lunch. The earth may have grown an inch or two larger between the time I had walked to school that morning and the time I went home to lunch, for some girls made a small space for me in their little band. But I couldn't pay much attention to them; my mind was on my new surroundings, my new teacher, what I had written in my nice new notebook with its black-all-mixed-up-with-white cover and smooth lined pages (so glad was I to get rid of my old notebooks, which had on their covers a picture of a wrinkled-up woman wearing a crown on her head and a neckful and armfuls of diamonds and pearls—their pages so coarse, as if they were made of cornmeal). I flew home. I must have eaten my food. I flew back to school. By half past one, we were sitting under a flamboyant tree in a secluded part of our schoolyard, our autobiographical essays in hand. We were about to read aloud what we had written during our morning of contemplation and reflection.

In response to Miss Nelson, each girl stood up and read her composition. 6 One girl told of a much revered and loved aunt who now lived in England

and of how much she looked forward to one day moving to England to live with her aunt; one girl told of her brother studying medicine in Canada and the life she imagined he lived there (it seemed quite odd to me); one girl told of the fright she had when she dreamed she was dead, and of the matching fright she had when she woke and found that she wasn't (everyone laughed at this, and Miss Nelson had to call us to order over and over); one girl told of how her oldest sister's best friend's cousin's best friend (it was a real rigmarole) had gone on a Girl Guide jamboree held in Trinidad and met someone who millions of years ago had taken tea with Lady Baden-Powell[1]; one girl told of an excursion she and her father had made to Redonda, and of how they had seen some booby birds tending their chicks. Things went on in that way, all so playful, all so imaginative. I began to wonder about what I had written, for it was the opposite of playful and it was the opposite of imaginative. What I had written was heartfelt, and, except for the very end, it was all too true. The afternoon was wearing itself thin. Would my turn ever come? What should I do, finding myself in a world of new girls, a world in which I was not even near the center?

It was a while before I realized that Miss Nelson was calling on me. My 7 turn at last to read what I had written. I got up and started to read, my voice shaky at first, but since the sound of my own voice had always been a calming potion to me, it wasn't long before I was reading in such a way that, except for the chirp of some birds, the hum of bees looking for flowers, the silvery rush-rush of the wind in the trees, the only sound to be heard was my voice as it rose and fell in sentence after sentence.

Excerpt from *Annie John* by Jamaica Kincaid. Copyright © 1985 by Jamaica Kincaid. Reprinted by permission of Farrar, Straus & Giroux, Inc.
1. Lady Baden-Powell: sister of founder of Boy Scouts, with whom she co-founded Girl Guides.

The Seam of the Snail

Cynthia Ozick

Cynthia Ozick grew up hearing Yiddish, the language of her Russian-born parents. As a child, she suffered "brutally difficult" prejudice. In his biography, Joseph Lowin records her memories of being called "Christ-killer" and of being pelted with stones as she passed neighborhood churches. In "A Drugstore in Winter," Ozick remembers the prejudices she encountered in grammar school when she refused to sing Christmas carols. In the following essay, first published as "Excellence" in MS., January 1985, Ozick recalls some childhood memories that bring out mother-daughter differences. She uses this contrast as a way of talking about what is important to her as a writer—precision: nothing matters to her "so much as a comely and muscular sentence." She likens herself to "a kind of human snail" and thinks of her sentences as "snail trails."

In my Depression childhood, whenever I had a new dress, my cousin Sarah 1 would get suspicious. The nicer the dress was, and especially the more expensive it looked, the more suspicious she would get. Finally she would lift the hem and check the seams. This was to see if the dress had been bought or if my mother had sewed it. Sarah could always tell. My mother's sewing had elegant outsides, but there was something catch-as-catch-can about the insides. Sarah's sewing, by contrast, was as impeccably finished inside as out; not one stray thread dangled.

My uncle Jake built meticulous grandfather clocks out of rosewood; he was a perfectionist, and sent to England for the clockworks. My mother built serviceable radiator covers and a serviceable cabinet, with hinged doors, for the pantry. She built a pair of bookcases for the living room. Once, after I was grown and in a house of my own, she fixed the sewer pipe. She painted ceilings, and also landscapes; she reupholstered chairs. One summer she planted a whole yard of tall corn. She thought herself capable of doing anything, and did everything she imagined. But nothing was perfect. There was always some clear flaw, never visible head-on. You had to look underneath, where the seams were. The corn thrived, though not in rows. The stalks elbowed one another like gossips in a dense little village. 2

"Miss Brrrroooobaker," my mother used to mock, rolling her Russian *r*'s, whenever I crossed a *t* she had left uncrossed, or corrected a word she had misspelled, or became impatient with a *v* that had tangled itself up with a *w* in her speech. ("*Vv*ventriloquist," I would say. "*Vv*ventriloquist," she would obediently repeat. And the next time it would come out "wiolinist.") Miss Brubaker was my high school English teacher, and my mother invoked her name as an emblem of raging finical obsession. "Miss Brrrroooobaker," my mother's voice hoots at me down the years, as I go on casting and recasting sentences in a tiny handwriting on monomaniacally uniform paper. The loops of my mother's handwriting—it was the Palmer Method[1]—were as big as soup bowls, spilling generous splashy ebullience. She could pull off, at five minutes' notice, a satisfying dinner for ten concocted out of nothing more than originality and panache. But the napkin would be folded a little off center, and the spoon might be on the wrong side of the knife. She was an optimist who ignored trifles; for her, God was not in the details but in the intent. And all these culinary and agricultural efflorescences were extracurricular, accomplished in the crevices and niches of a fourteen-hour business day. When she scribbled out her family memoirs, in heaps of dog-eared notebooks, or on the backs of old bills, or on the margins of last year's calendar, I would resist typing them; in the speed of the chase she often omitted words like "the," "and," "will." The same flashing and bountiful hand fashioned and fired ceramic pots, and painted brilliant autumn views and vases of imaginary flowers and ferns, and decorated ordinary Woolworth platters with lavish enameled gardens. But bits of the painted petals would chip away. 3

Lavish: my mother was as lavish as nature. She woke early and saturated the hours with work and inventiveness, and read late into the night. She was all profusion, abundance, fabrication. Angry at her children, she would run after us whirling the cord of the electric iron, like a lasso or a whip; but she never caught us. When, in seventh grade, I was afraid of failing the Music Appreciation final exam because I could not tell the difference between "To 4 a Wild Rose" and "Barcarole,"[2] she got the idea of sending me to school with a gauze sling rigged up on my writing arm, and an explanatory note that was purest fiction. But the sling kept slipping off. My mother gave advice like mad—she boiled over with so much passion for the predicaments of strangers that they turned into permanent cronies. She told intimate stories about people I had never heard of.

Despite the gargantuan Palmer loops (or possibly because of them), 5 I have always known that my mother's was a life of—intricately abashing word!—excellence: insofar as excellence means ripe generosity. She burgeoned, she proliferated; she was endlessly leafy and flowering. She wore red hats, and called herself a gypsy. In her girlhood she marched with the suffragettes and for Margaret Sanger[3] and called herself a Red.[4] She made me laugh, she was so varied: like a tree on which lemons, pomegranates, and prickly pears absurdly all hang together. She had the comedy of prodigality.

My own way is a thousand times more confined. I am a pinched perfec- 6 tionist, the ultimate fruition of Miss Brubaker; I attend to crabbed minutiae and am self-trammeled through taking pains. I am a kind of human snail, locked in and condemned by my own nature. The ancients believed that the moist track left by the snail as it crept was the snail's own essence, depleting its body little by little; the farther the snail toiled, the smaller it became, until it finally rubbed itself out. That is how perfectionists are. Say to us Excellence, and we will show you how we use up our substance and wear ourselves away, while making scarcely any progress at all. The fact that I am an exacting perfectionist in a narrow strait only, and nowhere else, is hardly to the point, since nothing matters to me so much as a comely and muscular sentence. It is my narrow strait, this snail's road; the track of the sentence I am writing now; and when I have eked out the wet substance, ink or blood, that is its mark, I will begin the next sentence. Only in treading out sentences am I a perfectionist; but then there is nothing else I know how to do, or take much interest in. I miter every pair of abutting sentences as scrupulously as Uncle Jake fitted one strip of rosewood against another. My mother's worldly and bountiful hand has escaped me. The sentence I am writing is my cabin and my shell, compact, self-sufficient. It is the burnished horizon—a merciless planet where flawlessness is the single standard, where even the inmost seams, however hidden from a laxer eye, must meet perfection. Here "excellence" is not strewn casually from a tipped cornucopia, here disorder does not account for charm, here trifles rule like tyrants.

I measure my life in sentences pressed out, line by line, like the lustrous 7 ooze on the underside of the snail, the snail's secret open seam, its wound, leaking attar.[5] My mother was too mettlesome to feel the force of a comma. She scorned minutiae. She measured her life according to what poured from the horn of plenty, which was her own seamless, ample, cascading, elastic, susceptible, inexact heart. My narrower heart rides between the tiny twin horns of the snail, dwindling as it goes.

And out of this thinnest thread, this ink-wet line of words, must rise a 8 visionary fog, a mist, a smoke, forging cities, histories, sorrows, quagmires, entanglements, lives of sinners, even the life of my furnace-hearted mother:

so much wilderness, waywardness, plenitude on the head of the precise and impeccable snail, between the horns. (Ah, if this could be!)

"The Seam of the Snail" by Cynthia Ozick was first published as "Excellence" in *Ms.* magazine, January 1985. Reprinted by permission of Ms. Magazine, © 1985.

1. Introduced in 1888, it taught penmanship using model letter forms (that adorned every elementary classroom) and free-flowing forearm exercises to practice loops and circles.
2. "To a Wild Rose" (1986): music by Edward MacDowell (1861–1908); "Barcarolle": by J. Offenbach, from *The Tales of Hoffman* (1881), with lyrics by Jules Paul Barbier (1822–1901).
3. Margaret Sanger (1883–1966), born in Corning, N.Y., led the birth-control movement in America. A trained nurse, she felt that the poor needed to control the size of their families. It was illegal to distribute birth-control information and she was arrested several times but helped get laws passed permitting doctors to give out information.
4. A communist.
5. A fragrant oil extracted from the petals of flowers.

Fish Cheeks

Amy Tan

Amy Tan wrote this essay before the publication of her first novel The Joy Luck Club, *a series of stories told by four Chinese mothers and their American-born daughters. In this essay, first published in* Seventeen, *December 1987, she recollects a Christmas Eve dinner and the lesson she learned years later.*

I fell in love with the minister's son the winter I turned fourteen. He was not 1 Chinese, but as white as Mary in the manger. For Christmas I prayed for this blond-haired boy, Robert, and a slim new American nose.

When I found out that my parents had invited the minister's family over 2 for Christmas Eve dinner, I cried. What would Robert think of our shabby Chinese Christmas? What would he think of our noisy Chinese relatives who lacked proper American manners? What terrible disappointment would he feel upon seeing not a roasted turkey and sweet potatoes but Chinese food?

On Christmas Eve I saw that my mother had outdone herself in creating 3 a strange menu. She was pulling black veins out of the backs of fleshy prawns. The kitchen was littered with appalling mounds of raw food: A slimy rock cod with bulging eyes that pleaded not to be thrown into a pan of hot oil. Tofu,[1] which looked like stacked wedges of rubbery white sponges. A bowl soaking dried fungus back to life. A plate of squid, their backs crisscrossed with knife markings so they resembled bicycle tires.

And then they arrived—the minister's family and all my relatives in a 4 clamor of doorbells and rumpled Christmas packages. Robert grunted hello, and I pretended he was not worthy of existence.

Dinner threw me deeper into despair. My relatives licked the ends of their 5 chopsticks and reached across the table, dipping them into the dozen or so plates of food. Robert and his family waited patiently for platters to be passed to them. My relatives murmured with pleasure when my mother brought out the whole steamed fish. Robert grimaced. Then my father poked his chopsticks just below the fish eye and plucked out the soft meat. "Amy, your favorite," he said, offering me the tender fish cheek. I wanted to disappear.

At the end of the meal my father leaned back and belched loudly, thank- 6 ing my mother for her fine cooking. "It's a polite Chinese custom to show you are satisfied," explained my father to our astonished guests. Robert was looking down at his plate with a reddened face. The minister managed to muster up a quiet burp. I was stunned into silence for the rest of the night.

After everyone had gone, my mother said to me, "You want to be the 7 same as American girls on the outside." She handed me an early gift. It was a miniskirt in beige tweed. "But inside you must always be Chinese. You must be proud you are different. Your only shame is to have shame."

And even though I didn't agree with her then, I knew that she under- 8 stood how much I had suffered during the evening's dinner. It wasn't until many years later—long after I had gotten over my crush on Robert—that I was able to fully appreciate her lesson and the true purpose behind our particular menu. For Christmas Eve that year, she had chosen all my favorite foods.

Copyright © 1987 by Amy Tan. Reprinted by permission of Amy Tan and the Sandra Dijkstra Literary Agency.
1. Soybean curd.

The Language We Know

Simon Ortiz

Simon Ortiz was born at Acomo Pueblo in New Mexico. His book From Sand Creek *won the Pushcart Prize for Poetry. In his autobiographical essay "The Language We Know," Ortiz addresses the relationship between language and culture. In the excerpts included here, he examines how the Acoma language and oral tradition he learned as a child nurtured and shaped him into a poet and writer.*

I don't remember a world without language. From the time of my earliest 1 childhood, there was language. Always language, and imagination, speculation, utters of sound. Words, beginnings of words. What would I be without language? My existence has been determined by language, not only the spoken but the unspoken, the language of speech and the language of motion. I can't remember a world without memory. Memory, immediate and far away in the past, something in the sinew, blood, ageless cell. Although I don't recall the exact moment I spoke or tried to speak, I know the feeling of something tugging at the core of the mind, something unutterable uttered into existence. It is language that brings us into being in order to know life.

My childhood was the oral tradition of the Acoma Pueblo people—Aaquu- 2 meh hano—which included my immediate family of three older sisters, two younger sisters, two younger brothers, and my mother and father. My world was our world of the Aaquumeh in McCartys, one of the two villages descended from the ageless mother pueblo of Acoma. My world was our Eagle

Ortiz

clan—people among other clans. I grew up in Deetziyamah, which is the Aaquumeh name for McCartys, which is posted at the exit off the present interstate highway in western New Mexico. I grew up within a people who farmed small garden plots and fields, who were mostly poor and not well schooled in the American system's education. The language I spoke was that of a struggling people who held ferociously to a heritage, culture, language, and land despite the odds posed them by the forces surrounding them since 1540 A.D., the advent of Euro-American colonization. When I began school in 1948 at the BIA (Bureau of Indian Affairs) day school in our village, I was armed with the basic ABC's and the phrases "Good morning, Miss Oleman" and "May I please be excused to go to the bathroom," but it was an older language that was my fundamental strength. In my childhood, the language we all spoke was Acoma, and it was a struggle to maintain it against the outright threats of corporal punishment, ostracism, and the invocation that it would impede our progress towards Americanization. Children in school were punished and looked upon with disdain if they did not speak and learn English quickly and smoothly, and so I learned it. It has occurred to me that I learned English simply because I was forced to, as so many other Indian children were. But I know, also, there was another reason, and this was that I loved language, the sound, meaning, and magic of language. Language opened up vistas of the world around me, and it allowed me to discover knowledge that would not be possible for me to know without the use of language. Later, when I began to experiment with and explore language in poetry and fiction, I allowed that a portion of that impetus was because I had come to know English through forceful acculturation. Nevertheless, the underlying force was the beauty and poetic power of language in its many forms that instilled in me the desire to become a user of language as a writer, singer, and storyteller. Significantly, it was the Acoma language, which I don't use enough of today, that inspired me to become a writer. The concepts, values, and philosophy contained in my original language and the struggle it has faced have determined my life and vision as a writer.

. . . . .

My first poem was for Mother's Day when I was in the fifth grade, and it was 3 the first poem that was ever published, too, in the Skull Valley School newsletter. Of course I don't remember how the juvenile poem went, but it must have been certain in its expression of love and reverence for the woman who was the most important person in my young life. The poem didn't signal any prophecy of my future as a poet, but it must have come from the forming idea that there were things one could do with language and writing. My mother, years later, remembers how I was a child who always told stories—that is, tall tales—who always had explanations for things probably better left unspoken, and she says that I also liked to perform in school plays. In remembering, I do know that I was coming to that age when the emotions and thoughts in me began to moil to the surface. There was much to experience and express in that age when youth has a precociousness that is broken easily or made to flourish. We were a poor family, always on the verge of financial disaster, though our parents always managed to feed us and keep us in clothing. We had the problems, unfortunately ordinary, of many Indian families who face poverty on a daily basis, never enough of anything, the feeling of a denigrating self-consciousness, alcoholism in the family and community, the feeling that something was falling apart though we tried desperately to hold it all together.

My father worked for the railroad for many years as a laborer and later as 4 a welder. We moved to Skull Valley, Arizona, for one year in the early 1950s, and it was then that I first came in touch with a non-Indian, non-Acoma world. Skull Valley was a farming and ranching community, and my younger brothers and sisters and I went to a one-room school. I had never really had much contact with white people except from a careful and suspicious distance, but now here I was, totally surrounded by them, and there was nothing to do but bear the experience and learn from it. Although I perceived there was not much difference between *them* and *us* in certain respects, there was a distinct feeling that we were not the same either. This thought had been inculcated in me, especially by an Acoma expression— *Gaimuu Mericano*—that spoke of the "fortune" of being an American. In later years as a social activist and committed writer, I would try to offer a strong positive view of our collective Indianness through my writing. Nevertheless, my father was an inadequately paid laborer, and we were far from our home land for economic-social reasons, and my feelings and thoughts about that experience during that time would become a part of how I became a writer.

Soon after, I went away from my home and family to go to boarding 5 school, first in Santa Fe and then in Albuquerque. This was in the 1950s, and this had been the case for the past half-century for Indians: we had to leave home in order to become truly American by joining the mainstream, which was deemed to be the proper course of our lives. On top of this was termination, a U.S. government policy which dictated that Indians sever their relationship to the federal government and remove themselves from their lands and go to American cities for jobs and education. It was an era which bespoke the intent of U.S. public policy that Indians were no longer to be Indians. Naturally, I did not perceive this in any analytical or purposeful sense; rather, I felt an unspoken anxiety and resentment against unseen forces that determined our destiny to be un-Indian, embarrassed and uncomfortable with our grandparents' customs and strictly held values. We were to set our goals as American working men and women, singlemindedly industrious, patriotic, and unquestioning, building for a future which ensured that the U.S. was the greatest nation in the world. I felt fearfully uneasy with this, for by then I felt the loneliness, alienation, and isolation imposed upon me by the separation from my family, home, and community.

Something was happening; I could see that in my years at Catholic 6 school and the U.S. Indian school. I remembered my grandparents' and parents' words: educate yourself in order to help your people. In that era and the generation who had the same experience I had, there was an unspoken vow: we were caught in a system inexorably, and we had to learn that system well in order to fight back. Without the motive of a fight-back we would not be able to survive as the people our heritage had lovingly bequeathed us. My

Ortiz

diaries and notebooks began then, and though none have survived to the present, I know they contained the varied moods of a youth filled with loneliness, anger, and discomfort that seemed to have unknown causes. Yet at the same time, I realize now, I was coming to know myself clearly in a way that I would later articulate in writing. My love of language, which allowed me to deal with the world, to delve into it, to experiment and discover, held for me a vision of awe and wonder, and by then grammar teachers had noticed I was a good speller, used verbs and tenses correctly, and wrote complete sentences. Although I imagine that they might have surmised this as unusual for an Indian student whose original language was not English, I am grateful for their perception and attention.

"The Language We Know" by Simon Ortiz was reprinted from *I Tell You Now: Autobiographical Essays by Native American Writers,* edited by Brian Swann and Arnold Krupat, by permission of the University of Nebraska Press. Copyright © 1987 by the University of Nebraska Press.

You can use childhood memories or family stories to reflect on an issue or to argue a point of view, as in this essay by Brenda Peterson and the one following by Alice Walker.

Growing Up Game

Brenda Peterson

Brenda Peterson works as an environmental writer in Seattle and is author of River of Light, *a novel. This essay was first published in Seattle's* The Weekly, *and is included in Peterson's nonfiction book* Living By Water: True Stories of Nature and Spirit *(1944).*

When I went off to college my father gave me, as part of my tuition, 50 1 pounds of moose meat. In 1969, eating moose meat at the University of California was a contradiction in terms. Hippies didn't hunt. I lived in a rambling Victorian house which boasted sweeping circular staircases, built-in lofts, and a landlady who dreamed of opening her own health food restaurant. I told my housemates that my moose meat in its nondescript white butcher paper was from a side of beef my father had bought. The carnivores in the house helped me finish off such suppers as sweet and sour moose meatballs, mooseburgers (garnished with the obligatory avocado and sprouts), and mooseghetti. The same dinner guests who remarked upon the lean sweetness of the meat would have recoiled if I'd told them the not-so-simple truth: that I grew up on game, and the moose they were eating had been brought down, with one shot through his magnificent heart, by my father—a man who had hunted all his life and all of mine.

One of my earliest memories is of crawling across the vast continent of 2 crinkled linoleum in our Forest Service cabin kitchen, down splintered back steps, through wildflowers growing wheat-high. I was eye-level with grasshoppers who scolded me on my first solo trip outside. I made it to the shed, a cool and comfortingly square shelter that held phantasmagoric metal parts; they smelled good, like dirt and grease. I had played a long time in this shed before some maternal shriek made me lift up on my haunches to listen to those urgent, possessive sounds that were my name. Rearing up, my head bumped into something hanging in the dark; gleaming white, it felt sleek and cold against my cheek. Its smell was dense and musty and not unlike the slabs of my grandmother's great arms after her cool, evening sponge baths. In that shed I looked up and saw the flensed body of a doe; it swung gently, slapping my face. I felt then as I do even now when eating game: horror and awe and hunger.

Growing up those first years on a forest station high in the Sierra was 3 somewhat like belonging to a white tribe. The men hiked off every day into their forest and the women stayed behind in the circle of official cabins, breeding. So far away from a store, we ate venison and squirrel, rattlesnake and duck. My brother's first rattle, in fact, was from a King Rattler my father killed as we watched, by snatching it up with a stick and winding it, whip-like, around a redwood sapling. Rattlesnake tastes just like chicken, but has many fragile bones to slither one's way through; we also ate salmon, rabbit, and geese galore. The game was accompanied by such daily garden dainties as fried okra, mustard greens, corn fritters, wilted lettuce (our favorite because of that rare, blackened bacon), new potatoes and peas, stewed tomatoes, barbecued butter beans.

I was 4 before I ever had a beef hamburger and I remember being disap- 4 pointed by its fatty, nothing taste and the way it fell apart at the seams whenever my teeth sank into it. Smoked pork shoulder came much later in the South; and I was 21, living in New York City, before I ever tasted leg of lamb. I approached that glazed rack of meat with a certain guilty self-consciousness, as if I unfairly stalked those sweet-tempered white creatures myself. But how would I explain my squeamishness to those urban sophisticates? How explain that I was shy with mutton when I had been bred on wild things?

Part of it, I suspect, had to do with the belief I'd also been bred on—we 5 become the spirit and body of animals we eat. As a child eating venison I liked to think of myself as lean and lovely just like the deer. I would never be caught dead just grazing while some man who wasn't even a skillful hunter crept up and konked me over the head. If someone wanted to hunt me, he must be wily and outwitting. He must earn me.

My father had also taught us as children that animals were our brothers 6 and sisters under their skin. They died so that we might live. And of this sacrifice we must be mindful. "God make us grateful for what we are about to receive," took on a new meaning when one knew the animal's struggle pitted against our own appetite. We also used *all* the animal so that an elk became elk steaks, stew, salami, and sausage. His head and horns went on the wall to watch us more earnestly than any babysitter, and every Christmas Eve we had a ceremony of making our own moccasins for the new year out of whatever Father had tanned. "Nothing wasted," my father would always say, or, as we munched on sausage cookies made from moosemeat or venison, "Think about who you're eating." We thought of ourselves as intricately linked to the food chain. We knew, for example, that a forest fire meant, at

Peterson

the end of the line, we'd suffer too. We'd have buck stew instead of venison steak and the meat would be stringy, withered-tasting because in the animal kingdom, as it seemed with humans, only the meanest and leanest and orneriest survived.

Once when I was in my early teens, I went along on a hunting trip as the 7 "main cook and bottle-washer," though I don't remember any bottles; none of these hunters drank alcohol. There was something else coursing through their veins as they rose long before dawn and disappeared, returning to my little camp most often dragging a doe or pheasant or rabbit. We ate innumerable cornmeal-fried catfish, had rabbit stew seasoned only with blood and black pepper.

This hunting trip was the first time I remember eating game as a con- 8 scious act. My father and Buddy Earl shot a big doe and she lay with me in the back of the tarp-draped station wagon all the way home. It was not the smell I minded, it was the glazed great, dark eyes and the way that head flopped around crazily on what I knew was once a graceful neck. I found myself petting this doe, murmuring all those graces we'd been taught long ago as children. *Thank you for the sacrifice, thank you for letting us be like you so that we can grow up strong as game.* But there was an uneasiness in me that night as I bounced along in the back of the car with the deer.

What was uneasy is still uneasy—perhaps it always will be. It's not easy 9 when one really starts thinking about all this: the eating game, the food chain, the sacrifice of one for the other. It's never easy when one begins to think about one's most basic actions, like eating. Like becoming what one eats: lean and lovely and mortal.

Why should it be that the purchase of meat at a butcher shop is some- 10 how more righteous than eating something wild? Perhaps it has to do with our collective unconscious that sees the animal bred for slaughter as doomed. But that wild doe or moose might make it without the hunter. Perhaps on this primitive level of archetype and unconscious knowing we even believe that what's wild lives forever.

My father once told this story around a hunting campfire. His own father, 11 who raised cattle during the Depression on a dirt farm in the Ozarks, once fell on such hard times that he had to butcher the pet lamb for supper. My father, bred on game or their own hogs all his life, took one look at the family pet on that meat platter and pushed his plate away from him. His siblings followed suit. To hear my grandfather tell it, it was the funniest thing he'd ever seen. "They just couldn't eat Bo-Peep," Grandfather said. And to hear my father tell it years later around that campfire, it was funny, but I saw for the first time his sadness. And I realized that eating had become a conscious act for him that day at the dinner table when Bo-Peep offered herself up.

Now when someone offers me game I will eat it with all the qualms and 12 memories and reverence with which I grew up eating it. And I think it will always be this feeling of horror and awe and hunger. And something else— full knowledge of what I do, what I become.

"Growing Up Game" by Brenda Peterson is from *Living by Water: True Stories of Nature and Spirit*, Ballentine/Fawcett, 1994. It first appeared in *The Weekly*, Seattle. Reprinted by permission of the author.

My Daughter Smokes

Alice Walker

Best known for The Color Purple, *Alice Walker has also written poetry, short stories, and essays. Watching her daughter smoke made Walker think about how smoking has affected her family. "My Daughter Smokes" was first published in* Living By the Word *(1988), a collection of essays. See "Beauty: When the Other Dancer Is the Self," an essay included earlier in this project.*

My daughter smokes. While she is doing her homework, her feet on the 1 bench in front of her and her calculator clicking out answers to her algebra problems, I am looking at the half-empty package of Camels tossed carelessly close at hand. Camels. I pick them up, take them into the kitchen, where the light is better, and study them—they're filtered, for which I am grateful. My heart feels terrible. I want to weep. In fact, I do weep a little, standing there by the stove holding one of the instruments, so white, so precisely rolled, that could cause my daughter's death. When she smoked Marlboros and Players I hardened myself against feeling so bad; nobody I knew ever smoked these brands.

She doesn't know this, but it was Camels that my father, her grandfather, 2 smoked. But before he smoked "ready-mades"—when he was very young and very poor, with eyes like lanterns—he smoked Prince Albert tobacco in cigarettes he rolled himself. I remember the bright-red tobacco tin, with a picture of Queen Victoria's consort, Prince Albert, dressed in a black frock coat and carrying a cane.

The tobacco was dark brown, pungent, slightly bitter. I tasted it more 3 than once as a child, and the discarded tins could be used for a number of things; to keep buttons and shoelaces in, to store seeds, and best of all, to hold worms for the rare times my father took us fishing.

By the late forties and fifties no one rolled his own anymore (and few 4 women smoked) in my hometown, Eatonton, Georgia. The tobacco industry, coupled with Hollywood movies in which both hero and heroine smoked like chimneys, won over completely people like my father, who were hopelessly addicted to cigarettes. He never looked as dapper as Prince Albert, though; he continued to look like a poor, overweight, overworked colored man with too large a family; black, with a very white cigarette stuck in his mouth.

I do not remember when he started to cough. Perhaps it was unnotice- 5 able at first. A little hacking in the morning as he lit his first cigarette upon getting out of bed. By the time I was my daughter's age, his breath was a wheeze, embarrassing to hear; he could not climb stairs without resting every third or fourth step. It was not unusual for him to cough for an hour.

It is hard to believe there was a time when people did not understand 6 that cigarette smoking is an addiction. I wondered aloud once to my sister— who is perennially trying to quit—whether our father realized this. I wondered how she, a smoker since high school, viewed her own habit.

It was our father who gave her her first cigarette, one day when she had 7 taken water to him in the fields.

Walker

"I always wondered why he did that," she said, puzzled, and with some 8
bitterness.

"What did he say?" I asked. 9

"That he didn't want me to go to anyone else for them," she said. "It 10
never really crossed my mind."

So he was aware it was addictive, I thought, though as annoyed as she 11
that he assumed she would be interested.

I began smoking in eleventh grade, also the year I drank numerous bot- 12
tles of terrible, sweet, very cheap wine. My friends and I, all boys for this
venture, bought our supplies from a man who ran a segregated bar and
liquor store on the outskirts of town. Over the entrance there was a large
sign that said COLORED. We were not permitted to drink there, only to buy.
I smoked Kools, because my sister did. By then I thought her toxic darkened
lips and gums glamorous. However, my body simply would not tolerate
smoke. After six months I had a chronic sore throat. I gave up smoking,
gladly. Because it was a ritual with my buddies—Murl, Leon, and "Dog"
Farley—I continued to drink wine.

My father died from "the poor man's friend," pneumonia, one hard win- 13
ter when his bronchitis and emphysema had left him low. I doubt he had
much lung left at all, after coughing for so many years. He had so little
breath that, during his last years, he was always leaning on something. I remember once, at a family reunion, when my daughter was two, that my father picked her up for a minute—long enough for me to photograph
them—but the effort was obvious. Near the very end of his life, and largely
because he had no more lungs, he quit smoking. He gained a couple of
pounds, but by then he was so emaciated no one noticed.

When I travel to Third World countries I see many people like my father and 14
daughter. There are large billboards directed at them both: the tough, "take-
charge," or dapper older man, the glamorous, "worldly" young woman,
both puffing away. In these poor countries, as in American ghettos and on
reservations, money that should be spent for food goes instead to the tobacco companies; over time, people starve themselves of both food and air,
effectively weakening and addicting their children, eventually eradicating
themselves. I read in the newspaper and in my gardening magazine that cigarette butts are so toxic that if a baby swallows one, it is likely to die, and
that the boiled water from a bunch of them makes an effective insecticide.

My daughter would like to quit, she says. We both know the statistics are 15
against her; most people who try to quit smoking do not succeed.[1]

There is a deep hurt that I feel as a mother. Some days it is a feeling of fu- 16
tility. I remember how carefully I ate when I was pregnant, how patiently I
taught my daughter how to cross a street safely. For what, I sometimes wonder; so that she can wheeze through most of her life feeling half her
strength, and then die of self-poisoning, as her grandfather did?

But, finally, one must feel empathy for the tobacco plant itself. For thou- 17
sands of years, it has been venerated by Native Americans as a sacred medicine. They have used it extensively—its juice, its leaves, its roots, its (holy)
smoke—to heal wounds and cure diseases, and in ceremonies of prayer and

peace. And though the plant as most of us know it has been poisoned by chemicals and denatured by intensive mono-cropping and is therefore hardly the plant it was, still, to some modern Indians it remains a plant of positive power. I learned this when my Native American friends, Bill Wahpepah and his family, visited with me for a few days and the first thing he did was sow a few tobacco seeds in my garden.

Perhaps we can liberate tobacco from those who have captured and 18 abused it, enslaving the plant on large plantations, keeping it from freedom and its kin, and forcing it to enslave the world. Its true nature suppressed, no wonder it has become deadly. Maybe by sowing a few seeds of tobacco in our gardens and treating the plant with the reverence it deserves, we can redeem tobacco's soul and restore its self-respect.

Besides, how grim, if one is a smoker, to realize one is smoking a slave. 19

There is a slogan from a battered women's shelter that I especially like: 20 "Peace on earth begins at home." I believe everything does. I think of a slogan for people trying to stop smoking: "Every home a smoke-free zone." Smoking is a form of self-battering that also batters those who must sit by, occasionally cajole or complain, and helplessly watch. I realize now that as a child I sat by, through the years, and literally watched my father kill himself: surely one such victory in my family, for the rich white men who own the tobacco companies, is enough.

"My Daughter Smokes" by Alice Walker appeared in *Living by the Word,* Harcourt Brace Jovanovich, 1988. Reprinted by permission.
1. Three months after reading this essay my daughter stopped smoking.

End-Project Writing Opportunities

1. Write about a significant childhood memory or memories. Interpret your recollections. How does your story fit into your larger family story or into the culture at large? Explain its significance. You could write about a memory or memories and then add some commentary or you could integrate the two.

Although experience can't be recovered, it can be narrated.

Linda Brodkey

2. You can use personal experience for other kinds of writing besides autobiography. You can use autobiographical material, for example, as a framework for an argument or as a means to lead you to reflect on an issue. Through your experience, you can speak with some authority. (See Brenda Peterson's "Growing Up Game" or Alice Walker's "My Daughter Smokes." See also Ricardo Sewell's "New Easter" ["Writer at Work"]. How could he use his story to reflect on the larger social problem of violence?)

3. Compare and contrast childhood memories with recent memories (of a place, for example, or an event or situation). Reflect on differences.

4. Write about a significant change of view in your life as a result of an experience. Include in your writing: (a) your view before the event, (b) the event that caused you to change your view, (c) your view after the event, and (d) your interpretation and evaluation of this experience in terms of your

life story. Do not write about a traumatic event that happened unless you have considerable distance from it. Alice Walker took thirty years to write about a scar from her childhood.

5. Virginia Woolf wrote memoirs for different audiences and occasions. For example, she wrote "A Sketch of the Past" to take a break from other writing she was doing that required considerable concentration, and also perhaps to divert her attention from the gloom of World War II. Also included in her book *Moments of Being* are several writings she delivered to the Memoir Club, a group of old friends who gathered from time to time to read memoirs. To suit her audience, her tone in these later writings is more intimate and less public. Even though everyone will be writing about memories, your class probably does not consist of old, close friends who have been meeting together for some time, and you cannot, therefore, naturally assume an intimate tone. Still, you may want to think of your class as a kind of Memoir Club and actually read your writing aloud during a class meeting. Your writing would then take more of the form of a talk about some recollections and reflections. Your writing could also take the form of a letter. You could invent an appropriate audience.

6. Review the approaches to writing about memories included in this project, and perhaps look at other autobiographical writing as well. Look at other writers' ways of writing: how they approached their lives and framed their stories. Use one writer's way of writing as a model, or perhaps invent your own way based on your reading of various approaches to autobiography.

Writer's Workshop 1: Trying Out Memories

Interviewer Anthony Whittier: How do you start a story?

Frank O'Connor: "Get black on white" used to be Maupassant's advice— that's what I always do. I don't give a hoot what the writing's like. I write any sort of rubbish which will cover the main outlines of the story, then I can begin to see it. When I write, when I draft a story, I never think of writing nice sentences about, "It was a nice August evening when Elizabeth Jane Moriarty was coming down the road." I just write roughly what happened, and then I'm able to see what the construction looks like. It's the design of the story which to me is most important, the thing that tells you there's a bad gap in the narrative. . . .[1]

Preworkshop Activity

You've already started writing. At the beginning of this project, before you began reading and listening to others, you tried tapping your memory. Next

---

1. Frank O'Connor, born (1903) in Cork, Ireland, is best known as a short story writer. This selection appeared in *Writers at Work: The Paris Review Interviews.* Second Series, ed. Malcolm Cowley. Copyright 1957, 1958 by The Paris Review, Inc.

you read autobiographical writing by others, and then you responded and continued to recollect and reflect on your own life. Before you actually begin this workshop, do the following things.

1. Review your writing-project folder now, perhaps making some notes about possible memories you could pursue.
2. Read again the suggested writing opportunities for recollecting and reflecting. Which one or ones interest you—or do you have another idea?
3. Begin writing about two or three memories, or a single memory if you have a direction you would like to try out. Return to the beginning of this project and reread the memories you wrote about then. Consider whether you want to pursue those or other memories that came to mind as you continued to read and write throughout this project (or perhaps other memories that come to mind now).
4. Then stop and write briefly about the kind of writing you think you would like to do and why. Also, write about any concerns you have or questions or problems you foresee.
5. Bring your writing-project folder and this work to class. Be prepared to read aloud and talk about your work with other writers.

Workshop Activity

Before getting into small discussion groups (of perhaps three members), you may want to go back and read what Will, Susan, and Darlene said about Darlene's writing on her childhood memories (see pp. 37–38). You could also ask some writers in your writing class to try their memories out on the whole class.

Get into your small discussion group to talk about memories and to get some suggestions for your writing project (or, listen to another writing group at work). Divide your time equally among group members, using the following writers' workshop guidelines.

Guidelines for Writers

1. Talk briefly about some memories you have written about. Help orient your listeners by providing some context.
2. Select one of your memories to *read aloud* to the group. Read it twice: once quickly so your listeners have a sense of the whole, and then a second time so they can take and make notes. (It's difficult to listen and take notes at the same time, and the whole is easily lost when listeners are paying attention to the parts.)

   Don't apologize for your writing ("If I only had more time . . ."; "I just dashed this off"; "I know this isn't any good"). This writing is a first effort, not a final one. Everyone will be rewriting. And everyone will be reading.

   Why read writing aloud instead of giving it to others to read? It's too easy to pay attention to surface errors (spelling and punctuation problems, for example) when you look at a piece of writing. That kind of attention is necessary when you are ready to present or go public with your writing; at this point, however, reading writing aloud forces listeners (as well as writers) to pay attention to meaning and sound. It's the design of the story that's important at first, says Frank O'Connor, not the writing (meaning, nice sentences). And if as a writer you are unused to reading your own writing aloud, as many experienced writers do, this workshop will give you an opportunity to see (and hear) the advantages of reading aloud.

3. Ask group members for their responses. Be an active writer (a "writer alive"). The purpose of this activity is not to sit back and absorb criticism. Rather, you seek responses that might help you decide which memories to pursue, how to make them significant, and how to frame them. *Take* notes.

4. At the end of this workshop, take a few minutes to write about the responses, including your plans for the next writing. *Make* notes. What direction do you plan to take?

Guidelines for Reviewers

1. The purpose of this workshop activity is to help writers decide what they want to write about and the significance or importance of selected memories. Keep these questions in mind: How can you help other writers? What kind of help would you like with your writing?

2. Remember that when you are listening, you are hearing the writer reading a first writing—a tryout. The writing is exploratory. In your role as a reviewer, ask yourself: Where did the act of writing take the writer? What did you hear the writer saying? The writer will use your comments as a guide for trying out a direction and writing a first draft.

3. Some writers may wander from one memory to another. Such wandering is natural when you are just beginning to think about what you want to write about. It would be inappropriate to tell a writer at this early point in the writing process that her writing is "disorganized" or that she needs to "expand" or "be more specific." Your goal as a reviewer is to help the writer center her writing or find out what she really wants to write about.

4. When you listen to writers read their work, be careful not to chase them away from some seemingly insignificant memories. Any event can be given significance, but the significance must be created by the writer and can only be suggested by readers: What is the significance of the event for the writer?

5. Listen once, pens down, to get a sense of the whole. Then read the Review Guide (Figure 3.8), and take and make notes during the second reading.

Talking with others while you are exploring ideas can help you think about what you want to write about. When writers work on a project, they talk over ideas with themselves and often with interested others. Take an active role in your writing group.

Figure 3.8

Writing Project: **Writer:** _____

Recollections & Reflections _____ **Reviewer:** _____

Draft: Tryout _____   **Date:** _____

REVIEW GUIDE

1. *Take* notes. Make a list of what the writer wrote about.
2. Review your list. *Make* notes. Here are some questions to guide your notemaking:
   a. Does any memory or group of memories dominate? If so, make a note ("The writer wrote mostly about . . .").
   b. In your view, where did the act of writing take the writer? What did you hear the writer saying? Tell the writer what you heard. (Sometimes a writer's intention is not realized. A reader and a writer might not agree about what the writer is saying. Your purpose here is to tell the writer your reading of this writing-in-progress to help the writer see from a different angle.)
   c. If the writer brings up different memories, are they connected? Did you have difficulty following the writer at any point? Did you get confused or wonder how something the writer included related to the whole? If so, make specific reference to the break or breaks in the story. Offer a suggestion if you can. How could a connection be made? Do you think one memory should be pursued for this writing or some part omitted?

Writer's Workshop 2: Moving Toward Significance

The purpose of this workshop is to help writers "disentangle the significant." Before you begin your review, go back and consider how the writers you've read in connection with this project made an event significant. Virginia Woolf, for example, made the viewing of the flowers on her mother's dress an event. An event doesn't have to be traumatic or dramatic; through writing you can create significance or what Woolf refers to as a "moment of being."

It is the business of writing and the responsibility of the writer to disentangle the significant—in character, incident, setting, mood, everything—from the random and meaningless and irrelevant that in real life surround and beset it.

     Eudora Welty

Writers:

 Read your first draft aloud to the whole class or to a small group of two or three other writers.

Reviewers:

1. Prepare to interview writers by familiarizing yourself with the Review Guide in Figure 3.9. Interview writers about their memories. What questions

Figure 3.9

Writing Project: **Writer:** _____

Recollections & Reflections _____   **Reviewer:** _____

Draft: _____ 1 _____   **Date:** _____

REVIEW GUIDE

1. *Questions:*

2. a. *The Writer's Intention:* I think your intention (what you are trying to do) in this piece of writing is:

   b. *The effect* on me as a reader/listener is:

3. *Suggestions for Improvement:*

---

do you have? What would you like to know more about? Were you confused at any point? If so, where? What would you like the writer to clarify?

2. a. How do you view the picture or story the writer has created? What do you think is the writer's intention?

   b. How did the writing affect you? What is significant to you?

3. How could the writer make her or his writing more significant/powerful/ meaningful to you as a reader/listener? Did the writing work for you? Was it effective? How and/or how not?

Writer's Workshop 3: Getting an Outside Review

Get into a different writing group. Exchange your writing with two other writers who are unfamiliar with your writing project. They will serve as outside reviewers.

Anthony Whittier:
Do you rewrite?
Frank O'Connor:
Endlessly, endlessly, endlessly.

Reviewers should respond to the drafts in writing, using the Outside Reviewer's Guide (Figure 3.10). Exchange written reviews toward the end of the workshop. Discuss them after writers have read them. Writers should make notes for revision.

Figure 3.10

Writing Project: **Writer:** _____

Recollections & Reflections _____   **Reviewer:** _____

Draft: _____   **Date:** _____

Working Title: _____

OUTSIDE REVIEWER'S GUIDE

Directions: Read the draft once through. Then reread the draft, this time taking notes. Make a list of what the writer brings up. Then address each of the following questions, using your list as a reference.

1. What do you think is the writer's intention in this piece of writing?

2. Is there anything you would like to know more about?
   ____ Yes   ____ No   If yes, what?

3. Is there anything that confused you? Did you find any sentence or section unclear? If so, write "I was confused about. . ." or ask a question (Why. . . ? What did you mean by. . . ? How. . . ?) Cite specific lines or passages from the text.

4. What about the order of presentation? Does the order make sense to you as a reader? Read again with attention to order, and review your list. Would another arrangement work better? Comment.

5. What do you like best about this piece of writing?

Additional comments:

Writer's Workshop 4: Introductions

Preworkshop Activity

It was Virginia Woolf's practice to write out one or more rough drafts of a work and then to type out complete revisions, sometimes as many as eight or nine.

Editor's note,
Moments of Being

In preparation for this workshop, read the introductory paragraphs in the autobiographical readings included in this chapter. How do the introductions compare? Make some notes. Copying a variety of introductions by hand will help slow down your reading, allowing you to pay close attention to the language. You may want to copy all the introductions by using a word processor and then look at one next to others.

Workshop Activity

1. Read aloud, one right after another, the introductions to autobiographical readings included in this chapter. Listen to the sounds of these introductions.

2. Return to your original writing group and read your introduction aloud.

3. Experiment with writing introductions. Try out two different ways of beginning this piece of writing. "Begin in the poem," Muriel Rukeyser used to advise poets in her writing workshop. What would happen if you took her advice and began *in* the event? What would happen, for example, if you deleted your current introduction and began with the second or third paragraph? How would that sound? What would happen if you began with some dialogue? What would happen if you began with a headnote or prologue? Try imitating an introduction by a writer you have read.

4. Report the results of your experimentation to your group. Which one does your group think is most effective?

5. Discuss your understanding of introductions and your background in writing them. Were you ever taught how to write an introduction? Is there only one way to write an introduction? How does writing an introduction for an autobiographical story differ from writing an introduction for a more academic piece of writing? How did the introductions written by the writers you read for this project differ? How were they alike? How do you go about writing an introduction? Do you try to "get it right" the first time? Do you usually rewrite your introduction? Talk about your introduction-writing process.

Writer's Workshop 5: Conclusions

1. Write for five to ten minutes about conclusions. What is the purpose of a conclusion? Have you been taught a particular way or ways to write conclusions? Do you usually have difficulty or experience frustration writing conclusions?

2. Turn to the writer next to you and talk about what you wrote. If you are writing with computers in class, you may want to have an electronic dialogue. Send your writing to other writers through electronic mail and then

receive their replies. It is also possible to look at the correspondence about conclusions between other writers in your class. (If everyone in class is going to have access to various conversations, however, everyone should know about the public nature of this dialogue beforehand.) This dialogue can be extended still further to include writers in other groups or other places, either through your own initiative or with the help of your instructor.

3. Have a whole-group discussion of introductions and conclusions. Read aloud the conclusion to Alice Walker's memoir and then go back and read the introduction. Talk about the relationship of the two in this piece of writing. Continue reading and discussing the relationship of introductions to conclusions in the readings included in this writing project (as well as those by other writers you may have added). A variety of introductions and conclusions could be made available for everyone to read and compare.

4. Get into your original writing group; first read your conclusion, and then read your introduction (again).

5. Tell your group your intention in your conclusion. How do you want to leave the reader? How does you conclusion relate to your introduction? Are you pleased with your conclusion? If you are displeased, explain why. Ask your group for responses.

6. Try rewriting your conclusion, and then read your revision to your group again for their responses.

Writers at Work

Writer at Work: Ricardo Sewell

After reading Alice Walker's description of an Easter memory, Ricardo Sewell began writing about the ritual of Easter when he was growing up, but he soon found himself contrasting his recent memories with childhood ones. Some of the notes Ricardo made and took are in Figure 3.11. During this process he began to think about the contrast of Easter as a child and as a teenager. He knew he wanted to write more and left a * to remind himself.

Ricardo worked steadily to get his story out and ready for reviewers. His unedited draft appears here just as he wrote it; Ricardo did not try to edit and write at the same time. (Writer David Bradley calls this writing a "get-it-out" draft. At this point in his writing process, Bradley likes to give his full attention to writing, letting the words pull his thoughts along, and then he goes back and rewrites and edits.)

A New Easter

When I was a little kid from the age of six to eleven, I used to look forward to Easter Sunday. I always wanted to color Easter eggs. In school the

Figure 3.11

NOTEMAKING	NOTETAKING
When I was a little kid from the age of 6–11, I used to look forward to Easter Sunday. I always wanted to color Easter eggs. In school the teacher used to make us color eggs and make Easter baskets to take home. Easter also meant candy and giant chocolate bunnies. When I received a bunny, it was always hollow, and I always wanted a solid one. This was a disappointment to me. . . . As I started to get older, Easter just wasn't really a religious holiday anymore, not to the people of New York City.*	Easter Sunday, 1950. Alice is 6. All dressed up. New dress. New shoes. Church. A speech. Alice feels admired more for her spirit than for her clothes.

teacher used to make us color eggs, and make Easter baskets to take home. Easter also meant candy and giant chocolate bunnies. When I received the bunny it was always hollow, and I always wanted a solid one. This was always a disappointment to me. Always around Easter time there were a lot of cartoons on TV. My favorite cartoon was "Here comes Peter Cotton-tail." I used to love this particular cartoon a lot. My mother used to take me to the department store and buy me a new suit. I was a pretty greedy kid so the big event of the day was Easter dinner. We always had a large ham and lots of pies. I went through this ritual for years. As I started to get older Easter just wasn't what it used to be. Easter took on a new meaning. Easter wasn't really a religious holiday anymore, not to the people in New York City.

I used to over hear my mother speaking about all the hypercritics on Easter. Then I started to notice what she was talking about. I notice how strange adults were. It's like Easter transformed every adult into a nice person. All the adults just play games with each other, especially the ones that hated each other. The ones that never spoke to each other all of a sudden started speaking to each other on this one particular day. When the last three hundred and sixty four days of the year they didn't even want to look at each other. Then there are the biggest hypercritics of them all. Its the Easter church hypercritics. It must be something in the air on Easter Sunday, because everyone goes to church. Even the teenagers find their way to church on Easter. It's like if you miss church on Easter you would be the biggest sinner in the world. The Pastor would have to bring out extra, extra chairs to accommodate the over sized crowd. People that you never saw before or in church just appeared out of no where, and you wondered where were they the whole year. Even with the extra chairs there still isn't enough seats for everyone. People would be piled into the aisles and the back of the church on Easter Sunday, because there were too many hypercritics.

I really started to notice the things the teenagers did on Easter in New York City. In school all the teenagers would talk about is all the new designer clothes they were going to get on Easter. You wouldn't be in the In crowd if you bought a suit, and not some famous designer outfit. Suits for Easter were out of style. And if you don't buy new clothes for Easter, you might as well stay inside the whole day. No one would even want to come near you if you had regular clothes on. All the guys would get new hair cuts, and the girls would get their hair done. The salons and the barber shops would make a lot of money around Easter time. The strangest thing on Easter Sunday is what the kids wore. It never fails but there is one particular outfit that just about everybody had on. No matter where you went in the city, you would see at least ten separate groups with the same thing on. I remember one year everyone had on leather suits. And other year everybody had on Guess jumpers, and Cocoa Cola shirts. The last year you had to have something Polo on. This would always make me and my friends laugh because everyone would look like they wanted to be twins with the same outfit.

There were four places that everyone would go on Easter Sunday every year—Coney Island, The City (42nd Street), Great Adventure, and the movies. They would go to these places after they finished attending church. This goes on every year in the city. Easter Sunday is always the day of reopening for Coney Island and Great Adventure. These two places would be packed to capacity with teenagers everywhere with their designer outfits.

The others would go to 42nd street in the city and just walk around for hours back and forth. All they would want to do was show off what they were wearing. It was like it was a fashion show walking back and forth to see what everyone had on and who had the best outfit. Then after a couple of hours of walking everyone went to the movies. The movie theatre made a lot of money too on Easter. I don't see the big deal of going to the movie and the city on Easter. I can do that any day of the week.

If you didn't live in the city you wouldn't know this, but Easter is the day that the jails are filled. So many people get robbed, shot, arrested or even killed on Easter. It is hard to believe until you experience it for yourself, because you couldn't imagine what goes on in New York on Easter. It's gotten so bad I don't even go outside on Easter any more. You would be surprised because all this robbing and shooting is done by kids of ages of twelve through twenty one. To some teenagers Easter is a day of "Getting Paid." This is what they call it when they go out to rob. They plan what they are going to do before Easter arrives. The things that I saw and heard are incredible. They form gangs of about 40 to 100 people, both guys and girls, and go out robbing. Oh yeah just about every teenager in the city carry razors and guns. Razor are very popular, especially the one everyone carries in their mouths. The robbing mostly goes on at Coney Island, the city, and Great Adventure. I remember one Easter I went to Coney Island with my brother and a couple of friends. It was very crowded. Kids were everywhere. We were having a good time laughing at everybody in just about the same outfits. We figured that nothing would happen because there were so many cops around. That didn't stop people from getting robbed at Coney Island. We were standing by the steeple chase, a ride in Coney Island that plays music as it goes around and around. It attracted a lot of people near it. It was very crowded during the whole day.

I remember this one particular guy with his girlfriend. He had a gold chain as thick as a jumprope. They call these chains cables in the city. On his cable he had a gold piece of sister Theresa as big as a plate. While he was standing waiting to get on the ride, six guys surrounded him and demanded his cable. He said no and pushed his girlfriend away. Then the six guys pulled out guns. He still refused and when one of the guys tried to snatch his cable he pulled out his gun and started shooting. The six guy's guns must have been unloaded because they started to run. He hit three of them. Then the cops started shooting so then the guy with the cable and his girlfriend got shot. In all, five people were shot that day in Coney Island and the other ones got caught.

While we were leaving the park after this incident another one broke out. I don't know what exactly happened, but I do know that about fifteen guys beat down two other guys with canes. They stomped one kid so much that when they ran, his body looked as if it was twisted. He was also knocked out. This incident started the crowd running and a lot of people fell and were trampled. One of my friends lost one of his sneakers while running and he found it later. What was so amazing is that all those guys got away with so many cops out there. I told my brother that I never wanted to go back to Coney Island on Easter.

We got on the train to go to the city, and we got off at 59th street and Columbus Circle where the carriage rides are. There were a lot of couples taking carriage rides getting on it. I guess it is romantic for girls to get on the horse ride. I went into the store with my friends while we were in the store, I heard a lot of screaming and firecrakers. When a friend and I came out of the store we, were surprised to see what was happening.

It was like a hundred teenagers just running down the block snatching jewelry and ripping men pockets. Ripping pockets is when someone runs up to you and rips your whole pocket off and takes your wallet at the same time. People were running and screaming everywhere. Out of all this confusion this one particular incident caught my eye. About ten guys ran over to the horse and buggy ride and attacked the couple in it. The guy tried to protect his girlfriend from the attackers; but more guys came and they dragged him out of the car and beat him down. The man that drove the buggy tried to help the lady, and got stabbed up about twelve times. One kid who looked about 10 years old pulled out a gun and fired a shot, this sent the horse running into the street. The horse ran wildly until he got hit by a yellow taxi cab. They kept running down the street like a tidal wave of destruction. This was the first time I ever saw anything like this.

The next year we decided not to go to the city or Coney Island. So we went to Great Adventure, the park was pretty crowded. I had a feeling something was going to happen. There were about fifteen of us and we almost got into a fight with another group of boys from Atlantic City. It just turn out to be an argument between us and them, so then we went about our business. I really didn't know how it started. We were there for about two hours. So around one o'clock that's when everything started.

While we were getting on the roller coaster my friend Pablo a college sophomore got into a fight. When we got off, we saw a crowd. When we got over there, we saw Pablo on the floor with five other guys they were all cut up by a razor. Pablo was cut in the neck, head, his thumb and shoulder. He was bleeding a lot. While we were waiting for the ambulance he told us that the other guys were being robbed by another group of guys. They thought he was with them. Pablo jewelry and money was gone. Pablo was in shock cause he couldn't believe that he was slash up like that just for his money and jewelry. As the park attendant was helping us with Pablo an other incident broke out.

It was like a tidal wave again. All you saw was guys grabbing people's pocketbooks, and throwing people on the floor for their money. They were also rushing all the souvenirs shops. It was like all the teenagers in the park were fighting too. I don't know who or why we were fighting for, but I just didn't want to get slashed up like Pablo. While everyone was fighting I heard gun shots. Thats when everyone started to run out of the park, people were panicing. When every thing cleared Pablo was still on the floor and my brother was shot in the shoulder. They had to close the park because so many people was hurt and robbed. Now great adventure will never reopened on Easter Sunday. This was the last Easter sunday that me and my brother ever went out. From now on we just stay in the house. The last Easter that past was just as wild as the others, every year it gets worse.

In cony Island a group of guy were coming home on the train. While they were riding home another group of guys entered the train and demanded there jackets. The train was filled with people, but no one did anything. The kids refused to hand over their jackets. So one of the demanders pulled out a gun and shot him in the head, and still took his jacket. Then they pulled two other guys off the train and shot them in the train station just for their jackets. The one that got shot in the head wasn't found till the train got in to Manhattan from Brooklyn. He died four days later in the hospital. The guys that shot him got caught two weeks later.

Easter just isn't the same anymore in the city. It not a religious holiday anymore. I don't look forward to Easter anymore like I used to. Now I wish they will just get rid of the holiday completely in the city. Maybe if they get rid of it some of these innocent people won't get robbed or killed. This is one holiday that I won't ever enjoy again.

Ricardo read a draft of "A New Easter" to two writing groups, his own and a nearby group whose members had overheard enough to get interested and had asked if they could listen. His middle-class Anglo-American female teacher, who was not from New York City, was captivated by Ricardo's story, which was outside her own experience. Other listeners were drawn to the story because they could identify with what he was writing about. Several added their own "New Easter" stories. A discussion of gang violence in cities followed. Later, prompted by a newspaper article entitled "Wolf Packs or Posses, Gang Violence Is Common" (*The New York Times,* May 9, 1989), this discussion continued. A group of graduate students, mostly Anglo-Americans who had not grown up in Ricardo's New York City and had come to school to study literature, found Ricardo's story and writing exciting. Had he made it up? they wondered.

Ricardo went on to work on paragraphing, the conclusion, and, finally, editing. He had gotten to the point at which he could edit for comma splices and verb-tense problems himself. He thought about writing a piece about gang violence. The presentation by *The New York Times,* from his view, was "wrong." As an insider, Ricardo believed he could see better than a reporter writing from the outside.

Writer at Work: Andrea Wilson

Excerpts from a lengthy piece of writing by Andrea Wilson illustrate how she handled her problem—not wanting to recall childhood memories—by making use of role-playing: one self (who didn't want to write to remember) to another self (the teller of memories or tales). The influence of Jamaica Kincaid's style is evident here (see "Girl," *At the Bottom of the River,* 1983).

I Burned My Memories

One night in 1986 I was feeling down, so I decided to write all about my memories as a child, coming up to the present. I knew I did not want anyone finding and reading my book of my memories inadvertently; therefore, I decided to write my memories in Spanish. Not even I could read my memories without a Spanish dictionary, since I wrote it with a Spanish dictionary. I don't remember if it was a day later that I burned it or a week later. All I know is that I burned it because I was afraid of anyone finding it and reading it. . . .

"I've a memory for you. Talk about Adrian."

"I am not sure if what I am going to say is what really happened, since I burned my memories."

Adrian and I attended Waterford Primary School in St. Catherine, Jamaica. Every day the children would pick on Adrian, and I had to stand up for him since he wouldn't stand up for himself. Day after day I would fight for Adrian. He refused to stand up for himself, although I constantly told him they would go on picking on him if he didn't put a stop to it. Adrian would not stand up for himself. One day I became sick of his pathetic crying ways and beat him up myself. I kept on telling him to hit me back, but he wouldn't at first. Then he started to fight back. I am not sure if this is true or not, since I burned my memories.

Whether this story is true or not, I forced Adrian to fight back. I know that I would not fight back if I were in Adrian's position; I'd probably just walk away; but then again, I burned my memories. However, I know that I never do anything that I am forced to do. Once my mother told me that when I was a baby girl, I would do the antithesis of what she told me. . . .

"You better tell about the diary."
"Okay, I will tell about the stupid diary. Are you satisfied?"

"Yes."

Once my mother bought me this red diary, but I never put anything of importance in it since I was afraid of anyone reading it. Therefore, I wrote silly things in it.

"I think the reason that you never wrote anything of significance in it is because it would become a concrete memory. You did not want that because there is always a memory that you don't want to remember. If you wrote memories in that diary, then you would be obliged to write good and bad memories in it. You want your memories to disappear, that is why you burned them!"
"Are you a psychiatrist? I have never thought of any of this profound stuff you are telling me."
"No, I am not a psychiatrist, but I know you better than you know yourself!"
"Well, this is boring me to death, so I will stop now. It is 19 minutes to midnight, and I don't want to write any more. And this place [computer facility] is too noisy."

"I think you should discuss Jamaica Kincaid. You love the name Jamaica, don't you?"

"Yes, I love, cherish, and adore the name Jamaica, so I will continue."

Ms. Kincaid informed us how she was raised in Antigua. She told us how her mother said: this is the way you cook food; this is the way you wash the clothes; this is the way you clean the house; this is the way you act and walk like a lady; and this is the way you conduct yourself in front of strangers, so they will not see the slut you are so bent on becoming.

"Stop looking at the [computer] screen in front of you and tell about the similar experiences you had as a child."

"That's my problem. I am procrastinating because what I am going to say is probably a lie!"

"Not anyone here knew you as a child. So if it's a lie, who cares? You do not care what anyone thinks anyway."

As a small girl going to school, my teacher used to beat me, make me walk like a lady and talk like a lady. However, I did not listen. I used to play in the dirt with the boys. My school uniform always got torn, since the boys played so roughly. I stood with my feet apart and hands on my hips. I also spoke the dirtiest words that would make an Angel cry for my shame. All of this contributed to the beatings I would get in school day after day. At home it wasn't much different. There were not many girls of my age living in the neighborhood; however, the few who were in my age group were told to stay away from me.

"Tell why they were threatened to keep away from you."

"I am trying to think if this is true or not, so please shut up and let me think."

"Hogwash! You know what you are going to say, so just tell it as it is in your mind at the present moment. Don't let me do it for you."

"I will tell the story if you do not interrupt me again."

"I promise."

The reason is this: I did almost everything the boys did. I would go on top of the roof and jump off, which was very dangerous. Many times I would jump across a very wide gully, which was not wise at all because a few times I did not jump over it successfully; sometimes I would fall in and get many cuts on my body. The mothers in the community called me Tomboy and Let-Go-Beast! They said that my brother and I would not come to anything good, since my brother was worse than I was. They said I would never become a lady and no man would every marry me, and furthermore I could not do any house duties since I was a lazy good-for-nothing.

I did not mind what they said because I had no intention of cooking or doing housework. Frankly, even now I hate house duties; I also have no intention of ever getting married. My mother, on the other hand, did not like what people had to say about her children. She told us to stay inside and keep away from those unruly boys. My brother and I did not obey her, since she was at work when we did our antics. Then she used force to get us to do what she wanted, but that did not work. Her next step was to increase my reading materials since she knew I loved reading the Hardy Boys, Nancy Drew, and the Bobbsey Twins. After a while I got bored, so I started to read her romance novels with a dictionary; that took me off the streets completely. People started saying what an industrious girl I was. I don't know if any of this is true since I burned my memories.

"What happened when you read romance novels for the first time?"

"It was great. Then I knew why my mother would ignore me when I asked for my dinner. I used to say, 'Mommy, I am hungry,' and she would say, 'Wait until I finish this chapter,' only for her to go to the next chapter and the next after that. I did the same thing to her when I started to read romance novels. She would say, 'Angie, come and set the table,' but I never went. The first time I went to Europe was grand. I think it was Italy. The novel's description of Italy was extremely distinctive. I don't remember what happened after that since I burned my memories. I do know that I would read romance novels at every opportunity I got, even in my classes. Even now I do it."

"Maybe the reason you do not have any memories is because your memories are of novels and also the fact that you burned them."

"You are probably right. One day I will go search for my memories and see if anything I said is true or not. If the ashes of my memories are all blown away, then maybe it was all for the best. It is probably better not knowing."

Writer at Work: Anthony Garraway

*By writing the autobi-
ography . . . I would
be rid of . . . the past
that had a hold on
me, that kept me
from the present.*

bell hooks
"writing
autobiography"

*What is always
needed in the appre-
ciation of art, or life,
is the larger perspec-
tive—to encompass
in one's glance at the
varied world the com-
mon thread, the uni-
fying theme through
immense diversity,
a fearlessness of
growth, of search, of
looking, that enlarges
the private and public
world. And yet, in our
particular society, it is
the narrowed and
narrowing view of life
that often wins.*

Alice Walker
"Saving the
Life That Is Your Own"

Anthony Garraway, who identifies himself as Guyanese, wrote these recollections and reflections his senior year in college in a writing workshop led
by Sharon Fellows, who gave him the opportunity to tell his story. He was
admitted to Binghamton University (State University of New York) through
the Educational Opportunity Program (EOP). "I've been waiting a long time
to get this out," Anthony said in an interview, "and it feels good. It's an important piece of writing for me. I know it needs work." He intends to keep
working on this essay and to write more. "It's a continuing story," explained
Anthony, who grew up in "the black section of Brooklyn." "It's a story of a
troubled childhood and the complexes I developed."

Complexes

I remember coming to this country as a young boy. I did not want to
come here because I enjoyed life with my grandparents in the old country.
My family is from Georgetown, Guyana, South America. My parents did not
give me a choice; I had to make the voyage to America: land of dreams. I
never expected the dreaded nightmare that was to come.

My preschool years in the United States were horrible. It was in these
tender years of my life that I was most severely scarred. While I was busy
trying to develop a personality, the other kids were busy taking away every
piece of self-confidence my parents were able to instill in me. I was about
four or five years old.

One of my first memories is the teasing and taunting that I suffered from
the kids in my class when I found out that I was not the same as they were.
Sure, we were all the same race, but I spoke differently. Only I did not realize this at the time. My schoolmates, however, wasted no time in letting me
know that I was a foreigner, different in speech and culture. They teased,
teased, and teased me about my uniqueness. The qualities that I had were
special to me. I loved myself and the things about me. The other children
just couldn't understand. Wouldn't understand.

I remember not wanting to go to school because of my classmates.
Afraid of the taunting, I would find myself sick in bed, unable to go to
school. At least that is what my mother thought. By not going to school,
I was missing out on an education. At the same time, I was lying to my
mother. I loved my mother and I had to lie to her. These conflicting feelings
overwhelmed me.

Slowly I began to have problems socializing. Slowly I became an introverted person. It became difficult for me to trust any of my fellow peers. Soon it was hard for me to trust anyone. Not being allowed to build trust, an important part of a child's normal development, leads to abnormal development in adulthood.

I later learned how to talk more like the other kids but continued to speak to my family in a soft West Indian accent. I didn't lose my accent until my teenage years. By then new problems were developing. The school bullies had found new things to tease me about. It was as if they went home and planned new ways to make fun of me. If only they put as much effort into their school work.

"Blacky." That was my new name. This one really threw me. Sure, I am black, but so was everyone else! What's this all about? I asked myself. Later, a friend of mine (yes, I managed to make a couple of friends) explained to me that we were known as "nerds," and bullies like to pick on nerds. The big news, my friend told me, was that I was darker than the average black person. I had never really paid much attention to this until one day when a boy pointed it out to me. Me and the whole laughing class. The laughter was unbearable. I wanted to cry. I did cry. It made me crazy. Psychologically, I was a wreck. I sometimes wished I was dead. I thought of killing them, making them pay for hurting me. I hadn't bothered them! I just didn't have the heart to commit a murder or to take my own life. The pressure building in me was like a volcano about to erupt. Erupt I did. All over that bully. We fought fiercely. I had the upper hand. My adreneline was in full force. I felt satisfaction.

That was the day that I realized that I have the power to take care of those bullies, and the day I found out that you have to pay for your actions. My parents were called to the principal's office. They could not understand why I had gotten into a fight. I never told them about the predators in my classes. I couldn't trust them.

It is a painful thought, the memory of when I was enlightened about the fact that I have strong, African features. This really messed me up. I knew that I was a foreigner, but I was not being identified with my homeland. I was said to look like a whole different group of people. They said that I had big lips like the Africans. I never noticed. Another startling revelation and another complex. Either way, a tease is a tease, and to me as a child, I was devastated.

"Short," that was my new nickname. One that I did not like. It was not meant to hurt me. It did. I wanted to be tall. To be a basketball jock. I wanted at least to be normal height. The girls were taller than me. I didn't know that I would later be taller than most of them.

By the beginning of high school, the pressure had begun to lessen in part thanks to the natural gift I had inherited. I was short but stout. The bullies realized that I could probably defend myself. Everyone asked me if I worked out. That made me want to work out, and I did.

I was big, but they came in more numbers than me. Now I had to deal with the high school bullies. They were not as bad as the previous set of child bullies. Even they had grown up. By this time the damage was already done. The bad childhood teasing and pranks that I suffered had taken effect on me.

Complexes were already formed. I had a problem dealing with being born outside of the United States, being dark-skinned, having African features, and being short. As an adult, I face new problems, ones that I did not know existed. I realized that I was always being stereotyped because of my appearance. Being judged prematurely by anyone and everyone destroys me. Like a life sentence, I am locked into this life of false attribution.

The problem of being stereotyped is magnified because of where I live. I am a student living in an upstate New York town, a place where there are few people like me. I feel the prejudice more. I can't hide. As a black adult male, I can understand and deal with the prejudice and the stereotyping a little better than I did as a child.

Another problem is that it is very difficult for a black student to be identified as a black crook. I realize that white people cannot tell the difference. Unfortunately, they choose to play it safe and pair me off with the crooks. When I walk by a white woman, she hunches down and takes on a defensive stance. I feel the tension. What should I do?

These experiences have had a tremendous psychological effect on me. They make me feel like an outsider. It hurts. I don't mean to scare people, I just do. This is not the same as the volcanic pressure that I spoke about earlier. It's older, more mature, more severe. There are no more bullies to beat up. How do I make a change? I sometimes want to stop and ask the frightened ladies what they are afraid of. Only I don't want to scare them. I try not to seem like a bad guy. Bad guys tend to dress and act a certain way. I try not to act that way. I don't wear the usual bad boy's gold jewelry and other attire known to be worn by them. I try to be friendly to everyone.

I smile even when I don't feel the part. Being courteous is something that I would do anyway. Only I do it with an extra touch of consciousness. I open doors and say "thank you," even to people who are jerks. It makes me know that I am better than them, or is it just another one of my complexes?

I have taken counseling to help me understand my feelings a little better. There are still a few obstacles that I need to overcome before I can live a life without complexes, without shame and distrust, without fear, and without emptiness.

The biggest help to me has been my education. The police are my biggest problem. I am afraid of them. It is a sad fact that they are paid to protect and make me feel safe, yet they help to tear down my self-esteem the most. They are not kind to me. Sometimes I wonder if it is all in my head. Just another complex. I don't think so. They are mean to me, never taking care to respect my civil rights. I do have them, or so the law says. They usually apologize and give me a sob story about why they were rough to me. They say they don't know if I am dangerous of not. Give me the benefit of the doubt. I think it's discrimination. I know it is. It hurts.

Anthony stopped here as if to pause after writing "It hurts." "I'm going to write more," he said. "I'm just getting going. Do you think you can use this story?"

Writer at Work: Lissette Norman

Lissette Norman, a former basic writing student, wrote this essay in an advanced writing class her senior year as part of a collection of writing she entitled *searching for drums.*

thank you bell hooks

If ever i were asked what about me i would like to change, i would have to say the silence that part of me carries like a swollen threat. However, that was never my answer. Although i sensed something was wrong, i didn't give much thought to how detrimental silence could be. It was something i hated about me and had a tough time dealing with. However, i gave little thought as to how i was going to rectify what i now call the "unbearable disease." I was a member of silence, but honestly could not understand that there was something wrong. Moreover, i did not know that silence was the name of my disease.

As a young child, i was often merited for being quiet, peaceful, and calm in my home. I was a good girl in mami's eyes and she was so proud. I had my own bedroom all my life, where i would go after school, after meals, and then to sleep, by myself. Very rarely did my brothers allow me into their bedroom to play. So once i closed my door, my room became my own little world—as a child, as a teenager, and still as an adult.

Now i notice how it bothers my mother when i come home from school for holidays or summer vacation and spend a lot of my time in my bedroom. She saids, "Lissette, why don't you come out here (into the dining room) and sit with us for a while and talk?" And then i think—how come when i was younger i wasn't asked to come out and talk? Was it not important what i had to say then?

I could relate to bell hooks (author of *Talking Back*) when she talks about wanting to join in on adult conversations when she was a child, but didn't because that would only have invited punishment, the backhand lick or a slap across the face. How come my mother didn't ask me to come into the kitchen to join the delicious kitchen talk she, my aunts, and her friends where having when i was younger? They'd sit around the kitchen table, talking, telling stories, exchanging recipes, talking, gossiping, laughing, and just talking. I would venture into that oral society praying not to be dismissed. How come instead i could only listen from the other side of my bedroom wall, after being sent to my room?

I also realized that this becomes a cycle, for my sister-in-law and i were conversing in her kitchen and we told my niece to leave the kitchen and go play, when she tried to partake in our conversation. It must have meant so much for her to have her say because we could hear her crying in the next room. So then i ask—what do we as mothers do with children who must speak in a kitchen full of adults?

I notice now that when i was in junior high school (maybe before then, but it was evident in these years) that outside of my home i transformed. It's as if i became another person, very loud. My choice of friends were a group of girls who were known to be bad. I was the class clown, i was disruptive in class and picked many fights. The dean of the school and i knew each other on a first name basis. But when i returned home there was that transformation back to silence.

This transformation also takes place when i first meet someone, i'll be very quiet and won't say too much, but after i get to know the person and feel comfortable, there is that transformation to my very talkative and joking self. Later my friends would tell me, "when i first met you, you were so quiet, what happened?" As i try to focus in on this picture of self, i believe i used my silence as a cover up. A simple tool for the sake of acceptance. If i am quiet and don't say too much, i won't give a negative impression. My mother taught me that. Nice girls were supposed to be quiet. And that's all i knew. But somewhere deep inside me there was protest which explains those feelings of resistance within me that i expressed when i stepped out-side of my house.

I have searched deeply for answers and try to pin-point the reasoning for the conflicting selves within me and conclude this writing with a much clearer and sharper picture. It's taken me until my senior year in college, but i think i have a lot more answers as to my position in silence. My silence was something i hated, something i didn't want to try to understand because it was too complicated, too painful, and something i didn't want to talk or write about. But in reading bell hooks' *Talking Back*, i found out that my silence was not unusual, for there were many like me. bell hooks has helped me in my fight to end the silence. She was instrumental in helping me affirm my voice, validating it and celebrating it. And so for this i say— thank you bell hooks.

Suggestions for Further Reading

Angelou, Maya. 1969. *I Know Why the Caged Bird Sings.* New York: Random House.

Anzaldúa, Gloria. 1987. *Borderlands/La Frontera: The New Mestiza.* San Francisco: spinsters/aunt lute.

Baker, Russell. 1982. *Growing Up.* New York: Signet.

Baldwin, James. 1954. "Fifth Avenue, Uptown: A Letter From Harlem," *Nobody Knows My Name.* New York: Dell.

Begley, Louis. 1991. *Wartime Lies.* New York: Knopf.

Berger, John. 1986. "Her Secrets." *The Graywolf Annual Three: Essays, Memoirs & Reflections.* Scott Walker (ed). St. Paul, MN: Graywolf Press.

Cliff, Michelle. 1985. "If I Could Write This in Fire, I Would Write This in Fire," *The Land of Look Behind.* Ithaca, NY: Firebrand Books.

Cofer, Judith Ortiz. 1991. *Silent Dancing: A Partial Remembrance of a Puerto Rican Childhood.* Houston: Arte Publico Press.

Coles, Robert. 1989. *The Call of Stories.* Boston, MA: Houghton Mifflin.

Crews, Harry. 1978. *A Childhood: The Biography of a Place.* New York: Harper & Row.

Dillard, Annie. 1987. *An American Childhood*. New York: Harper & Row.

Dorris, Michael. 1987. *A Yellow Raft in Blue Water*. New York: Holt.

Erdrich, Louise. 1984. *Love Medicine*. Orlando, FL: Holt, Rinehart & Winston.

Galarza, Ernesto. 1971. *Barrio Boy*. Notre Dame, IN: University of Notre Dame Press.

Giovanni, Nikki. 1979. "Nikki Rosa," *Black Feeling, Black Talk, Black Judgement*. New York: William Morrow.

Haley, Alex. 1965. *The Autobiography of Malcolm X as Told to Alex Haley*. New York: Ballantine Books.

Hampl, Patricia. 1986. "Parish Streets." *The Graywolf Annual Three: Essays, Memoirs & Reflections*. Scott Walker (ed). St. Paul, MN: Graywolf Press.

Hodge, Merle. 1981. *Crick Crack Monkey*. London: Heinemann.

Hoffman, William. 1978. "Amazing Grace" in *Virginia Reels*. Carbondale, IL: University of Illinois Press.

Hughes, Langston. 1986. *The Big Sea*. New York: Thunder's Mouth Press, Inc.

Hurston, Zora Neale. 1942. *Dust Tracks on a Road: An Autobiography*. Urbana & Chicago: University of Illinois Press.

Jones, Suzanne W. (Ed.) 1991. *Growing Up in the South: An Anthology of Modern Southern Literature*. New York: Penguin.

Kincaid, Jamaica. 1983. *At the Bottom of the River*. New York: Farrar, Straus, & Giroux.

Kincaid, Jamaica. 1985. *Annie John*. New York: Plume.

Kincaid, Jamaica. 1990. *Lucy*. New York: Farrar, Straus & Giroux.

Kingston, Maxine Hong. 1976. *The Woman Warrior: Memoirs of a Girlhood Among Ghosts*. New York: Random House.

Lamming, George. 1983. *In the Castle of My Skin*. New York: Schocken.

Lovelace, Earl. 1984. *The Wine of Astonishment*. New York: Vintage Books.

Lyons, Robert. 1984. *Autobiography: A Reader for Writers*. New York: Oxford University Press.

Marshall, Paule. 1981. *Brown Girl, Brownstones*. New York: The Feminist Press.

Marshall, Paule. 1983. *Reena & Other Stories*. New York: The Feminist Press.

McCarthy, Mary. 1981. *Memories of a Catholic Girlhood*. New York: Harcourt Brace Jovanovich.

Mohr, Nicholasa. 1973. *Nilda*. New York: Harper & Row.

Mohr, Nicholasa. 1975. *El Bronx Remembered*. New York: Harper & Row.

Mohr, Nicholasa. 1990. *Felita*. New York: Bantam.

Moody, Anne. 1968. *Coming of Age in Mississippi*. New York: Dell.

Nunes, Susan. 1990. "A Moving Day" in *Home to Stay: Asian American Women's Fiction*. Sylvia Watanbe and Carol Bruchac (eds). Greenfield Center, NY: Greenfield Review Press.

Olson-Fallon, Judith. (Ed.). 1992. *Growing Up, Growing Old*. New York: Harper-Collins.

Paley, Grace. 1985. "The Loudest Voice" and "A Subject of Childhood," *The Little Disturbances of Man*. New York: Penguin.

Peterson, Brenda. 1994. "Growing up Game." *Living by Water: Essays on Life, Land, and Spirit*. Seattle: Alaska Northwest Books.

Riley, Patricia. (Ed.). 1993. *Growing Up Native American*. New York: Morrow, 1993.

Rivera, Edward. 1983. *Family Installments: Memories of Growing Up Hispanic*. New York: Penguin Books.

Rodriguez, Richard. 1982. *Hunger of Memory: The Education of Richard Rodriguez*. Boston: David R. Godine.

Shange, Ntozake. 1985. *Betsey Brown*. New York: St. Martin's Press.

Simpson, Eileen. 1987. *Orphans*. New York: Plume.

Smith, Lee. 1981. "Artists" in *Cakewalk*. New York: Putnam.

Spencer, Elizabeth. 1960. "A Southern Landscape" in *The Stories of Elizabeth Spencer*. New York: Doubleday.

Staples, Brent. 1994. *Parallel Time: Growing Up in Black and White*. New York: Pantheon.

Toth, Susan Allen. 1978. *Blooming*. New York: Ballantine Books.

Villarreal, Jose Antonio. 1970. *Pocho*. Garden City, NY: Anchor Books.

Walker, Alice. 1971. "A Sudden Trip Home in the Spring" in *You Can't Keep a Good Woman Down*. New York: Harcourt Brace Jovanovich.

Welty, Eudora. 1979. "The Little Store" and "A Sweet Devouring," *The Eye of the Story: Selected Essays and Reviews*. New York: Vintage Books.

Wolff, Tobias. 1989. *This Boy's Life: A Memoir*. New York: Harper & Row.

Woolf, Virginia. 1985. *Moments of Being*. New York: Harcourt Brace Jovanovich.

4 Going to College: Educational Histories

For me, not to go to college was, in a sense, not to become a full human being.

Margaret Mead, anthropologist

The past is present. We are all part of our background.

Susan Howe, poet and historian

"**G**oing to College" is the title of a piece of writing you'll be asked to do at the end of this project. You could write about going to college without doing any of the reading, writing, and talking included here. In fact, you'll be asked to begin this writing project by writing about what comes to mind when you think about going to college. The activities in this project, however, will encourage you to reflect and write a more complete and richer response. This project is designed to take you beyond a superficial account of a going-to-college story that you might write in class without reading, talking, and listening. Readings will help you think about how you want to shape your educational story. The notetaking and notemaking you are asked to do in response to the readings for this project will help you think more critically about going to college. This project invites you to think about the story of your education and to place yourself in the larger context of your family and culture. You are asked to situate yourself in relation to your immediate family and relatives and cultural background with regard to education and to reflect critically about going to college in the 1990s.

Your instructor may want to collect some of your project-related writings for response. You may be asked to submit a project portfolio or to select some of these writings to include in a course portfolio. As a class you may want to publish a collection of "Going to College" stories in order to share them with each other and perhaps with future groups of developing writers. You may even want to extend the dialogue by corresponding with writers who are also working on this project in another class at your school or perhaps even at another school. You could use regular or electronic mail to exchange responses to readings as well as to drafts. Collections of end-project writings could be published and exchanged.

Prereading Activities

Writing to Learn

Freewriting

Write or type "Going to College" at the top of a page or computer screen and write whatever comes to your mind. Begin writing without planning what to say. Perhaps write "Going to College" and then just keep writing. Write by association. Think of someone walking up to you and asking you what the words "Going to College" mean to you, or visualize these words appearing on a screen. What comes to mind? Keep writing—keep moving your pen or striking the keys. Do not worry now about using correct grammar, spelling, or punctuation. If you get stuck, stop and say to yourself (or visualize, or even write again) the words "Going to College," and then continue writing. Don't worry about paragraphing or organization now. You are writing to learn what you have in your mind now about this subject. This writing is not for formal presentation; rather, it will serve as a starting point for discussion and for a preliminary draft for your end-project writing.

Key Words Activity

What words do you associate with "college"? What words come to mind? Quickly write a list of "key words." You can work as a whole class from the start, perhaps using a blackboard or overhead projector or computer network. You could also start with individual lists, which you then share with others. Discuss the "key words" that come out of your class. Try repeating this activity after reading and talking about going to college, perhaps part way through this project and then again at the end. Compare lists.

Guided Writing

After writing on your own about going to college until you come to a stop, use the following questions to help you continue writing:

1. When did you first know you were going to college? Was it a decision you made in recent years, or had you always known you would go to college?
2. "For me," wrote Margaret Mead, "not to go to college was, in a sense, not to become a full human being." Does this statement ring true for you? What does "going to college" mean to you? What are your expectations?
3. Did your parents or other family members go to college? To what extent were they formally educated?
4. Are there people you admire and look up to who are going or have gone to college?
5. What is your family's attitude toward your going to college?
6. How did you come to choose this particular college?

Listening to Developing Writers at Work

Stop and listen to some students who worked on this project.

Cynthia: Going to college was one of the things I dreamed of since I was a kid. Not attending college would have been a disgrace, not only to me but to my family as well.

Josefina: As I was growing up, my parents always emphasized that an education would bring me success, and they still do. I knew I had to attend college, not because my parents expected me to, but because I wanted to.

Petra: I know that my parents are excited and very happy that I am attending college, but I do not really know what they expect from me.

Sakeena: My family has always valued education. My grandmother is an electrical engineer. My mother graduated from college with a degree in psychology and works with disturbed children. She did not ask me if I were going to college. She just took it for granted that I would go.

Narda: I come from a large Hispanic family. My mother never finished school, and my father dropped out at a very early age. I have two brothers and two sisters. My eldest sister went to college but only completed a year and a half. The others never completed high school. My family is very proud of me for going to college and for being the second in my family to have graduated from high school.

Joann: My mother and father regretted not going to college and encouraged me to go and get a college degree.

Reread your own writing now and write some more if you wish.

Talking About Going to College: Researching Your Educational Story

Read or talk about your writing to another writer in your writing class/community. Compare your backgrounds with regard to going to college. Ask each other questions about your educational stories. What questions do you have about others' writing? Here are some questions to consider:

1. What would you like to know more about?
2. Were you confused at any point? Because the writer is present, you have the opportunity to ask the writer to clarify. Remember that in the end (product), the writing must stand alone, apart from the writer.
3. Can you think of something else that could be included that would help others better understand the personal and family story behind the writer's going to college?

At the end of your conversation/interview, write about what you talked about, what you learned, and what else you might include in the story of your own education. Keep all your notes and writing in your "Going to College" writing-project folder for reference.

Turn now to some readings to help you think still further about your own education.

Reading and Reflecting on Going to College

Jane Ellen Wilson

Jane Ellen Wilson

Jane Ellen Wilson's story was first published in Jake Ryan and Charles Sackrey's Strangers in Paradise: Academics from the Working Class *(1984), a collection of oral histories of professional academicians who come from marginalized social groups. Wilson describes her difficulty negotiating between her home culture (the farming background of her family) and academic culture (the elite intellectual world of the university).*

I was born in a hospital, and I grew up on my family's farm three miles east of the Susquehanna River in a fertile valley of central Pennsylvania. My great-grandfather was a druggist in a small town for most of his life, but when his health demanded it he bought this farm and moved his family upriver twenty miles. My grandfather and father were actually born here, as well as my great aunt, great uncle, and uncle. My sister grew up here with me. 1

My father's family, of their generation in this country, boasts a few ministers, some schoolteachers, and a lawyer ("Uncle George"). They also farmed and worked in factories. When I got my Ph.D., I became the most educated person in the family—a subject much and proudly discussed at the recent family reunions. My mother's family holds farmers, loggers, laborers, and many nameless women. 2

I grew up close to all four of my grandparents. My father's father farmed all his life, raising bumper crops and building up a Holstein dairy herd. Towards the end of his life he wrote poetry: about the land, the animals, the weather. He showed me plants and trees and taught me some of their names and uses. His wife farmed, cooked, milked cows and taught me to read at the age of four. I learned to play piano using her old upright and the pump organ in the parlor. 3

My mother's father was a cheerful man with a strong sense of justice. He smoked Camels, tickled me with his whiskers, and let me play with his wooden leg (I liked to put things in the holes in it). He left his real leg in the Argonne during the first World War. Even with his wooden one he farmed, worked in the limestone quarry, and, as he got older, began sharpening saws for a living. My grandmother grew up on farms and in logging camps, helping her mother cook for the loggers. In spite of her irregular education she was valedictorian of her high school class. She married and quickly had three children, going on to work as a cook, a nurse's aide, and finally an LPN.[1] In her fifties she began to paint, and now paints wonderful pictures of the activities of her early life in the woods and farmland of Pennsylvania. 4

My father graduated from high school and wanted to go to college, but was prevailed upon by his family to stay and help with the farm. In addition to farming, he was interested in music, and learned to play guitar and call 5 square dances. After he and my mother married they put together a country and western band (she played bass and sang) and played for local festivals, at square dances, and on the local radio station. They still do this, taking off very little time from their work. When his father died, my father went on to become a carpenter and local contractor, farming in the evenings and on weekends, trying to make ends meet. Besides helping with all the farm work, my mother has worked as a cook, housekeeper, and companion to elderly ladies.

The people I come from get up at dawn, work hard all day, go to the 6 Lutheran church on Sunday, abstain from liquor, get married, stay married and have children (there are a few old maids), and live close to their family and close to the earth. We had little cash but lots of food and a beautiful piece of land to live on.

Among these people farms pass to sons, not daughters. Although my par- 7 ents had no sons—only two daughters—it was expected that we would marry and leave. It was never expected that we would become farmers and stay there. This bothered me; I felt dispossessed by default. My family decided that I had a gift for music, so they brought me up to play in their band. They had me sing as soon as I could talk, and taught me to play guitar as soon as my hands were big enough. They decided I had a gift for schooling, too. I read everything I could find and was "smart." Like everyone else on the farm, I did all I could to help in the fields, at the barn, and in the house: making hay, butchering, doing daily chores, sewing, cooking, gardening. They imagined futures for me: I could be a nurse or a teacher; I could marry a farmer or a factory worker and stay near home; I could marry a rich man (that future came highly recommended and in fact my mother still mentions it); I could go to Nashville and become a country music star. They had no better idea than I did how to reconcile my abilities (which they wanted me to develop) with traditional women's roles (which they wanted me to follow).

By the time I was twelve I had opinions about everything, most of them 8 different from my parents'. Country music: didn't like it; Christianity: thought it was hypocritical; country living: I wanted to go to the city, hear "folk music" (i.e., Bob Dylan), and visit Europe; government: I was generally against it; war: didn't like it in general and in particular was concerned about Vietnam (this was 1965). My folks were appalled; a revolutionary ancestor was ok, but a revolutionary teenager was another story. My voracious reading and musical taste had given me ideas. I was stuck with these ideas, however, three miles out of town in a household with strict parents. I was sure the exciting, real world was going on elsewhere and I was missing it. By the time I graduated from high school I had built up a tremendous head of steam and was out to find what I had been missing.

I went to college. Getting married or going to school were the two ac- 9 ceptable ways to leave my family and I bet on education. However, I was still only sixteen, and my parents wanted me to stay close to home; of the nearby colleges I chose the most intellectual and radical and moved to the dorm to enter another world. What I found was more middle and upper class people than I knew existed; and for the first time I met people who didn't know that trees had names.

Wilson

I expected to find intellectual stimulation and community; fun and companionship; new ideas and political concern; and all the things I had been missing just ten miles away in Rural Delivery Route 2. I also strongly expected academia not to discriminate against women. I knew that if I married someone who worked at Chef Boyardee or AC & F that I'd be expected to conform to traditional women's roles. I also knew that physically I couldn't work the way that men did; I didn't like baling hay when I had my period, for example. And though I had a lot of endurance for physical work, that didn't seem like strength to me; strength meant picking up a hundred pound sack of grain. (Little did I realize how hard that was for men, too). But clearly (I thought), being an academic didn't involve physical labor or childbearing, so I trustingly assumed that the academic world did not discriminate against women. 10

What I found at college was disillusioning; but I had invested heavily in my bet on education, and I lasted two years the first time. I found some intellectual stimulation; and I found lots of people making themselves miserable with their intellect: agonizing over Hegel and Nietzsche and talking in (I thought) circles. I found a great deal of personal freedom: to come and go, talk and dress as I pleased. I found some companionship; my first boyfriend was from upper class suburbia. While I had no expectations about women's roles there, I did believe (for years) that the long-haired pacifist men of the late sixties extended their gentleness and egalitarianism to women as well as to the Vietnamese. 11

I had a scholarship and I borrowed money; I worked in the library. I found people who shared my taste in music and I played with them and by myself in college coffeehouses. I tried to be a music major, since I was more interested in music than anything, but found that I didn't have enough of the right kind of training—classical—to do much, instrumentally. My music instructors were very authoritarian, I thought, demanding class attendance and sign-in sheets at concerts; although I breezed through music theory, I couldn't bring myself to abide by the letter of their law. Finally the chairman politely told me I wasn't suited to being a music major, and suggested if I couldn't get up in the mornings for his class, I should see a psychiatrist. This was my first major disappointment with academia. 12

I dropped out and spent the summer on the farm. Eventually I got a job as a waitress at a local Pancake House. In a few months, I had saved money and wanted to go to England, although I couldn't quite figure out how to go about it; in the meantime, two of my former professors convinced me to return to college as an English major, saying that the campus needed "creative people" like me, and that they had designed a new program with more freedom. I believed (I was nineteen) and signed up again only to be told by the dean that I was, as a junior, too old to be part of this new program. I slogged through English courses, writing poems and songs instead of term papers. 13

Because academic reality seemed reductive, flat, lifeless to me, I kept seeking other realities. I worked occasionally as a musician (coffeehouses) and as a music instructor for children, in summer arts programs and in a hospital. I also worked at a small, local hotel as an all night desk clerk. Although just downtown—seven blocks—this was a world away from the college. I had begun to realize—through my high-class, crazy boyfriend—that most people 14 at the college came from a middle class suburban world, with its own trappings, values, customs—most of which I did not find congenial, even though I was supposed to be aspiring to them (by virtue of betting on education). At the Hotel I dealt with truck drivers and their girlfriends, with women from New York and Philadelphia come to visit their husbands and lovers in the nearby federal penitentiary, with small town dramas and informal prostitution. In a way I felt at home with this—country music on the juke box, drinking, adultery, high drama in a small pond. I did not feel at home with truck driver machismo, but started to learn to deal with it. When I became friends with a driver from Cincinnati, I was shocked to learn that his wife wrote poetry and he thought it was great. Mostly I was shocked by my own arrogance in assuming that this class of people wouldn't know or care about art. After I realized that my own assumptions had been cutting me off from people, I started to feel a little more at home in the world.

I graduated from college and moved to my boyfriend's hometown. He 15 lived in the high class Philadelphia suburbs, and I lived in a house in town, as did some students, and all the black people. For many reasons, I wasn't very happy there. Thus, having discovered that there wasn't much room for my voice in the working world, and seeing little room for my voice in a suburban lifestyles [sic], I bet again on education. Well, maybe I couldn't get an interesting job because I wasn't educated enough. (The extent to which this was also influenced by my being a woman and by my class background was just beginning to dawn on me.) And maybe, I thought, I just hadn't found the right subject to study in academia.

I had always felt there was something missing in academia's view of the 16 world. In literature, for example, they studied Englishmen writing literature; I knew that people exercised verbal creativity in many more ways than that. My grandfather told stories, my father told stories, every truck driver that walked into the hotel had a story to tell. In music, academics studied classical (mostly European) music; I knew that people exercised musical creativity in more ways than that. My political concerns had led me from the first to an interest in folk music (and vice versa). From somewhere, it occurred to me that people in the academy might actually study these things. Maybe one of my professors told me how I could look that up—maybe it was a librarian that showed me the index where universities were listed according to the majors they offered; I don't remember. But in any case, I started applying to graduate school in folklore; I also applied to my alma mater to study for an M.A. in English. My experience in the working world had upped the ante on my bet on education.

Another reason to keep betting on education was that I had rejected my 17 family's way of life and values. More accurately, I couldn't see any place for myself in it. Laboring from dawn to dark was not my idea of a good time, even if I had been a man. Still, I love living in the country and growing food. But what farmer wanted a "smart" wife? That was not part of my family's imagined future for me.

My family didn't always see much sense in my ongoing education. When 18 my friends from suburbia wanted to drop out of school and become carpenters, farmers, musicians, their families were horrified. The family of one woman I knew threatened to have her committed to an asylum when she

Wilson

persisted in her desire to do physical labor and live in the country. My family, on the other hand, often said they thought I should go to Nashville and become a country music star. While they saw some sense in going to college for four years, they hoped I would become a teacher at the end of that (one of their Wilsonfew models of educated people, I guess). When I found only menial jobs and then went back to school, they were mystified. To their credit, they were fairly supportive. But, even when I was an undergraduate, they had little money to spare for education, and when I persisted in this system, they told me I was on my own.

Two schools accepted me as a graduate student in folklore; neither could 19 offer any financial assistance. My alma mater offered me a scholarship to get an M.A. in English. It seemed easy to do. I had also figured out a way to deal with their system, I thought, and I was already living in that town. So I deferred folklore for a year and went back to my first school.

Taking four courses a semester didn't daunt me; in fact, I was quite non- 20 chalant about the experience at the time. Nights, I worked at the hotel again, taught some music, and lived cheap (the garden vegetables helped). In twelve months I had an M.A., and it was on to grad school in folklore in the big city . . . and, at a famous Ivy League school.

Again with some nonchalance, I borrowed money to finance the first 21 year. I was very excited about having found a field that, I thought, expressed my innermost concerns and would provide me with the socially, intellectually acceptable means to bring forth those concerns into the world. The second year, I got a scholarship which paid my tuition. I still had to meet my living expenses. By this time I felt comfortable enough in the city to begin playing music for money. I did this with the new man I had taken up with, a good talker and interesting character, a high school dropout from the Jewish suburban middle class. The rigors of being straight academically were compensated for by the fieldwork I was doing as part of that—I had begun to interview people in my home county about folk medicine.

Active as I was as a graduate student, the methods of academia still seemed 22 alien to me. Although I conceived of my discipline as subversive within the larger intellectual reality of our culture (as did a number of my colleagues, explicitly), on a day-to-day basis, we felt as oppressed by our own discipline as by those disciplines we had come from. The hierarchies and game playing which seemed essential for survival in the system were offensive to me. It also made me sad to see my fellow students so cowed by authority.

I was disillusioned when my discipline (committed at least intellectually 23 to the views of the "folk," the peasants, the poor, the disenfranchised) had to debate whether or not to become involved in political issues. Many folklorists said that an academic group should not have political views. It seemed so obvious to me that we were living in the same world as Phyllis Schlafly, Gloria Steinem and millions of women and should recognize the fact (that mysterious, physical, universal world which we were all part of—although my faith in this had become hazy). *The Journal of American Folklore* published a scholarly article on the involvement of folklorists in the Third Reich. A number of women and I planned a conference on Women and Folklore and boycotted the larger meetings in Utah, which had not ratified the ERA.

During these years I was also playing music three or four nights a week in 24 city and suburban bars. Being in the city was stimulating musically as well as intellectually. I felt that I had finally learned to use my mind, to stretch my abilities. I felt I had finally met large numbers of people who were just as smart and smarter than me, just as talented and more talented musically than me, as crazy, radical, poetic, visionary, anything! In the city I was no longer the eccentric I was at my rural High School. I had finally been to the place where everything was happening and had measured myself against it, had jumped in with both feet and found the water fine. I got comfortable with my abilities and felt less disenfranchised than I ever had. However, at the same time, living in the city and being a graduate student was strenuous and downright dangerous.

The whole process of becoming highly educated was for me a process of 25 losing faith. I was taught not to trust my perceptions, but to refer to the bibliography and the traditions of my field; my original reasons for taking up folklore had been translated into the particulars of twenty courses and many conferences, parties, guest speakers, administrative wranglings, by the interdepartmental feuds and machinations, by papers and newsletters and meetings, by the anger I felt at my discipline's shortcomings and its treatment of women, by the cultivating of professors, by the hairsplitting which is essential in European intellectual culture.

As I did my studies, I also began working by myself in the city. It was an 26 educational and terrifying experience. Fortunately for my financial situation, I was hired to play three nights a week in a little bar/restaurant near the waterfront, near a newly hip section of the city. What I liked most about the place was its mixed clientele: longshoremen, businessmen, beautiful people on dates from center city, gay men and women, artists and craftspeople of every ilk, Catholic Italians from south Philly, and occasionally some of my fellow graduate students. Because I played mostly for tips, I had to learn to communicate musically and verbally with all these people. I enjoyed that challenge and its contrast to the academic world across the river. Crazy as the Left Bank was, I felt at home with the folks there and gained a lot more poise. I also learned how to deal with obnoxious drunks of all ages and classes; and noticed that the whole scene got crazier when the moon was full.

The main drawback to working at the Left Bank and elsewhere as a musi- 27 cian was that I was no longer under a man's protection. Aside from the expected barroom hassles, I often went home alone, and had to park far from my house and walk there—four, five blocks, in the middle of the night. In order to survive, I had to think defensively. That sounds sensible enough, but what that meant was walking home from work every night considering how I might or might not be jumped, robbed or raped. That made me very angry.

Finally, after a few minor street incidents, I tangled with serious crime. I 28 found that my house had been broken into, robbed, and set on fire. I lost cash, instruments, all my clothes, personal belongings, stereo, everything valuable. Most of my papers and all my notes for my dissertation were o.k. The police thought it was the work of a psychopath, but had no clues. My friends and neighbors were freaked out, and so was I. I pulled myself together enough to finish writing a paper and delivered it at the folklore society meetings that month, and then I left the city and my close association with the academic world.

What living in the city and living in the academy have in common, 29 for me, are two things: Both took me closer to the realities of mainstream American culture than I had ever been (you know what I mean: official culture, high culture, the majority consensus of reality; the trappings of the American dream, or depending on your point of view, the "heart of the dragon"); and both were the opposite of what I grew up with, the farthest poles, that I had to explore in seeking what was missing from what I knew. Well, what I discovered (as many people before me) was that what I was searching for didn't exist "out there." Only by coming to terms with my own past, my own background, and seeing that in context of the world at large, have I begun to find my true voice and to understand that, since it is my own voice, that no pre-cut niche exists for it; that part of the work to be done is making a place, with others, where my and our voices can stand clear of the background noise and voice our concerns as part of a larger song.

As I have come to realize this, to come full circle to where I started, I have 30 found more and more people who share some part of my vision. This makes me very hopeful and also makes confronting the realities of America somewhat less grim. I have also come to believe that most people feel like strangers in the world.

Specifically, my sense of community comes from both inside and outside 31 the academy. Recently I have found a number of people my age who now have Ph.D.s and are functioning inside universities—often we share some past in the 1960s, some transformation of those concerns and times; and recently I have come to realize that many folklorists come from working class backgrounds. Last year at our annual meetings (which have the character of a festival, family reunion, academic racetrack, business luncheon, and singles bar) I had several conversations with people about coming from "the folk" and how strange academia was, how strange the assumptions of the middle class, and how strange our families found our bet on education (though not necessarily in principle: A number of our families espoused onward and upward). What they found strange was either that we were women doing it, or that the realities of it—years of study, poverty, academic power trips—did not match their image of the dream. One of my fellow graduate students, from a working class English background, had difficulty explaining the ins and outs of academic life to his family until he compared interdepartmental politics to the cutthroat business practices with which his family was familiar. And then they were appalled to realize how similar academics were to the rest of the people.

A more positive connection for me, comes from the subject of my field, 32 and my own interests in that field. It's no accident that I've studied the people that I came from. It's their reality I'm trying to describe, to affirm, to give voice to. Doing this gives me great satisfaction, because I can put my intellect (whose restlessness forced me to leave what I knew) and my academic experience (for better or for worse, it's part of me now) to use for the people and the place where my heart lies.

When writing my dissertation I lived on my family's farm. Instead of paying rent, I worked in the fields and garden. What I resented as a child, I then enjoyed as a choice that I made; I came to see the positive values in my family's way of life as well as all the negative ones which I had rebelled against. I came to see that those values have been part of me even while I thought I was doing something very different. My folks, too, while they couldn't understand the purpose of my education while I was going through it, enjoyed reading my dissertation (which is about a kind of folk medicine they both know and is written in a style meant to be useful to both academics and the people whom it's about). 33

I feel the same way about academia; it's like an eccentric member of my family whose company I enjoy at annual reunions and family dinners. My intellect, as well as my background, is a part of me that I can't deny. I would rather give a lecture on mythology for an honorarium than work as a waitress for the same amount of money. (I would also rather play music in smokey bars than work as a factory supervisor for the same amount of money.) I'd rather spend the day writing than driving a tractor, five days a week. I would rather do any of the above than be wife to someone whose support bought my subservience. 34

What I value and begin to find, even in the academy, is: cooperation, a sense of community, a concern for the disenfranchised, an attempt to lead a balanced life. My first job teaching was at a community college where most of the students majored in forestry, nursery management, horticulture, welding, wood products technology, graphic arts, nursing, etc. I taught freshman composition; a required course, though there were no English majors there. I liked this job because these people were "down to earth." That's how I find myself putting it. What I mean is they came from the same class background as I did. This made me comfortable. I tell myself that I enjoyed these people more than students with pretensions about themselves and their backgrounds, and with illusions about the class value of education. I felt silly, sometimes, teaching them English grammar (I call myself the grammar police) and I felt ambivalent about the fact that it might have enabled them to get on in the system that values education; but I liked to talk to them about writing, about communication, about ideas, about how to write resumes and letters to the editor. 35

I found it significant that some of my former professors considered this a low class job. But it's all the same to me whether I correct grammar or whether I try to impose some standard of writing style. While I might rather have been talking about some fine points of folklore, still, it was a job; and one way or another, my working class background makes me want to keep working in my second job. It makes me want to survive in this cash economy, and to work to bring forth in the world a voice that speaks for my vision and for the vision of the people and place that I come from. Those people and that place gave me life, beauty, dreams, and purpose, and to speak for them is the least I can do. 36

Reprinted with permission of South End Press, Boston.
1. LPN: *Licensed Practical Nurse.*

Reader's Dialogue

A Guide for Rereading, Notemaking & Writing an Essay

Contrast Jane Ellen Wilson's background to your own. Consider culture, class, and educational background of family. Use the following list as a guide for rereading, and then make notes (from your notes) using the comparison frame in Figure 4.1.

1. "I expected," says Wilson, "to find intellectual stimulation and community; fun and companionship; new ideas and political concern; and all the things I had been missing. . . . I also strongly expected academia not to discriminate against women." Reread paragraphs 9, 10, and 11. Compare Wilson's expectations about college to your own.
2. "[M]ost people at the college came from a middle class suburban world" (paragraph 14). Would you say this is true about students at the college you attend? Does Wilson's description fit your own background?
3. What assumptions had Wilson made about people who didn't go to college? See paragraph 14.
4. "I had always felt there was something missing in academia's view of the world" (paragraph 16). What do you think Wilson means here?

Figure 4.1

Comparison Frame

Points of Comparison	Self	Wilson
1. Expectations about college		

2. Class
    own class
    class of students
    at college		

3. Assumptions about people who didn't go to college		
4. Attitude of family toward going to college		
5. Degree of comfort in academic environment		
6. Other categories		

5. Wilson talks about her "family's imagined future" for her (paragraph 17). Can you identify with her? Does anyone in your family imagine your future for you? In paragraph 18 she remarks, "My family didn't always see much sense in my ongoing education." How does this attitude compare to the attitude of your family toward your going to college?

6. "[T]he methods of academia still seemed alien to me," Wilson says in paragraph 22. What is she talking about, and can you relate to what she's saying? Do the methods of academia seem alien to you?

7. "Well, what I discovered," Wilson continues in paragraph 29, "was that what I was searching for didn't exist 'out there.'" What do you understand her to mean here?

8. How did Wilson finally come to regard academia (the world of college)? See paragraphs 33–36. How did she make peace with these different worlds (her world, the world of her family, and the world of academia or school)?

Look over the notes you made in the comparison frame, and reorder the points of comparison in the order you want to present to a reader. What makes sense to you to bring up first? The attitudes of their families? Their own expectations about college? After organizing some points of comparison, write about Wilson first in one or more paragraphs; then, following the same order, write about yourself.

Next, rewrite going back and forth for each point of comparison. Finally, read both versions aloud. Which version do you think is more effective?

Writer at Work: Karen Wong

Karen Wong, a Chinese-American, believes everyone should go to college. She begins this draft of her going-to-college story with a quotation from her grandmother, who grew up in a different time and in a different place. You may notice a few mechanical and grammatical errors when you read this draft. Some errors—problems with verb tenses or articles (a, an), for example—persist because she has not internalized usage rules for standard American English. Listen to what she has to say and, again, think of your own story and what you want to say.

Going to College

"We were a product of a culture that said women existed to serve their husbands and to stay home to cook and clean," my grandmother used to say. She would always advise us not to take education for granted, and to learn as much as possible. Coming from a large Chinese family, my mother used to watch Kaiti Tong and Connie Chung daily on the NBC or ABC news and admire their achievements and recognition in society, and around the world. I believe that they have given me the sense of opportunities, upward mobility and capacity for young Asian students to accomplish their goals and to never give up. I understood that they have worked hard and went through many years of school in order to become what they are today. Another reason why I looked up to these two Asian broadcasters is because I can sympathize how diligently they work in order to be accepted in a predominantly white society. The same is true for other minorities, such as Italians. I have just recently read an article about Mario Cuomo, the successful governor of New York, and how difficult it was for him to enter the best law firms because of his Italian background. Nevertheless, after hard work and a loving family, and of course, a full education, he was able to have a successful career.

Today I feel that everyone should go to college. I believe that it is necessary for a student to attend college, not only to further their academic knowledge and skills, but also to understand and be content with their identity. In addition, it is important to further and advance this country by inventing new medicine, science, literature and bringing fresh inspiration to our future children. When I look back at my grandmother's words, I realize her best interest in our lives in wanting us to be someone, and not just a wife. She wanted us to have a good career and to prove that Asians also have a voice in society; they can contribute some value to society.

College Is a Waste of Time and Money

Caroline Bird

Caroline Bird does not believe that college is the best place for all high-school graduates, male or female. She attended Vassar College, the first women's college to have the equipment and resources equal to those of men's colleges. Bird went on to earn a B.A. degree from the University of Toledo and an M.A. degree from the University of Wisconsin. She is author of Born Female, The Crowding Syndrome, Everything a Woman Needs to Know to Get Paid What She's Worth, *and* The Case Against College. *In addition to writing books and articles for various magazines, she has also taught courses on the status of women and lectured on college campuses across the country. "College Is a Waste of Time and Money" first appeared in the May 1975 issue of* Psychology Today. *Although some issues and figures are dated, this article raises some objections about going to college that continue to be relevant.*

A great majority of our nine-million college students are not in school because they want to be or because they want to learn. They are there because it has become the thing to do or because college is a pleasant place to be;   1 because it's the only way they can get parents or taxpayers to support them without working at a job they don't like; because Mother wanted them to go, or some other reason entirely irrelevant to the course of studies for which college is supposedly organized.

As I crisscross the United States lecturing on college campuses, I am dismayed to find that professors and administrators, when pressed for a candid opinion, estimate that no more than 25 percent of their students are turned on by classwork. For the rest, college is at best a social center or aging vat, and at worst a young folks' home or even a prison that keeps them out of the mainstream of economic life for a few more years.

The premise—which I no longer accept—that college is the best place for all high-school graduates grew out of a noble American ideal. Just as the United States was the first nation to aspire to teach every small child to read and write, so, during the 1950s, we became the first and only great nation to aspire to higher education for all. During the '60s we damned the expense and built great state university systems as fast as we could. And adults— parents, employers, high-school counselors—began to push, shove and cajole youngsters to "get an education."

It became a mammoth industry, with taxpayers footing more than half the bill. By 1970, colleges and universities were spending more than 30-billion dollars annually. But still only half our high-school graduates were going on. According to estimates made by the economist, Fritz Machlup, if we had been educating every young person until age 22 in that year of 1970, the bill for higher education would have reached 47.5-billion dollars, 12.5 billion more than the total corporate profits for the year.

The Baby Boom Is Over

Figures such as these have begun to make higher education for all look financially prohibitive, particularly now when colleges are squeezed by the pressures of inflation and a drop-off in the growth of their traditional market.

Predictable demography has caught up with the university empire builders. Now that the record crop of postwar babies has graduated from college, the rate of growth of the student population has begun to decline. To keep their mammoth plants financially solvent, many institutions have begun to use hard-sell, Madison-Avenue techniques to attract students. They sell college like soap, promoting features they think students want: innovative programs, an environment conducive to meaningful personal relationships, and a curriculum so free that it doesn't sound like college at all.

Pleasing the customers is something new for college administrators. Colleges have always known that most students don't like to study, and that at least part of the time they are ambivalent about college, but before the student riots of the 1960s educators never thought it either right or necessary to pay any attention to student feelings. But when students rebelling against the Vietnam war and the draft discovered they could disrupt a campus completely, administrators had to act on some student complaints. Few understood that the protests had tapped the basic discontent with college itself, a discontent that did not go away when the riots subsided.

Bird

Today students protest individually rather than in concert. They turn in- 8
ward and withdraw from active participation. They drop out to travel to
India or to feed themselves on subsistence farms. Some refuse to go to college at all. Most, of course, have neither the funds nor the self-confidence for
constructive articulation of their discontent. They simply hang around college unhappily and reluctantly.

All across the country, I have been overwhelmed by the prevailing sad- 9
ness on American campuses. Too many young people speak little, and then
only in drowned voices. Sometimes the mood surfaces as diffidence, wari-
ness, or coolness, but whatever its form, it looks like a defense mechanism,
and that rings a bell. This is the way it used to be with women, and just as
society had systematically damaged women by insisting that their proper
place was in the home, so we may be systematically damaging 18-year-olds
by insisting that their proper place is in college.

Sad and Unneeded

Campus watchers everywhere know what I mean when I say students are 10
sad, but they don't agree on the reason for it. During the Vietnam war some
ascribed the sadness to the draft; now others blame affluence, or say it has
something to do with permissive upbringing.

Not satisfied with any of these explanations, I looked for some answers 11
with the journalistic tools of my trade—scholarly studies, economic analyses, the historical record, the opinions of the especially knowledgeable, conversations with parents, professors, college administrators, and employers,
all of whom spoke as alumni too. Mostly I learned from my interviews with
hundreds of young people on and off campuses all over the country.

My unnerving conclusion is that students are sad because they are not 12
needed. Somewhere between the nursery and the employment office, they
become unwanted adults. No one has anything in particular against them.
But no one knows what to do with them either. We already have too many
people in the world of the 1970s, and there is no room for so many newly
minted 18-year-olds. So we temporarily get them out of the way by sending
them to college where in fact only a few belong.

To make it more palatable, we fool ourselves into believing that we are 13
sending them there for their own best interests, and that it's good for them,
like spinach. Some, of course, learn to like it, but most wind up preferring
green peas.

Educators admit as much. Nevitt Sanford, distinguished student of higher 14
education, says students feel they are "capitulating to a kind of voluntary
servitude." Some of them talk about their time in college as if it were a sentence to be served. I listened to a 1970 Mount Holyoke graduate: "For two
years I was really interested in science, but in my junior and senior years I
just kept saying, 'I've done two years; I'm going to finish.' When I got out I
made up my mind that I wasn't going to school anymore because so many
of my courses had been bullshit."

But bad as it is, college is often preferable to a far worse fate. It is better 15
than the drudgery of an uninspiring nine-to-five job, and better than doing
nothing when no jobs are available. For some young people, it is a graceful

way to get away from home and become independent without losing the financial support of their parents. And sometimes it is the only alternative to an intolerable home situation.

It is difficult to assess how many students are in college reluctantly. The 16 conservative Carnegie Commission estimates from five to 30 percent. Sol Linowitz, who was once chairman of a special committee on campus tension of the American Council on Education, found that "a significant number were not happy with their college experience because they felt they were there only in order to get the 'ticket to the big show' rather than to spend the years as productively as they otherwise could."

Older alumni will identify with Richard Baloga, a policeman's son, who 17 stayed in school even though he "hated it" because he thought it would do him some good. But fewer students each year feel this way. Daniel Yankelovich has surveyed undergraduate attitudes for a number of years, and reported in 1971 that 74 percent thought education was "very important." But just two years earlier, 80 percent thought so.

An Inside View of What's Good

The doubters don't mind speaking up. Leon Lefkowitz, chairman of the de- 18 partment of social studies at Central High School in Valley Stream, New York, interviewed 300 college students at random, and reports that 200 of them didn't think that the education they were getting was worth the effort. "In two years I'll pick up a diploma," said one student, "and I can honestly say it was a waste of my father's bread."

Nowadays, says one sociologist, you don't have to have a reason for 19 going to college; it's an institution. His definition of an institution is an arrangement everyone accepts without question; the burden of proof is not on why you go, but why anyone thinks there might be a reason for not going. The implication is that an 18-year-old is too young and confused to know what he wants to do, and that he should listen to those who know best and go to college.

I don't agree. I believe that college has to be judged not on what other 20 people think is good for students, but on how good it feels to the students themselves.

I believe that people have an inside view of what's good for them. If a 21 child doesn't want to go to school some morning, better let him stay at home, at least until you find out why. Maybe he knows something you don't. It's the same with college. If high-school graduates don't want to go, or if they don't want to go right away, they may perceive more clearly than their elders that college is not for them. It is no longer obvious that adolescents are best off studying a core curriculum that was constructed when all educated men could agree on what made them educated, or that professors, advisors, or parents can be of any particular help to young people in choosing a major or a career. High-school graduates see college graduates driving cabs, and decide it's not worth going. College students find no intellectual stimulation in their studies and drop out.

If students believe that college isn't necessarily good for them, you can't 22 expect them to stay on for the general good of mankind. They don't go to

Bird

school to beat the Russians to Jupiter, improve the national defense, increase the GNP, or create a market for the arts—to mention some of the benefits taxpayers are supposed to get for supporting higher education.

Nor should we expect to bring about social equality by putting all young 23 people through four years of academic rigor. At best, it's a roundabout and expensive way to narrow the gap between the highest and lowest in our society anyway. At worst, it is unconsciously elitist. Equalizing opportunity through universal higher education subjects the whole population to the intellectual mode natural only to a few. It violates the fundamental egalitarian principle of respect for the differences between people.

The Dumbest Investment

Of course, most parents aren't thinking of the "higher" good at all. They send 24 their children to college because they are convinced young people benefit financially from those four years of higher education. But if money is the only goal, college is the dumbest investment you can make. I say this because a young banker in Poughkeepsie, New York, Stephen G. Necel, used a computer to compare college as an investment with other investments available in 1974 and college did not come out on top.

For the sake of argument, the two of us invented a young man whose 25 rich uncle gave him, in cold cash, the cost of a four-year education at any college he chose, but the young man didn't have to spend the money on college. After bales of computer paper, we had our mythical student write to his uncle: "Since you said I could spend the money foolishly if I wished, I am going to blow it all on Princeton."

The much respected financial columnist Sylvia Porter echoed the com- 26 mon assumption when she said last year, "A college education is among the very best investments you can make in your entire life." But the truth is not quite so rosy, even if we assume that the Census Bureau is correct when it says that as of 1972, a man who completed four years of college would expect to earn $199,000 more between the ages of 22 and 64 than a man who had only a high-school diploma.[1]

If a 1972 Princeton-bound high-school graduate had put the $34,181 27 that his four years of college would have cost him into a savings bank at 7.5 percent interest compounded daily, he would have had at age 64 a total of $1,129,200, or $528,200 more than the earnings of a male college graduate, and more than five times as much as the $199,000 extra the more educated man could expect to earn between 22 and 64.

The big advantage of getting your college money in cash now is that you 28 can invest it in something that has a higher return than a diploma. For instance, a Princeton-bound high-school graduate of 1972 who liked fooling around with cars could have banked his $34,181, and gone to work at the local garage at close to $1,000 more per year than the average high-school graduate. Meanwhile, as he was learning to be an expert auto mechanic, his money would be ticking away in the bank. When he became 28, he would have earned $7,199 less on his job from age 22 to 28 than his college-educated friend, but he would have had $73,113 in his passbook—enough to buy out his boss, go into the used-car business, or acquire his own new-car dealership. If successful in business, he could expect to make more than the average college graduate. And if he has the brains to get into Princeton, he would be just as likely to make money without the four years spent on campus. Unfortunately, few college-bound high-school graduates get the opportunity to bank such a large sum of money, and then wait for it to make them rich. And few parents are sophisticated enough to understand that in financial returns alone, their children would be better off with the money than with the education.

Rates of return and dollar signs on education are fascinating brain 29 teasers, but obviously there is a certain unreality to the game. Quite aside from the economic benefits of college, and these should loom larger once the dollars are cleared away, there are grave difficulties in assigning a dollar value to college at all.

Status, Not Money

In fact there is no real evidence that the higher income of college graduates 30 is due to college. College may simply attract people who are slated to earn more money anyway; those with higher IQs, better family backgrounds, a more enterprising temperament. No one who has wrestled with the problem is prepared to attribute all of the higher income to the impact of college itself.

Christopher Jencks, author of *Inequality,* a book that assesses the effect of 31 family and schooling in America, believes that education in general accounts for less than half of the difference in income in the American population. "The biggest single source of income differences," writes Jencks, "seems to be the fact that men from high-status families have higher incomes than men from low-status families even when they enter the same occupations, have the same amount of education, and have the same test scores."

Jacob Mincer of the National Bureau of Economic Research and Colum- 32 bia University states flatly that of "20 to 30 percent of students at any level, the additional schooling has been a waste, at least in terms of earnings." College fails to work its income-raising magic for almost a third of those who go. More than half of those people in 1972 who earned $15,000 or more reached that comfortable bracket without the benefit of a college diploma. Jencks says that financial success in the U.S. depends a good deal on luck, and the most sophisticated regression analyses have yet to demonstrate otherwise.

But most of today's students don't go to college to earn more money any- 33 way. In 1968, when jobs were easy to get, Daniel Yankelovich made his first nationwide survey of students. Sixty-five percent of them said they "would welcome less emphasis on money." By 1973, when jobs were scarce, that figure jumped to 80 percent.

The young are not alone. Americans today are all looking less to the pay 34 of a job than to the work itself. They want "interesting" work that permits them "to make a contribution," "express themselves" and "use their special abilities," and they think college will help them find it.

Bird

Jerry Darring of Indianapolis knows what it is to make a dollar. He worked 35 with his father in the family plumbing business, on the line at Chevrolet, and in the Chrysler foundry. He quit these jobs to enter Wright State University in Dayton, Ohio, because "in a job like that a person only has time to work, and after that he's so tired that he can't do anything else but come home and go to sleep."

Jerry came to college to find work "helping people." And he is perfectly 36 willing to spend the dollars he earns at dull, well-paid work to prepare for lower-paid work that offers the reward of service to others.

Psychic Income

Jerry's case is not unusual. No one works for money alone. In order to deal 37 with the nonmonetary rewards of work, economists have coined the concept of "psychic income," which according to one economic dictionary means "income that is reckoned in terms of pleasure, satisfaction, or general feelings of euphoria."

Psychic income is primarily what college students mean when they talk 38 about getting a good job. During the most affluent years of the late 1960s and early 1970s college students told their placement officers that they wanted to be researchers, college professors, artists, city planners, social workers, poets, book publishers, archeologists, ballet dancers, or authors.

The psychic income of these and other occupations popular with stu- 39 dents is so high that these jobs can be filled without offering high salaries. According to one study, 93 percent of urban university professors would choose the same vocation again if they had the chance, compared with only 16 percent of unskilled auto workers. Even though the monetary gap between college professor and auto worker is now surprisingly small, the difference in psychic income is enormous.

But colleges fail to warn students that jobs of these kinds are hard to 40 come by, even for qualified applicants, and they rarely accept the responsibility of helping students choose a career that will lead to a job. When a young person says he is interested in helping people, his counselor tells him to become a psychologist. But jobs in psychology are scarce. The Department of Labor, for instance, estimates there will be 4,300 new jobs for psychologists in 1975 while colleges are expected to turn out 58,430 B.A.s in psychology that year.

Of 30 psych majors who reported back to Vassar what they were doing a 41 year after graduation in 1972, only five had jobs in which they could possibly use their courses in psychology, and two of these were working for Vassar.

The outlook isn't much better for students majoring in other psychic-pay 42 disciplines: sociology, English, journalism, anthropology, forestry, education. Whatever college graduates want to do, most of them are going to wind up doing what there is to do.

John Shingleton, director of placement at Michigan State University, ac- 43 cuses the academic community of outright hypocrisy. "Educators have never said, 'Go to college and get a good job,' but this has been implied, and now students expect it. . . . If we care what happens to students after college, then let's get involved with what should be one of the basic purposes of education: career preparation."

In the 1970s, some of the more practical professors began to see that jobs 44
for graduates meant jobs for professors too. Meanwhile, students themselves reacted to the shrinking job market, and a "new vocationalism" exploded on campus. The press welcomed the change as a return to the ethic of achievement and service. Students were still idealistic, the reporters wrote, but they now saw that they could best make the world better by healing the sick as physicians or righting individual wrongs as lawyers.

No Use on the Job

But there are no guarantees in these professions either. The American Enter- 45
prise Institute estimated in 1971 that there would be more than the target ratio of 100 doctors for every 100,000 people in the population by 1980. And the odds are little better for would-be lawyers. Law schools are already graduating twice as many new lawyers every year as the Department of Labor thinks will be needed, and the over-supply is growing every year.

And it's not at all apparent that what is actually learned in a "profes- 46
sional" education is necessary for success. Teachers, engineers and others I talked to said they find that on the job they rarely use what they learned in school. In order to see how well college prepared engineers and scientists for actual paid work in their fields, The Carnegie Commission queried all the employees with degrees in these fields in two large firms. Only one in five said the work they were doing bore a "very close relationship" to their college studies, while almost a third saw "very little relationship at all." An overwhelming majority could think of many people who were doing their same work, but had majored in different fields.

Majors in nontechnical fields report even less relationship between their 47
studies and their jobs. Charles Lawrence, a communications major in college and now the producer of "Kennedy & Co.," the Chicago morning television show, says, "You have to learn all that stuff and you never use it again. I learned my job doing it." Others employed as architects, nurses, teachers and other members of the so-called learned professions report the same thing.

Most college administrators admit that they don't prepare their gradu- 48
ates for the job market. "I just wish I had the guts to tell parents that when you get out of this place you aren't prepared to do anything," the academic head of a famous liberal-arts college told us. Fortunately, for him, most people believe that you don't have to defend a liberal-arts education on those grounds. A liberal-arts education is supposed to provide you with a value system, a standard, a set of ideas, not a job. "Like Christianity, the liberal arts are seldom practiced and would probably be hated by the majority of the populace if they were," said one defender.

The analogy is apt. The fact is, of course, that the liberal arts are a religion 49
in every sense of that term. When people talk about them, their language becomes elevated, metaphorical, extravagant, theoretical and reverent. And faith in personal salvation by the liberal arts is professed in a creed intoned on ceremonial occasions such as commencements.

Bird

Ticket of Admission

If the liberal arts are a religious faith, the professors are its priests. But dis- 50
seminating ideas in a four-year college curriculum is slow and most expensive. If you want to learn about Milton, Camus, or even Margaret Mead you
can find them in paperback books, the public library, and even on television.

And when most people talk about the value of a college education, they 51
are not talking about great books. When, at Harvard commencement, the
president welcomes the new graduates into "the fellowship of educated men
and women," what he could be saying is, "here is a piece of paper that is a
passport to jobs, power and instant prestige." As Glenn Bassett, a personnel
specialist at G.E. says, "In some parts of G.E., a college degree appears completely irrelevant to selection to, say, a manager's job. In most, however, it is
a ticket of admission."

But now that we have doubled the number of young people attending 52
college, a diploma cannot guarantee even that. The most charitable conclusion we can reach is that college probably has very little, if any, effect on
people and things at all. Today, the false premises are easy to see:

First, college doesn't make people intelligent, ambitious, happy, or lib- 53
eral. It's the other way around. Intelligent, ambitious, happy, liberal people
are attracted to higher education in the first place.

Second, college can't claim much credit for the learning experiences that 54
really change students while they are there. Jobs, friends, history, and most
of all the sheer passage of time, have as big an impact as anything even indirectly related to the campus.

Third, colleges have changed so radically that a freshman entering in the 55
fall of 1974 can't be sure to gain even the limited value research studies assigned to colleges in the '60s. The sheer size of undergraduate campuses of
the 1970s makes college even less stimulating now than it was 10 years ago.
Today even motivated students are disappointed with their college courses
and professors.

Finally, a college diploma no longer opens as many vocational doors. Em- 56
ployers are beginning to realize that when they pay extra for someone with
a diploma, they are paying only for an empty credential. The fact is that
most of the work for which employers now expect college training is now or
has been capably done in the past by people without higher educations.

College, then, may be a good place for those few young people who are 57
really drawn to academic work, who would rather read than eat, but it has
become too expensive, in money, time, and intellectual effort to serve as a
holding pen for large numbers of our young. We ought to make it possible
for those reluctant, unhappy students to find alternative ways of growing
up, and more realistic preparation for the years ahead.

Caroline Bird, "College Is a Waste of Time and Money." From *Psychology Today* 8 (12), May
1975. Reprinted by permission of the author.
1. According to the 1984 Statistical Abstract of the United States, a person who completed
four years of college in 1979 could expect to earn $309,000 more than a non-college
graduate.

Reader's Dialogue

Making Connections: A Guide for Rereading & Notemaking

What is your response to paragraphs 12–15? Caroline Bird is not addressing students directly but indirectly—she is talking (from her view) about the sad state of students in the mid-1970s. How would you describe her tone (the way she relates as a writer to her readers)?

Do you think there is some truth in the 1990s to what she wrote in 1975 about "newly minted 18-year-olds" (paragraph 12)?

Some people think 18-year-olds are too young and confused to know what they want to do, so they should listen to those who know best and go to college (paragraph 19). Bird does not agree. She believes "that college has to be judged not on what other people think is good for students, but on how good it feels to the students themselves" (paragraph 20). What is your view? Where would you position yourself in this debate?

"Equalizing opportunity through universal higher education subjects the whole population to the intellectual mode natural only to a few. It violates the fundamental egalitarian principle of respect for the differences between people" (paragraph 23). Is Bird saying that going to college should be for a select few? Paraphrase (put in your own words) what you think she's saying here and give your opinion. Do you follow her argument? Do you agree with her?

Copy the following quotation in the notetaking side of your notebook:

> Americans today are all looking less to the pay of a job than to the work itself. They want "interesting" work that permits them "to make a contribution," "express themselves" and "use their special abilities," and they think college will help them find it. (paragraph 34)

Then, on the notemaking side and just opposite the quotation, address the following question: Would you say that what Caroline Bird wrote in 1975 about American values and the role of college is true today?

Continue reading the last three sections (beginning at paragraph 37). List the major points she makes (about the relation of college and work and so on). Then reread her conclusion and respond. Should college be a place "for those few young people who are really drawn to academic work"? Why do students seem to be going to college in the 1990s?

Readers at Work

Letters to the Editor: Responses to Caroline Bird

These "Letters to the Editor" appeared in *Psychology Today* in October 1975 in response to Bird's essay.

Some students may be bored with 90 percent of their classes and be "interested" in only the remaining 10 percent. Does that mean that they are wasting their time and money? I don't think so. A valuable learning experience can be wrapped up in that 10 percent.

I do agree with Bird that students are unable to recognize the relevance of most of the course work to their jobs. However, I have found that the longer people are out of school, the more they recognize the importance and relevance of many of their college courses.

Jerry Horgesheimer
D.B.A.
Ogden, Utah

In some European countries the compulsory attendance age extends to 9th or 10th grade. Much of the emphasis is placed on reading, writing and arithmetic. Many college graduates in the U.S. lack the mastery of these vital skills. The lowering of the compulsory-attendance age in the United States would leave the opportunity of higher education only to those students who are attracted to education's liberality.

Sam Maravich Jr.
Steelton, Penn.

High schools should equip students with an awareness of society and the availability of jobs, provide them with marketable skills, and require courses that will help students examine and develop their own value systems, learn to make decisions and to achieve "personhood." Giving high-school students this knowledge would enable them to make better decisions as to what they chose to do after high school. Students who opted for work would have difficulty as the labor market, also, is certainly unprepared to accommodate a good percentage of high-school graduates. So college becomes a good stopgap.

Parents who want their children to have it "as good as they do," if not better, feel that college will guarantee their children upward mobility (generally equated in dollar signs). This is unrealistic because of current and predicted labor demands, as well as the changing role of education that is becoming a life-long process instead of one ending at age 23. In addition, jobs will exist that cannot be prepared for now, as they do not exist. Flexibility is the key word, as well as societal reappraisal of the value of work and the prestige of vocational training.

Judith Sacks, Counselor
Baldwin Senior High School
Baldwin, N.Y.

Bird doesn't recognize that a large proportion of the staggering sums asked collectively by colleges and universities are in the forms of loans, scholarships and grants that would not be available if one chose to invest in the world of business instead.

John Michelsen
Gusatavus Adolphus College
Mound, Minn.

I know a number of people with B.A.s who are for all intents and purposes ignorant of 90 percent of what they supposedly went to college to learn. I attribute this to immaturity at the time of instruction, poor secondary education, and the lowering of academic standards at many institutions. I started university study at 28. As an older student, I am self-motivated and have a clear goal I wish to attain. I feel strongly that students not academically inclined (as I was not, at age 18) should not be pushed into or pandered to at a university.

Susan Gilbertsen
Eugene, Ore.

We at the Boatshop raise our oar in salute to Caroline Bird.

We educators dropped our hammers and saws too soon! Observing that our college-degree success has led to Wall Street failure, we have turned to tools to discover excitement and satisfaction. Using their hands to discipline their minds, our apprentices create marketable products of both.

Stefan P. Galazzi, Director
The Experience on Cape Cod
South Orleans, Mass.

College will continue to be a waste of time and money for the taxpayer and the student until colleges start getting what should be their product; trained students that can successfully and skillfully apply what they have learned and do. Of course the first prerequisite to this is that what is taught *can* be used.

Glen J. Doe
Hamilton, Ontario

I worked my way through a private college because I wanted to. As one of my professors once said, "The more we know, the more increase of mystery; the more we know, the more unknown we meet." He compared it to a light bulb of 60 watts that illuminates to a certain perimeter of light, and a 100-watt bulb that illuminates only to increase the perimeter of darkness. College, for me, was all this and more.

Christine Masi
Maspeth, N.Y.

One overwhelming fact that Bird cannot explain is that once students grow into adulthood, they come back to the university, not for a degree ("that glorious piece of wallpaper," as Mark Twain called it), but to immerse themselves in ideas, literature, and the arts. Although undergraduate programs are finding themselves bankrupt—in more ways than one—programs for adults, schools of continuing education, are alive and flourishing all over the country. For the first time in American history, part-time, adult students outnumber full-time undergraduates. This does not indicate that our universities are obsolete.

I certainly do not wish to "blame" undergraduates for not living up to our expectations. They, too, are victims of a society that systematically destroys intellectual curiosity and interpersonal sensitivity, a society that has replaced reading and discussion with the TV. But neither must we blame the universities for the widespread apathy found among undergraduates. And I suspect Bird knows this very well.

Victor B. Marrow, Associate Director
Division of Liberal Studies
Assistant Professor of Social Philosophy
School of Continuing Education
New York University

Liberal arts should be taught in high schools, community-based "continuing education" programs, and small colleges. Vocational curricula should be available, in separate or coordinated programs, to complement the liberal arts. Large universities could then stick to academics and research. People could then know what to expect from whatever institution they attend, and clearer purpose would improve performances by both students and schools.

Eric T. MacKnight
College Dropout
Washington, D.C.

Does Bird make a case against College (*College,* like Plato's *Republic*) or a case against the American postsecondary-education system that bores students for four (or more) years and then has the audacity not to reward those students for their stoical endurance (and dad's dough) with the lump of sugar, carrot or cigar? Worse, take her use of the word "good" like a college Freshman would—"I believe that college has to be judged not on what other people think is good for students but on how good it feels to students themselves [outrage mine]." But, Caroline, at least in language one "good" does not another make. What about a case for wasting more time and money on education?

John M. de Jong
Long Beach, Calif.

I lasted one year on a State university campus and three years later took up in an experimental University Without Walls program, primarily because I was faced with a salary cut without a degree. The responsibility of the UWW program was placed squarely upon my shoulders. I learned not only the necessary academics and some practical skills that I was able to test out on the job, but I also learned to direct and take responsibility for my own learning, my own career, my own life.

I think most young people ought to give themselves a few years between high school and college (if they so desire—let's not go the other way and say that all 18-year-olds should delay college). They might see what the world is really like when one has to support oneself, and they might get the opportunity to discover what offers "psychic income" to them.

Karen Trisko
Chicago

To make higher education more relevant to more people would certainly make my job (recruiter for Education Opportunity Program applicants) a lot easier and more worthwhile. If the impact of your ideas has this effect, then

I hope more people get wind of your message. If the waste in higher education is reduced by "better" selection procedures and more effective education methods, then I say let's push your ideas forward. If, on the other hand, what occurs is reduced funding that results in less incentives to create more relevant curricula, or, if "more" selectivity rather than "better" selectivity results in the continued "meat-market" tactics of selection based only on GPAS and test scores (which have proven to discriminate against minorities and women), then I feel your statements may amount to a shortcut to the dark ages.

Ramon Cruz, Assistant Director
Educational Opportunity Program
California State University
Long Beach

In one sense I can say that college was indeed a waste of time and money. I am not working in my chosen field of study and the chances are that I won't be in the future. In another sense, college was an invaluable experience that I will never forget. I am not today the person I was when I entered college. My views on many subjects have made a 180° turnabout. Some of these changes would have occurred anyway as a result of a process of maturing, but other changes needed the stimulus the university and its population provided.

Linda Slepicka
Chicago

Reprinted with permission from *Psychology Today* magazine, copyright © 1975 (Sussex Publishers, Inc.).

More Readers at Work

Stop and listen now to some students who worked on this project:

Lee: I think it is true that the majority of students are not in college because they want to be or because they want to learn. Some students describe going to college as if it were a sentence to be served. It's difficult to assess how many students are in college reluctantly. If we have a college degree, we are not guaranteed a well-paying job. A college degree no longer opens as many vocational doors.

Marina: I agree that 'college doesn't make people intelligent, ambitious, happy, or liberal.' Those who have these qualities are the ones who succeed in achieving a higher education. Watching my sisters and friends graduate from college, I can see that college afterlife can be indecisive. Many have questioned their lives while confronting the working world. Some have graduated with top honors yet have not received a secure, agreeable or suitable occupation.

    Sure, I want to make a good living—who doesn't? This summer one of my friends decided not to attend college. She felt that she was not ready to commit herself to four years of working hard for no reason.

Besides, what she wanted to do in life had nothing to do with what college could offer her. Right now, she is working in the fashion industry, marketing the sales of new lines of clothing, where there are guarantees for advancement. She is happy but is still unsure of what she really wants. What I am trying to say is that each one of us has to experience some kind of life, whether it's in college or in the working world, to find out what is best for ourselves.

Now I am dedicated to learning in college. My sister Mary graduated from New York University with a B.S. in banking/finance. She is now working for the New York Stock Exchange as an examiner. She has plans to attend graduate school. Who is to say that a college education is of value or not?

Lee and Marina included this notemaking in their writing-project folders and referred to them later. If you keep writing about going to college after doing some reading and listening to others, you'll find that when you begin to write your own story, you'll have done considerable writing and thinking already.

So Who Needs College?

Carrie Tuhy

In 1982, in this article that appeared in Money *magazine, Carrie Tuhy questions whether a college diploma is worth the price. However, she also says not to overlook "values that cannot be measured in dollars."*

Career seekers, the want ads are trying to tell you something. Despite the 1 highest unemployment rate since 1941, Sunday papers across America are thick with job postings for specialized skills. Employers seem unable to find enough qualified people for such positions as bank teller, commercial artist, computer programmer, data processor, electronics technician, medical technologist, nurse, office manager, salesperson and secretary. Fewer and fewer classified ads stipulate college as a requirement.

The message is clear: even a severe recession hasn't caused a labor surplus 2 in certain occupations. But the message goes deeper. In good times as well as bad, a bachelor's degree is becoming less valuable for some careers. As students head off to college this month, they and their parents may wonder whether the diploma is still worth its price in tuition, room, board and four years of forgone income.

The majority of openings, now and for the economic recovery that could 3 be getting under way, require types of skills more likely to be acquired in a technical or trade school or on the job than on an ivied campus. Technical school graduates are routinely landing jobs with higher starting pay than newly minted bachelors of arts can command. A computer programmer fresh from a six-month course can earn up to $14,000 a year while an English major is rewriting his resume for the umpteenth time. Clearly, the $5,000 certificate of technical competence is gaining on the $50,000 sheepskin.

While graduates of four-year colleges still have a small financial edge, 4 that advantage is narrowing. In the 1960s, beginning salaries for college men started an average of 24% higher than for the work force as a whole. That differential is now down to 5%. Projections of the lifetime return on an investment in a college education are still more disillusioning. The foremost specialist in such estimates, Richard Freeman of the National Bureau of Economic Research, predicts that the class of '82 will realize only 6% or 7% a year on its education costs in the form of higher earnings compared with the 11% return projected for the class of '62. Concludes Finis Welch, an economist at UCLA: "A college degree today is not a ticket to a high-paying job or an insurance policy against unemployment. . . ."

In fact, going to college may even be a hindrance for some people with 5 extraordinary talent or ambition. They often feel that college bottles up their drive. Still, you shouldn't overlook educational values that cannot be measured in dollars. Pursuing a bachelor's degree can stretch the mind, help a young person gain maturity and generally enrich anyone's life. Indisputably too, college remains essential in preparing for the professions and advantageous in getting interviews for some occupations. You may not need a B.A. to do the work of an advertising copywriter, broker or journalist—to cite some conspicuous examples—but a diploma still helps you to get in the door. Degreeless applicants may have to start lower or fight harder to enter such fields, and they may be passed over for promotions, particularly to management levels.

Conversely, doors stand wide open to rewarding careers, especially in 6 technical fields, for those with the right nonacademic training. Trade and technical schools are quickly outgrowing their matchbook-cover image— DRAW THIS DOG AND EARN BIG MONEY! Despite the continuing shabby practices of a few institutions, most of the nation's 7,000 private vocational schools for high school graduates competently provide training for all manner of careers from actor to X-ray technician.

The emphasis in vocational education is switching from training blue- 7 collar factory hands and brown-collar repairmen to preparing gray-collar technicians. Also, high-tech companies with a vested interest in a competent work force have taken it upon themselves to educate people in specialized skills. The list of those companies starts with AT&T, IBM and Xerox but goes on to include such somewhat smaller firms as Bell & Howell, Control Data and Wang. One of several courses sponsored by Bell & Howell's DeVry Institute of Technology in Chicago trains technicians to build product prototypes by following engineering drawings; the course takes 20 months and leads to jobs starting at $18,000 a year.

Profit-making trade schools are flourishing even as university enroll- 8 ments dwindle. One of the country's largest commercial schools, National Education Corp. (NEC), based in Newport Beach, Calif., has more than 100,000 students in 70 branches. Graduates repair jets (average starting salary: $15,000), manage radio stations ($30,000), write computer programs and design microprocessor chips (both $12,000).

Fees are often substantial at a high-tech school, but because the training 9 is condensed it costs far less than getting a university degree. A six-month course in computers at NEC's National Institute of Technology costs $5,000; a two-year program in electronics engineering is $7,900. Says Wayne Gilpin, president of the institute, with a touch of braggadocio: "Our students may not be able to quote Byron, but they are technically sharp. They can sit alongside four-year graduates from Purdue and MIT."

Trade school students should face the fact that they won't sit beside 10 many of those Purdue and MIT graduates. Electrical engineers, for example, can get jobs researching and developing new technology at salaries ranging from $23,000 to $30,000, while technicians are more likely to work at repairing those creations at $18,000 to $22,000.

Even so, bright people can advance surprisingly far on trade school train- 11 ing. One example: Ronald Billodeaux, now 29, who completed an electronics course at Little Rock's United Electronics (now called Arkansas College of Technology) and got a job maintaining equipment for Geophysical Services Inc., a Texas Instruments subsidiary that provides exploration data for oil companies. Over the years, Billodeaux helped search for oil in Africa, South America and Australia. Last year the company wanted to move him to London to oversee Middle Eastern and African operations, but he balked at further travel. Almost immediately, Mobil hired him away as a supervisor to scout oil prospects in the Gulf of Mexico.

Two-year community colleges and private junior colleges offer voca- 12 tional training at a considerably lower cost than private technical schools do. Tuition averages $500 a year for such job-oriented studies as auto mechanics, data processing, police science and real estate sales. Says Roger Yarrington, until recently executive director of the American Association of Junior and Community Colleges: "The use of these schools has shifted from university preparation to job preparation." But community colleges, with their multitude of majors, may not have the resources to give as thorough and up-to-date training as you can get at single-subject technical schools. NEC, for example, is spending more than $1 million this year on new equipment.

What is most valuable in vocational education—whether at a commu- 13 nity college or a technical school—is hands-on training. In choosing a program, you should ask about not only the school's resources but also about the time devoted to learning by doing and the companies that hire the most students. Then query those companies' personnel managers on how they rate the school's courses.

Employers say the best preparation combines study with work alongside 14 people in the field. At the Fashion Institute of Design and Merchandising, a California junior college with branches in San Francisco and Los Angeles, Constance Bennett, 23, spent her second year working as an intern at Hang Ten, a sportswear manufacturer. The experience serves her well in her present job at Koret of North America, a San Francisco sportswear company. During a 21-month course at the Culinary Institute of America in Hyde Park, N.Y., the Harvard of *haute cuisine*, students get experience in some of the nation's best-known kitchens. John Doherty, 24, spent more than a quarter of his course at the Waldorf Astoria in New York City. After graduation in 1978, he was hired as a cook there; he has since risen to second in command of a kitchen with 170 cooks.

The best deal, of course, is getting paid to learn a skill. Competition for 15 apprenticeships is always stiff, and a slack economy has cut the number of openings. But as business revives, so will the need for trainees. Along with the standard apprenticeships for plumbers, pipefitters and carpenters, there are programs in hundreds of occupations including biomedical equipment technician, film and video editor, recording engineer, meteorologist and chef. Frank Ruta, 24, learned to cook and run a kitchen in a three-year apprenticeship arranged by the American Culinary Federation. Instead of forking out more than $13,000 to attend the Culinary Institute of America, he hired on at the Lemon Tree, a restaurant in his home town of McKeesport, Pa., at $3.25 an hour and got a 25¢ raise every six months. Ruta learned to cook well enough to satisfy a range of tastes, in politics as well as palates. As personal chef to the First Family, he has served the Carters and the Reagans.

The Labor Department's Bureau of Apprenticeship and Training supervises programs in some 500 trades. Thirty years ago, federal regulation was aimed against racism, favoritism and exploitation in handing out job assignments. Today the bureau mainly monitors wages: apprentices at first average about $6 an hour, 40% to 50% of skilled workers' pay. State agencies with information about apprenticeships are listed in phone directories; look under "state government" for the employment security administration. 16

However, some of the most respected employer-sponsored programs, such as those run by Kodak, General Electric and Westinghouse, are not listed with government offices. You can find them by asking major employers in your chosen field. Apprenticeships are investments of time rather than money; it takes five years to qualify as a journeyman machinist—only a year less than it usually requires to earn a bachelor's degree and an M.B.A. Though apprentices start with no job guarantee, a company that spends up to six years training a person is likely to keep him. 17

Even without training, high school graduates sometimes can land worthwhile jobs in marketing, retailing and a few other fields. Continental Illinois National Bank in Chicago occasionally hires promising teenagers as trainees at $10,000 a year. In five years, they can rise to loan service representative at $27,000—a position and a salary few people fresh from a liberal arts college would qualify for in less than two or three years. 18

In some government-regulated sales fields—particularly real estate, securities and insurance—a mere office clerk can impress the boss by passing the licensing exam. Judith Briles, 36, started as a secretary in a brokerage house with just a high school diploma and a housewife's experience. She quickly learned the business and got a stockbroker's license. After 10 years in the field, she was earning $150,000 a year in commissions at E.F. Hutton in San Jose. 19

Only after opening her own investment advisory company in 1978 did she go to college—to hone her management skills. At Pepperdine University in Malibu, Calif., she took an entrance exam to determine how much her life's experience should count toward her degree. It counted a lot. In two years of part-time study, she bypassed a bachelor's degree and won an M.B.A. 20

Reprinted from the September 1982 issue of *Money* magazine by special permission; copyright 1982; Time Inc. Please note that the financial data in this article refer to the year 1982 and earlier.

Reader's Dialogue

Make notes (freewrite) in response to the two quotations used in the comparison frame of Figure 4.2. Select and copy other lines or passages and respond. Notice where you stop as a reader to ponder or question and write back to the text. Discuss your reading with others.

In the advertisement for the Education Savings Bond Program (Figure 4.3), the Mobil Corporation stresses the extrinsic or economic value of a college education. Although the cost of learning will increase dramatically in the 1990s, Mobil maintains that higher education is also becoming more valuable.

Reader's Dialogue

Making Connections

Reread Mobil's advertisement for an education savings plan, paying careful attention to the value placed on a college education. (See especially the first and last paragraphs.) Take notes and make notes. Compare and contrast this viewpoint of the value of a college degree with the viewpoints of others you have read or heard. Why is Mobil running an ad like this?

Sharing Connections: Expanding Dialogue

In the 1970s Caroline Bird predicted going to college would become a trend, and in her book *The Case Against College* (1975) she attacked the myth that every 18- to 22-year-old American should go to college. Over the past two decades, more and more students have indeed been going to college. The number of nontraditional students has increased (the average age is now 25);

Figure 4.2

NOTEMAKING		NOTETAKING
		"Going to college may even be a hindrance for some people."
		"Still, you shouldn't overlook values that cannot be measured in dollars."

Figure 4.3

The price of learning: Academic year 2005-06

Tuition	$42,000
Books	3,500
Lab & computer fees.	1,200
Room and board.	12,000

You owe: $58,700

Years hence, when today's toddler goes off to college, costs are likely to be far higher than at present. Yet, then as now, nothing we can provide our children will be of larger economic value than a college education. So the Treasury Department has come up with a new way to help most families save—not for a rainy day but for that bright, sunny morning when their teenager embarks upon higher education.

The ticket for that trip to a top school—estimated above for the freshman term of a child now three years old—will surely put a dent in anybody's pocketbook. But with the new Education Savings Bond Program, launched this past New Year's Day, many parents can sock away tax-free savings toward tuition and fees for their children's college years. And if they do this by means of a payroll savings plan at work, setting aside a certain sum each payday to buy U.S. Savings Bonds, building the fund for college can be relatively painless.

The federal tax exemption on these Education Bonds—which are <u>triple</u> tax-free if used for education—begins to phase out for single parents once their income exceeds $40,000 a year, and for married couples filing a joint return when they earn more than $60,000 a year. But income limitations will be adjusted every year to account for inflation. Purchasers have to be at least 24 years old.

The bonds—already exempt from state and local income taxes—feature market-based interest rates. You'll have a guaranteed minimum (currently six percent) for bonds held at least five years, but will probably do better. No fees or commissions are ever charged when the bonds are bought or sold. Since they are backed by the government, and replaced if lost, destroyed, or stolen, they are surely one of the safest long-term investments parents can make.

Higher education is becoming more expensive—yet simultaneously more valuable as the knowledge-based economy places a growing emphasis on brain power. If you have children, your family has already launched its investment in the future. One way to assure its success is to sign up now for the U.S. Treasury's Series EE Savings Bonds. They'll help you manage what that old song about college life labeled—with surely no irony intended—the children's "Golden Days."

Reprinted with permission of Mobil Corporation. © 1990 Mobil Corporation.

the number of non-Anglo/Euro-Americans within the traditional student population has increased as well, comprising about one-third of that group; and the number of women going to college has almost doubled since 1970. (More women now attend college than men.) Higher education has also become more expensive. Has it become more valuable? How would you describe the value of a college education today?

Talk with others in your class and listen; then write a brief summary of the discussion to put in your writing-project folder.

Now See What Others Say About the Value of College

A. Jerome Jewler and John N. Gardner

A. Jerome Jewler and John N. Gardner, authors of Step By Step to College Success, *do not agree with Caroline Bird that college is a waste of time. Read their introduction to "Step 2: Now See What Others Say About the Value of College" for a glimpse of their view.*

In our earlier book, *College Is Only the Beginning,* college professor and administrator Hilda F. Owens explained the difference college can make. She reported that many wonderful, challenging, and satisfying experiences would accrue to the fortunate individuals who chose to work toward a college degree. On the other hand, she warned that going to college could also be a stressful and frustrating experience. 1

You should know that you may experience what some call "cognitive dissonance," or resistance to ideas which are foreign to you. This exposure is essential for further learning and development. If you were not exposed to new ideas which proved challenging and often disturbing to you, how on earth could you become better educated? 2

Notwithstanding the fact that this risk is there, it appears that the good outweighs the bad in the college experience. For example, studies indicate that students in college tend to be more accepting of new ideas and more able to control their own destinies. What's more, they feel better about themselves (self-esteem), display a greater appreciation for the cultural and esthetic values of life, and are better able to grasp broad theoretical issues. 3

But the news is even better. From all the evidence to date, colleges seem to do a very good job at what they claim to do best: increase the knowledge and development of their students. Furthermore, educational achievement has a very definite positive correlation with career opportunities and income level. In an age when many are questioning the investment of time and money in a college education, evidence still shows that it is a sound investment. 4

As one educator has expressed it, "If you think education is expensive, try ignorance." 5

Students tend to leave college not only more competent, but more *confident.* They tend to have a better sense of who they are, where they fit in the 6 scheme of things, and how they might make a difference in the world about them. You can expect to experience changes in your attitudes, values, behaviors, and self-concepts as a result of college, but mostly in positive directions.

So why are college graduates generally more able to adapt to most future 7 situations than those who didn't attend college? Among the reasons are that they tend to adopt more liberal views, develop greater interest in political and public affairs, are more likely to vote and be active in community affairs, and are less likely to lead a life of crime.

College also helps people develop the flexibility, mobility, and knowl- 8 edge needed to adapt to the changing demands of work and life. It also seems to contribute to increased on-the-job productivity and satisfaction.

But college offers even more. It is an important influence on family life. 9 As women earn more of the family income, matters of child care and household responsibilities tend to be shared by husband and wife. College graduates tend to delay the age of marriage, have fewer children, and spend more time, thought, energy, and money on child rearing. They also tend to divorce less, and their children seem to have greater abilities and to enjoy greater achievements of their own than other children.

College-educated people tend to save more of their money, take greater 10 but wiser investment risks, and spend considerably more on their homes, intellectual and cultural interests, and their children. They also tend to spend more wisely in the marketplace, and are better able, because of their education, to deal with misleading advertising, tax laws, and the legal system.

They spend less time and money on television and movies and more time 11 on intellectual and cultural pursuits, including adult education, hobbies, community and civic affairs, and vacations.

College graduates are also likely to be more concerned with the preven- 12 tion, rather than just treatment, of physical and mental health matters. Diet, exercise, stress management, and other factors result in longer life spans and fewer disabilities. Attention to health is probably related to an increased self-concept and sense of personal worth.

Perhaps Kingman Brewster, a former president of Yale University, said 13 it best when asked to define the primary goals of a college education. He claimed those goals consisted of the development of three senses: a sense of place, a sense of self, and a sense of judgment. Brewster clearly argued for the broader and more liberating view of education when he concluded:

> The most fundamental value of education is that it makes life more interest- 14 ing. This is true whether you are fetched up on a desert island or adrift in the impersonal loneliness of the urban hurly-burly. It allows you to see things which the uneducated do not see. It allows you to understand things which do not occur to the less learned. In short, it makes it less likely that you will be bored with life. It also makes it less likely that you will be a crashing bore to those whose company you keep. By analogy, it makes the difference between the traveler who understands the local language and the traveler to whom the local language is a jumble of nonsense words.

College, then, is much more than just a place where learning happens 15 in the classroom. Many students, unfortunately, fail to realize this, and although their grades are impressive, they never realize their full potential

Jewler & Gardner

because their education starts and stops with the ringing of the bell. We have a profoundly different idea about learning and college. We believe, first, that learning is a lifelong process and that college is where it can blossom. We further believe that an educated person is a person who has grown in all six of the dimensions we have discussed.[1] Finally, we declare that the day you stop learning, that day you stop living.

16 To engage students in thinking about the purpose of higher education, the authors offer for discussion the following statements made by educators:

17 1. Years ago, college was only for a select group of people. Today, we urge everyone to try to get a college education, even if they are not fully prepared for it. As a result, a college education is more valuable to us than before.

18 2. Years ago, people who attended college were more interested in getting a liberal education (learning how to think about new things) than in preparing for careers. Today, students seem to be more interested in learning the specific skills they will need for their chosen careers. As a result, college graduates are better off than before.

19 3. Years ago, colleges allowed students to sink or swim on their own in the belief that those who were college material would make it through. Today we have advisement programs, orientation programs, special freshman seminars, career and counseling centers, and more. As a result, college students are more able to make it on their own when they graduate.

20 4. Grades, tests, and lectures interfere with the learning process. Get rid of them, and real learning will take place. (What would you do in place of grades, tests, and lectures?)

21 5. Teaching isn't just throwing information at students and hoping they will remember it for the quiz. In a true learning environment, teachers and students are learning from one another and share the role of "information giver." (What is an information giver, how can teachers learn from students, and why does this tend to make it easier for students to learn?)

From *Step By Step to College Success* by A. Jerome Jewler and John N. Gardner. Copyright © 1987 by A. Jerome Jewler and John N. Gardner. Reprinted by permission of Wadsworth Publishing Co., Belmont, CA.
1. These six dimensions are intellectual, occupational, emotional, physical, social, and spiritual development.

Reader's Dialogue

Making Connections

Reread critically each statement at the end of Jewler and Gardner's argument. Number your responses to correspond with the numbered statements. Do you agree with each statement? If so, to what extent? Do you disagree? If so, why? Give reasons for your opinions. What is the basis of each of your opinions? Then write an end-response informed by your thoughts on items 1–5.

Sharing Connections

Discuss your reading of Caroline Bird's viewpoint that college is a waste and the contrasting viewpoint and tone of Jewler and Gardner, who administer a freshman orientation seminar that helps students both understand why they are going to college and learn, through a positive approach, how to get what they want out of college.

The Questionnaire

Lynne Hall

Lynne Hall, a pseudonym for an African-American female student at Yale University in the 1970s, describes how close she came to being swept into life as a drug peddler and how she chose to go to college instead. Her story is one of many personal stories collected by Harriet Harvey in Stories Parents Seldom Hear: College Students Write About Their Lives and Families *(New York: Delacorte Press/ Seymour Lawrence, 1983).*

Yale University
Application Form

2. Personal Commentary

Instructions:

This is the part of your application that belongs to you. Use it in any way you wish to enable us to get to know you as a person, not as a statistic. . . . If you submit a sample of your work, we will have it examined and evaluated by a Yale faculty member knowledgeable in the particular area. . . .

We are most interested in anything of importance to you that will help us better understand you, your abilities, your interests, your reasons for wanting to attend college, and why you feel that your attending Yale will be a mutually beneficial experience. . . .

White people are always asking this sort of question and then making judg- 1 ments against a person if he or she gives them the truth. They think they won't but they do.

I believe that the experiences I shall relate not only describe who I am 2 but have given me a strong motivation to go to college, to finish it, and to use my education to help people less fortunate than myself. I don't know which of your professors is "knowledgeable in the particular area" of my essay, but I leave that up to you. I hope that all of you who read my essay will agree that what I have learned from my experience will make my attending Yale a "mutually beneficial" experience.

I learned most about myself and other people between the ages of thir- 3 teen and sixteen, when my boyfriend and I hung around the streets of our city. If it hadn't been for Greg, I probably would not have come in contact with the people and the experiences that I did.

Looking back, it's hard for me to understand why I went along with Greg 4 and why I stayed with him as long as I did. At the time I was extremely shy

Hall

and passive, and Greg was the only person with whom I had any relationship at all. I needed him, I think, to make contact with the world I was too timid to approach on my own. I just went along with anything he did.

I lived with my mother and five sisters in a two-family house on a pleas- 5 ant street not far from a district that contained five hospitals and nursing homes. A large park was just two blocks away. Although we lived on the edge of a black district, we were the only black family on our particular street. My mother and father were separated, and although my father owned the house in which we lived, he lived in an apartment on the other side of town, where he was the reading specialist for a local elementary school.

My mother, my sisters, and I occupied both sides of the two-family house, 6 and we had knocked an opening through the wall between two upstairs bedrooms in order to join the two sides of the house together. On the ground floor, however, there was no passage between the two sides, and we had to go upstairs to reach the other side of the house. I lived alone, in the unused ground-floor living room and kitchen on one side, which meant I had both a front and back door exit of my own. This arrangement made it possible for Greg to come and go without anyone in the house—especially my mother—knowing anything about it.

During this period, as I look back on it, my mother was unhappy and 7 worried, and she didn't approve of much of anything my sisters and I did. So we just went our individual ways, not paying too much attention to one another and not telling anything to my mother. My oldest sister worked in an insurance company and my mother as a secretary to a doctor. The rest of us went to school.

Greg lived a block and a half away. We first started going together when I 8 was thirteen and he was fourteen and we were both in eighth grade. He was quite short, light-skinned, and had short hair. I began going out with him, I suppose, because I was competing with my girlfriend for his attention. At first Greg did everything he could to heighten the competition between us, but later I won him over and just the two of us hung around together.

From the very beginning, my mother didn't like him. She thought his 9 mother was a phony and she didn't like his father because he ran around with other women. When my mother first saw Greg with me, she warned him not to hang around me, so I was careful that she didn't see us together. Greg's own mother and father didn't like him much either. When he was sixteen and had grown bigger, he beat them up and they would throw him out of the house.

We'd been going together for about three months when our juvenile de- 10 linquency started at the hospital gift shop, quite by accident. Because it was closer than the nearest store, Greg and I went to the hospital often to get snacks and Cokes from the vending machines and Life Savers and potato chips from the gift shop. The shop was usually tended by a single woman volunteer. One day, as the volunteer turned her back to us to get the potato chips we'd asked for, Greg snatched a pair of earrings off the rotating stand on the counter and stuffed them into his pocket. The old lady didn't see us—nor, I think, did she suspect us. Having discovered that we could get away with lifting earrings, we visited the gift shop often and devised tricks to get the lady to turn her back on us. We would change our minds about whether we wanted potato chips or potato sticks and stage fake fights to divert her attention. Then we would slip the earrings into our pockets. When we weren't wearing clothes with pockets, we would stuff them into our mouths or half-filled Coke cups. In less than two months we had "liberated" more than $125 worth of earrings. I was very proud of my collection and kept it in a jewelry box made just for earrings that one of my eighth-grade classmates had given me. The box itself I hid under my mattress so my ten-year-old sister wouldn't help herself to a few.

After this start we expanded our operations by discovering a way to break 11 into the local recreation center. The center, which was run by the parks department, sat in a small playground midway between Greg's house and mine. In spring and summer it offered outdoor recreation such as basketball and handball for older kids and swings and sandboxes for younger ones. In winter and fall the building itself was opened, offering indoor basketball, Ping-Pong, pool. Throughout the year the director ran competitions in the various sports, and the winner usually won prizes of candy. On weekends, however, the center was not open and the building was locked tight. A set of double doors at the back were fastened together by a chain that ran through the handles. Greg and I discovered that these doors could be forced open just wide enough for a skinny person to squeeze through an opening at the top. Greg would give me a boost to the top of the doors, I would wiggle through and then run down the hall and unlock the side door for Greg. So we spent our Saturdays and Sundays playing pool or basketball and trying to find a way to unlock the cellar door to get at the prize candy in the center's refrigerator. This was an exciting enterprise. We had to be very quick and secretive so that the neighbors and their kids wouldn't become suspicious and call the police. On Saturday nights we'd put everything back in its proper place and lock the center up again.

One day some neighborhood kids heard us inside and we had to let them 12 in so they wouldn't tell on us. They of course soon told their friends, and before long the activity inside the center was just as great on weekends as it was during the week, when the center was open. As time went on, it became more and more difficult to cover everybody's tracks; eventually some little kids told the director and he put new locks on the doors. Greg and I were never caught, because after a while there were so many of us that the little kids didn't know who was responsible for opening the doors. Others had learned the trick.

With the recreation center closed to us, we looked for new enterprises. 13 One day we broke into the local junior high school, which was Greg's school and also the school where my father taught. We went to the homemaking room, stole all the edible food, and stored it at my house. On another day, when we were on our way home from our early morning paper route, we broke into a candy wagon parked at a gas station for the night. Greg broke a window and opened the door from inside. We filled our paper-route bags and our pockets with all the candy we could carry. We hid the candy in my room at home and opened up what turned out to be an unprofitable business. At first we tried to sell the candy, but because most of the kids had no money, we were forced to take IOU's. These were never paid, so we soon accepted the inevitable and just gave the candy to our friends or ate it ourselves. Eventually my little sister discovered our business and, in spite of being bribed on many different occasions, told my mother. At least I was fortunate in that I was leaving for camp in a few days and all I had to do was pack the candy with my clothes and tell my mother I had gotten rid of it.

That summer, ironically enough, I had been hired as a junior counselor 14 for nine weeks at an overnight camp for ghetto children. It was located in the Connecticut hills and had formerly been a Jewish resort hotel. Although drab and ugly, it was well equipped, with a swimming pool, fields for archery and baseball, and an arts and crafts room. There were woods nearby for nature walks. All thirty-two girl campers and four girl counselors lived in one large building; the forty or so boys in two others.

I was the counselor for the seven- and eight-year-old girls, who came for 15 two-week sessions and were usually frightened and homesick for the first week. Most of them were black or Puerto Rican, and some of the Puerto Rican girls could hardly speak any English. The counselors were very young—all under eighteen—but at fourteen I was the youngest. It was my first time away from home and my first experience in communal living with people my own age. I was to learn a lot from it.

Until I went to camp, I had difficulty talking to people I didn't know very 16 well. At camp I was forced to come out of my shell in order to take care of the little girls and to work with the other counselors and kitchen help. I was impressed by these people: they weren't flawless, but they were down to earth, and they were trying very hard to make something out of their lives. They were all struggling hard to survive the inhuman conditions that had been forced on them by the sick urban ghettoes in which they had grown up. It was the first time I had seen people make a real effort to overcome their difficulties. After camp was over, I was to learn that some of these new friends of mine had succeeded in their struggle to survive while others had been pulled down and defeated. The dishwasher, Mike (who was nice but looked like a thug), had been sent to camp as an alternative to reform school, where he had been sentenced for assault and burglary. After camp he was caught taking LSD and was returned to reform school. George, a counselor for eight- to ten-year-old boys, was tall, skinny, and comical. He kept us all laughing. He had a drug habit which he tried hard to lick at camp, and if he took anything at camp, I never knew about it. After he left, he was caught in the LSD episode with Mike and sent to prison. I never heard what became of Bill. A dishwasher like Mike, he was vulgar, dirty, and nasty, and all the other girl counselors and I hated him. Although he was only twenty, he had already been married, but his marriage had broken up. Some say this breakup was the cause of his bisexuality, but I suspect that sexuality had been a problem for him all his life. In any case he made constant passes at the girl counselors, and Mike, his roommate, caught him having sexual relations with a cat on one occasion and with a small boy camper on another. Although Alan, the director of the camp, was later arrested in Ohio for abusing a young boy sexually, at camp he was straight.

On the other hand, there was Ann, the counselor of the ten- to twelve- 17 year-old girls. She married the next winter and is living happily with her husband and their baby girl. Curtis, the counselor of the eight- to ten-year-old boys, has joined the army, and John is now at divinity school. Two other counselors, Sandy and Dianne, have gone to college. I spent a lot of time with Dianne. She came from Virginia, where she had been sheltered and brought up strictly. Although she was only seventeen, she seemed older and wiser, and I found her nice to be with. My favorite person at camp, however, was the cook, Mac. He was handsome, and I had a girlish crush on him from the first moment I saw him. Much older—twenty-two—he had been married but was separated from his wife. At first I would just sit and stare at him, not daring to show him I liked him. But he was so nice to me that I gradually started talking to him, and he looked after me. He gave me extra food and taught me how to swim. One night, Mac and all the counselors went on a hike in the woods, trying to follow the north star. We lost our way, had a cookout, and came back to camp in the early dawn. For the first time in my life, I was having fun. So when Greg turned up to visit one day, I wasn't happy to see him at all. I just introduced him around, and after a few hours he left—but not before threatening to beat up Charlie, whom he erroneously suspected of being my boyfriend.

From all these people I began to gain an understanding of why people— 18 myself included—behave the way they do. I also was learning to handle difficult situations, particularly personal confrontations from people who were messed up. For the first time, I had begun to learn to deal with people on my own without Greg or anyone else acting as intermediary. For the next year, however, much of what I learned that summer lay dormant within me while my delinquent life expanded.

A few days after I returned home, Greg returned from another camp, 19 where he had been a camper. While I came back with a new appreciation of people, Greg came back with a new appreciation of marijuana, hashish, speed, LSD, cocaine, and who knows what else. In spite of my camp experiences, I was still very much under Greg's influence. I had not yet found any goal for my life nor formed any judgments about what activities were good or bad for me. In a desultory sort of way, I was antiestablishment. I had no strong feelings against taking drugs and told myself I should at least have some knowledge of what it was I wasn't supposed to be doing.

And so I began. I spent New Year's Eve with Greg at a pot party. Someone 20 has said that whatever you do on New Year's Eve you will do for the rest of the year. That was true for me—almost completely.

For the better part of the next year I played with drugs. I used marijuana, 21 hash, speed, and cocaine frequently. I experimented with LSD, DMT, and downs. I watched people shoot up, turn on, and freak out. Through Greg I met an assortment of hippies, drug pushers, black militants, street corner artists—many of whom were simply passing back and forth from Boston to New York. On street corners and in alleyways and little stores, I saw many business transactions and watched the arrival and distribution of large shipments of drugs. This was different from the year before, when our activities were restricted to our own neighborhood and just to young kids like ourselves.

All this scared me. (If I saw someone with a rubber strap around his arm 22 about to shoot heroin, I would have to leave the room.) At most times, I was

Hall

a passive tagalong, just following Greg and watching mindlessly, not considering the consequences nor really feeling much of anything at all.

In fact, I didn't particularly like drugs. And internally I must have resisted quite strongly, because I never freaked out; all the time I was under, I would concentrate on keeping control. The one time I took LSD Greg told me it was something else; if I had known that he was giving me LSD, I would have refused. When I found out, I fought the drug and sat still, simply controlling myself and waiting for the trip to be over. 23

The same was not true of Greg. He liked to take drugs and to peddle them as well—a thing I could not bring myself to do. Experimenting with drugs on myself was one thing; pushing them on other people was, for me, another thing altogether. It was true that I would sometimes go with Greg when he dealt nickel bags of pot at the evening concerts in the park. Because policemen couldn't shake down girls without first bringing them to the police station, it was safer if I carried the bags in my pocketbook and handed him one when he made a sale. But I did this only to reduce the chances of Greg's being arrested. I never went with him when he made other transactions or peddled stronger stuff. On one of these occasions, in April, he was arrested for selling LSD and speed to an undercover agent. He was in jail for about a month, and I visited him there once. When he came to trial, he was convicted but given a suspended sentence, because it was his first offense and he was only sixteen. He was put on probation. On the day he was released from jail, he returned to his usual activities, making no attempt to give up drugs or to stop selling them. 24

It didn't take me long to realize that Greg was hooked and had a serious problem. Slowly, during that year, he had turned weird. He would frequently imagine that people and objects were trying to harm him. At night he'd lie in bed, afraid that his overhead light was plotting to explode, emitting gaseous fumes that would kill him. School authorities had enrolled him in a drug rehabilitation program, and he told me, rather proudly, that the psychiatrists there had said that he was "a paranoid schizophrenic" and was "psychologically addicted to drugs." I, too, felt that his persecution feelings caused him to seek refuge in drugs. When he was high, he seemed oblivious to the things he normally saw as threats, and could be quite gentle. Although he would frequently promise me he was going to swear off, he attended the rehabilitation clinic only sporadically and then usually when he was high. To reduce his paranoia the clinic gave him tranquilizers, but he would take overdoses of these in order to get high again. He was proud of deceiving people and would spend his time thinking of new ways to "blow people's minds" or "psych them out." 25

He was also violent. Whenever he was in his paranoid state, he would beat me for some imagined wrong—usually that I was going out with someone else. I grew to dislike him, but I was afraid to leave him because he threatened to kill me if I did. On rare occasions when he wasn't having a fight with his family, he lived at home, but mostly he stayed wherever he could find a bed. Sometimes he stayed with me. 26

Meanwhile, I lived a schizophrenic life of my own. After I graduated from junior high school, I had been given a full scholarship to an elite private girls' day school in the suburbs. The rules were strict: knee-length skirts and 27 saddle shoes were required; bare legs were forbidden—they must be covered with stockings or knee socks; makeup was outlawed; and of course no one was to have a thought about swearing or drinking. The catchphrase was "ladylike behavior" and along with it went a set of unspoken rules that I sometimes had difficulty figuring out. "Polished" was another word frequently laid on us.

And so, by day, I wandered politely over green lawns in my knee socks, 28 studied French, and mingled with middle- and upper-middle-class white girls in a New England prep school. My first year I was the only black in my class and one of six in the whole school. A few more blacks were added in subsequent classes, and in my senior year, when our school merged with a private boys' school, there were over twenty. On the playgrounds or between classes, the other girls talked mostly about school, but gradually, as I became somewhat friendly with them, I described to them—in very general terms—another kind of life, where people used drugs and had different ideas about sex and money. (You can be sure I gave no hint of being connected with these people in any way. I was the "sociological observer.") They had never met any black people before except their maids, and they never accepted the fact that I was different from them, or to be more accurate, they never admitted it openly. I don't know if they let themselves learn anything from me. I didn't belong to any of the cliques, and most of the time I felt as if I was just part of the furniture. At one of the school dances the girls met Greg and flocked around him—fascinated and vying for his attention. On this occasion, I felt even more like an inanimate object and silently resented them all. Of course I told them nothing about our nighttime activities.

Academically the school was good for me and taught me a great deal 29 more than I could have learned in the public high school in our neighborhood. I was fortunate to find an understanding English teacher who realized the position I was in and encouraged me to speak from my own point of view, and write from my own experience. She did a lot for all the black students. I was active in sports and played on the hockey, lacrosse, baseball, and basketball teams.

Each day, I'd return home from school about five o'clock, work at my 30 chores around the house, do a little homework, and pick up what I could to eat. My mother hated to cook and so never prepared any real dinner. About ten, I would put on my pajamas, go upstairs, pass through the door that connected us with the other side of the house, and continue on to the bathroom. En route, I'd stop in my sisters' and mother's rooms to find out what time each one needed to get up in the morning. It was my job to wake everyone up. Then I'd say my good-nights and, returning to my room, would turn out the lights, get dressed again, and wait long enough for my mother and sisters to think I was asleep. When enough time had elapsed, I would sneak out the front door on my side of the house.

Greg would usually be waiting for me at the corner. We'd walk through 31 the park and across town to Charlie's Drug Store—"the dope dealer's haven." Out front, middlemen would be standing in little groups; inside, buyers, sellers, and middlemen would be milling around trying to negotiate without looking suspicious. When a seller located a buyer, they'd go outside to score. Inside, the game was to see how many cigarettes, papers, pipes, magazines, and other small items could be liberated without rousing Charlie's attention. After midnight, the place was so full of weird-looking people that it was like a circus. At Charlie's, Greg and I would say hello to our friends, and after a while Greg would wander outside to do whatever business he had in mind. We would hang around there for a bit and then make our way to the dairy, where products for the next day's delivery would be set out on the loading ramps behind the factory. There we would pick up a couple of gallons of chocolate milk, some cream cheese, and some eggs, and proceed to the People's Pad.

The People's Pad was a five-room apartment located in one of a long line 32 of apartment buildings near the milk factory. The area was known for its many busts, and many young kids and dope dealers lived in the apartments there. I never knew exactly who rented the People's Pad, but it was open all night to anyone who wanted to go there and smoke dope, take drugs, or just hang around. Anyone who had no other place to sleep could always spend the night there.

After arriving, Greg and I would fill up the refrigerator with our haul, 33 have something to eat, and sit around and listen to music from a record player. All night, people came in and out of the apartment; they'd sit down for a while, pass around a couple of joints, and talk about the places they'd been and the things they'd seen. Greg and I would sit and listen to their tales or catch a few catnaps until about four, when we would go back to my house. Sometimes Greg would stay with me, but mostly he went off to wherever he was staying that week. At 6:45 I'd be up and ready to catch my school bus. No one ever knew that I had left my house the night before or suspected that I was using drugs.

Sometime in the spring term, a few of my girl friends at school started 34 smoking pot. They were obvious and foolish. They would come to school visibly stoned, their eyes red and their hair and breath smelling like reefers. Or during class hours they would sneak out behind the school buildings and get stoned on campus. Occasionally they experimented with LSD and speed, but they smoked pot almost continuously. I never joined them. Even cigarette smoking meant automatic suspension, but I wasn't worried about that; as the only black in my class, I knew they wouldn't suspend me. It was just that I felt that school was not an appropriate place for pot and the girls behaved stupidly when they smoked. Everyone else at school knew what they were doing—even the administration, who simply pretended that the situation didn't exist. My guess is that the headmistress didn't want to take the chance of having a pot scandal. Occasionally she would talk to me, always very guardedly and in general terms, about pot and other drugs. I think she felt that I, as a black, understood the world of dope and might be able to give her advice on how she could handle the situation. Speaking in a saccharine voice, she was always falling over herself to "understand blacks," but she wasn't sincere.

In the spring of that year, when I was fifteen, I began to look at myself 35 and the people around me. I realized that the way I was living was stagnant. I wasn't doing anything that I could actually call "something." I was just sitting around wasting time, and not even enjoying that. I wasn't taking advantage of the educational opportunities in front of me, nor was I doing anything to help the less fortunate people who would have liked to have the scholarship I had. I decided that I would stop playing at being into drugs, and fighting the establishment, and give up all my strong opinions on things I really knew nothing about. I thought that I would just give up my night life and start taking school seriously.

After making this decision, I discovered that I was pregnant. I couldn't 36 tell my parents, so I was dependent on Greg for all the financial and moral support I was to get. Marriage to Greg was out of the question, and more than anything else I wanted to finish high school; so we agreed that I should get an abortion. Greg knew a chemist at an airplane manufacturing company who performed illegal abortions on the side. Earlier in his life he had been rejected by medical school and so took up abortions both as a money-making enterprise and as a vendetta against the medical profession. He charged two hundred dollars, so Greg and I planned to make the money over the summer. Time was the only cause for concern. In two weeks I had to leave to be a camp counselor for the second year. I would be gone for two months, so it was absolutely essential that we have the money and all the arrangements made before the end of August and be able to proceed with the abortion on the day I came home.

That summer was taxing. I worked very hard with my girls, trying to 37 make an impression on their lives and to teach them to live with each other. I was in charge of eleven- and twelve-year-olds, and the cultural and language differences caused more conflicts than I had had with the younger ones. In my care were three black girls, one white girl, and two Puerto Ricans, one of whom spoke no English at all. In addition, we had a new camp director who was a slavedriver. He ran the camp like a military training camp, insisting that each camper and counselor participate in some organized activity all day long. I was the exercise teacher and my job, apart from counseling the girls, was to lead the campers and counselors in exercises for a half hour every morning in the blazing sun. I began to gain weight and had to fight against morning sickness. Throughout the day I made what seemed a superhuman effort to stay awake to play baseball or basketball, when all I wanted to do was crawl into bed and sleep.

All summer I successfully hid the fact that I was pregnant, but I couldn't 38 wipe out my own fears. I was beset by fantasies: I would be deserted by Greg; I wouldn't be able to have the abortion; I would be found out by my parents.

Greg came to see me once that summer, just three weeks before the end 39 of the season. He told he that he hadn't any money but assured me that he could raise it in less than two weeks dealing dope.

When I returned home three weeks later, Greg was nowhere to be seen. 40 For the next week I sat around waiting for him to show up and trying not to believe what I knew was true: when the chips were down, Greg didn't want to know me. He didn't care what happened to me. Just at this point, Mac called me from out of town, asking if he could come see me on my birthday. (I had seen him only once since my first year at camp; he hadn't been cooking there the second summer.) I spent the day with him, and just before he left I told him about my pregnancy and Greg's disappearance. We discussed the problem and agreed that the most sensible thing to do would be to tell my parents. Since Greg obviously was not concerned with my well-being, we decided that if he should show up, I wouldn't proceed with his abortionist. He, too, might turn out to be a fake—or worse. The matter, we concluded, should be taken out of Greg's hands altogether except for whatever financial aid he could contribute.

So on my sixteenth birthday I came home about seven, went to my mother's room, and I told her I was pregnant. At first she didn't believe me, but when she realized that I wasn't joking, she took it calmly. The next day she told my father. Both my parents said they would go along with the abortion as long as I was sure that was what I wanted. Through friends they were put in touch with a retired doctor in New York City, and the appointment was set for two weeks later. It would cost five hundred dollars. A week later, Greg showed up, penniless. 41

My father wanted to break Greg's neck and my mother wanted to have him thrown in jail. They didn't act on their feelings, however, because they needed whatever money he could produce; instead, he was warned against ever again setting foot on my parents' property. Before two weeks passed, Greg had come up with $180. I still had $120 of my summer earnings and my father had been able to raise another $200. 42

When the day arrived, I was outwardly calm, but inside I was scared. I took a bus to Bridgeport, where I met my parents. My father had been working and living there for a couple of years and my mother was attending a two-day Masonic convention and staying at a hotel. The moment I saw her in her hotel room, I knew my mother was frightened. She told me that on the previous night she had dreamed that I had died. Some of her friends had told her that she shouldn't let me have an abortion, because if anything went wrong she and my father could get into a lot of trouble. She told me that I could go away somewhere and have the baby and come back in a year or so. She had already concocted a story we could tell our relatives about my absence. But I had made up my mind to go through with it. School was going to start in four days and I was determined not to miss a day. So as soon as my father turned up, we got into his car and started for New York. All during the trip my mother and father discussed possible alternatives to the abortion. 43

In New York we first went to the house of a woman who was acting as intermediary and, I surmise, a check against police investigation. She sat us all down, offered us some coffee, and then interviewed us about my age, physical condition, and length of pregnancy. After she had finished taking my history, she went into the next room and called the doctor. When she returned, she told us the doctor had been reluctant to proceed when he found out I was only sixteen and was three and a half months pregnant. But because I was in good health and had come so far, he had finally decided it would be all right to go ahead. None of this made my mother a bit happier. 44

The woman gave us the doctor's address on 125th Street and told us to leave the car and go there by cab an hour later at eight o'clock. To kill time we went to a small store around the corner and ate some pickles and, after what seemed like a long time, proceeded to the doctor's address as advised. 45

The doctor lived above a small variety store, and the hallway off the street was narrow and dark. We walked up two flights of stairs, passing garbage cans crowded around the apartment doors on each floor. The walls of the stairwell were dirty brown and the paint was peeling. The whole place smelled of garbage.

When we knocked on the appointed door, we were admitted by the doc- 46
tor himself. He was a small man with snow-white hair and a full snow-white beard. Against his very dark skin his hair looked even whiter than it was. He looked about eighty, but was still spry and had a pleasant face. He was dressed in a dingy white doctor's jacket and black pants. He greeted us and led us into an office where there was a scale, two medicine chests, a stool, two chairs, a table with medical instruments on it, and an examining table. Everything in the room, except for some colored pills and the steel instruments, was the same dingy white as the doctor's jacket. Plaques and medical certificates—from Vienna, London, Stockholm—hung on the walls. The doctor was such a friendly little old man that I felt at home.

The doctor told us that I would have to stay there two days, which sur- 47
prised us all and made my mother and father more uneasy than they already were. He patiently explained that the operation took time and that it was necessary for me to remain twenty-four hours after it was over so that he could watch over me to be sure there were no complications. He reassured my parents that everything would be all right and told them to go home and stop worrying. Because it was the policy to pay in advance, my father, looking terrified, took out the money and gave it to the doctor. Then he gave me some money to come home on the train. They paused for a moment, looking at me as if it were the last time they would see me, and left.

Their look made me feel eerie for a moment. But, for myself, I was no 48
longer frightened. I had made up my mind that everything was going to be all right. I had too much to live for. I was going to finish school and go on to college in order to study psychology. I wanted to do something for people whose minds had been messed up—people who no longer believed they had any worth or purpose. I was going to help these people regain their self-esteem by showing them that they were victims of a system devised to keep them down. Then I was going to get married and have a large family. I had talked all this over with Mac before I had come to New York, and he told me he had faith in me and that everything would be all right. I knew he expected me to be brave, so I had promised myself that for him I would take it all like a woman.

After the doctor's wife had searched about and found an old nightgown, 49
many sizes too big, the doctor put me on the examining table and gave me a knockout shot. I must have wanted very much to stay conscious because I fought the medication even after a second shot. I could not tell exactly what the doctor was doing to me but I felt as if he were pulling my insides out, piece by piece. I wanted to scream or cry or jump off the table, but I remembered that I was supposed to be brave, and the doctor scolded me every time I moved a muscle. At midnight, when my parents called to check on me, the doctor told them I was fine. He continued to work on me until, about an hour later, the water broke—something I knew happened to women before

they went into labor. His wife brought me a dry nightgown and I heard the doctor mumbling something about how strange it was and how he had never seen anything quite like this before. He then took me into a small bedroom next to his office and I fell asleep.

When I woke up, it was morning, and the doctor's wife gave me breakfast 50 in the kitchen. After breakfast the doctor asked me to remove a tube he had put in me the night before, and when nothing happened, he looked worried. He then gave me a large black pill and told me to lie down and rest.

Late in the afternoon I began having terrible pains in my abdomen and 51 could feel something moving around inside of me. When I called for the doctor, he told me I was going into labor and that I should walk around the room to reduce the pain and hasten the process. He warned me not to make any noise, because another patient would soon be arriving in the next room. He left me a pail and told me to use it. I paced for another few hours before I fully understood what I was to use it for.

That night, all alone, I aborted. It was a boy. I called the doctor, and he 52 examined me. Because I had lost a lot of blood, he gave me a variety of iron pills and I fell asleep. The next morning I drank tea and soup, and by mid-afternoon I was up and dressed. My clothes were falling off me; I had lost seven pounds from Friday night to Sunday afternoon. The doctor gave me instructions about more medications and advised me not to get into any more trouble. He and his wife then walked me around the apartment twice to be sure I was steady. They told me how to get to the train station, gave me their address, and said good-bye.

I arrived home all right, and after answering my mother's questions, fell 53 into bed, exhausted. The next day I went to school to buy books. I was offered a ride by some of my classmates, but it was no joyride; they had chosen this day to tell their favorite jokes about abortions and knitting needles. For the rest of the week I attended school, but by the following Monday I was feeling too weak to move from my bed. I had tried to do too much too soon. I rested for a week and after that I was fine.

All during that week I saw the little boy in my mind's eye, and over and 54 over again I thought what a waste it had all been. I felt that I had deprived him of his chance to make something of his life. When I stopped thinking, I hated myself and I hated Greg. I decided I wouldn't see him anymore. When I told him what happened and how I felt about the baby, he shrugged it off. He laughed and said I'd get over it—he'd known lots of girls who'd been through it. When I told him I didn't want to see him anymore, he beat me.

For the next year I tried to get away from him, and for a year he beat me. 55 I didn't dare not see him when he came around because I thought he would kill me if I didn't. He threatened many times to do so and I believed that he was capable of it. I couldn't tell my mother because I wasn't supposed to be seeing him, and besides, I couldn't see what she could do to prevent his coming. If I brought up the subject of our breaking up, he'd beat me. If I tried to give him the cold shoulder, he'd beat me. If I tried to avoid him completely, he'd beat me. Every day he would wait for me along the route I took coming home from school. When I changed routes, he'd wait for me in the small yard beside our house, where he could hide in the bushes if my mother came along. If, when I arrived, I didn't let him in, he would threaten to kill me. Sometimes he wouldn't be waiting for me in the afternoon but would come later, at night. If I turned off the light and pretended I wasn't there, he would bang so loud at the door or the window that I would open it in fear my mother would hear him. Sometimes I would move upstairs with one of my sisters for a few days, but it was so crowded that I had no room to study and barely room enough to sleep.

All this time I was looking for some large guy who could walk home with me from the school bus stop and confront Greg. I thought that when Greg saw I was serious about seeing other people he would realize he was wasting his time and would no longer force me to go out with him. Especially if the guy was bigger than he was. Mac was working in another city, but he too was trying to find someone whom he trusted and who could stand up to Greg. Then, one day, Larry, a school friend, offered to walk me home. He knew nothing about the situation, and I couldn't bring myself to tell him. But he was bigger than Greg, and I thought Greg would back off when he saw him. 56

As usual, Greg was waiting for me at the corner of my street. He was shocked but he didn't hesitate to walk right up to us. 57

"Who's that guy with you?" he asked in a growly voice. I explained that he was a good friend of mine. "And just what does that mean?" he asked. I answered as I had many times before—that it meant that we were no longer going steady and that I didn't want to see him anymore. The next thing I knew, quick as lightning, he struck me across the face. Larry stepped between us and they started arguing. Greg asked for his ring, and when I handed it to him, he jumped around Larry and slapped me again. I dropped the ring on the sidewalk. Larry took my arm and said, "Let's get out of here." We left Greg on his knees looking for the ring in the dark. 58

When I arrived home, I was so angry I told my mother what had happened and we went down to the police station and filed a warrant for Greg's arrest. For a long time the police took no action. But when I told Greg what I'd done, he no longer tried to meet me on the street or at the house. He did, however, phone almost every night to harass me. He wasn't served with the warrant until four months after we first filed it. Then he was jailed for two weeks, but when his case came to court, he was freed because I failed to give testimony against him. Too much time had elapsed for my anger to be hot. After the warrant, he made no attempt to contact me. 59

In October my mother and sisters moved to Middlebury. I stayed behind so that I could graduate from my prep school in the spring. I live in an upstairs apartment in our house; the rest of it has been rented to another family. 60

Each evening now I spend filling out the long application forms for college, and like all personal questionnaires they force me to reflect. More and more, I feel my experiences have helped me shape many of the values and ideas I hold. I hope you too will realize the value of my experiences and decide to admit me to your university. I am a responsible and stable person. 61

Copyright © 1983 by Harriet Harvey. Reprinted by permission of Delacorte Press/Seymour Lawrence, a division of Bantam Doubleday Dell Publishing.

Reader's Dialogue

Making Connections

After reading Lynne Hall's story, write your immediate response in a page or two. Begin writing and continue writing until you come to a natural stop. Then listen to some responses by other first-year college students.

Readers at Work

Reynoldo: In this essay, there were no lies. I truly liked this kind of writing. It caught my attention.

Kim: I was surprised someone would write of an experience that wasn't a positive part of their lives. I was very impressed with her total honesty.

Evans: This story was electrifying. The application states 'We are most interested in anything of importance to you that will help us better understand you, your abilities, your interests, your reasons for wanting to attend college. . . .' But do they really want to hear the mystical glass side of your life? If the applicants are smart enough, they will have figured out the only way of being accepted is by playing the untold rules of the administration board. I am betting this essay raised their hair on ends. She did what most applicants would not have done—she gave a realistic account of her life and why going to college was so important to her.

Heather: The introduction to her story was very thoughtful. She tells her readers she wants to make something of her life: 'I believe that the experiences I shall relate not only describe who I am but have given me a strong motivation to go to college, to finish it, and to use my education to help people less fortunate than myself.' She then builds her story. While reading, a shocking feeling came over me to know that a human could suffer that way, whether an adult or child. She taught me a lot about drugs (what they can do to you), pregnancy (how you can be deserted), and street life itself. After reading this writing, I would like to meet Hall and see what became of her.

Marina: In this application, a different style of writing is presented to us. We as incoming students to college would not think of writing this way. It's a unique form of writing that lets us readers be involved.

Kim: Why would the people at Yale who judge applications let her in? Were they worried that if they didn't accept her another terrible thing would happen to her? Or was her essay so moving they said OK, and anyway, we have to accept a certain number of minorities? Or it is really possible, as I wish, that there sat someone on the committee who was educated enough to see her as an asset to Yale?

Suimen: It is quarter to one on a Thursday morning. I am sitting here in the computer room reading Lynne Hall's article about going to college. The more I read, the more ideas I have for my own writing. I often wonder what it means to go to college. What are reasons to go? Is college a place to learn or is it a place to get me rich someday? Is knowledge what this world is looking for, or is it money that this world is after?

After reading these responses, write some more (if you wish) before talking with others in your own class.

Sharing Connections

Extend your dialogue now by talking with other readers and writers in your class about Lynne Hall's experiences and about this writing as part of an application letter to college. You may also want to talk about informal and formal education.

Only Daughter

Sandra Cisneros

Sandra Cisneros, the "only daughter" of a Mexican father and a Mexican-American mother, writes about Latino culture. She is perhaps best known for her book The House on Mango Street *(1984). (See "My Name," a selection included in "Recollections & Reflections.") She has also written a collection of poetry,* My Wicked Ways *(1987), and a collection of stories entitled* Woman Hollering Creek *(1991). This essay, which appeared in* Glamour *magazine in November 1990, reveals her father's attitude about "girls" going to college and the alienation she experienced in a family of six sons.*

Once, several years ago, when I was just starting out my writing career, I was 1 asked to write my own contributor's note for an anthology I was part of. I wrote: "I am the only daughter in a family of six sons. *That* explains everything."

Well, I've thought about that ever since, and yes, it explains a lot to me, 2 but for the reader's sake I should have written: "I am the only daughter in a *Mexican* family of six sons." Or even: "I am the only daughter of a Mexican father and a Mexican-American mother." Or: "I am the only daughter of a working-class family of nine." All of these had everything to do with who I am today.

I was/am the only daughter and *only* a daughter. Being an only daughter 3 in a family of six sons forced me by circumstance to spend a lot of time by myself because my brothers felt it beneath them to play with a *girl* in public. But that aloneness, that loneliness, was good for a would-be writer—it allowed me time to think and think, to imagine, to read and prepare myself.

Being only a daughter for my father meant my destiny would lead me to 4 become someone's wife. That's what he believed. But when I was in the fifth grade and shared my plans for college with him, I was sure he understood. I remember my father saying, *"Que bueno, mi'ja, that's good."* That meant a lot to me, especially since my brothers thought the idea hilarious. What I didn't realize was that my father thought college was good for girls—good for finding a husband. After four years in college and two more in graduate school, and still no husband, my father shakes his head even now and says I wasted all that education.

In retrospect, I'm lucky my father believed daughters were meant for husbands. It meant it didn't matter if I majored in something silly like English. After all, I'd find a nice professional eventually, right? This allowed me the liberty to putter about embroidering my little poems and stories without my father interrupting with so much as a "What's that you're writing?"

But the truth is, I wanted him to interrupt. I wanted my father to understand what it was I was scribbling, to introduce me as "My only daughter, the writer." Not as "This is only my daughter. She teaches." *Es maestra*—teacher. Not even *profesora*.

In a sense, everything I have ever written has been for him, to win his approval even though I know my father can't read English words, even though my father's only reading includes the brown-ink *Esto* sports magazines from Mexico City and the bloody *¡Alarma!* magazines that feature yet another sighting of *La Virgen de Guadalupe* on a tortilla or a wife's revenge on her philandering husband by bashing his skull in with a *molcajete* (a kitchen mortar made of volcanic rock). Or the *fotonovelas*, the little picture paperbacks with tragedy and trauma erupting from the characters' mouths in bubbles.

My father represents, then, the public majority. A public who is uninterested in reading, and yet one whom I am writing about and for, and privately trying to woo.

When we were growing up in Chicago, we moved a lot because of my father. He suffered bouts of nostalgia. Then we'd have to let go our flat, store the furniture with mother's relatives, load the station wagon with baggage and bologna sandwiches and head south. To Mexico City.

We came back, of course. To yet another Chicago flat, another Chicago neighborhood, another Catholic school. Each time, my father would seek out the parish priest in order to get a tuition break, and complain or boast: "I have seven sons."

He meant *siete hijos,* seven children, but he translated it as "sons." "I have seven sons." To anyone who would listen. The Sears Roebuck employee who sold us the washing machine. The short-order cook where my father ate his ham-and-eggs breakfasts. "I have seven sons." As if he deserved a medal from the state.

My papa. He didn't mean anything by that mistranslation, I'm sure. But somehow I could feel myself being erased. I'd tug my father's sleeve and whisper: "Not seven sons. Six! and *one daughter.*"

When my oldest brother graduated from medical school, he fulfilled my father's dream that we study hard and use this—our heads, instead of this—our hands. Even now my father's hands are thick and yellow, stubbed by a history of hammer and nails and twine and coils and springs. "Use this," my father said, tapping his head, "and not this," showing us those hands. He always looked tired when he said it.

Wasn't college an investment? And hadn't I spent all those years in college? And if I didn't marry, what was it all for? Why would anyone go to college and then choose to be poor? Especially someone who had always been poor.

Last year, after ten years of writing professionally, the financial rewards 15 started to trickle in. My second National Endowment for the Arts Fellowship. A guest professorship at the University of California, Berkeley. My book, which sold to a major New York publishing house.

At Christmas, I flew home to Chicago. The house was throbbing, same as 16 always; hot *tamales* and sweet *tamales* hissing in my mother's pressure cooker, and everybody—my mother, six brothers, wives, babies, aunts, cousins—talking too loud and at the same time, like in a Fellini film, because that's just how we are.

I went upstairs to my father's room. One of my stories had just been 17 translated into Spanish and published in an anthology of Chicano writing, and I wanted to show it to him. Ever since he recovered from a stroke two years ago, my father likes to spend his leisure hours horizontally. And that's how I found him, watching a Pedro Infante movie on Galavisión and eating rice pudding.

There was a glass filmed with milk on the bedside table. There were sev- 18 eral vials of pills and balled Kleenex. And on the floor, one black sock and a plastic urinal that I didn't want to look at but looked at anyway. Pedro Infante was about to burst into song, and my father was laughing.

I'm not sure if it was because my story was translated into Spanish, or be- 19 cause it was published in Mexico, or perhaps because the story dealt with Tepeyac, the *colonia* my father was raised in and the house he grew up in, but at any rate, my father punched the mute button on his remote control and read my story.

I sat on the bed next to my father and waited. He read it very slowly. As 20 if he were reading each line over and over. He laughed at all the right places and read lines he liked out loud. He pointed and asked questions: "Is this So-and-so?" "Yes," I said. He kept reading.

When he was finally finished, after what seemed like hours, my father 21 looked up and asked: "Where can we get more copies of this for the relatives?"

Of all the wonderful things that happened to me last year, that was the 22 most wonderful.

"Only Daughter" by Sandra Cisneros appeared in *Glamour* magazine, November 1990. Courtesy *Glamour*. Copyright © 1990 by The Conde Nast Publications, Inc.

Reader's Dialogue

"Isn't college an investment?" asks Sandra Cisneros. Using the comparison frame of Figure 4.4, consider the different views of this father and "only daughter" about going to college.

Readers at Work

My parents believed that daughters weren't capable of taking care of themselves, while sons were meant to go away to college to explore the

Figure 4.4

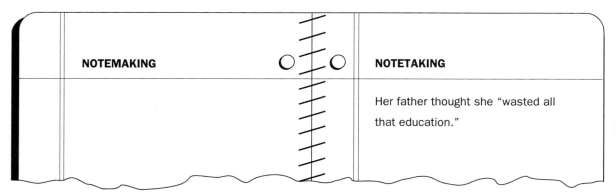

world and become a man. I knew that in order for me to get equal treatment I would have to go away to college. I'm the only daughter in my [Chinese] family and that's why they don't want me to go away to college. My brother was allowed to do almost anything. . . . Sometimes I just wish I was another son instead of a daughter. I wanted the same freedom my brother got. That's why I wanted to go away to college. —Betty Tang

My family's attitude towards college is of two different opinions. My mother expects me to go to college and make money. She does not think I need a husband to support me. She is happy for me that I am going to college because she never had the opportunity so she wants her daughter to go and she knows what is best for me. I want her to know that she did an excellent job raising me. On the other hand, my father is a little old-fashioned and he thinks that once a girl has children and a husband, she should stay home and care for them. My father thinks my husband will take care of me and that I should be a housewife. For me, being a housewife would not be an ideal thing in my life because I would never want to stay in a house to watch after children and clean the house day after day. I know for myself that college is for me. With what my father thinks, it reminds me of what Jane Ellen Wilson said: "Although my parents had no sons—only two daughters—it was expected that we would marry and leave. It was never ex-pected that we would become farmers and stay there." My father has this assumption that after he raised my sister and I, we would leave our home to enter our husband's family. He never expected me to go to college. To him, college was never a necessity, so when I entered college, it was a surprise for him. —Erika Dea

College

Anzia Yezierska

Anzia Yezierska (born in the 1880s) emigrated with her parents from the Russian part of Poland to the United States. She sought a college education to escape poor living conditions as a Jewish immigrant in Manhattan's crowded Lower East Side. She attended night school, graduated from Teachers College (Columbia University) in 1904, and went on to become a successful writer. Fiercely independent, she re-jected traditional family roles for women, sympathized with the oppressed, and was outraged by tyranny of any kind. "College" is taken from her autobiographical novel, Bread Givers: A Struggle Between a Father of the Old World and a Daughter of the New *(1925), about a young woman's struggle to free herself from Jewish immigrant life and from the "woman's role" assigned to her by men. This selection describes some of her experiences her first year at an American college.*

That burning day when I got ready to leave New York and start out on my 1
journey to college! I felt like Columbus starting out for the other end of the
earth. I felt like the pilgrim fathers who had left their homeland and all their
kin behind them and trailed out in search of the New World.

I had stayed up night after night, washing and ironing, patching and 2
darning my things. At last, I put them all together in a bundle, wrapped
them up with newspapers, and tied them securely with the thick clothes line
that I had in my room on which to hang out my wash. I made another bundle of my books. In another newspaper I wrapped up my food for the journey: a loaf of bread, a herring, and a pickle. In my purse was the money I
had been saving from my food, from my clothes, a penny to a penny, a dollar to a dollar for so many years. It was not much but I counted out that it
would be enough for my train ticket and a few weeks start till I got work out
there.

It was only when I got to the train that I realized I had hardly eaten all 3
day. Starving hungry, I tore the paper open. *Ach!* Crazy-head! In my haste I
had forgotten even to cut up the bread. I bent over on the side of my seat,
and half covering myself with a newspaper, I pinched pieces out of the loaf
and ripped ravenously at the herring. With each bite, I cast side glances like
a guilty thing; nobody should see the way I ate.

After a while, as the lights were turned low, the other passengers began to 4
nod their heads, each outsnoring the other in their thick sleep. I was the
only one on the train too excited to close my eyes.

Like a dream was the whole night's journey. And like a dream mounting 5
on a dream was this college town, this New America of culture and education.

Before this, New York was all of America to me. But now I came to a town 6
of quiet streets, shaded with green trees. No crowds, no tenements. No hur-
rying noise to beat the race of the hours. Only a leisured quietness whispered in the air: Peace. Be still. Eternal time is all before you.

Each house had its own green grass in front, its own free space all around, 7
and it faced the street with the calm security of being owned for generations,
and not rented by the month from a landlord. In the early twilight, it was

like a picture out of fairyland to see people sitting on their porches, lazily swinging in their hammocks, or watering their own growing flowers.

So these are the real Americans, I thought, thrilled by the lean, straight 8 bearing of the passers-by. They had none of that terrible fight for bread and rent that I always saw in New York people's eyes. Their faces were not worn with the hunger for things they never could have in their lives. There was in them that sure, settled look of those who belong to the world in which they were born.

The college buildings were like beautiful palaces. The campus stretched 9 out like fields of a big park. Air—air. Free space and sunshine. The river at dusk. Glimmering lights on passing boats, the floating voices of young people. And when night came, there were the sky and the stars.

This was the beauty for which I had always longed. For the first few days 10 I could only walk about and drink it in thirstily, more and more. Beauty of houses, beauty of streets, beauty shining out of the calm faces and cool eyes of the people! Oh—too cool. . . .

How could I most quickly become friends with them? How could I come 11 into their homes, exchange with them my thoughts, break with them bread at their tables? If I could only lose myself body and soul in the serenity of this new world, the hunger and the turmoil of my ghetto years would drop away from me, and I, too, would know the beauty of stillness and peace.

What light-hearted laughing youth met my eyes! All the young people I 12 had ever seen were shut up in factories. But here were young girls and young men enjoying life, free from the worry for a living. College to them was being out for a good time, like to us in the shop a Sunday picnic. But in our gayest Sunday picnics there was always the under-feeling that Monday meant back to the shop again. To these born lucky one's joy seemed to stretch out forever.

What a sight I was in my gray pushcart clothes against the beautiful gay 13 colours and the fine things those young girls wore. I had seen cheap, fancy style, Five- and Ten-Cent Store finery. But never had I seen such plain beautifulness. The simple skirts and sweaters, the stockings and shoes to match. The neat finished quietness of their tailored suits. There was no show-off in their clothes, and yet how much more pulling to the eyes and all the senses than the Grand Street richness I knew.

And the spick-and-span cleanliness of these people! It smelled from 14 them, the soap and the bathing. Their fingernails so white and pink. Their hands and necks white like milk. I wondered how did those girls get their hair so soft, so shiny, and so smooth about their heads. Even their black shoes had a clean look.

Never had I seen men so all shaved up with pink, clean skins. The richest 15 store-keepers in Grand Street shined themselves up with diamonds like walking jewellery stores, but they weren't so hollering clean as these men. And they all had their hair clipped so short; they all had a shape to their heads. So ironed out smooth and even they looked in their spotless, creaseless clothes, as if the dirty battle of life had never yet been on them.

I looked at these children of joy with a million eyes. I looked at them 16 with my hands, my feet, with the thinnest nerves of my hair. By all their differences from me, their youth, their shiny freshness, their carefreeness, they pulled me out of my senses to them. And they didn't even know I was there.

I thought once I got into the classes with them, they'd see me and we'd 17 get to know one another. What a sharp awakening came with my first hour!

As I entered the classroom, I saw young men and girls laughing and talk- 18 ing to one another without introductions. I looked for my seat. Then I noticed, up in front, a very earnest-faced young man with thick glasses over his sad eyes. He made me think of Morris Lipkin, so I chose my seat next to him.

"What's the name of the professor?" I asked. 19

"Smith," came from his tight lips. He did not even look at me. He pulled 20 himself together and began busily writing, to show me he didn't want to be interrupted.

I turned to the girl on my other side. What a fresh, clean beauty! A crea- 21 ture of sunshine. And clothes that matched her radiant youth.

"Is this the freshman class in geometry?" I asked her. 22

She nodded politely and smiled. But how quickly her eyes sized me up! It 23 was not an unkind glance. And yet, it said more plainly than words, "From where do you come? How did you get in here?"

Sitting side by side with them through the whole hour, I felt stranger to 24 them than if I had passed them in Hester Street. Wasn't there some secret something that would open us toward one another?

In one class after another, I kept asking myself, "What's the matter with 25 me? Why do they look at me so when I talk with them?"

Maybe I'd have to change myself inside and out to be one of them. But how? 26

The lectures were over at four o'clock. With a sigh, I turned from the col- 27 lege building, away from the pleasant streets, down to the shabby back alley near the post office, and entered the George Martin Hand Laundry.

Mr. Martin was a fat, easy-going, good-natured man. I no sooner told 28 him of my experience in New York than he took me on at once as an ironer at fifty cents an hour, and he told me he had work for as many hours a day as I could put in.

I felt if I could only look a little bit like other girls on the outside, maybe 29 I could get in with them. And that meant money! And money meant work, work, work!

Till eleven o'clock that night, I ironed fancy white shirtwaists. 30

"You're some busy little worker, even if I do say so," said Mr. Martin, 31 goodnaturedly. "But I must lock up. You can't live here."

I went home, aching in every bone. And in the quiet and good air, I so 32 overslept that I was late for my first class. To make matters worse, I found a note in my mailbox that puzzled and frightened me. It said, "Please report at once to the dean's office to explain your absence from Physical Education I, at four o'clock."

A line of other students was waiting there. When my turn came I asked 33 the secretary, "What's this physical education business?"

"This is a compulsory course," he said. "You cannot get credit in any 34 other course unless you satisfy this requirement."

At the hour when I had intended to go back to Martin's Laundry, I en- 35 tered the big gymnasium. There were a crowd of girls dressed in funny short black bloomers and rubber-soled shoes.

Yezierska

The teacher blew the whistle and called harshly, "Students are expected 36 to report in their uniforms."

"I have none." 37

"They're to be obtained at the bookstore," she said, with a stern look at 38 me. "Please do not report again without it."

I stood there dumb. 39

"Well, stay for today and exercise as you are," said the teacher, taking 40 pity on me.

She pointed out my place in the line, where I had to stand with the rest 41 like a lot of wooden soldiers. She made us twist ourselves around here and there, "Right face!" "Left face!" "Right about face!" I tried to do as the others did, but I felt like a jumping-jack being pulled this way and that way. I picked up dumbbells and pushed them up and down and sideways until my arms were lame. Then she made us hop around like a lot of monkeys.

At the end of the hour, I was so out of breath that I sank down, my heart 42 pounding against my ribs. I was dripping with sweat worse than Saturday night in the steam laundry. What's all this physical education nonsense? I came to college to learn something, to get an education with my head, and not monkeyshines with my arms and legs.

I went over to the instructor. "How much an hour do we get for this 43 work?" I asked her, bitterly.

She looked at me with a stupid stare. "This is a two-point course." 44

Now I got real mad. "I've got to sweat my life away enough only to earn 45 a living," I cried. "God knows I exercised enough, since I was a kid—"

"You properly exercised?" She looked at me from head to foot. "Your pos- 46 ture is bad. Your shoulders sag. You need additional corrective exercises out- side the class."

More tired than ever, I came to the class next day. After the dumbbells, 47 she made me jump over the hurdles. For the life of me, I couldn't do it. I bumped myself and scratched my knees on the top bar of the hurdle, knock- ing it over with a great clatter. They all laughed except the teacher.

"Repeat the exercise, please," she said, with a frozen face. 48

I was all bruises, trying to do it. And they were holding their sides with 49 laughter. I was their clown, and this was their circus. And suddenly, I got so wild with rage that I seized the hurdle and right before their eyes I smashed it to pieces.

The whole gymnasium went still as death. 50

The teacher's face was white. "Report at once to the dean." 51

The scared look on the faces of the girls made me feel that I was to be 52 locked up or fired.

For a minute when I entered the dean's grand office, I was so confused I 53 couldn't even see.

He rose and pointed to a chair beside his desk. "What can I do for you?" 54 he asked, in a voice that quieted me as he spoke.

I told him how mad I was, to have piled on me jumping hurdles when I 55 was so tired anyway. He regarded me with that cooling steadiness of his. When I was through, he walked to the window and I waited, miserable. Finally he turned to me again, and with a smile! "I'm quite certain that physical education is not essential in your case. I will excuse you from attending the course."

After this things went better with me. In spite of the hard work in the 56 laundry, I managed to get along in my classes. More and more interesting became the life of the college as I watched it from the outside.

What a feast of happenings each day of college was to those other students. 57 Societies, dances, letters from home, packages of food, midnight spreads and even birthday parties. I never knew that there were people glad enough of life to celebrate the day they were born. I watched the gay goings-on around me like one coming to a feast, but always standing back and only looking on.

One day, the ache for people broke down my feelings of difference from 58 them. I felt I must tear myself out of my aloneness. Nothing had ever come to me without my going out after it. I had to fight for my living, fight for every bit of my education. Why should I expect friendship and love to come to me out of the air while I sat there, dreaming about it?

The freshman class gave a dance that very evening. Something in the 59 back of my head told me that an evening dress and slippers were part of going to a dance. I had no such things. But should that stop me? If I had waited till I could afford the right clothes for college, I should never have been able to go at all.

I put a fresh collar over my old serge dress. And with a dollar stolen from 60 my eating money, I bought a ticket to the dance. As I peeped into the glittering gymnasium, blaring with jazz, my timid fears stopped the breath in me. How the whole big place sang with their light-hearted happiness! Young eyes drinking joy from young eyes. Girls, like gay-coloured butterflies, whirling in the arms of young men.

Floating ribbons and sashes shimmered against men's black coats. I took 61 the nearest chair, blinded by the dazzle of the happy couples. Why did I come here? A terrible sense of age weighed upon me; yet I watched and waited from someone to come and ask me to dance. But not one man came near me. Some of my classmates nodded distantly in passing, but most of them were too filled with their own happiness even to see me.

The whirling of joy went on and on, and still I sat there watching, cold, 62 lifeless, like a lost ghost. I was nothing and nobody. It was worse than being ignored. Worse than being an outcast. I simply didn't belong. I had no existence in their young eyes. I wanted to run and hide myself, but fear and pride nailed me against the wall.

A chaperon must have noticed my face, and she brought over one of 63 those clumsy, backward youths who was lost in a corner by himself. How unwilling his feet as she dragged him over! In a dull voice, he asked, "May I have the next dance?" his eyes fixed in the distance as he spoke.

"Thank you. I don't want to dance." And I fled from the place. 64

I found myself walking in the darkness of the campus. In the thick shad- 65 ows of the trees I hid myself and poured out my shamed and injured soul to the night. So, it wasn't character or brains that counted. Only youth and beauty and clothes—things I never had and never could have. Joy and love were not for such as me. Why not? Why not? . . .

Yezierska

I flung myself on the ground, beating with my fists against the endless 66
sorrows of my life. Even in college I had not escaped from the ghetto. Here
loneliness hounded me even worse than in Hester Street. Was there no escape? Will I never lift myself to be a person among people?

I pressed my face against the earth. All that was left of me reached out in 67
prayer. God! I've gone so far, help me to go on. God! I don't know how, but
I must go on. Help me not to want their little happiness. I have wanted their
love more than my life. Help me be bigger than this hunger in me. Give me
the love that can live without love . . . .

Darkness and stillness washed over me. Slowly I stumbled to my feet and 68
looked up at the sky. The stars in their infinite peace seemed to pour their
healing light into me. I thought of the captives in prison, the sick and the
suffering from the beginning of time who had looked to these stars for
strength. What was my little sorrow to the centuries of pain which those
stars had watched? So near they seemed, so compassionate. My bitter hurt
seemed to grow small and drop away. If I must go on alone, I should still
have silence and the high stars to walk with me.

Selections from *Bread Givers* by Anzia Yezierska, copyright © 1925 by Doubleday. Copyright
renewed 1952 by Anzia Yezierska, transferred to Louise Levitas Henriksen in 1970. Reprinted by permission of Persea Books, Inc.

Reader's Dialogue

Write about your own adjustments to college, perhaps in the form of a letter
to a friend. Or write a first letter from college to your parents or a relative or
friend. Use the comparison frame of Figure 4.5 as a jumping-off point.

Writer at Work: Melissa Greer

Coping With College

After arriving on campus and barely surviving the first week, I was faced
with the reality that college wasn't everything I had expected it to be. After
reading Jane Ellen Wilson's story, it seems that I was not alone in my feelings of false expectations. In her story about going to college she expected
to "find intellectual stimulation and community; fun and companionship;
new ideas and political concern." Wilson was also faced with an unfortunate
reality during her experiences with college, as I was. First of all, I was in an
over-occupied room with two other roommates. Being used to my own room
at home I was astonished that three girls could ever fit their belongings in
one of those tiny rooms.

Figure 4.5

NOTEMAKING	NOTETAKING
How did you feel when you left for college?	A.Y. tells about how she felt when she left for college.
What were your first impressions of your college or university? How did the buildings and campus impress you?	
What were your expectations about college and how did those expectations compare to your life at college the first few weeks? Was it different from what you expected?	
From your own observations, what would you say "going to college" means to others at your school?	"Going to college to them was being out for a good time."
How would you define your appearance (dress or style, for example) in comparison to others at your school? Did you feel that you fit in? In what ways did you feel different or out of place? Did you feel you were an outsider? Did you feel invisible?	"And they didn't even know I was there."

Fortunately, I was the first to arrive so I was able to choose all the best furniture, but I still had to share a closet. None of us were comfortable; we were all crammed for space. I got along with one of my roommates, but my other roommate was not very friendly. . . . Although I met so many other people the first week, I had no good friends yet. No one to just talk with, no one like my friends from home. And this is where the homesickness began. I had several pictures of all of my friends and family throughout my room and was constantly thinking of home. . . . I cried a lot and looked through my photo albums several times a day, not to mention I wrote all my friends, keeping in close contact with them all. The highlight of my day was receiving around two or three letters from home.

Also, within the first week I felt that I was constantly busy. I never had time to just sit down and relax. My classes were all going well, but I had lots of work. I couldn't believe how much work I had to do. It's not as if it was impossible as I had thought it would be, but there was just so much of it. I never felt that I accomplished anything because if I finally caught up with one class I would fall behind in another; it was a never ending cycle. Because of my work overload, I rarely found time to sleep or to even go running. At home I couldn't function without at least seven hours of sleep and I would run around two or three miles a day. My body was constantly tired, not to mention the fact that I wasn't eating right. The food in the dining hall was nothing compared to Mom's cooking and I was lucky if I found the time to eat three meals a day. Altogether I just felt awful. College didn't seem to be anything I expected at all.

After that first miserable week, I learned to come to terms with the situation. I accepted the fact that I wasn't going to make good friends right away, but I eventually would. I actually did start forming some closer friendships. It didn't happen overnight, but day by day we got to know each other a little more. I learned to manage my time so I could get most of my work done, socialize, get some sleep, and still find time to eat. I might not ever get to run every day anymore, but I try to find some other form of exercise at least once a week. I do not expect to ever have all of my work done, but if I take time for each class, I have found I am better prepared. I try to save most of my socializing for the weekends, although I often find myself spending hours talking in the dining halls or just hanging out in someone's room. I cannot expect to have everything run exactly on schedule, but I will get it done, and now I know I can. Although I am doing better, I still miss home. At least now I know that things will get better with time and somehow, some way I will survive.

Note: Melissa wrote this during her first semester at college. Her instructor was Barb Adams. At the time this book went to press, Melissa was a junior.

When she came to my office to reread this piece and to give me permission to use it, a flood of memories of first days of college came back to her. "I didn't even write well!" she exclaimed, wanting to pick up a pen and revise. "I was so miserable," she said. "And I was such an outsider in that class. Everyone was from the city and I was from upstate. But now I love college." We made a copy of her essay, which she decided she wanted to keep to look back and remember.

Optional Listening & Writing Opportunities

Interview a college graduate about her or his experiences of going to college. Tape record your interview if possible. Here are some writing options:

1. Transcribe your interview, complete with questions and responses. Add your analysis or some commentary about what you learned.
2. Omit your questions and piece together the responses of the person you interviewed so that your writing reads as a kind of oral narrative about going to college.
3. Write an essay about the person's "Going to College" story. Include some quotations. Perhaps interview more than one person.

In class, discuss the possibilities for some people to interview (professors, students, family members, friends, members of the community).

Writing good interview questions is not easy. Once you have made arrangements for one or more interviews, jot down some notes about each person to be interviewed and what you'd like to know or think would be appropriate to ask. Perhaps invite a skilled interviewer from the campus or larger community to come to class to discuss interviewing techniques.

Try out your questions in small groups and then revise them. As a whole class, discuss what kinds of questions might be appropriate for most people you might interview. Prepare a list of backup questions to use if some of your questions do not elicit much response. Conduct one or two interviews in class, perhaps with one student taking the lead and others joining in. Afterward review your interview questions and methodology, first in small groups and again in the class as a whole. Then revise your questions yet again. You may also want to discuss with your interviewee the changing views of going to college as presented in some of your reading.

Invite one or more college graduates to class to tell their "Going to College" stories. Write informally in your Writing Project notebooks about what you learned or found interesting.

End-Project Writing Opportunities

Write your own story about going to college. Think of this writing either as a chapter in your autobiography or as a personal essay to be included with your college application form.

Review your notes in your project folder, and then write a first draft. You will be revising your writing later; at this point, try to write as much as you can. Here are some questions you might want to address in your essay:

What do you think going to college means to your parents?

What do you think your going to college means to them?

What is your family's attitude about going to college?

To what extent were other family members formally educated?

Refer to the "key words" activity. What does going to college mean to you?

When did you first know you were going to college?

What are your expectations and goals about college?

Connect your story with the stories or views expressed in project-related readings. In what ways are your story or views similar or different? What issues about college did some of the readings raise for you?

Do not write your draft by answering these questions one after another, as if you were filling out a questionnaire! These questions are intended to be read as a departure point for your writing. You could read them over to help you get started with your story, which will probably unfold during the process of writing. After you get started writing and you come to a natural stop, you could read over these questions again to help you think about what else to include. Do look back at all the work you've done on this project—your responses to readings, your notes, and so on. Write a draft. Allow your story to begin to take shape.

Writer's Workshop 1: Getting Started

Workshop Activity

Get into a small writing group (of perhaps three members) to talk about what you wrote and to get some response. Divide the time equally among group members. One group member could serve as workshop leader to keep track of time and keep the discussion going (and on track). Suggested time: forty-five minutes (fifteen minutes per writer) for a group of three.

As an alternative, meet as a whole class. Respond to up to three writers and then take notes for rereading your own writing. Perhaps work in pairs following some whole-class response to help you get oriented. Read the guidelines that follow for writers and listeners. Before you begin, you may want to turn to "Writers at Work," page 167, for one writer's in-class reading and the class's questions in response to it.

Guidelines for Writers

1. Talk briefly about getting started. How did you get started? Did you write with ease? Did you get stuck? Do you feel you have written most of what you want to say? Don't apologize for not writing a perfect first draft. Talk about how you got started on your writing project.
2. Read your writing to the group.
3. Reread your writing, and this time, ask your listeners to write down any questions they have. Take an active role. Ask them what they want to

know more about. Do they have any questions about something they were confused about?

4. Take notes and/or collect the written questions. If you are in a whole-class workshop, you may want to take a few questions orally and then collect the rest of the written questions.

5. At the end of this workshop or soon after, take a few minutes to make some notes about the responses to your writing. Did some questions surprise you? Did some seem inappropriate? What did you learn from listening to the kinds of questions listeners asked? Did you realize you needed to write or explain more? Then write about your plans for the next writing. What do you need to add or clarify? Should you address all the questions? Which ones are appropriate for you to address for this writing?

Guidelines for Listeners

1. Listen once through without taking notes.

2. After listening once, write down what you liked about this piece of writing. Next, review the guide in Figure 4.6. Then listen to the writing a second time and write down any questions or concerns you have. Sometimes in writing, especially in a first draft, writers assume that readers have more background than they do and fail to supply the necessary context. At this point, writers are still working out ideas and have probably not thought fully about their readers. You can help writers move along now toward rewriting with their readers more and more in mind. Form some questions to help writers resee and reconsider. This is a great opportunity to interview a writer at work.

3. Give your written response to the writer for future reference. Include your name so the writer can talk with you further if there is not enough opportunity during class.

Revision Focus: Completeness

Alone with only the hum of the computer, accompanied by all my faces . . . , the monitor's screen reflects back the dialogue among "us."
Gloria Anzuldúa
Making Face, Making Soul

Review the responses you received in the writer's workshop and continue writing, trying to make your draft as complete as possible. Do not necessarily address all the questions reviewers asked—some may not be appropriate for this writing project. You could add some details that would not necessarily add to the quality of writing.

Decide what to expand or clarify. Place an asterisk (*) wherever you are considering making additions or clarifications. Make some notes to yourself in the margins to help you when you rewrite. Label your rewriting "Draft 2."

If you are writing with a word processor, make your notes on the printout of Draft 1 and make any insertions or changes at the computer keyboard. You may find you want to write more, especially if you are writing with a word processor. The questions and the process of rereading your own writing may also bring more ideas to mind. Keep writing. This writing is what author David Bradley calls a "get-it-out" draft. Bring as complete a draft as you can to the next writers' workshop.

Figure 4.6

Writing Project: **Writer:** _____

Going to College   **Reviewer:** _____

Draft: _____   **Date:** _____

REVIEW GUIDE

1. What interests you about this piece of writing?

2. What would you like to know more about? Ask a question or two.

3. Did the writer mention some event or make a reference that left you wondering? Were you confused at any point? Do you need some clarification? Express your confusion in the form of a specific question.

4. Did the writer include family educational history?   ___ Yes ___ No
Do you have any questions you'd like to ask the writer related to this history or any suggestions to offer?

5. Did the writer discuss attitudes about going to college (of family or friends)?   ___ Yes ___ No

6. Summarize what you "hear" the writer doing in this draft, and then summarize your comments for the writer's reference during the rewriting process. Begin by telling what you liked or found interesting and then summarize comments that you think would be helpful to this "writer at work."

Writer at Work

Prescott Harris read his first draft to the whole class.

Going to College

My decision to go to college was based on not wanting to let my mind go to waste. All through the period of time I was in the army and working I felt that I wasn't applying what I had learned in school. I was yearning for text-books and a classroom setting. I really missed waking up to go to school in the morning, doing homework, and meeting people through school. With all of this in mind I decided to apply and get out of a life that I wasn't happy with and into a classroom. Since I also didn't care much for being in the city, I decided to go away to college. I narrowed my choices down to the State University of New York at Binghamton because my intended major is nursing and the academic reputation of this school is excellent. I am glad that I made this choice, though some of my relatives feel that I should work and learn to take care of myself since I am of age now. My grandparents who raised me didn't have much education but a lot of work experience, which was more important than continuing their education because it was neces-sary for them to survive when they were growing up. All of my family is proud because I am in such a good college and because I will be a role model to my two younger brothers. Having a job and making money was nice, but I am happier in a classroom. Though I have cousins in college and aunts who have graduated from college, I am the first in my family to go away to col-lege, so I am proud of that. I feel very confident now, though I didn't in the beginning, and look forward to some rough roads along the way that I am confident enough to handle now.

Because Prescott wrote one page and did not know what else to write, we began interviewing him. Everyone had questions:

"Did you go right into the army after high school, or did you go to work first?"

"What kind of work did you do? Why didn't you like it?"

"Why weren't you happy in the army? Where did you go in the army? What did you do? What didn't you like?"

"Did you like high school? Did you like a particular class or just going to school? Was it the routine you missed?"

"What don't you like about the city?"

"What made you decide to major in nursing? Did someone influence you, or did you have some experience in a hospital?"

"Why do your relatives feel you should go to work? Are these close relatives? Why do you think they have this attitude? Do they think college is not a good investment?"

"What kind of work did your grandparents do? Do they support your wanting to go to college?"

"Did your cousins and aunts influence you in your decision to go to college?"

"Why didn't you go to college right after high school?"

"Why weren't you confident about going to college at first, and why are you more confident now?"

Prescott began taking down these questions. "Oh, OK, you want to know more about that?" After listening to a few questions to get an idea about how to go about continuing his writing, he collected the rest of the questions for later review.

Then another writer, Marie, read her writing. She mentioned that her aunt was an important influence in her life. Like her aunt, Marie was science-minded, but unlike her aunt, she was going to college, something her aunt had wanted to do. We wanted to know more about her aunt. Why didn't she go to college? What was her story? How did she impress Marie?

Everyone liked getting questions. It's easy when writing to assume that readers can fill in the background or provide context. In the context of the classroom, of course, you can ask the writer questions, but ultimately everyone's writing must stand alone without the writer's literal presence.

Writer's Workshop 2: Keeping Going

Workshop Activity

An idea . . . is not a "point" so much as a branching tree of elaboration and demonstration.

Mina Shaughnessy

Writers: Read your second draft to two other writers, who will serve as peer reviewers. If you worked with a small group for the first draft review, you may want to remain with this group so they can compare the two drafts. After each writer has been heard, exchange written or printed copies for review.

Reviewers: For this draft, the focus was on detailing the story about going to college. The focus for the next draft is on organization and unity. As a reviewer, look back to see if the story is told fully and clearly enough, and also comment particularly on the order of presentation. Make any other comments that you think may help the writer revise.

On a sheet of looseleaf paper or on a computer screen, use the format in Figure 4.7 to formulate your responses. (If you are using a word processor,

Figure 4.7

Writing Project: **Writer:** _____

Going to College _____   **Reviewer:** _____

Draft: _____   **Date:** _____

REVIEW GUIDE

1. *Overall response:* What stands out for you in this piece of writing? What do you think the writer is trying to express here? How would you characterize this "Going to College" story? How would you compare it to your story, for example, or others you have heard? What is different? What concerns or background does this writer have in common with others?

2. *Development and clarity:* Do you have any questions? Would you like to know more about some point or event the writer has included? Are you confused by any line or passage? Cite specific references from the writer's text.

3. *Organization:*
   (a) Reread and make an informal outline of this draft. What does the writer bring up first? Next? Keep going.

   (b) Review your outline and consider the organization. Would it make sense to change the order at all? What do you suggest?

4. *Unity:* Does something seem out of place in this piece? Did the writer go offtrack? Should a line or passage be omitted? is there a gap at some point? If so, where? What do you suggest the writer should add?

5. *Other Comments:*

you may want to exchange drafts through electronic mail. Or you could exchange disks, or you could sit at another writer's computer and make comments.) After completing your comments, give them to the writers. If there is time in class, compare and discuss the reviews. Writers could also read them and make notes for a follow-up discussion in the next class (or perhaps in a conversation through electronic mail).

Revision Focus: Organization & Unity

After reading peer commentary and talking with your reviewers, write a response, perhaps to your instructor. What did you find useful? What comments will you use? Which ones will you discard and why? What are your plans for rewriting? Perhaps have a writing consultation (oral or written) with your instructor or with another writing consultant. If you and your instructor are using a computer with electronic-mail capability, you could have a consultation via the computer, at least as a starting point for an in-person discussion. It would also be helpful to your reviewers if they saw a copy of your responses to their critiques, for they are working on developing their critical reading abilities. Your instructor may also find it helpful to receive the critiques and your response to reviewers with your draft.

Everyone in your writing class/community will work in different ways, as writing is not a lockstep, unified process. It is helpful, however, if each workshop has a focus, as a starting point for review. Listen to the ways writers are writing. Use review questions as a guide for responding until you feel comfortable actively reading another writer's text. Learn what's helpful to a writer who is at work on a piece of writing. What kind of response do you find helpful?

Writer's Workshop 3: Rewriting

Workshop Activity

If you have been working with the same writing group, this may be a good time to get an outside review. Try to get readings from those who are unfamiliar with your story. Exchange written drafts either in person or electronically. If you are using electronic mail, you may want to continue the conversation through the mail and talk in person later.

As a starting point, reviewers should refer to questions 3 and 4 on organization and unity in Figure 4.7. Comment again on organization and unity, and then make any other comments you think would be useful as the writer moves toward a final draft. At this point, continue to focus on the story rather than on any mechanical or grammatical problems.

Read peer and perhaps teacher commentary on the previous draft. Then read the writer's new version and make observations on how this draft addressed concerns expressed in the commentaries.

Revision Focus: Introductions & Conclusions

After reviewing comments, making notes, and talking with your reviewers (if possible), reread aloud both your introduction and your conclusion. How could they be improved? How do they relate? Read your whole piece of writing aloud, paying particular attention to how the introduction and conclusion sound. Read the opening line again. How do you first engage your readers? With what thought or image or impression do you leave the reader? Rewrite your introduction and conclusion to try out on other writers or on a writing consultant (or instructor or tutor).

Writer's Workshop 4: Experimenting

Workshop Activity

As a whole class (or in small groups again), take turns reading introductions aloud. Listen to one introduction after another. How do these introductions suit the purposes of these writers?

Writers at Work

Look at the variety of ways five writers began their writing.

Ainsley tried beginning by writing about Jamaican families:

In some Jamaican families living in a bad community, parents feel college is an opportunity for their children to obtain a career and a good job. They see going to college as a way of preventing their children from becoming members of a ruthless posse or becoming juvenile delinquents.

In her Draft 3, Marie began:

My parents feel that an education is the key to success. At an early age I was taught the value of education.

After experimenting some, Marie wrote this opening line:

If I went to college, my parents could say Marie did something right. My parents feel that . . .

Evans wrote this attention-getting opener:

For me, not to go to college would be like being a skunk without its streak.

Suimen, after many drafts, wrote this eye-opener:

Born a child of war, a victim caught in the greed for power played by the elite pool of Cambodian society, college was not denoted in my book of knowledge. The first time I tasted the beauty of life, I was captive in the world of rice fields and cow herding. A world where books contain no value and knowledge is a crime. A world where hunger is the common theme in every child's mind, and mourning for the dead is seen in every family's eyes.

Marina, a first-generation Chinese-American, began her larger "Going to College" story with a little story:

As I was growing up, my sisters and I were told countless stories by our great grandmother. Each of these stories had an educational meaning behind it. I recall one story. . . .

Later, Marina wrote, "Although my great grandmother did not have any education in school, she is my inspiration." This line could serve as the opening line, but Marina chose to embed it in the second paragraph. Compare this line with the opening line she used ("As I was growing up, my sisters and I were told countless stories by our great grandmother."). What would happen if she began with this line? Compare the two effects on you as a reader.

Try moving some of your sentences around. Experiment with your introduction. Ask yourself: What would happen if I began here? Read some conclusions. Experiment. Rewrite your conclusion and try out different possibilities in class.

Writer's Workshop 5: Editing for Grammar & Mechanics

Workshop Activity

Review "Developing an Editing System" on page 356 of the appendix, "Guidelines for Editing Your Own Writing," and follow the procedures. Take out your Editing Projects notebook, which should contain your most recent editing list and notes. If you have enough information about the kinds of errors you tend to make, then proceed to edit your latest draft using your notebook as a guide. Check your work with your instructor and/or peers if you set up an editing workshop in class.

Small groups in your class could work together on a common problem and then list questions to ask a consultant. If there isn't enough time in class, questions could be written down for the instructor to address in the next class. Each time you are preparing a piece of writing for presentation (publication or evaluation), try controlling for particular kinds of errors, beginning with those that most interfere with a reader's understanding of what you are trying to say. As you gain control, try adding a different grammar convention for subsequent editing sessions.

Editing Progress Report

Use your revised editing notebook as a starting point for writing about your progress. What kinds of errors did you try to eliminate in this final draft? Give examples of some of the kinds of errors you often make and ones you found and changed. Is editing for certain kinds of errors easier for you now? What difficulties are you having with editing? What questions do you have? Are you developing a way of editing now? Has your editing changed? What do you need to work on next?

Date your report and keep a copy in your Editing Projects notebook for reference. Your instructor may want a copy attached to your final draft.

In-Class Publication

Ask volunteers to read their "Going to College" stories in class and/or make an anthology and distribute copies. Perhaps invite students from another class in for a reading, or have volunteers from two classes read their stories. If you interviewed others about their "Going to College" stories, you could invite them to a reading to enjoy, respond, and/or share their stories.

Writer at Work: Carol Bell

Going to College

As a child, the highlight of my week was going to the library with my father. Each book on the shelf seemed to be a new world that I could take home and make my own. I loved school. Every semester was a new adventure with new books and new things to learn. My parents taught me that knowledge was the key to becoming a complete human being. Their plans for my future, for college, were so beautiful; I never imagined it would be over twenty years before I made that dream come true.

I envisioned college as ivy-covered walls, grey-haired professors that would engage in intellectual dissertations, a feast for the curious mind. I dreamt of the days I would spend having deep and esoteric conversations with my peers about the vast array of subjects I was studying. My parents reveled in my visions and fed my desires. I was to be the first one in our family to go to college.

My dream died when I was sixteen. Family and financial problems forced me to quit school and take a job in a shoe factory. I told myself it didn't matter, but I felt cheated. Worst of all, I felt like a failure. I married within a year and set my sights on being a wife and eventually a mother. However, deep inside I knew that a part of me had been short-changed.

After years of feeling cheated and embarrassed, I decided to go back and get my equivalency diploma. I was ashamed to be in those classes. It took all the courage I had to walk into the classroom each week. I saw it as an admission of my failure just to be there. The teacher made matters worse. She was condescending and looked down on her students. I remember how she spoke slowly and in a loud voice the way people do to children or the elderly, as if I would have difficulty understanding the simplest lesson. Instead of respecting me for my efforts to improve myself, she treated me like a second-class citizen, a loser. The work was easy, and I got my equivalency diploma but still felt defeated. I continued to see myself as a failure.

Eight years ago, at the age of thirty-five, I became a single parent and breadwinner for my four children. I had advanced myself to a position as a computer operator in a local industry, but I still did not earn enough money to support my family. With a lot of hard work and study I landed a job as a software engineer. My boss was happy with my work, but he made it clear that if I wanted to advance, I would need a degree.

I started evening classes at a community college; however, I no longer viewed college as a way of improving my mind. I had one purpose. I needed that piece of paper that would be my ticket to a higher-paying job. Attempting to be both mother and father and working a full-time job left me little time for my own schoolwork. I had to travel and was assigned projects at work that required more and more of my time, and my schoolwork had to take second place. I grew discouraged and angry with what I viewed to be an uphill climb. College became a drudgery for me because the only reward I sought was a fatter paycheck. The love of learning that I once held so dear seemed to wither and die.

My feelings of failure came back with a vengeance and I just quit trying. The minute a course required more time than I could give, I quit going to class. I felt stupid when I couldn't "ace" a course and I told myself that I was too old to do this. College was for young people and I had missed my chance. I had disappointed my parents years ago and now I was disappointing my children.

Six years later I remarried. My new husband knew exactly what I needed. He assured me I would do well in college if I put all my feelings of failure behind me. Eventually, he persuaded me to try again. He told me not to do it for money and career advancement; he encouraged me to do it for myself, to learn. He told me to take a course that interested me, one that would challenge me as a person. Hesitant and afraid of failing, I set off to college again.

I enrolled in an upper-level literature class. My professor was demanding, but he only demanded my best. He challenged me, and I worked to live up to my professor's expectations. School became the highlight of my week. I would get out of work and run home to do my homework. Books became wondrous things again. The more I learned, the more I wanted to learn. All my old dreams started to come to life again.

Each semester became an adventure again, and I knew that this time there was no stopping me. Last semester my mother became critically ill. I missed a full month of school sitting at her bedside before she died. I had my lectures taped and borrowed notes from other students. I read at Mom's bedside and wrote my essays in the ICU waiting room. Before she died, I knew that she was proud of me. She told me not to quit: I passed my class with an A–.

I believe I have been a positive example for my children. My oldest daughter is married and takes evening classes at a community college. My son is a senior at Niagara University and will attend law school when he graduates. My sixteen-year-old daughter will graduate from high school next year and plans to study biology here. My youngest daughter is only twelve, but she is already talking about going to college.

Being in college has made me a happier person. I feel fulfilled and full of energy. It has forced me to examine my values, my thoughts, and has broadened my horizons. At last, instead of being just a wife, mother, or employee, I am becoming my own person. Last month I quit my job to become a full-time student. I am majoring in literature and mathematics and will obtain a Master's degree in teaching. I want to teach high-school students and encourage them to continue their education. I hope to share my love of books and learning with young people. I want to keep alive the dream my parents had given me and pass it on to others.

Writer at Work: Michelle Espinal

A woman's role in a Latino family is basically staying home, having a job, doing house chores, having babies and raising them at home. The average level for a Latino woman is going to high school and maybe graduating from high school. This is the traditional Latino woman. And most Latino women go by this. I do not.

I have relatives who are very traditional. These are the women who were disappointed to hear that I had decided to go to college. They thought that I would go with the tradition; get married to my boyfriend and give them great nieces, nephews, grandchildren, and so on. But they were wrong. I would not allow myself to live that type of life, nor would my parents allow it. I did not want to get married and have children. I think I can do this later on in my life but in the meantime I can continue my education.

These women and many others outside a Latino family have this tradition as well. Most of these women have the potential to have a profession and be great at it. But since these women did not have the willpower to leave the tradition behind and better themselves, they hung onto it. I could never continue with the tradition. I believe that there is so much a person can do after high school besides getting married and having children. It would be like giving yourself away. I do not think that I am a baby factory. Let alone anyman's maid. The way I see it is that by going with the tradition it is proving that women could never be equal to men. This is why I decided to go to college, as well as for other reasons.

When I was in high school, I would see girls pregnant and hear how some of them felt that they had realized that they had messed their lives up as well as themselves because they were not going to college but wanted to go. I saw girls looking in the brides' magazines and saying how their wedding in the spring was going to be wonderful and "magical." I saw all this in my freshman year. To make things worse, I would hear my great aunts and my grandmother talking about how I was getting older, soon graduating, and how they were going to have great nieces, great nephews, and great-grandchildren. Also, hoping they would live to see them. I would just laugh at what they would say. What threw me off the most was how they would gossip in their rockers about teenagers in the family. They could not wait for us to get married and have children of our own!

So as the years passed by, I continued to hear these conversations. I heard how the girls I knew were criticized by others and how these "baby producing" girls would talk about how their lives had been thrown down the drain. I would also see how the girls that were looking at their wedding dresses in the magazines and were preparing everything for that beautiful, wonderful, spring wedding, were now pregnant and single. If not, these girls were now widows because their newly wed husband had been shot, wounded, or killed in a drive-by-shooting at his drug spot.

With all this and the other family talks, I started to become more aware about my future. I started to think about the future and it did not involve following this tradition. I had to better myself and my relatives' thoughts of women being housewives, baby bearers, and maids to their husbands. As I continued to think more about going to college, I did not know what profession I would go into but that was the least of the matter. I just did not want to continue with this tradition and end up like some of these girls. I also thought about the struggles that I as a minority woman might go through. I had to go to college and educate myself more. I did not know about the different colleges or which were better or not.

When I got to my senior year, it was a hectic year. This was the year where I had to fill out all these papers, applications, and/or financial aid papers. Everyone who was graduating that June was running around filling these papers out, studying for the SAT's, studying harder, trying to pass all their classes, keeping their grades up and writing their college essays. So was I. I was making sure all my papers were in place so I could graduate on time and go to college. I really wanted to go.

I had decided to apply to city colleges. Then I started to think back about the girls who were pregnant and some of my drug-dealing friends who had died in my arms over their "profession" and I needed to get away from this and the tradition. So I then decided to apply to state colleges as well as city colleges. That way I could get away, at least for a while. I could go to a different scene and broaden my horizons outside the city life and style.

I let my parents and relatives know this. My parents were happy, but of course my relatives were disappointed. But what could I do. There is always one bad child in the batch, this time it happened to be me.

As I waited for the responses from the colleges, I continued to think of going away. The responses from the colleges had finally come in. I had gotten accepted to the city colleges as well as two out of three of the state colleges. I had never visited these schools, let alone been outside the city limits. So whichever school I would decide to go to, it would be a different environment as well as a change of lifestyle.

I decided to go to a university upstate. Away from the city. Since I had decided upon going to this school and under the circumstances I applied, I had to go away for a summer program.[1] When I returned to the city after the program was over, I had a different attitude and view of things. I explained these views to my mother and she understood. She also understood my reasons and decision for not following the tradition. Now she is in college and she is also continuing her education. Now my relatives can complain about both of us going to college and not following this stupid tradition!

Writer at Work: Onyo Brown

Why Did I Come Here?

Amityville Horror, the movie, is the first reason that my town became known. The town I lived in is Amityville. There are two parts to this town; there's the north side and there's the south side. I lived on the north side of Amityville. In this part of town, there's an area called by the people "The Block" and by the news media "The Corner." I can understand it being called "The Corner" because it is on the corner of an intersection, but why it was and still is called "The Block" I have absolutely no idea. I remember when I was younger, the kids were able to go up on "The Block" without having drug peddlers try to push drugs on them. We were able to go past there with a 95 percent chance of not getting shot. Females, including the young ones, could walk past there and not have anyone whistle, call, or chase after [them]. Most of the people who were and still are high-school dropouts sold drugs, and 99.9 percent of them WERE guys. On the streets where we lived, our parents didn't have to worry about us getting shot or caught in a fight, whether it was between two or more people. We were able to leave our bikes outside, knowing that they were going to be where we left them in the morning. In the summer, we were able to sleep with our windows open and

---

1. Michelle was admitted through the Educational Opportunity Program.

our doors unlocked, knowing that no one would try to steal from the house. There were so many things that we, my generation and back, were able to do that seem impossible or too deadly for the generations of today to do.

Today, as I'm sure you can imagine, things have changed tremendously. Nowadays, if anyone walked up on "The Block," someone would try to push whatever drug he/she might have on to that person. If a female with a nice body and form-fitting clothes walked on or passed by, things like this may be said to her: "YO! baby wut chu doin' t'nite. 'Cawz I would like ta take you out t'nite. Ya know wut I'm sayin'?" or maybe, "Excuse me miss but uhhh I been watchin' you and uhhh I was wunderin' if uhhh, you know, we could get t'getha one night and go out." Then he would take out his money and say, "I kin take you out to dinna, and I don't mean McDonald's, Burger King, or White Castle, dhen we could go to dha movies or to a club; wut evah you like. Ya know wut I'm sayin'." There are times when things like this may be said, and she may be dumb enough and fall for it or he may not know who or what she is or who her boyfriend might be. What I mean by that is, she could be the girlfriend of the most ruthless drug seller in the next seven towns. Another thing, she could be the best thief there is in town, so if a guy was to get together with her, he could lose everything. The worst thing of all is that she could be an undercover cop, and by messing around with her, he could get arrested.

If you leave your bike outside without anyone watching it, you're lucky if it's there when you get back. When children go outside today, you have to keep an eye on them constantly. Why? Because there is a possibility of that child getting shot or caught in a fight by accident. Bullets have no names on them, even though there is a specific target. When you walk past "The Block," it's best to walk on the other side of the street so that someone doesn't "hawk" (stare at) you.

This did have an effect on me. I plan to return to my town to somehow, some way, teach the children a better way of living. I don't want my kids growing up perpetually surrounded by this kind of garbage. It's bad enough that my brother, who is eleven, and my sister, who is six, know how to make some of these drugs. These are just some of the things that convinced me to choose college over PathMark, McDonald's, Burger King, and other fast-food restaurants. Another thing that led me in this direction is my mother. I saw the way she was struggling to support herself as well as three kids, and

I didn't want to have to go through all of those things. When I have my children, I want to be financially stable to the point where I won't have to be worried about having my electricity cut off and things of that nature. I didn't hate living in Amityville; I just hated the things that went on in the town. The effect that this had on me was to do whatever I could to change my hometown. I want to become a lawyer, specializing in juvenile criminals, and to become that, I have to go to college. The decision to become a lawyer was made by me when I was in the seventh grade walking down the hallway to get to class. How that thought came to my mind, I will never know. But what I do know is that one of my goals is to CLEAN UP Amityville. One way that I'm going to do that is by getting rid of all the drug dealers the best way possible. Another way that this is going to happen is when I begin to teach the children to respect themselves and their neighbors. What was that you said—How do you know I'm going to become a lawyer? I know that I am going to become a lawyer because I believe and have faith in GOD. As long as I have that I have nothing to worry about.

I was influenced by some of the things that happened there. I started drinking when I started going out with this guy. He was nineteen, and I was sixteen or seventeen. Yes, my mother met him. Every Friday we went out somewhere, and he always bought two or three forty-ounce bottles of Old English. After a while I went on to the harder stuff: Brass Monkey, L.I. Ice Tea, Peach Tree Schnapps, Wild Irish Rose, etc. I began to stay out past my curfew, not giving a hoot about the consequences I would receive. . . . [My mother] threatened to send me to Madonna Heights, a girls home. . . . Then one night I came home from somewhere and she told me that I was no longer a part of her family and that she was going to take my room away from me. When she did that, it punched me into reality very quickly and very hard. For a long time I had to buy my own food, wash my own things, and ask to use the telephone. This was hurting me to the point where I thought that no one loved me. When I left the house, I had to make it seem as if there was nothing wrong, but deep down inside I had a hole in my heart. I realized that I was becoming like the girls who were destroying their lives in whatever ways that they were. I didn't want those things to happen to me because I had plans for myself, and I had to be a role model for my younger siblings. So I began to straighten up; and after a while I started going back to church and that's when things began to get better.

I could never call Amityville "home," but the place that I talked about above is my "home" and if I lose it, at this time in my life, my world will be nothing but dust. All of the things that I went through I don't want my brother and sister to even think about trying to do. I know that they have to learn from their own mistakes, but I will do all that I can to lead them down the right road.

A lot of the girls in my neighborhood have babies. Most of them are between the ages of fourteen and eighteen. Most of them tend to drop out of school, and then there are some who let their mothers take care of the child or they don't take care of them at all. They are out in the streets at parties getting drunk or high and their children are at home with God knows who. I needed to get away from all of those depressing, agitating, sad things. I wanted and still want to make something of myself before I have to take care of such a BIG responsibility.

By coming to college, I knew that I would be able to make enough money some day to buy my mother what she wants and give my brother and sister money to start them off into the profession that they want to go in. All of this may take a long time, but I am positive that it will be worth the wait.

These are the reasons why I came to college. This story may sound sad or boring but there is a reason for everything. This is the life that I have lived and still am living in certain ways. If you did not like this story, I am sorry to say "It's like that and that's the way it is!!!"

Suggestions for Further Reading

Moody, Anne. 1968. "College," a chapter in *Coming of Age in Mississippi*. New York: Dial.

Rodriguez, Richard. 1982. *The Education of Richard Rodriguez*. Boston: Godine.

Walker, Alice. 1983. "A Talk: Convocation 1972," from *In Search of Our Mothers' Gardens*. New York: Harcourt Brace Jovanovich.

Part III

Writing Projects: Becoming Educated/Defining, Analyzing, & Arguing

It is through and by means of education that [individuals] may become empowered to think about what they are doing, to become mindful, to share meanings, to conceptualize, to make varied sense of their lived worlds. It is through education that preferences may be released, languages learned, intelligences developed, perspectives opened, possibilities disclosed.

Maxine Greene

It is through and by means of education . . . that individuals can be provoked to reach beyond themselves. . . . It is through and by means of education that they may become empowered to think about what they are doing, to become mindful, to share meanings, to conceptualize, to make varied sense of their lived worlds. It is through education that preferences may be released, languages learned, intelligences developed, perspectives opened, possibilities disclosed.

Maxine Greene, *The Dialectic of Freedom*

And my mama said it was bad to live in ignorance because that way it was easier for them to cheat you; you'd be more at the mercy of intelligent people.

Manlio Argueta, *One Day of Life*

[T]o spend time with a subject. That, to me, is what it means to be a writer at a university. David Bartholomae, "Writing Assignments: Where Writing Begins"

This project calls for you to explore what it means to you to become an educated person. After some reading, talking, and exploratory writing, write an essay based on your reflections about getting an education. When you talk about going to college to become educated, what do you mean?

This end-project writing could follow your educational history ("Going to College" story). Your story could be Part A, and your exploration of education could be Part B. You could, of course, also work on this project without having written your educational history.

In this essay you could focus on what it means to you, after reading and reflection, to be an educated person. You could also choose to focus on a related topic, such as formal and informal education, education and cultural dislocation or alienation, women and education, or enrollment and related issues. You could read a book related to this project. Use as sources your own experiences and observations as well as readings. These choices depend on how much time your class spends on this project and also on how much time you have to invest.

This chapter provides a framework and some resources for reflecting on "Becoming Educated." After some initial work on defining *educated*, you may want to work with several related topics or focus on one or on a book. This is slow work and difficult, especially if you examine the story (history) and various stories or readings of this word. You could build a whole course around going to college and becoming educated. Your final Writing Project portfolio could include selected written reflections on readings and discussion about becoming educated as well as your final essay. It could be interesting to reread this writing at the end of your college education and consider how you would rewrite this essay based on your educational experience.

Working Toward a Definition

To get started, begin a list of key words you associate with the word *educated* and then read Raymond Williams' story about this word.

Educated

Raymond Williams

Raymond Williams wrote about the social and cultural history of England for many years. In Keywords: A Vocabulary of Culture and Society, *Williams demonstrates how words that are key to understanding our society take on new meanings and how these changes reflect the political bent and values of society. Here he traces some changes in the meaning of the word* educated.

To **educate** was originally to rear or bring up children, from rw *educare*, L— to rear or foster (rather than from *educere*—lead forth, develop, of which *educare* is an intensive form) and fw *educationem*, L, in the same general sense. The wide sense has never quite been lost but it has been specialized to organized teaching and instruction since eC17 and predominantly so since lC18. When a majority of children had no such organized instruction the distinction between **educated** and **uneducated** was reasonably clear, but, curiously, this distinction has been more common since the development of generally organized education and even of universal education. There is a strong class sense in this use, and the level indicated by **educated** has been continually adjusted to leave the majority of people who have received an education below it. The structure has probably been assisted by the surviving general sense of bringing-up, as in *properly brought-up* which can be made to mean anything a particular group wants it to mean. **Over-educated** and **half-educated** are mC19 and especially lC19 formations; they are necessary to preserve a specializing and distinguishing use of **educated** itself. This use interacts with the specialized use of *intelligent* to distinguish a particular level or form of a faculty from the common faculty which it originally indicated. It remains remarkable that after nearly a century of universal education in Britain the majority of the population should in this use be seen as **uneducated** or **half-educated**, but whether **educated people** think of this with self-congratulation or self-reproach, or with impatience at the silliness of the usage, is for them to say.

Abbreviations

> fw: immediate forerunner of a word, in the same or another language.   2
>
> rw: ultimate traceable word, from which "root" meanings are derived.
>
> C: followed by numeral, century (C19: nineteenth century).
>
> eC: first period (third) of a century.
>
> mC: middle period (third) of a century.
>
> lC: last period (third) of a century.
>
> L: Latin.

From *Keywords: A Vocabulary of Culture and Society,* 2nd edition, by Raymond Williams, Copyright © 1976, 1983 by Raymond Williams. Reprinted by permission of Oxford University Press, New York.

What did you learn about the background of *educated?* Write three or four sentences summarizing what Williams has to say. What, according to Williams, was the original meaning of this word? How has the meaning changed?

What do you make of the use of *educated* in the advertisement for *The New York Times Magazine* (Figure 5.1)? Raymond Williams pointed out that sometimes *educated* carries a "strong class sense." Do you associate this ad with a particular class? Who reads this magazine? Why would this ad be appealing?

Defining: Educated and Uneducated

Tom McArthur

EDUCATED AND UNEDUCATED. Contrastive terms especially in sociology   1 and linguistics, used to refer to people who have or have not had formal schooling (usually to at least the end of secondary or high school), and to their usage. The contrast is often used to suggest a continuum (*more educated/less educated*), and there are three broad approaches to its use: (1) That the terms are self-evidently useful and do not risk either the self-esteem of the people discussed or the reputation of those engaged in the discussion. (2) That they can sometimes be helpful but should be used with care, because they are at least as much social as scientific judgements. A precaution often taken is to place the terms in quotation marks: *an 'educated' speaker of English.* (3) That they are best avoided unless they can be rigorously defined for certain purposes, because they risk oversimplifying or distorting complex issues and relationships and may in effect be euphemisms for distinctions of social class. The contrast appears in some contexts to be stereotypical and patronizing, implying that people are performing on an unusual level: *Educated Indian English* (compare *Cultivated Australian*). The phrase *an educated accent* is widely used to denote the accent of someone educated to at

Figure 5.1

Here's what people are saying about
The New York Times Magazine:

"*Learned;
cultured;
educated;
wise.*"

Gregory Georgieff
Senior Vice President &
Managing Director
Chubb & Son, Inc.

𝕿𝖍𝖊 𝕹𝖊𝖜 𝖄𝖔𝖗𝖐 𝕿𝖎𝖒𝖊𝖘 𝕸𝖆𝖌𝖆𝖟𝖎𝖓𝖊

There's something important in it for you.

What do you have to say about The New York Times Magazine? Send a description on the back of your
business card to: C.T. Coyle, The New York Times Advertising Department, 229 West 43d Street, New York,
N.Y. 10036. You may see your description "in print" like the ones above.

Copyright © 1994 by The New York Times Company. Reprinted by permission.

least college level, often (for some of the time at least) at a private school,
and implying (especially in Britain) that such an accent is not marked as regional, lower-class, or non-standard. See ACCENT, EDUCATED ENGLISH, STAN-
DARD ENGLISH. [EDUCATION, STYLE, VARIETY].

From *The Oxford Companion to the English Language,* edited by Tom McArthur, 1992, OUP.
Reprinted by permission.

Figure 5.2

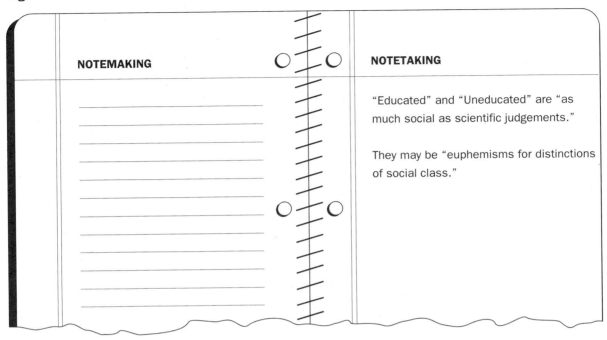

Copy the lines of Figure 5.2 in the note*taking* side of your notebook and write what you make of them on the note*making* side.

Based on your reading of the following essay, and other reading and critical thinking you've been doing, begin a page of writing with "An educated person is. . ."

Who's Educated? Who Knows?

Margo Kaufman

What is an educated person? Someone who watches public television voluntarily and cites *The Atlantic* magazine and *Harper's* instead of *People* and *Us?* Is it someone who breaks into Tennyson at odd moments or programs a computer in machine language? 1

Confucius believed that the educated person knows "the ordinances of Heaven," "the rules of propriety" and the "force of words." But some people envision a walking course catalogue. Dr. H. Keith H. Brodie, president of Duke University, suggested that the all-knowing should know "something of history and literature; of the rules and laws of the universe; of human laws, government and behavior; and something of art—how to understand and respect the play of imagination, and how to be enriched and kept whole by it." 2

Of course, while such a smartypants would do very well on a game show like "Jeopardy," he or she might be judged lacking by someone with different 3 priorities—which is just about everyone, since in high-minded circles nobody agrees on what educated people should know.

This Is Serious!

There does seem to be consensus that this is no laughing matter; even the 4
most amusing turn solemn if not downright ponderous when the subject is broached. Take Bertice Berry, a former university professor who is now a stand-up comic. "I'd have to include curriculums from a diverse group of people, whether they won the battle or not," Ms. Berry said. "Works of women, Native Americans, Hispanics and African-Americans. And they'd probably take precedence over the dead white men."

At least the well-schooled dead white men. "An educated person is often 5
an idiot," said the comedian Jackie Mason. "Having a lot of information doesn't mean you know how to deal with the reality of making intelligent adjustments in terms of real life and society. An educated person should be the kind of person who understands how to deal with people, with his job, and with his family." Not surprisingly, Mr. Mason says that by his standards he is "one of the most educated people who ever lived." But then, people often define education in self-flattering terms.

"It's someone who always wants to learn more," said the Pulitzer 6
Prize–winning playwright Wendy Wasserstein. "Someone who questions. Someone who thinks he doesn't know anything yet." Does she consider herself educated? "I still need to learn more, too," Ms. Wasserstein said.

Marjorie David, a Los Angeles writer-producer who says she was overeducated at Harvard and Columbia, suggested this definition: "It's the ability to 7
critically assess material. People who can't put information in a context respond to the most superficial things. When they watch TV and are told to buy soap they buy it. But an education teaches you to assess the soap pitch." And to be suspicious of any product described as "feminine" or "all natural" or pitched by an old coot who looks as if he stepped out of a Norman Rockwell painting.

John Callahan, the syndicated cartoonist whose latest collection is titled 8
"Do What He Says! He's Crazy!!!" declared that an educated person "knows what a cat wants for dinner" and "can read George Bush's lips." Sha-ri Pendleton, better known as Blaze on the television program "American Gladiators," felt that the educated man or woman combines the "insight of Dr. David Viscott," a radio psychologist, "the intelligence of a Nobel Peace Prize winner and the drive of Michael Jackson."

Ms. Pendleton, whose specialty is playing a female Little John in a high- 9
altitude, high-technology version of his encounter with Robin Hood on the log, said she "aspires to possess all these qualities."

English and Calculus?

Back in academia, Steven B. Sample, president of the University of Southern 10
California, said that, for an American, "to be educated means proficiency in English and the second major language of our time, calculus." Mastery of English entails "not just reading billboards and making oneself understood

in supermarkets, but having a real understanding of the literature past and present and the ability to communicate, to move people."

As for calculus, a subject that has led many a math phobic to a university 11 without distribution requirements, "it has become the lingua franca of science and technology," said Mr. Sample, a professor of electrical engineering. Fortunately, it's still not a big icebreaker at parties.

Hanna H. Gray, president of the University of Chicago, offered what 12 could be a recipe for smarts. The main ingredients include "the capacity for independent thought, a sense of relationship between different questions, a sense of history, respect for evidence and a sense of how to define and approach important questions."

L. Jay Oliva, president of New York University, seasoned the soup with 13 "strength of character, ethical behavior, understanding one's role in society as an active participant and feeling that helping other people is one of the most instructive and beneficial things you can do."

Lloyd Richards, professor emeritus at the Yale School of Drama, threw in 14 "wit, wisdom, tolerance and the ability and willingness to share."

Experts ascribe the variety of definitions to the complexity of the subject. 15 "There's no way either temporally or spatially of limiting what it means to be educated," said George Rupp, president of Rice University. "Knowledge is continually escalating, and spatially we don't have any easy limits to set around what we need to know."

Mr. Rupp pointed out that 1,000 years ago, a person who grew up in 16 Christian Europe needed to understand the traditions of biblical and Greek culture to be considered educated. "Today we ask, 'Do we have to know about Buddhism, the history of Japan prior to Westernization and all the ranges of experience the Chinese have?' And there are exactly the same kinds of questions in social sciences and natural sciences."

Luckily for those of us who never heard of Gondwanaland, fractals or 17 semiotics, Samuel Johnson postulated that knowledge is of two kinds—that which you know and that which you know how to find.

More than 2,000 years ago, Plato wrote that "The sum and substance of 18 education is the right training, which effectively leads the soul of the child at play onto the love of the calling in which he will have to be perfect when he is a man."

By this definition, Steve Smith, director of the Ringling Bros. and 19 Barnum & Bailey Clown College, is a sage. "You need the vision to know the world doesn't revolve around your ego," Mr. Smith said, "and in our case, juggling, magic, pantomime and how to ride a unicycle."

From *The New York Times*, November 1, 1992. Copyright © 1992 by The New York Times Company. Reprinted by permission.

Discuss with your peers your attempt at defining an "educated person." How do your definitions differ? Consider the viewpoints presented in the ads of Figures 5.3, 5.4, and 5.5. After your discussion, go back and write a few more lines, working further on your definition. You may want to raise a question to consider as you work your way through this project.

Figure 5.3

THERE ARE THREE THINGS EVERYONE SHOULD READ BEFORE ENTERING COLLEGE:

PLATO'S REPUBLIC, THE COMPLETE WORKS OF ARISTOTLE, AND THIS AD.

Not so fast.

If you think you can get away with ignoring the first two works and get right into this ad, stop. Rip this page out and stick it in your sock drawer.

Don't read this ad until you've first savored Plato. And discovered Aristotle, if not the complete works at least the incomplete collection, maybe the *Ethics* or the *Politics*.

Then you'll be able to deal with the Madison Avenue manipulators who market universities the same way they market sausages or deodorant soap.

Your mind will then be keen enough to dismiss the vapid slogans that university marketers conjure up to attract you, the consumers, who enter the education marketplace each spring. Slogans also designed to soothe parents whose checks enter the universities' treasuries each autumn.

(Used to be a school's slogan would be a nice Latin phrase such as *lux et veritas* or *semper paratus* or *ut omnes te cognoscant*. Now we get corporate gobbledy-gook like: People making successful people ever more successful, successfully).

If you're heading for business school, for example, you'll not only note the obvious: how many successful graduates in all fields that Adelphi can point to. You'll also investigate what you can learn at Adelphi besides LIFO, FIFO, and the other Principles of Accounting. What is it that a liberal arts environment imparts that a trade school can't?

The same is true of the psychology student or the communications major. Or the pre-law and pre-med students who are, after all, students of the Arts and Sciences, respectively.

When you visit our school, ask to see a dean, even the President. (The President of Adelphi still teaches his philosophy class every Thursday at 5:10 PM. If you drop in with an inquiring mind, he'll welcome you, albeit argumentatively).

The premise of Adelphi is that all students (whether of nursing, psychology, business, the humanities, the physical sciences, education, the fine arts) deserve the opportunity to enrich themselves by exposure to ideas.

Now: will your day-to-day involvement in those ideas make you a better investment banker? Or social worker? Or lawyer? Or high school teacher? Or nurse? Or statesman? Or accountant? Or psychologist? Or doctor? Does a liberal education make a difference in one's ability to make a living in 20th Century America. not to mention 21st Century America?

Yes. And we believe a profound difference. It has done that for 2,500 years in every corner of the world. It will be no less efficacious today in the Western Hemisphere, in the United States, on Long Island 45 minutes from Manhattan and a five-block stroll from the Nassau Blvd. station of the Long Island Railroad.

Now that you've removed this ad from your sock drawer, there are three more things to do before entering college. One, give us a call. Two, read our publications and look at our video. And three, visit our campus and say hello.

ADELPHI UNIVERSITY

Garden City, NY 11530. (516) 663-1100. For application materials and a video, write or call.

Used by permission of Adelphi University.

What does an educated person read according to the ad in Figure 5.3? What's the underlying assumption? In what ways does this ad appeal and/or not appeal to you? "An education teaches you to assess the . . . pitch," says Marjorie David (quoted in "Who's Educated? Who Knows?"). What's your assessment of this pitch? Read the advertisements of Figures 5.4 and 5.5, one for Hofstra University and one for American Indian colleges. What are they talking about when they talk about education?

Getting a "Centric" Education

School as Spin Control

Russell Baker

Russell Baker, whose autobiographical writing appears in the "Recollections & Reflections" Writing Project, writes in his Observer column for The New York Times *(October 30, 1990) about "-Centrism," an issue he says that makes education-minded people today "see red and gnash their teeth." What's he so heated up about? Read and take and make notes, then summarize his position.*

The issue that makes education-minded people see red and gnash their teeth 1
these days is -centrism. You thought it would be the swinishness of college sports programs, didn't you? If you're a behind-the-times kind of person, you probably thought it would be college graduates not knowing which country Abraham Lincoln was President of.

You were wrong. -Centrism is where the heat is. There are many varieties 2
of -centrism. Among people who like to shout at each other, the most popular are ethnocentrism, Eurocentrism and Afrocentrism.

Yes, these are the kinds of words that affect the brain like chloroform, but 3
ours is an age when people talk like the boilerplate in sociology textbooks. This enables them to talk a long time while trying to think of something to say. Nevertheless, dull though it sounds, -centrism has the power to make blood boil.

This is because it's about how education should make people feel good. It 4
assumes that education has a duty to affect people's feelings in a positive way. Let's try to illustrate:

Who do you think discovered America? If you say Columbus, it's because 5
you had a Eurocentric education. If you say Leif Ericsson, you're still from the Eurocentric school, but we are seeing obvious signs of ethnocentrism. Your education may have been Nordocentric, possibly even Norse-ocentric.

It doesn't matter here. Under -centrism theory, having America discov- 6
ered by either Ericsson or Columbus makes Americans of white European background feel good about themselves. Recently, some Americans of African background have been saying that America was actually discovered by unknown Africans who crossed the Atlantic ages ahead of the two usual European suspects.

Eurocentric education's failure to teach the African discovery is said to be 7
typical of a white racism that suffuses and poisons Eurocentric education. (You can see how -centrism could bring people to a boil.) In short, we are now seeing pressure for a more Afrocentric education.

Figure 5.4

What does it take to be the best?

Determination and hard work, at any age, can lead to being the best.
   Hofstra University, just 50 years old, is already among the
   top ten percent of American colleges and universities in
   almost all academic criteria and resources.
Professionally accredited programs in such major areas as business,
   engineering, law, psychology and education.
A library with over 1.1 million volumes *on campus*—a collection
   larger than that of 95% of American universities.
Record enrollments with students from 31 states and 59 countries—
   with a student-faculty ratio of only 17 to 1.
The largest, most sophisticated non-commercial television facility
   in the East. A high technology undergraduate teaching
   resource with broadcast-quality production capability.
A ranking in *Barron's Guide to the Most Prestigious Colleges*—one of
   only 262 colleges and universities chosen from almost 4,000.
At Hofstra, determination, inspiration and hard work are qualities
   our faculty demands in itself and instills in our students.
These qualities are what it takes to be the best. In anything.

HOFSTRA UNIVERSITY
WE TEACH SUCCESS.

50th Anniversary
Hempstead, L.I., New York 11550

Used by permission of Hofstra University.

The aim is to help Americans of black African background feel just as   8
good about themselves as Americans of white European background feel
when the discovery is discussed.

Where does this leave American Indians? Since they were here before ei-   9
ther Africans or Europeans, they surely deserve all the credit for the discovery.

Figure 5.5

LET US PUT OUR MINDS TOGETHER AND SEE WHAT LIFE WE CAN MAKE FOR OUR CHILDREN."

SITTING BULL, DAKOTA SIOUX, 1877

IN THE PAST 500 YEARS, NATIVE AMERICANS HAVE LOST MUCH OF WHAT THEY HELD DEAR. THE AMERICAN INDIAN COLLEGES REPLACE THE HARSH MEMORIES OF THE PAST WITH DIGNITY AND ACHIEVEMENT IN THE FORM OF A COLLEGE EDUCATION. THE 27 TRIBAL COLLEGES ADDRESS ECONOMIC REALITIES AND CULTURAL HERITAGE, SO THAT WHILE NATIVE AMERICANS ARE LEARNING TO BECOME FINANCIALLY INDEPENDENT, THEY ARE REAFFIRMING THEIR CULTURE AND PASSING VALUABLE LESSONS ON TO THEIR CHILDREN, THEIR COUNTRY AND THEIR WORLD. HELP SAVE A CULTURE THAT COULD SAVE OURS. GIVE TO THE AMERICAN INDIAN COLLEGE FUND, 21 WEST 68TH ST., DEPT. PS, NY, NY 10023. 1-800-776-FUND.

AMERICAN
INDIAN
COLLEGE
FUND

With your charter membership to the American Indian College Fund you'll receive this 24"x 36" poster of Sitting Bull, a timeless reminder of your concern and generosity.
Photo courtesy Paul Harbaugh and Denver Public Library, Western History Department.

Used by permission of the American Indian College Fund.

Baker

Wouldn't American Indians feel much, much better about themselves if Leif and Columbus were dropped from the curriculum, the early African discoverers put aside, and the discovery properly credited to unknown Indians?

Of course they would, and Indians have pressed the point by observ- 10 ing that since they are not a people of the East Indies and Asian subcontinent—which is to say, Indians—they prefer to be called "Native Americans." In pressing for change in the dominant Eurocentric vocabulary, these longtime Americans have taken the first step toward demanding a Native-Americocentric education.

Unforeseen problems can result from mounting evidence that Native 11 Americans descend from prehistoric Siberians who discovered the ancient New World by walking over to Alaska. It's entirely possible, such is the fierceness for control of education's powerful bias, that Americans of Siberian background will demand a more Russocentric education.

The battle for control of the schoolhouse is not confined to racial and 12 ethnic competitors, of course. Women complain that education's chauvinistocentrism denies them the chance to feel as good as men when contemplating civilization's noblest achievers.

They want a more feminocentric syllabus exalting the likes of Queen 13 Boadicea and Emily Dickinson. Homosexuals are having too tough a time right now to fling themselves with gusto into the fray. Still, they have made it clear in the past that they want American education to become gayocentric enough to start hauling more of civilization's greatest stars out of the closet.

Nor should we overlook the religious pressure groups ever busy censoring 14 textbooks and cleansing literature departments of writers who shouldn't be allowed to walk the streets with decent people. This group wants education to be upliftocentric.

What is depressing about these conflicts over -centrism is the disputants' 15 indifference to the idea that education involves training people to think clearly. Instead, they treat education as a propaganda system to be manipulated for transient social or political purposes. Which is to say, with contempt.

From *The New York Times*, October 30, 1990. Copyright © 1990 by The New York Times Company. Reprinted by permission.

Readers at Work

Education, for Baker, "involves training people to think clearly." Those educators concerned about the issue of -centrism, according to Baker, "treat education as a propaganda system." Two college students respond in the following selection.

Take and make notes. What are these college students saying? What are they upset about? What do you *make* of this issue? How do you position yourself in this argument?

Eurocentrism? We Aren't the World...

Letters

To the Editor:

When Russell Baker attacks "-centrism" in education, as in ethnocen- 1 trism ("School as Spin Control," column, Oct. 30), he fails to realize that education, especially in history, has always been partly "a propaganda system to be manipulated for transient social or political purposes."

I spent the summer of 1987 researching changes in the way the discovery 2 of America is treated in primary and secondary level textbooks published between 1870 and 1980, and found that texts have changed with the values of the times. While Mr. Baker ridicules the idea that an account that credits Leif Ericsson with the discovery could be "Nordocentric," Ericsson is most prominent in texts published in the first decade of this century, after a war with Spain and during a period in which many Anglo-Saxon Americans were calling for an end to immigration from Southern Europe.

As for Columbus, he has appeared since the Civil War as both a historical 3 figure and a hero to be emulated. As the nation changed, the positive qualities ascribed to him as a role model varied from manliness to intelligence and the persistence and hard work of a Horatio Alger Jr. hero.

The lesson this teaches is that value judgments are inherent in any ac- 4 count, so there can be no purely objective history that seeks only to "train people to think clearly." Rather than chase such a chimera, we should ask of our educational system two things: that the facts it teaches be accurate and that the values it promotes be noble.

ZACHARY SCHRAG
Cambridge, Mass., Nov. 2, 1990

The writer is a student at Harvard College.

To the Editor:

Russell Baker, in his Oct. 30 column, which attacks "-centrism," assumes 1 the reason for an educational system that is not centered on Europe is to "make people feel good." But the focus is quite different: it is the continuation of the academic responsibility to search for truth.

To ignore the possibility that America was discovered by Africans because 2 these explorers are "unknown" is irresponsible and arrogant; if we are unaware of an event, does that mean it never happened? Similarly, Mr. Baker's contention that Native Americans prefer that term "to feel good" is condescending. What justification can there be for ignoring history on which there is virtually no disagreement: namely, that the Native Americans were here first?

Mr. Baker complains that these attempts at an end to Eurocentrism "treat 3 education as a propaganda system to be manipulated for transient social or political purposes." For Mr. Baker it is "political" to search for the roots of our civilization in places other than Europe.

Universities have been "political" since they began focusing on Europe as the single base of American society. The appropriate attack rests at that point, and not with today's academics who attempt to set the record straight.

ANDREW J. PERRIN
Swarthmore, Pa., Nov. 1, 1990

The writer is a student at Swarthmore College.

Informal and Formal Education

Confessions of a Blue-Collar Worker

Linda Lavelle

"Educated stands for a whole range of experiences and feelings that may in fact have little to do with formal schooling," wrote Richard Sennett and Jonathan Cobb in The Hidden Injuries of Class *(1973). Linda Lavelle writes about her informal education, knowledge that "wasn't taught in any classroom or found in any text."*

The large brick building was a factory that made circuit breakers. There were assembly lines, spot welding machines, riveting machines, and hundreds of people handling the same small parts over and over. There were several of us naive eighteen-year-olds who, courtesy of thoughtful relatives, entered the world of concrete and noise that day. This was a place where youth had an advantage. It was bonus work, and we couldn't believe it was possible to earn so much money for performing such simple tasks. 1

As the weeks passed, and the overwhelming boredom set in, we began to realize what we were really being paid for. Forty hours a week, while our hands moved with lightning speed, our minds were free—to wander, to dwell on problems, to rot. We were being subjected to a form of mental torture—for a paycheck. Still, we were not discouraged because most of us planned to make it a temporary stay. I, for one, had my future mapped out: work for a year, buy a new car, fatten my bank account, then join VISTA (the application was safely tucked away in my desk drawer), and later start college. My plans had not allowed for getting caught in the quicksand of money and machinery. 2

A year passed, and another, and another. We were all still there, still planning to leave. Only now we looked differently at the young women, always on the verge of divorce, popping their valium, while the life was slowly sucked out of them with each movement of the assembly line. We looked differently too at the old ladies with knotted hands and varicose veins who were struggling to keep pace. It became frightening to realize these stoop-shouldered old ladies with the bitter smiles had once been young and full of dreams. We looked into their empty eyes and saw the ghost of things to come. 3

I lost my VISTA application, but I did acquire my new car, and another, 4
and a houseful of furniture—not to mention the house and husband. I
applied and was hired for more dignified positions, but I always changed
my mind. I just couldn't walk away from the high pay and good benefits. So
I continued to fill circuit breakers with little parts as the assembly line
moved on.

Like many of the others, I tried to continue my formal education. And 5
like those others, in the face of frustration and fatigue, I finally gave up. At
the same time, my informal education flourished beneath the fluorescent
lighting, although the knowledge I was acquiring wasn't taught in any classroom or found in any text. I studied business up close. I learned the intrica-
cies of the numbers operations and the going price of stolen goods. I learned
how management and unions function on the intimidation of workers, and
how to fight for rights against both of them.

I met people who taught me volumes about human behavior. I saw peo- 6
ple take amphetamines to keep up with ever-rising production rates. I saw
good friends, and even relatives, physically attack each other over job assignments that would mean a few cents' difference. I observed women
cheating on their husbands and men cheating on their wives. I watched
women hand over their entire paycheck to a bookie. I saw pregnant women,
their feet too swollen for shoes, come to work in slippers. I saw women with
colds stuff pieces of tissue up their nostrils so they wouldn't have to keep
stopping to blow their nose.

I even studied a new language—"Shop Talk"—which consists of insults 7
and profanities shouted by supervisors and workers at each other. Fluency in
this language is essential to blue-collar work, as the need for it occurs frequently. I had lessons in vocabulary as well. I learned the definitions of ob-
scenities I had never even heard before. And while the words "self respect"
were being driven from my vocabulary, the definition of dehumanization
was being driven home each day. I learned the meaning of many words, like
humiliation, when I heard two foremen referring to their workers as "the
stupid whores."

In time all the vulgarities became part of the scenery, like the peeling 8
paint on the machines or the faded partitions that covered the windows.
And when, six years after that first day, I climbed out of the quagmire to ring
out my time card for the last time, I had learned the value of a good sense of
humor. We had laughed a great deal. We joked about our "prison uniforms"
and being replaced by chimpanzees. We joked that some people pay large
sums of money to have their fingerprints removed while we were having it
done for free. We laughed about our "fringe benefits," like being able to buy
"hot items" on our breaks. We laughed at so many things that weren't
funny. We laughed at the office workers, with their small paychecks, who
looked down their prissy noses at us. We laughed, but we always glanced at
our calloused fingers and knew that we were becoming something less than
human beings.

Copyright © 1986, from *Student Writers at Work*, second edition, by Nancy Sommers and
Donald McQuade. Reprinted with permission of St. Martin's Press, Incorporated.

Rereading and Reflecting

1. What would you say Lavelle's goal was in writing this piece? How is she trying to educate her readers?
2. Write and talk about your own informal education or any significant learning experience outside school.

You could read (or listen to) some other accounts of informal education. See, for example, Maya Angelou's autobiographical account of informal education (*I Know Why the Caged Bird Sings*) or Toni Cade Bambera's short story "The Lesson." Reread Lynne Hall's account of her informal education in relation to her request that Yale University give her an opportunity for a formal education. See also Alex Haley's story ("My Furthest-Back Person—'The African'") about how he educated himself about his cultural roots. There are many reading possibilities to stimulate your thinking about the nature of education.

Education and Separation from Family & Community

Moving to an Academic Culture: A Story of Cultural Dislocation

Richard Rodriguez

Richard Rodriguez was educated at Stanford, Columbia, and Berkeley. In this selection from "Going Home Again: The New American Scholarship Boy," he draws on his own experiences and questions the price of an education that increasingly separated him from his Mexican-American parents. (See another selection, "I Remember . . .", from Hunger of Memory *in the "Recollections & Reflections" Writing Project.)*

At each step, with every graduation from one level of education to the next, the refrain from bystanders was strangely the same: "Your parents must be so proud of you." I suppose that my parents were proud, although I suspect, too, that they felt more than pride alone as they watched me advance through my education. They seemed to know that my education was separating us from one another, making it difficult to resume familiar intimacies. Mixed with the instincts of parental pride, a certain hurt also communicated itself—too private ever to be adequately expressed in words, but real nonetheless.

The autobiographical facts pertinent to this essay are simply stated in two sentences, though they exist in somewhat awkward juxtaposition to each other. I am the son of Mexican-American parents, who speak a blend of Spanish and English, but who read neither language easily. I am about to receive a Ph.D. in English Renaissance literature. What sort of life—what tensions, feelings, conflicts—connects these two sentences? I look back and remember my life from the time I was seven or eight years old as one of constant movement away from a Spanish-speaking folk culture toward the world of the English-language classroom. As the years passed, I felt myself becoming less like my parents and less comfortable with the assumptions of visiting relatives that I was still the Spanish-speaking child they remembered. By the time I began college, visits home became suffused with silent embarrassment: there seemed so little to share, however strong the ties of our affection. My parents would tell me what happened in their lives or in the lives of relatives; I would respond with news of my own. Polite questions would follow. Our conversations came to seem more like interviews.

A few months ago, my dissertation nearly complete, I came upon my father looking through my bookcase. He quietly fingered the volumes of Milton's tracts and Augustine's theology with that combination of reverence and distrust those who are not literate sometimes show for the written word. Silently, I watched him from the door of the room. However much he would have insisted that he was "proud" of his son for being able to master the texts, I knew, if pressed further, he would have admitted to complicated feelings about my success. When he looked across the room and suddenly saw me, his body tightened slightly with surprise, then we both smiled. 3

For many years I kept my uneasiness about becoming a success in education to myself. I did so in part because I wanted to avoid vague feelings that, if considered carefully, I would have no way of dealing with; and in part because I felt that no one else shared my reaction to the opportunity provided by education. When I began to rehearse my story of cultural dislocation publicly, however, I found many listeners willing to admit to similar feelings from their own pasts. Equally impressive was the fact that many among those I spoke with were *not* from nonwhite racial groups, which made me realize that one can grow up to enter the culture of the academy and find it a "foreign" culture for a variety of reasons, ranging from economic status to religious heritage. But why, I next wondered, was it that, though there were so many of us who came from childhood cultures alien to the academy's, we voiced our uneasiness to one another and to ourselves so infrequently? Why did it take *me* so long to acknowledge publicly the cultural costs I had paid to earn a Ph.D. in Renaissance English literature? Why, more precisely, am I writing these words only now when my connection to my past barely survives except as nostalgic memory? 4

Looking back, a person risks losing hold of the present while being confounded by the past. For the child who moves to an academic culture from a culture that dramatically lacks academic traditions, looking back can jeopardize the certainty he has about the desirability of this new academic culture. Richard Hoggart's description, in *The Uses of Literacy*, of the cultural pressures on such a student, whom Hoggart calls the "scholarship boy," helps make the point. The scholarship boy must give nearly unquestioning allegiance to academic culture, Hoggart argues, if he is to succeed at all, so different is the milieu of the classroom from the culture he leaves behind. For a time, the scholarship boy may try to balance his loyalty between his concretely experienced family life and the more abstract mental life of the classroom. In the end, though, he must choose between the two worlds: if he in- 5

Rodriguez

tends to succeed as a student, he must, literally and figuratively, separate himself from his family, with its gregarious life, and find a quiet place to be alone with his thoughts.

After a while, the kind of allegiance the young student might once have given his parents is transferred to the teacher, the new parent. Now without the support of the old ties and certainties of the family, he almost mechanically acquires the assumptions, practices, and style of the classroom milieu. For the loss he might otherwise feel, the scholarship boy substitutes an enormous enthusiasm for nearly everything having to do with school.

How readily I read my own past into the portrait of Hoggart's scholarship boy. Coming from a home in which mostly Spanish was spoken, for example, I had to decide to forget Spanish when I began my education. To succeed in the classroom, I needed psychologically to sever my ties with Spanish. Spanish represented an alternate culture as well as another language—and the basis of my deepest sense of relationship to my family. Although I recently taught myself to read Spanish, the language that I see on the printed page is not quite the language I heard in my youth. That other Spanish, the spoken Spanish of my family, I remember with nostalgia and guilt: guilt because I cannot explain to aunts and uncles why I do not answer their questions any longer in their own idiomatic language. Nor was I able to explain to teachers in graduate school, who regularly expected me to read and speak Spanish with ease, why my very ability to reach graduate school as a student of English literature in the first place required me to loosen my attachments to a language I spoke years earlier. Yet, having lost the ability to speak Spanish, I never forgot it so totally that I could not understand it. Hearing Spanish spoken on the street reminded me of the community I once felt a part of, and still cared deeply about. I never forgot Spanish so thoroughly, in other words, as to move outside the range of its nostalgic pull.

Such moments of guilt and nostalgia were, however, just that—momentary. They punctuated the history of my otherwise successful progress from *barrio* to classroom. Perhaps they even encouraged it. Whenever I felt my determination to succeed wavering, I tightened my hold on the conventions of academic life.

Spanish was one aspect of the problem, my parents another. They could raise deeper, more persistent doubts. They offered encouragement to my brothers and me in our work, but they also spoke, only half jokingly, about the way education was putting "big ideas" into our heads. When we would come home, for example, and challenge assumptions we earlier believed, they would be forced to defend their beliefs (which, given our new verbal skills, they did increasingly less well) or, more frequently, to submit to our logic with the disclaimer, "It's what we were taught in our time to believe. . . ." More important, after we began to leave home for college, they voiced regret about how "changed" we had become, how much further away from one another we had grown. They partly yearned for a return to the time before education assumed their children's primary loyalty. This yearning was renewed each time they saw their nieces and nephews (none of whom continued their education beyond high school, all of whom continued to speak fluent Spanish) living according to the conventions and assumptions of their parents' culture. If I was already troubled by the time I graduated from high school by that refrain of congratulations ("Your parents must be so proud. . . ."), I realize now how much more difficult and complicated was my progress into academic life for my parents, as they saw the cultural foundation of their family erode, than it was for me.

Yet my parents were willing to pay the price of alienation and continued 10 to encourage me to become a scholarship boy because they perceived, as others of the lower classes had before them, the relation between education and social mobility. Lacking the former themselves made them acutely aware of its necessity as prerequisite for the latter. They sent their children off to school in the hopes of their acquiring something "better" beyond education. Notice the assumption here that education is something of a tool or license—a means to an end, which has been the traditional way the lower or working classes have viewed the value of education in the past. That education might alter children in more basic ways than providing them with skills, certificates of proficiency, and even upward mobility, may come as a surprise for some, but the financial cost is usually tolerated.

Copyright © 1975 by Richard Rodriguez. Reprinted by permission of Georges Borchardt, Inc., for the author.

Rereading and Reflecting

"Key Words" Activity

Reread the last paragraph of the reading selection and underline "key words" Richard Rodriguez associates with getting an education.

 ## Reader's Dialogue

Reread the essay and take and make notes. Figure 5.6 presents the beginning of notes one writer took. Discuss your notemaking with two other writers in your class/community or as a whole class. Leave enough time to write briefly about the discussion.

Women and Education

A Will to Freedom

Ida Tarbell

Only men were allowed to attend Harvard University when it opened in 1636 as the first institution of higher learning in the United States. Radcliffe College, a private liberal arts college for women, was founded in 1879 as an affiliate of Harvard. In 1943 courses offered by Harvard faculty were opened to Radcliffe students, and

Figure 5.6

NOTEMAKING	NOTETAKING
(Do you think your getting a college education will separate you from your parents?)	"Your parents must be so proud of you."
	". . .my education was separating us from one another. . ."
	"As the years passed, I felt myself becoming less like my parents. . ."
	"By the time I began college, visits home became suffused with silent embarrassment: there seemed so little to share, however strong the ties of our affection."
	"Our conversations came to seem more like interviews."
	His father—mixed feelings about Richard's success
	Richard—uneasy about becoming a success in education
	Cultural dislocation
	". . .one can grow up to enter the culture of the academy and find it a 'foreign' culture for a variety of reasons. . ."

since 1963 Radcliffe graduates have received degrees from Harvard. The undergraduate school of Yale, the third oldest university (1701), was open only to men until 1969.

Cornell first opened to women in 1872. Ida Tarbell planned to attend Cornell but decided to attend Allegheny College instead, as you will learn in this selection from her autobiography All in the Day's Work (1929). Her History of the Standard Oil Company (1904) exposed the practices of some large corporations *and established her reputation as an investigative reporter. She also wrote biographies of Napoleon Bonaparte and Abraham Lincoln. According to one reviewer, "her life was a model for intelligent, independent women."*

1 Out of the agitation for rights as it came to me, two rights that were worth going after quite definitely segregated themselves: the right to an education, and the right to earn my living—education and economic independence.

2 The older I grew, the more determined I became to be independent. I saw only one way—teach; but if I was to teach I must fit myself, go to college. My father and mother agreed. I had a clear notion of what I wanted to teach—natural science, particularly the microscope, for I was to be a biologist. I made my choice—Cornell, first opened to women in 1872; but at the moment when the steps to enter Cornell were to be taken, there appeared in the household as an over-Sunday guest the president of a small college in our neighborhood, only thirty miles away, Allegheny. Among the patrons of that college was the Methodist organization known as the Erie Conference, to which the Titusville church belonged. I had heard of it annually when a representative appeared in our pulpit, told its story, and asked for support. The president, Dr. Lucius Bugbee, was a delightful and entertaining guest and, learning that I was headed Cornellward, adroitly painted the advantages of Allegheny. It was near home; it was a ward of our church. It had responded to the cry of women for educational opportunity and had opened its doors before the institution I had chosen.

3 Was not here an opportunity for a serious young woman interested in the advancement of her sex? Had I not a responsibility in the matter? If the few colleges that had opened their doors were to keep them open, if others were to imitate their example, two things were essential: women must prove they wanted a college education by supporting those in their vicinity; and they must prove by their scholarship what many doubted—that they had minds as capable of development as young men. Allegheny had not a large territory to draw from. I must be a pioneer.

4 As a matter of fact the only responsibility I had felt and assumed in going to college was entirely selfish and personal. But the sense of responsibility was not lacking nor dormant in me. It was one of the few things I had found out about myself in the shanty on the flats when I was six years old and there was a new baby in the family.

5 The woman looking after my mother had said, "Now you are old enough to make a cup of tea and take it to her." I think, in all my life since, nothing has seemed more important, more wonderful to me than this being called upon by an elder to do something for my mother, be responsible for it. I can feel that cup in my hand as I cautiously took it to the bed, and can see my mother's touching smile as she thanked me. Perhaps there came to her a realization that this rebelling, experimenting child might one day become a partner in the struggle for life so serious for her at the moment, always to be more or less serious.

6 But to return to Dr. Bugbee and his argument; before he left the house I had agreed to enter Allegheny in the fall of 1876. And that I did.

7 What did I take with me? Well, I took what from my earliest years I had been told was necessary to everyone—a Purpose, always spelled with a capital. I had an outline of the route which would lead to its realization. Making

Tarbell

outlines of what was in my mind was the one and only fruit that I had gathered so far from long terms of struggle over grammar, rhetoric, composition. Outlines which held together, I had discovered, cleared my mind, gave it something to follow. I outlined all my plans as I had diagramed sentences. It was not a poor beginning for one who eventually, and by accident rather than by intention, was to earn her living by writing—the core of which must be sound structure.

One thing by choice left out of the plan I carried from high school was 8
marriage. I would never marry. It would interfere with my plan; it would fetter my freedom. I didn't quite know what Freedom meant; certainly I was far from realizing that it exists only in the spirit, never in human relations, never in human activities—that the road to it is as often as not what men call bondage. But above all I must be free; and to be free I must be a spinster. When I was fourteen I was praying to God on my knees to keep me from marriage. I suspect that it was only an echo of the strident feminine cry filling the air at that moment, the cry that woman was a slave in a man-made world. By the time I was ready to go to college I had changed my prayer for freedom to a will to freedom. Such was the baggage I carried to college, where I was soon to find several things I had not counted on.

Excerpt from *All in the Day's Work* by Ida M. Tarbell, first published by Macmillan in 1939, and reprinted in 1985 by G. K. Hall.

Reader's Dialogue

Take and make notes on your responses to the preceding selection, using the same frame as in earlier Dialogues. Notice how Tarbell links education with independence and freedom.

Why Go to College?

Alice Freeman Palmer

In 1897, when this address was given by former Wellesley College president Alice Freeman Palmer, few women were going to college. (Ida Tarbell was an exception.) Wellesley, founded in 1870 as a private liberal arts college for women, had been open since 1875. In her address, Palmer argues that more "girls" should be going to college. Now women students make up over half of the enrollment in most colleges and universities across the nation.

Palmer's whole address, over 30 pages, is too long to include here. The selected passages, however, will help you think about differences in attitude then and now—over 100 years later—with regard to women's (and men's) going to college. Read in one sitting the opening remarks that set the tone of the address and then the excerpts included.

To a largely increasing number of young girls college doors are opening 1
every year. Every year adds to the number of men who feel as a friend of mine, a successful lawyer in the great city, felt when in talking of the future

of his four little children he said, "For the two boys it is not so serious, but I lie down at night afraid to die and leave my daughters only a bank account." Year by year, too, the experiences of life are teaching mothers that happiness does not necessarily come to their daughters when accounts are large and banks are sound, but that on the contrary they take grave risks when they trust everything to accumulated wealth and the chance of a happy marriage. Our American girls themselves are becoming aware that they need the stimulus, the discipline, the knowledge, the interests of the college in addition to the school, if they are to prepare themselves for the most serviceable lives.

But there are still parents who say, "There is no need that my daughter should teach; then why should she go to college?" I will not reply that college training is a life insurance for a girl, a pledge that she possesses the disciplined ability to earn a living for herself and others in case of need; for I prefer to insist on the importance of giving every girl, no matter what her present circumstances, a special training in some one thing by which she can render society service, not amateur but of an expert sort, and service too for which it will be willing to pay a price. The number of families will surely increase who will follow the example of an eminent banker whose daughters have been given each her specialty. One has chosen music, and has gone far with the best masters in this country and in Europe, so far that she now holds a high rank among musicians at home and abroad. Another has taken art; and has not been content to paint pretty gifts for her friends, but in the studios of New York, Munich, and Paris, she has won the right to be called an artist, and in her studio at home to paint portraits which have a market value. A third has proved that she can earn her living, if need be, by her exquisite jellies, preserves, and sweetmeats. Yet the house in the mountains, the house by the sea, and the friends in the city are not neglected, nor are these young women found less attractive because of their special accomplishments.

While it is not true that all girls should go to college any more than that all boys should go, it is nevertheless true that they should go in greater numbers than at present. They fail to go because they, their parents, and their teachers, do not see clearly the personal benefits distinct from the commercial value of a college training. I wish here to discuss these benefits, these larger gifts of the college life—what they may be, and for whom they are waiting.

It is undoubtedly true that many girls are totally unfitted by home and school life for a valuable college course. These joys and successes, these high interests and friendships, are not for the self-conscious and nervous invalid, nor for her who in the exuberance of youth recklessly ignores the laws of a healthy life. The good society of scholars and of libraries and laboratories has no place and no attraction for her who finds no message in Plato, no beauty in mathematical order, and who never longs to know the meaning of the stars over her head or the flowers under her feet. Neither will the finer opportunities of college life appeal to one who, until she is eighteen (is there such a girl in this country?), has felt no passion for the service of others, no desire to know if through history, or philosophy, or any study of the laws of society, she can learn why the world is so sad, so hard, so selfish as she finds it, even when she looks upon it from the most sheltered life. No, the college

Palmer

cannot be, should not try to be, a substitute for the hospital, reformatory, or kindergarten. To do its best work it should be organized for the strong, not for the weak; for the high-minded, self-controlled, generous, and courageous spirits, not for the indifferent, the dull, the idle, or those who are already forming their characters on the amusement theory of life. All these perverted young people may, and often do, get large benefit and invigoration, new ideals, and unselfish purposes from their four years' companionship with teachers and comrades of a higher physical, mental, and moral stature than their own. I have seen girls change so much in college that I have wondered if their friends at home would know them—the voice, the carriage, the unconscious manner, all telling a story of new tastes and habits and loves and interests, that had wrought out in very truth a new creature. Yet in spite of this I have sometimes thought that in college more than elsewhere the old law holds, "To him that hath shall be given and he shall have abundance, but from him who hath not shall be taken away even that which he seemeth to have." For it is the young life which is open and prepared to receive which obtains the gracious and uplifting influences of college days. What, then, for such persons are the rich and abiding rewards of study in college or university?

Pre-eminently the college is a place of education. That is the ground of its 5 being. We go to college to know, assured that knowledge is sweet and powerful, that a good education emancipates the mind and makes us citizens of the world. No college which does not thoroughly educate can be called good, no matter what else it does. No student who fails to get a little knowledge on many subjects, and much knowledge on some, can be said to have succeeded, whatever other advantages she may have found by the way.

. . . . .

. . . I want to point out some of these collateral advantages of going to 6 college, or rather to draw attention to some of the many forms in which the winning of knowledge presents itself.

The first of these is happiness. Everybody wants "a good time," especially 7 every girl in her teens. A good time, it is true, does not always in these years mean what it will mean by and by, any more than the girl of eighteen plays with the doll which entranced the child of eight. It takes some time to discover that work is the best sort of play, and some people never discover it at all. But when mothers ask such questions as these: "How can I make my daughter happy?" "How can I give her the best society?" "How can she have a good time?" the answer in most cases is simple. Send her to college—to almost any college. Send her because there is no other place where between eighteen and twenty-two she is so likely to have a genuinely good time. Merely for good times, for romance, for society, college life offers unequalled opportunities. Of course no idle person can possibly be happy, even for a day, nor she who makes a business of trying to amuse herself. For full happiness, though its springs are within, we want health and friends and work and objects of aspiration. "We live by admiration, hope, and love," says Wordsworth. The college abounds in all three.

. . . . .

Yet a girl should go to college not merely to obtain four happy years, but 8
to make a second gain, which is often overlooked, and is little understood
even when perceived; I mean a gain in health. The old notion that low vitality is a matter of course with women; that to be delicate is a mark of superior
refinement, especially in well-to-do families; that sickness is a dispensation
of Providence—these notions meet with no acceptance in college.

· · · · ·

It is significant that already statistical investigation in this country and 9
in England shows that the standard of health is higher among the women
who hold college degrees than among any other equal number of the same
age and class.

· · · · ·

Until a girl goes away from home to school or college, her friends are 10
chiefly chosen for her by circumstances. Her young relatives, her neighbors
in the same street, those who happen to go to the same school or church—
these she makes her girlish intimates. She goes to college with the entire
conviction, half unknown to herself, that her father's political party contains all the honest men, her mother's social circle all the true ladies, her
church all the real saints of the community. And the smaller the town, the
more absolute is her belief. But in college she finds that the girl who earned
her scholarship in the village school sits beside the banker's daughter; the
New England farmer's child rooms next the heiress of a Hawaiian sugar plan-
tation; the daughters of the opposing candidates in a sharply fought election
have grown great friends in college boats and laboratories; and before her
diploma is won she realizes how much richer a world she lives in than she
ever dreamed of at home. The wealth that lies in differences has dawned
upon her vision.

The old fairy story which charmed us in childhood ended with—"And 11
they were married and lived happy ever after." It conducted to the altar, having brought the happy pair through innumerable difficulties, and left us
with the contented sense that all the mistakes and problems would now
vanish and life be one long day of unclouded bliss: I have seen devoted and
intelligent mothers arrange their young daughters' education and companionship precisely on this basis. They planned as if these pretty and charming
girls were going to live only twenty or twenty-five years at the utmost, and
had consequently no need of the wealthy interests that should round out
the full-grown woman's stature, making her younger in feeling at forty than
at twenty, and more lovely and admired at eighty than at either.

Emerson in writing of beauty declares that "the secret of ugliness consists 12
not in irregular outline, but in being uninteresting. We love any forms, however ugly, from which great qualities shine. If command, eloquence, art, or
invention exists in the most deformed person, all the accidents that usually
displease, please, and raise esteem and wonder higher. Beauty without grace
is the head without the body. Beauty without expression tires.

· · · · ·

But her elders know, looking on, that our American girl, the comrade of 13
her parents and of her brothers and their friends, brought up from baby-
hood in the eager talk of politics and society, of religious belief, of public action, of social responsibility—that this typical girl, with her quick sympa-
thies, her clear head, her warm heart, her outreaching hands, will not
permanently be satisfied or self-respecting, though she have the prettiest
dresses and hats in town, or the most charming of dinners, dances, and teas.
Unless there comes to her, and comes early, the one chief happiness of life—
a marriage of comradeship—she must face for herself the question, "What
shall I do with my life?"

.   .   .   .   .

. . . Our serious, non-producing classes are chiefly women. It is the regu- 14
lar ambition of the chivalrous American to make all the women who depend
on him so comfortable that they need do nothing for themselves. Machinery has taken nearly all the former occupations of women out of the
home into the shop and factory. Widespread wealth and comfort, and the
inherited theory that it is not well for the woman to earn money so long as
father or brothers can support her, have brought about a condition of things
in which there is social danger, unless with the larger leisure are given high
and enduring interests. To health especially there is great danger, for nothing breaks down a woman's health like idleness and its resulting *ennui*. More
people, I am sure, are broken down nervously because they are bored, than
because they are overworked; and more still go to pieces through fussiness,
unwholesome living, worry over petty details, and the daily disappoint-
ments which result from small and superficial training. And then, besides
the danger to health, there is the danger to character. I need not dwell on
the undermining influence which men also feel when occupation is taken
away and no absorbing private interest fills the vacancy.

.   .   .   .   .

. . .The regular occupations of women in their homes are generally dis- 15
connected and of little educational value, at least as those homes are at present conducted. Given the best will in the world, the daily doing of household details becomes a wearisome monotony if the mere performance of
them is all. To make drudgery divine a woman must have a brain to plan and
eyes to see how to "sweep a room as to God's laws." Imagination and knowledge should be the hourly companions of her who would make a fine art of
each detail in kitchen and nursery.

. . . And why should our daughters remain aloof from the most absorbing 16
work of modern city life, work quite as fascinating to young women as to
young men? . . . It has been well said that the ability to see great things large
and little things small is the final test of education. The foes of life, especially of women's lives, are caprice, wearisome incapacity, and petty judgments. From these oppressive foes we long to escape to the rule of right reason, where all things are possible, and life becomes a glory instead of a grind.

No college, with the best teachers and collections in the world, can by its own power impart all this to any woman. But if one has set her face in that direction, where else can she find so many hands reached out to help, so many encouraging voices in the air, so many favoring influences filling the days and nights?

Excerpts from *Why Go to College? Selections from an Address* by Alice Freeman Palmer, published in 1897 by Thomas Y. Crowell & Company, Boston.
Note: I thank Susie Williams for finding this book for me in a used bookstore in Ithaca, New York. She was a basic writing instructor and is now an Educational Opportunity Program (EOP) counselor and study skills instructor (Binghamton University, State University of New York). She also helps with T.A. training for the summer Binghamton Enrichment Program.

Reader's Dialogue

Making Connections: A Guide for Rereading and Notemaking

Focus: As you reread, think about the contrast between parental expectations of daughters (and sons) in the late 1800s, as described by Palmer, and parental expectations you have observed in recent times. Consider gender, race, and class differences then and now. The comparison frame of Figure 5.7 is a way of assessing your results.

Guiding Questions

The questions that follow are not provided to check your reading; rather, they are meant to stimulate your thinking about what you are reading and to help you consider more fully your own background with regard to going to college.

Read through the first group of questions once and then reread the corresponding excerpts of Palmer's talk, using the comparison frame following the questions as a way of noting differences. Some categories (the value of college, for example) are more speculative than others and invite you to try out some reflections which you may want to adjust later as you continue to read, write, and talk with others. You may want to add other categories or rephrase a category. You can use this way of notetaking about comparisons for other reading and writing as well.

1. Locate phrases or lines that help you as a reader determine the social class of people Palmer is talking about here. Do you think Palmer's description holds across classes or is it limited to a particular class? What class of people were likely to be in the audience she was addressing? What race were most women going to Wellesley College in 1897 likely to be?
2. Who goes to college today? Could anyone go to college in the late 1800s? Can anyone go to *any* college today? How have admission criteria changed?

Figure 5.7

	Comparison Frame	
Category	**Then**	**Now**
Admission standards (selectivity)		
Gender, no. of women in college		
Parental attitude & gender		
Career/ Occupations & gender		
Race		
Class		
The value of college		

3. Would you say most parents today believe it is equally important for daughters as for sons to go to college?
4. If women did go to college in the late 1800s, what occupations were they likely to pursue? What changes do you see now with regard to careers for women? What occupations are women you know considering? Would these have been likely choices during Palmer's time?

Palmer argues that more "girls" should go to college. "They fail to go," she says, "because they, their parents, and their teachers, do not see clearly the personal benefits distinct from the commercial value of a college training." To what extent today do you think students (male and female) go to college for the "commercial value"—or extrinsic rather than intrinsic rewards?

More Notes

What, according to Palmer, are the "larger gifts" of college life? Why is happiness going to college? Read the last excerpts related to this subject, take notes, and summarize. Then reread your notes and write briefly about your reading.

Reread the last excerpt, the closing of Palmer's address. What do you take Palmer to mean when she says that "no college, with the best teachers and collections in the world, can by its own power impart all of this to any woman"? What is your reading? What do you make of this line?

Then & Now

Return to the *focus* at the beginning of "Reader's Dialogue." Reread your notes and write a page or two (as long as you can write) about differences, then and now, with regard to going to college.

Claiming an Education

Adrienne Rich

"It is only within the last hundred years that higher education has grudgingly been opened up to women at all, even to white, middle-class women," explained Adrienne Rich in a talk given to new students at Douglass College, the Women's College of Rutgers University, on September 6, 1977. This talk was later included in her book On Lies, Secrets, and Silence *(1979). Rich, a noted teacher, essayist, and feminist, won the National Book Award for poetry in 1974.*

For this convocation, I planned to separate my remarks into two parts: some 1 thoughts about you, the women students here, and some thoughts about us who teach in a women's college. But ultimately, those two parts are indivisible. If university education means anything beyond the processing of human beings into expected roles, through credit hours, tests, and grades (and I believe that in a women's college especially it *might* mean much more), it implies an ethical and intellectual contract between teacher and student. This contract must remain intuitive, dynamic, unwritten; but we must turn to it again and again if learning is to be reclaimed from the depersonalizing and cheapening pressures of the present-day academic scene.

The first thing I want to say to you who are students, is that you cannot 2 afford to think of being here to *receive* an education; you will do much better to think of yourselves as being here to *claim* one. One of the dictionary definitions of the verb "to claim" is: *to take as the rightful owner; to assert in the face of possible contradiction.* "To receive" is *to come into possession of; to act as receptacle or container for; to accept as authoritative or true.* The difference is that between acting and being acted-upon, and for women it can literally mean the difference between life and death.

One of the devastating weaknesses of university learning, of the store of 3 knowledge and opinion that has been handed down through academic training, has been its almost total erasure of women's experience and thought from the curriculum, and its exclusion of women as members of the academic community. Today, with increasing numbers of women students in nearly every branch of higher learning, we still see very few women in the upper levels of faculty and administration in most institutions. Douglass College itself is a women's college in a university administered overwhelmingly by men, who in turn are answerable to the state legislature, again composed predominantly of men. But the most significant fact for you is that

Rich

what you learn here, the very texts you read, the lectures you hear, the way your studies are divided into categories and fragmented one from the other— all this reflects, to a very large degree, neither objective reality, nor an accurate picture of the past, nor a group of rigorously tested observations about human behavior. What you can learn here (and I mean not only at Douglass but any college in any university) is how *men* have perceived and organized their experience, their history, their ideas of social relationships, good and evil, sickness and health, etc. When you read or hear about "great issues," "major texts," "the mainstream of Western thought," you are hearing about what men, above all white men, in their male subjectivity, have decided is important.

Black and other minority peoples have for some time recognized that 4 their racial and ethnic experience was not accounted for in the studies broadly labeled human; and that even the sciences can be racist. For many reasons, it has been more difficult for women to comprehend our exclusion, and to realize that even the sciences can be sexist. For one thing, it is only within the last hundred years that higher education has grudgingly been opened up to women at all, even to white, middle-class women. And many of us have found ourselves poring eagerly over books with titles like: *The Descent of Man; Man and His Symbols; Irrational Man; The Phenomenon of Man; The Future of Man; Man and the Machine; From Man to Man; May Man Prevail?; Man, Science and Society;* or *One-Dimensional Man*—books pretending to describe a "human" reality that does not include over one-half the human species.

Less than a decade ago, with the rebirth of a feminist movement in this 5 country, women students and teachers in a number of universities began to demand and set up women's studies courses—to *claim* a woman-directed education. And, despite the inevitable accusations of "unscholarly," "group therapy," "faddism," etc., despite backlash and budget cuts, women's studies are still growing, offering to more and more women a new intellectual grasp on their lives, new understanding of our history, a fresh vision of the human experience, and also a critical basis for evaluating what they hear and read in other courses, and in the society at large.

But my talk is not really about women's studies, much as I believe in 6 their scholarly, scientific, and human necessity. While I think that any Douglass student has everything to gain by investigating and enrolling in women's studies courses, I want to suggest that there is a more essential experience that you owe yourselves, one which courses in women's studies can greatly enrich, but which finally depends on you, in all your interactions with yourself and your world. This is the experience of *taking responsibility toward yourselves*. Our upbringing as women has so often told us that this should come second to our relationships and responsibilities to other people. We have been offered ethical models of the self-denying wife and mother; intellectual models of the brilliant but slapdash dilettante who never commits herself to anything the whole way, or the intelligent woman who denies her intelligence in order to seem more "feminine," or who sits in passive silence even when she disagrees inwardly with everything that is being said around her.

Responsibility to yourself means refusing to let others do your thinking, 7
talking, and naming for you; it means learning to respect and use your own
brains and instincts; hence, grappling with hard work. It means that you do
not treat your body as a commodity with which to purchase superficial intimacy or economic security; for our bodies and minds are inseparable in this
life, and when we allow our bodies to be treated as objects, our minds are in
mortal danger. It means insisting that those to whom you give your friendship and love are able to respect your mind. It means being able to say, with
Charlotte Brontë's *Jane Eyre:* "I have an inward treasure born with me, which
can keep me alive if all the extraneous delights should be withheld or offered only at a price I cannot afford to give."

Responsibility to yourself means that you don't fall for shallow and easy 8
solutions—predigested books and ideas, weekend encounters guaranteed to
change your life, taking "gut" courses instead of ones you know will challenge you, bluffing at school and life instead of doing solid work, marrying
early as an escape from real decisions, getting pregnant as an evasion of already existing problems. It means that you refuse to sell your talents and aspirations short, simply to avoid conflict and confrontation. And this, in
turn, means resisting the forces in society which say that women should be
nice, play safe, have low professional expectations, drown in love and forget
about work, live through others, and stay in the places assigned to us. It
means that we insist on a life of meaningful work, insist that work be as
meaningful as love and friendship in our lives. It means, therefore, the
courage to be "different"; not to be continuously available to others when
we need time for ourselves and our work; to be able to demand of others—
parents, friends, roommates, teachers, lovers, husbands, children—that they
respect our sense of purpose and our integrity as persons. Women everywhere are finding the courage to do this, more and more, and we are finding
that courage both in our study of women in the past who possessed it, and
in each other as we look to other women for comradeship, community, and
challenge. The difference between a life lived actively, and a life of passive
drifting and dispersal of energies, is an immense difference. Once we begin
to feel committed to our lives, responsible to ourselves, we can never again
be satisfied with the old, passive way.

Now comes the second part of the contract. I believe that in a women's 9
college you have the right to expect your faculty to take you seriously. The
education of women has been a matter of debate for centuries, and old, negative attitudes about women's role, women's ability to think and take leadership, are still rife both in and outside the university. Many male professors
(and I don't mean only at Douglass) still feel that teaching in a women's college is a second-rate career. Many tend to eroticize their women students—
treat them as sexual objects—instead of demanding the best of their minds.
(At Yale a legal suit [*Alexander v. Yale*] has been brought against the university
by a group of women students demanding a stated policy against sexual ad-
vances toward female students by male professors.) Many teachers, both
men and women, trained in the male-centered tradition, are still handing
the ideas and texts of that tradition on to students without teaching them to
criticize its antiwoman attitudes, its omission of women as part of the

Rich

species. Too often, all of us fail to teach the most important thing, which is that clear thinking, active discussion, and excellent writing are all necessary for intellectual freedom, and that these require *hard work*. Sometimes, perhaps in discouragement with a culture which is both anti-intellectual and anti-woman, we may resign ourselves to low expectations for our students before we have given them half a chance to become more thoughtful, expressive human beings. We need to take to heart the words of Elizabeth Barrett Browning, a poet, a thinking woman, and a feminist, who wrote in 1845 of her impatience with studies which cultivate a "passive recipiency" in the mind, and asserted that "women want to be made to *think actively:* their apprehension is quicker than that of men, but their defect lies for the most part in the logical faculty and in the higher mental activities." Note that she implies a defect which can be remedied by intellectual training; *not* an inborn lack of ability.

I have said that the contract on a student's part involves that you demand to be taken seriously so that you can also go on taking yourself seriously. This means seeking out criticism, recognizing that the most affirming thing anyone can do for you is demand that you push yourself further, show you the range of what you *can* do. It means rejecting attitudes of "take-it-easy," "why-be-so-serious," "why-worry-you'll-probably-get-married-anyway." It means assuming your share of responsibility for what happens in the classroom, because that affects the quality of your daily life here. It means that the student sees herself engaged *with* her teachers in an active, ongoing struggle for a real education. But for her to do this, her teachers must be committed to the belief that women's minds and experience are intrinsically valuable and indispensable to any civilization worthy the name; that there is no more exhilarating and intellectually fertile place in the academic world today than a women's college—*if* both students and teachers in large enough numbers are trying to fulfill this contract. The contract is really a pledge of mutual seriousness about women, about language, ideas, methods, and values. It is our shared commitment toward a world in which the inborn potentialities of so many women's minds will no longer be wasted, raveled-away, paralyzed, or denied.

10

Reprinted from *On Lies, Secrets, and Silence: Selected Prose 1966–1978*, by Adrienne Rich, by permission of the author and W.W. Norton & Company, Inc. Copyright © 1979 by W.W. Norton & Company, Inc.

Reader's Dialogue

The notes in the comparison frame of Figure 5.8 are intended to help you get started. You could begin here and continue with your own reading notes. Use Rich's talk as a resource for helping you reflect further on "getting an education." Continue with your own notes now. How can you incorporate your reading and reflections on "women and education" into your end-project essay? Your reflections could become part of what you want to say or could become the focus.

Figure 5.8

NOTEMAKING	NOTETAKING
What do you understand Rich to mean here?	"You cannot afford to think of being here to *receive* an education; you will do much better to think of yourselves as being here to *claim* one."
Rich made this statement in the 1970s. Would you say this is true in the 1990s? Is this true in the courses you are now taking or took in college? The number of women and men going to college is now roughly equal. What about the faculty at your school? Are there more males than females?	"One of the devastating weaknesses of university learning. . . has been its almost total erasure of women's prior experience and thought from the curriculum and its exclusion of women as members of the academic community."

Enrollment Issues in Education

Intense College Recruiting Drives Lift Black Enrollment to a Record

Michel Marriott

Black enrollment in colleges and universities reached record highs in the 1 late 1980's largely because the schools developed extensive recruiting programs to tutor, counsel and provide financial aid to prospective students, educators and sociologists say.

Seeking to explain a surge in enrollment figures released last month by 2 the Federal Department of Education, the experts said in interviews that efforts to stress to black young people the importance of higher education had found an increasingly receptive audience, mostly among young women.

The Department of Education figures showed that black enrollment had 3 ended a long downward trend. Young women accounted for much of the increase, and the sociologists and educators said that fact supported the view

Marriott

that young black men generally seemed to find it difficult to believe college was a viable option for them.

But now colleges and universities are using more and more tutoring and guidance counseling programs to raise black interest. They have also expanded their student financial assistance programs to make up for a shrinkage in Federal budgets of the 1980's. The result has been a reversal of a troubling trend, educators say. 4

"We are beginning to see a collection of institutions, both black and white, that are helping black students understand again that the single most important route out of poverty is education," said Benjamin F. Payton, president of Tuskegee University in Alabama. "To have a high school diploma alone is not considered to be an adequate education in a world increasingly driven by science and technology." 5

Sexes' Enrollments: A Gulf?

From 1986 to 1988, the Federal Department of Education says, non-Hispanic black college enrollment rose to 1.13 million students from 1.08 million. The previous high was 1.10 million students in 1980. 6

Total enrollment in American colleges was 12 million in 1980 and 13 million in 1988. 7

Among young black women, enrollment rose to 687,000 from 646,000 from 1986 to 1988, but in the same period, black male enrollment rose only to 443,000 from 436,000, raising concern that an economic gulf was developing between black men and women. 8

Dr. Troy Duster, a sociologist at the University of California at Berkeley, said poor black men were more likely than poor black women to be influenced by "macho" attitudes, and that those attitudes made it likely that they would be driven into crime. 9

"Girls don't tend to get involved as much in these kinds of male bonding activities: gang life, sports," said Dr. Duster, the director of the Institute for the Study of Social Change of the University of California at Berkeley. But he added that black culture itself has always affirmed the importance of education; black females simply had fewer counterforces to keep them from responding. 10

Why Not the Ivy League?

Last month, the National Institute of Independent Colleges and Universities, based in Washington, said in a report based on the Education Department's findings that the greatest increase in black enrollment had come at private institutions. In the period examined, black enrollment increased by 7.1 percent in private institutions as against 0.2 percent in public colleges and universities. 11

There is concern on the part of educators and parents, however, that fewer black students are attending Ivy League and similarly prestigious institutions. 12

"This year we saw a decrease in black applicants," said Jennifer Carey, the senior admissions and financial aid officer at Harvard University. "We've been listening to other Ivy League schools and the message is fairly consistent: there is a noticeable decline." 13

A Rise in College Fund Schools

Most black college students are in public institutions of higher education, 14 whose costs and requirements are comparatively modest. There were 881,000 black students in publicly supported colleges and universities in 1988, as against 248,000 in private institutions, the Education Department says.

Officials of the United Negro College Fund concurred in the Federal findings, but spokesmen for the fund said their research had not found a decrease in black male enrollment among the 41 black colleges and universities that are affiliated with the fund.

From *The New York Times,* April 15, 1990. Copyright © 1990 by The New York Times Company. Reprinted by permission.

Reader's Dialogue

A Guide to Notetaking & Notemaking

1. From 1980 to 1986, black enrollment in higher education fell nationally. According to this article, why did black enrollment in colleges and universities reach record highs in the late 1980s?
2. What was the total enrollment in American colleges in 1980? In 1988?
3. Contrast the enrollment figures for young black women and young black men in 1986 and 1988. What question does this difference raise?
4. What are some possible explanations for this difference? Reread paragraphs 3, 9, and 10. Take notes and summarize and then make a notebook entry response in which you continue speculating and/or questioning the explanations given in this article.
5. Why were fewer black students applying to Ivy League schools during this period? What can you infer from reading this article?
6. According to a report by the American Council on Education (February 28, 1994), there has been a 5 percent drop in university enrollment by black men over the last two years.

   Rate of Enrollment of High School Graduates, ages 18-24
   1992   33.8 percent   Black
           37.1 percent   Hispanic
           42.2 percent   White

   Black Males Enrolled in College
   1972   21.0 percent
   1980   17.3 percent
   1990   26.1 percent
   1992   21.2 percent

   College enrollment for black women, on the other hand, has almost doubled in the past 20 years.
   1972   15.7 percent
   1992   28.8 percent

Hispanic Males Enrolled in College
1972 15.1 percent
1987 18.5 percent
1992 17.8 percent
Study these enrollment figures and speculate further, adding to your notebook entry in preparation for some class discussion.

More Dialogue

Speculate

While access to higher education has increased for many underrepresented groups, graduation rates for "blacks and Hispanics" were down at the beginning of this decade. According to a 1991 report by the American Council on Education (ACE) only 30.3 percent of blacks and 32.3 percent of Hispanics going right from high school to a four-year college earned their degrees, compared to 55.5 percent among white students and 49.8 percent among Asian-Americans. Speculate about the reasons for the differences reported. (See also articles about admission quotas for Asian-Americans in Chapter 6, the "Reading the News" Writing Project.)

Talk Back

Talk back to the next three articles in whatever form you choose. You could do some focused freewriting based on a sentence or passage, or on your overall response. Voice your views from your position based on your cultural background and interactions with students from different backgrounds.

Pedagogy and Political Commitment: A Comment

bell hooks

bell hooks has written widely on the politics of race, gender, and class. This essay is a chapter from her book Talking Back: Thinking Feminist, Thinking Black *(1989). More of her writing (about her name change) appears on page 25 in the "Recollections & Reflections" Writing Project.*

Education is a political issue for exploited and oppressed people. The history of slavery in the United States shows that black people regarded education—book learning, reading, and writing—as a political necessity. Struggle to resist white supremacy and racist attacks informed black attitudes toward education. Without the capacity to read and write, to think critically and analytically, the liberated slave would remain forever bound, dependent on the will of the oppressor. No aspect of black liberation struggled in the United States has been as charged with revolutionary fervor as the effort to gain access to education at all levels.

From slavery to the present, education has been revered in black com- 2
munities, yet it has also been suspect. Education represented a means of radical resistance but it also led to caste/class divisions between the educated
and the uneducated, as it meant the learned black person could more easily
adopt the values and attitudes of the oppressor. Education could help one as-
similate. If one could not become the white oppressor, one could at least
speak and think like him or her, and in some cases the educated black person assumed the role of mediator—explaining uneducated black folks to
white folks.

Given this history, many black parents have encouraged children to ac- 3
quire an education while simultaneously warning us about the danger of education. One very real danger, as many black parents traditionally perceived
it, was that the learned black person might lose touch with the concrete reality of everyday black experience. Books and ideas were important but not
important enough to become barriers between the individual and community participation. Education was considered to have the potential to alien-
ate one from community and awareness of our collective circumstance as
black people. In my family, it was constantly emphasized that too much
book learning could lead to madness. Among everyday black folks, madness
was deemed to be any loss of one's ability to communicate effectively with
others, one's ability to cope with practical affairs.

These ambivalent attitudes toward education have made it difficult for 4
black students to adapt and succeed in educational settings. Many of us have
found that to succeed at the very education we had been encouraged to seek
would be most easily accomplished if we separated ourselves from the experience of black folk, the underprivileged experience of the black underclass
that was our grounding reality. This ambivalent stance toward education has
had a tremendous impact on my psyche. Within the working-class black
community where I grew up, I learned to be suspicious of education and suspicious of white folks. I went for my formative educational years to all-black
schools. In those schools, I learned about the reality of white people but also
about the reality of black people, about our history. We were taught in those
schools to be proud of ourselves as black people and to work for the uplift of
our race.

Experiencing as I did an educational environment structured to meet our 5
needs as black people, we were deeply affected when those schools ceased to
exist and we were compelled to attend white schools instead. At the white
school, we were no longer people with a history, a culture. We did not exist
as anything other than primitives and slaves. School was no longer the place
where one learned how to use education as a means to resist white-suprema-
cist oppression. Small wonder that I spent my last few years of high school
depressed about education, feeling as though we had suffered a grave loss,
that the direction had shifted, the goals had changed. We were no longer
taught by people who spoke our language, who understood our culture; we
were taught by strangers. And further, we were dependent on those strangers
for evaluation, for approval. We learned not to challenge their racism since
they had power over us. Although we were told at home that we were not to
openly challenge whites, we were also told not to learn to think like them.

hooks

Within this atmosphere of ambivalence toward education, I, who had been dubbed smart, was uncertain whether or not I wanted to go to college. School was an oppressive drag. Yet the fate of smart black women had already been decided; we would be schoolteachers. At the private, mostly white women's college where I spent my first year, I was an outsider. Determined to stay grounded in the reality of southern black culture, I kept myself aloof from the social practices of the white women with whom I lived and studied. They, in their turn, perceived me as hostile and alien. I, who had always been a member of the community, was now a loner. One of my white teachers suggested to me that the alienation I experienced was caused by being at a school that was not intellectually challenging, that I should go to Stanford where she had gone. 6

My undergraduate years at Stanford were difficult ones. Not only did I feel myself alienated from the white people who were my peers and teachers, but I met black people who were different, who did not think the way I did about black culture or black life—who seemed in some ways as strange to me as white people. I had known black people from different classes in my hometown, but we still experienced much the same reality, shared similar world views. It was different at Stanford. I was in an environment where black people's class backgrounds and their values were radically different than my own. 7

To overcome my feelings of isolation, I bonded with workers, with black women who labored as maids, as secretaries. With them I felt at home. During holiday break, I would stay in their homes. Yet being with them was not the same as being home. In their houses I was an honored guest, someone to be looked up to, because I was getting a college education. My undergraduate years at Stanford were spent struggling to find meaning and significance in education. I had to succeed. I could not let my family or the race down. And so I graduated in English. I had become an English major for the same reason that hundreds of students of all races become English majors: I like to read. Yet I did not fully understand that the study of literature in English departments would really mean the study of works by white males. 8

It was disheartening for me and other non-white students to face the extent to which education in the university was not the site of openness and intellectual challenge we had longed for. We hated the racism, the sexism, the domination. I began to have grave doubts about the future. Why was I working to be an academic if I did not see people in that environment who were opposing domination? Even those very few concerned professors who endeavored to make courses interesting, to create a learning atmosphere, rarely acknowledged destructive and oppressive aspects of authoritarian rule in and outside the classroom. Whether one took courses from professors with feminist politics or marxist politics, their presentations of self in the classroom never differed from the norm. This was especially so with marxist professors. I asked one of these professors, a white male, how he could expect students to take his politics seriously as a radical alternative to a capitalist structure if we found marxist professors to be even more oppressively authoritarian than other professors. Everyone seemed reluctant to talk about the fact that professors who advocated radical politics rarely allowed their critique of domination and oppression to influence teaching strategies. The 9 absence of any model of a professor who was combining a radical politic opposing domination with practice of that politic in the classroom made me feel wary about my ability to do differently. When I first began to teach, I tried not to emulate my professors in any way. I devised different strategies and approaches that I felt were more in keeping with my politics. Reading the work of Paulo Freire greatly influenced my sense that much was possible in the classroom setting, that one did not simply need to conform.

In the introduction to a conversation with Paulo Freire published in *idac,* 10 emphasis is placed on an educative process that is not based on an authoritarian, dominating model where knowledge is transferred from a powerful professor to a powerless student. Education, it was suggested, could be a space for the development of critical consciousness, where there could be dialogue and mutual growth of both student and professor:

> If we accept education in this richer and more dynamic sense of acquiring 11 a critical capacity and intervention in reality, we immediately know that there is no such thing as neutral education. All education has an intention, a goal, which can only be political. Either it mystifies reality by rendering it impenetrable and obscure—which leads people to a blind march through incomprehensible labyrinths—or it unmasks the economic and social structures which are determining the relationships of exploitation and oppression among persons, knocking down labyrinths and allowing people to walk their own road. So we find ourselves confronted with a clear option: to educate for liberation or to educate for domination.

In retrospect, it seems that my most radical professors were still educating 12 for domination. And I wondered if this was so because we could not imagine how to educate for liberation in the corporate university. In Freire's case, he speaks as a white man of privilege who stands and acts in solidarity with oppressed and exploited groups, especially in their efforts to establish literacy programs that emphasize education for critical consciousness. In my case, as a black woman from a working-class background, I stand and act as a member of an oppressed, exploited group who has managed to acquire a degree of privilege. While I choose to educate for liberation, the site of my work has been within the walls of universities peopled largely by privileged white students and a few non-white students. Within those walls, I have tried to teach literature and Women's Studies courses in a way that does not reinforce structures of domination: imperialism, racism, sexism, and class exploitation.

I do not pretend that my approach is politically neutral, yet this disturbs 13 students who have been led to believe that all education within the university should be "neutral." On the first day of classes, I talk about my approach, about the ways the class may be different from other classes as we work to create strategies of learning to meet our needs—and of course we must discover together what those needs are. Even though I explain that the class will be different, students do not always take it seriously. One central difference is that all students are expected to contribute to class discussion, if not spontaneously, then through the reading of paragraphs and short papers. In this way, every student makes a contribution, every student's voice is heard. Despite the fact that this may be stated at the onset of class, written clearly on the syllabus, students will complain and whine about having to speak. It is only recently that I have begun to see much of the complaining

hooks

as "change back" behavior. Students and teachers find it hard to shift their paradigms even though they have been longing for a different approach.

Struggling to educate for liberation in the corporate university is a 14 process that I have found enormously stressful. Implementing new teaching strategies that aim to subvert the norm, to engage students fully, is really a difficult task. Unlike the oppressed or colonized, who may begin to feel as they engage in education for critical consciousness a newfound sense of power and identity that frees them from colonization of the mind, that liberates, privileged students are often downright unwilling to acknowledge that their minds have been colonized, that they have been learning how to be oppressors, how to dominate, or at least how to passively accept the domination of others. This past teaching year, a student confronted me (a black male student from a middle-class urban experience) in class with the question of what I expected from them (like his tone of voice was: did I have the right to expect anything). Seriously, he wanted to know what I wanted from them. I told him and the class that I thought the most important learning experience that could happen in our classroom was that students would learn to think critically and analytically, not just about the required books, but about the world they live in. Education for critical consciousness that encourages all students—privileged or non-privileged—who are seeking an entry into class privilege rather than providing a sense of freedom and release, invites critique of conventional expectations and desires. They may find such an experience terribly threatening. And even though they may approach the situation with great openness, it may still be difficult, and even painful.

This past semester, I taught a course on black women writers in which 15 students were encouraged to think about the social context in which literature emerges, the impact of politics of domination—racism, sexism, class exploitation—on the writing. Students stated quite openly and honestly that reading the literature in the context of class discussion was making them feel pain. They complained that everything was changing for them, that they were seeing the world differently, and seeing things in that world that were painful to face. Never before had a group of students so openly talked about the way in which learning to see the world critically was causing pain. I did not belittle their pain or try to rationalize it. Initially, I was uncertain about how to respond and just asked us all to think about it. Later, we discussed the way in which all their comments implied that to experience pain is bad, an indication that something is wrong. We talked about changing how we perceive pain, about our society's approach to pain, considering the possibility that this pain could be a constructive sign of growth. I shared with them my sense that the experience should not be viewed as static, that at another point the knowledge and new perspectives they had might lead to clarity and a greater sense of well-being.

Education for liberation can work in the university setting but it does not 16 lead students to feel they are enjoying class or necessarily feeling positive about me as a teacher. One aspect of radical pedagogy that has been difficult for me is learning to cope with not being seen positively by students. When one provides an experience of learning that is challenging, possibly threatening, it is not entertainment, or necessarily a fun experience, though it can be. If one primary function of such a pedagogy is to prepare students to live and act more fully in the world, then it is usually when they are in that context, outside the classroom, that they most feel and experience the value of what they have shared and learned. For me, this often means that most positive feedback I receive as a teacher comes after students have left the class and rarely during it.

Recently talking with a group of students and faculty at Duke University, 17 we focussed on the issue of exposure and vulnerability. One white male professor, who felt his politics to be radical, his teaching to be an education for liberation, his teaching strategies subversive, felt it was important that no one in the university's bureaucratic structure know what was happening in the classroom. Fear of exposure may lead teachers with radical visions to suppress insight, to follow set norms. Until I came to teach at Yale, no one outside my classes had paid much attention to what was going on inside them. At Yale, students talked a lot outside about my classes, about what happens in them. This was very difficult for me as I felt both exposed and constantly scrutinized. I was certainly subjected to much critical feedback both from students in my classes and faculty and students who heard about them. Their responses forced recognition of the way in which teaching that is overtly political, especially if it radically challenges the status quo, requires acknowledgement that to choose education as the practice of freedom is to take a political stance that may have serious consequences.

Despite negative feedback or pressures, the most rewarding aspect of 18 such teaching is to influence the way students mature and grow intellectually and spiritually. For those students who wish to try to learn in a new way but who have fears, I try to reassure them that their involvement in different types of learning experiences need not threaten their security in other classes; it will not destroy the backing system of education, so they need not panic. Of course, if all they can do is panic, then that is a sign that the course is not for them. My commitment to education as the practice of freedom is strengthened by the large number of students who take my courses and, by doing so, affirm their longing to learn in a new way. Their testimony confirms that education as the practice of liberation does take place in university settings, that our lives are transformed there, that there we do meaningful radical political work.

From *Talking Back: Thinking Feminist, Thinking Black*. Reprinted by permission of South End Press.

A Primer for Black Students on White Campuses

Nikki Giovanni

Writer Nikki Giovanni—poet, essayist, activist—is a professor of English at Virginia Polytechnic Institute and State University at Blacksburg, Virginia. This piece, renamed "Campus Racism 101," is included in Giovanni's book Racism 101 *(1994).*

There is a bumper sticker that reads: "Too bad ignorance isn't painful." I like 1 that. But ignorance is.

We just seldom attribute the pain to it or even recognize it when we see 2 it. Like the postcard on my corkboard. It shows a young man in a very hip jacket smoking a cigarette. In the background is a high school with the American flag waving. The caption says: "Too cool for school. Yet too stupid for the real world." Out of the mouth of the young man is a bubble enclosing the words "Maybe I'll start a band." There could be a postcard showing a jock in a uniform saying "I don't need school. I'm going to the NFL or NBA." Or one showing a young man or woman studying and a group of young people saying, "So you want to be white." Or something equally demeaning. We need to quit it.

I am a professor of English at Virginia Tech. I've been here for four years, 3 though for only two years with academic rank. I am tenured, which means I have a teaching position for life, a rarity on a predominantly white campus. Whether from malice or ignorance, people who think I should be at a predominantly black institution will say, "Why are you at Tech?" Because it's here. And so are black students.

But even if black students weren't here, it's painfully obvious that this 4 nation and this world cannot allow white students to go through higher education without interacting with blacks in authoritative positions. It is equally clear that predominantly black colleges cannot accommodate the numbers of black students who want and need an education.

Is it difficult to attend a predominantly white college? Compared with 5 what? Being passed over for promotion because you lack credentials? Being turned down for jobs because you are not college-educated? Joining the armed forces or going to jail because you cannot find an alternative to the streets?

Let's have a little perspective here. Where can you go and what can you 6 do that frees you from interacting with the white American mentality? You're going to interact; the only question is, will you be in some control of yourself and your actions, or will you be controlled by others? I'm going to recommend control.

What's the difference between prison and college? They both proscribe 7 your behavior for a given period of time. They both allow you to read books and develop your writing. They both give you time alone to think and time with your peers to talk about issues. But four years of prison doesn't give you a passport to greater opportunities. Most likely that time only gives you greater knowledge of how to get back in. Four years of college gives you an opportunity not only to lift yourself but to serve your people effectively.

What's the difference when you are called nigger in college from when 8 you are called nigger in prison? In college you can, although I admit with effort, follow procedures to have those students who called you nigger kicked out or suspended. You can bring issues to public attention without risk of your life. But mostly college is and always has been the future. We, neither less nor more than other people, need knowledge. There are discomforts attached to attending predominantly white colleges, though no more so than living in a racist world. Here are some rules to follow that may help:

Go to class. No matter how you feel. No matter how you think the pro- 9 fessor feels about you. It's important to have a consistent presence in the classroom. If nothing else, the professor will know you care enough and are serious enough to be there.

Meet your professors. Extend your hand (give a firm handshake) and tell 10 them your name. *Ask them what you need to do to make an A.* You may never make an A but you have put them on notice that you are serious about getting good grades.

Do assignments on time. Typed or computer-generated. You have the 11 syllabus. Follow it. If for some reason you can't complete an assignment on time, let your professor know before it is due and work out a new due date— then meet it.

Go back to see your professor. Tell him or her your name again. If an as- 12 signment received less than an A, ask why, and find out what you need to do to improve the next assignment.

Yes, your professor is busy. So are you. So are your parents, who are work- 13 ing to pay or help with your tuition. Ask *early* what you need to do if you feel you are starting to get into academic trouble. Do not wait until you are failing.

Understand that there will be professors who do not like you; there may 14 even be professors who are racist or sexist or both. You must discriminate among your professors to see who will give you the help you need. You may not simply say "They are all against me." They aren't. They mostly don't care. Since you are the one who wants to be educated, find the people who want to help.

Don't defeat yourself. Cultivate your friends. Know your enemies. You 15 cannot undo hundreds of years of prejudicial thinking. Think for yourself and speak up. Raise your hand in class. Say what you believe no matter how awkward you may think it sounds. You will improve in your articulation and confidence.

Participate in some campus activity. Join the newspaper staff. Run for of- 16 fice. Join a dorm council. Do *something* that involves you on campus. You are going to be there for four years, so let your presence be known, if not felt.

You will inevitably run into some white classmates who are troubling be- cause they often say stupid things, ask stupid questions—and expect an an- swer. Here are some comebacks to some of the most common inquiries and comments.

Q. What's it like to grow up in a ghetto? 17

A. I don't know. 18

Q. From the teacher: Can you give us the black perspective on Toni 19 Morrison, Huck Finn, slavery, Martin Luther King Jr., and others?

A. I can give you *my* perspective. (Do not take the burden of 22 million 20 people on your shoulder. Remind everyone that you are an individual, and don't speak for the race or any other individual within it.)

Q. Why do all the black people sit together in the dining hall? 21

A. Why do the white students sit together? 22

Q. Why should there be an African-American studies course? 23

Giovanni

A. Because white Americans have not adequately studied the contribu- 24
tions of Africans and African Americans. Both black and white students need
to know our total common history.

Q. Why are there so many scholarships for "minority" students? 25

A. Because they wouldn't give my great-grandparents their 40 acres and 26
the mule.

Q. How can whites understand black history, culture, literature and so 27
forth?

A. The same way we understand white history, culture, literature and so 28
forth. That is why we're in school: to learn.

Q. Should whites take African-American studies courses? 29

A. Of course. We take white studies courses, though the universities don't 30
call them that.

Comment: When I see groups of black people on campus, it's really in- 31
timidating.

Comeback: I understand what you mean. I'm frightened when I see 32
white students congregating.

Comment: It's not fair. It's easier for you guys to get into college than for 33
other people.

Comeback: If it's so easy, why aren't there more of us? 34

Comment: It's not our fault that America is the way it is. 35

Comeback: It's not our fault either, but both of us have a responsibility to 36
make changes.

It's really very simple. Education progress is a national concern; educa- 37
tion is a private one. Your job is not to educate white people; it is to obtain
an education. If you take the racial world on your shoulders, you will not get
the job done.

Deal with yourself as an individual worthy of respect, and make every- 38
one else deal with you the same way. College is a little like playing grown-
up. Practice what you want to be. You have been telling your parents you are
grown. Now is your chance to act like it.

From *Racism 101*, published by Wm. Morrow and Company, Inc., New York, 1994. Copyright © 1991 Nikki Giovanni. Reprinted by permission of the author.

Racism 101

Ruth Conniff

*"Real change requires a reevaluation of the basic philosophy of college educa-
tion—who is qualified to be educated and what constitutes an education?" asks
Ruth Conniff in the following article she wrote for* The Progressive *(1988) when
she was an undergraduate editorial intern studying at Yale University.*

At the University of Wisconsin in Madison, the brothers of Phi Gamma 1
Delta fraternity are known as Fijis, and each spring they throw what they
call a Fiji Island Party. For the festivities of May 1987, they painted themselves

in blackface and set up, on the lawn outside their fraternity house, a large caricatured cutout of a black man with a bone through his nose.

At about the same time, black students at the University of Michigan 2 found fliers slipped under their doors declaring "open hunting season on jigaboos and porch monkeys." At the University of Massachusetts, white students attacked an interracial couple and several black students on campus.

These incidents and others like them have been widely reported as evidence of a resurgence of racism on campus. University administrators have responded to the outcry by announcing plans to combat the problem. 3

But for minorities, the news is old. Long after the civil-rights movement 4 and desegregation, black students worry about their safety at universities all over the country. Name-calling and even violent threats are routine. And campus racism is no new phenomenon. The Fiji party, for example, had been going on every spring for years before anyone called attention to it.

But tensions between black and white students are just the most visible 5 part of the problem. Hispanics, Asians, and Native Americans, as well as blacks, struggle against racism, deeply rooted in the universities. It starts when they apply for admission and financial aid, continues in the classroom, and extends to daily life on campus.

"You have to look at the mindset of minority students when they get 6 here," says Charles Holly of the University of Wisconsin's Black Student Union. "You're going to class on the first day, and you're the only black in with 300 white students, all staring at you like, 'What are you doing here?' My first football game here, freshman year, I had garbage thrown at me and was called 'nigger.' That was my last football game, too."

Many white students, however, resent the recent surge of attention to 7 issues of race.

"We've been stabbed from all sides," says Dan Mose, a Wisconsin Fiji. 8

"It seems like the way the university and the black students went after 9 them was just for attention," says a member of a sorority on campus. "They always pick on the Greek system. It's gotten to the point now where you hear so much about it [racism] that people are watching everything they say."

Fewer nonwhites are enrolling in college these days, and fewer can stay. 10 Blacks and Hispanics are increasingly underrepresented on campus—26,000 fewer blacks attend college now than in 1980—because cuts in financial aid and the shift from grants to loans under the Reagan Administration make tuition unaffordable for most minorities.

More black students graduate from high school now than ten years ago, 11 but more and more blacks and Hispanics join the military or enroll in vocational schools instead of going to college. The current emphasis on "raising standards" at universities, rather than on opening doors to students from ethnically and economically diverse backgrounds, has aggravated this trend.

In Albuquerque last year, the University of New Mexico began referring 12 students who once qualified for the school's General College, or remedial program, to local community colleges. The state legislature imposed the plan to raise standards at the university by phasing out a special-admissions program for students who don't meet the regular grade and test-score requirements.

Going to the nearby Technical Vocational Institute is more reasonable for students than paying university tuition for basic courses, says Gary Kerkendal, assistant head of admissions at the university. "We feel very comfortable that there is an alternative for students to come back to us better prepared." 13

The alternatives are less comfortable for New Mexico's low-income Hispanic, Native American, and black students. Extra years in school mean a bigger accumulation of loans to pay off and more time before beginning careers. These factors, plus rising tuition rates, push the state university beyond the reach of many. 14

"The thing is," says Maximiliano Madrid, a senior at UNM who was admitted as a General College student, "now you're told you're going to have to take two years at the community college and then comes the university and it takes four or five more years. You're behind to start off with and you're going to stay behind." 15

In Albuquerque's public high schools, the Industrial Cooperative Training Program encourages low-income students to learn job skills and start working before they graduate. Most continue in their jobs afterwards or go on to the Technical Vocational Institute. 16

At the University of California at Berkeley, Asian-American students are engaged in a different kind of struggle with the administration. 17

Enrollment by Asians has not declined, but in the last few years it has leveled off. Students charge that some admissions policies are deliberately designed to keep them out. Berkeley awards extra points, for example, to students who pass achievement tests in European foreign languages, but no points are awarded to students who know Chinese or Vietnamese. Asian students, like Hispanics and blacks, also say they feel alienated and receive inadequate support while at the university. 18

Chancellor Ira Michael Heyman denies that the university's admissions policies are discriminatory, but he recently made a public apology for not responding "more openly and less defensively" to Asian students' concerns. 19

One major bone of contention is the English-language program. More than half of the Asian students at Berkeley are recent immigrants, and they represent 80 per cent of those enrolled in the three-semester English as a Second Language sequence. As with all the university's remedial programs, a student who fails more than one ESL course flunks out, regardless of grade-point average. Many Asian immigrants who pass their other classes do not graduate because of the English requirement. 20

"U.C. Berkeley considers that there are too many Asians on campus in the first place, and not enough are flunking out to need help," says Richard Ehara, a tutor at Berkeley and a member of a committee protesting the university's Asian policies. "There are no Asian counselors and they are not considered a priority for tutoring." 21

Student activists claim the ESL program is culturally discriminatory. 22

"That's why a lot of Asians flunk out of Berkeley," says Nam Nguyen, a Vietnamese-American student, "not because they can't do the work. You 23 have to write an essay on a subject that you don't understand because of cultural differences. For instance, they ask you to debate a point in the Constitution. First of all, if you're a recent immigrant, you might not know the Constitution as well. And secondly, if it's someone from an Asian culture, most people don't debate in Asian culture. When you write a paper, it's more of a discussion. You use a lot of philosophy and a lot of quotes and stuff. And teachers don't understand why the students are writing this way."

In New Mexico, students also complain about ethnocentrism in the 24 classroom.

"There are certain pieces of literature that are very offensive," says Madrid. 25 "You study long enough and all of a sudden you say, 'Hey, maybe that's not right,' even the way the Pulitzer Prize-winning authors depict things in Southwest Studies. You're from the area and you're proud of your people and you're sitting here reading something by Willa Cather about fat, greasy Mexicans who all they want to do is have kids. And you know, it may be written so it sounds kind of nice, but you're sitting there saying, 'God, this is offensive.' That's what your professors want you to read. They don't want you to read something by Raulfo Acuna, talking about occupied America. And you don't study people like Rejes Tijerina, or the disputes over the treaty of Guadalupe Hidalgo land grants. You've got to teach yourself that stuff."

Institutional callousness to nonwhites fosters an atmosphere among stu- 26 dents that is hostile to minorities in several ways:

- White students don't see or know much about other cultures and eth- 27 nic groups because groups are underrepresented on campus.
- White culture dominates the curriculum, and that reinforces white students' assumption that theirs is the only legitimate culture.
- With the tightening of educational funds and the conservative political climate, many white students resent such measures as affirmative action, which seem to coddle minorities.

Given this set of circumstances, it is not surprising that white students 28 are confused by and resentful of the sudden surge of attention to issues of race.

Many of the gains achieved by the civil-rights movement in the 1960s 29 and 1970s are slipping away. Cultural centers and special programs set up to accommodate nonwhite students have dwindled or disappeared.

Gerald Thomas, who now conducts race-awareness training sessions at 30 the University of Wisconsin, has watched the atmosphere on campus change since he started teaching Afro-American studies in 1970.

"We had the sensitivity and the awareness of racial issues culminating to- 31 ward the end of the 1960s," he says. "The white community was sensitized and the minority community's interest was heightened. And then it died out. Students moved on, and administrators and institutions got weary of dealing in a half-assed way with racism."

After recent racist incidents, black student activists have rallied to de- 32 mand that university administrators protect their safety and address the declines in enrollment, financial aid, and supportive resources.

Conniff

The United Coalition Against Racism at Michigan played host in the 33
summer of 1987 to students from twenty other campuses to discuss building
a new movement. At several such conferences held that summer, students
discussed strategies for dealing with a racism that is more subtle and insidi-
ous than that confronted by their predecessors a generation ago. Members of
UCAR are working to form a national student movement against racism.

"Mainly, we're not talking about white students," says Barbara Ransby of 34
the Michigan coalition, "but rather a racist administration." Efforts to combat racism among students can be useful, she says, "but it's really not the
crux of the problem. If whites are nicer and more polite to black students, it
doesn't change the underlying oppressive power structure."

Although student activists have made some gains recently in the struggle 35
against campus racism, it will take a deep revision of universities' structures
and values to make a lasting change.

Mandatory ethnic-studies programs, which would teach students about a 36
variety of cultures, are a big item among the reforms student activists are demanding and university administrators are discussing on various campuses,
including Stanford, Berkeley, Wisconsin, Michigan, and Massachusetts.

In Madison, University of Wisconsin chancellor Donna Shalala, with the 37
help of student and faculty committees, has formulated a plan to combat
racism that includes awareness training for students, a cross-departmental
ethnic-studies requirement, and a pledge to increase recruitment of minority
students and faculty. The university has instituted workshops and classes on
race relations, a pledge to recruit more minority staff and students, and
stricter penalties for racial harassment. After the Fiji party, the university
temporarily suspended the fraternity. It was reinstated last spring with the
understanding that members would attend one of the new racism-awareness
sessions.

"The model for these training sessions describes racism as a series of 38
stages varying between ignorance and intentional discrimination," says
Roger Howard, associate dean of students. "If you go by that model, then,
yes, the members of the Fiji fraternity were racist in that they were ignorant
and insensitive. But what feels like racism from the point of view of a minority doesn't seem like racism to white students."

Charles Holly, who attended the fraternity's training sessions, has a dif- 39
ferent view.

"The university's idea was just to parade black students in there," Holly 40
says. "They said, 'Okay, we have this racial ignorance, you go in and educate
them.' It was like when you're four years old and your parents sit you down
and try to make you learn your multiplication tables. One guy stood up and
said, 'I don't know why we're here.' That set the tone. 'We don't think we
need to be here. We just had a party, and they're making us into villains.'

"It was the whole blame-the-victim thing. We [black students] were 41
wrong for even raising the issue, because it had been going on for years. If it
was okay then, why not now? There was this alumnus standing there in the
background clapping and saying, 'Yeah!' The whole thing was based on the
idea that the fraternity guys were ignorant. But their idea was that what they
do shouldn't offend anyone. That's racist. It's one thing to say, 'Damn, I'm
sorry, Charles, I didn't know that would offend you,' and another to say, 'I

don't care if it does.' That's the attitude the fraternity has: 'I don't know and I don't care.' "

The same attitude is evident in the argument that Stanford's Pulitzer 42 Prize–winning historian Carl Degler makes against multicultural education: "It is difficult, to say the least, to name the important institutions and values in modern American culture that can be shown to have been derived from Africa, China, Japan. . . ."

Changes like those made by Stanford in its required study of Western civ- 43 ilization—which is now called "Culture and Ideas" and includes works by minorities and women—are still the subject of much debate. Many academics fear that in embracing such a diverse program of studies, universities may fail to educate students in the foundations of American society. While this is a legitimate concern, it must be considered alongside the all-too-visible failings of a university atmosphere traditionally hostile to minorities. 44

Before they can hope to combat campus racism, students, professors, and administrators must change the deeply ingrained attitude that Western culture is the most important culture, that nonwhite cultures are separate from "real" American culture.

Real change requires a reevaluation of the basic philosophy of college 45 education—who is qualified to be educated and what constitutes an education? When white students say there is no reason for them to challenge their racist assumptions, they merely reflect a world view fostered by the university.

Meanwhile, back in Madison at the University of Wisconsin, in late 46 October, the Zeta Beta Tau fraternity dressed its pledges up in Afro wigs and blackface and held a slave auction. Eight students who protested were arrested. The fraternity has been suspended by the Interfraternity Council. Its president told one of the protesters the event "wasn't intended to be racist."

First published in *The Progressive,* 1988. Used by permission.

Look Back & Plan Ahead

Every academic essay could be read as a story told. . .
Linda Brodkey

In your end-project essay, you may want to incorporate some of your reflections on these readings or you may want to focus on some aspect of this topic. You could, for example, write about some difficulties underrepresented groups encounter in college and draw on these and perhaps other readings as well as your own experience or observations. You could write as an outsider-observer or as an insider if you consider yourself a member of an underrepresented group. You could research racial tensions on college campuses, including perhaps your own campus. (See also reports in the "Reading the News" Project—Chapter 6.) You could research possible causes for the high dropout rates for Latino and African-American students. You could incorporate interviews, following the ethnographic interview guide in the "Ethnic Identification" Writing Project (Chapter 7). What are the retention rates at your college? How does ethnic background (or gender or class) relate to academic success? What is your college doing to increase retention? Are any students considered "at risk"? If you decide not to use these readings and related thinking in your end-project essay, a notebook entry or some written reflections could be included in your project portfolio as part of your work.

Suggestions for Further Reading

Angelou, Maya, 1969. *I Know Why the Caged Bird Sings.* New York: Random House.

Haley, Alex. 1976. *Roots.* Garden City, NY: Doubleday.

Report of the American Council on Education. 1994.

Walker, Alice. 1973. "Everyday Use," *In Love and Trouble.* New York: Harcourt Brace Jovanovich.

6 Reading the News: Questioning the Word & the World

All the News That's Fit to Print   Masthead of *The New York Times*

And that's the way it is. . . .   Walter Cronkite

Becoming educated is not about acquiring a body of knowledge—it's a process of knowing or of coming to know. Educated readers are not passive recipients or consumers of news. They take into account various perspectives and question and position themselves from an informed and reasoned viewpoint. This project will help you read "the news" more critically and consider how print media affects our perceptions of events.

First, you will examine various reports of the "same" event and consider how these presentations tell different stories and leave readers with different impressions. Can readers ever know what "really happened"? Do we expect too much of the media? Are all news reports stories or re-presentations? Are readers responsible for reading "through" the news? You will also have an opportunity to observe an event, to compare your reading, and to explore what makes for different readings of a text. (A text could be a scene from a classroom as well as a scene from a play or story.)

After considering your own bias as a reader and writer of news, you'll learn that all news, even in mainstream newspapers, is biased. You'll look in on a "Reader at Work" struggling to read a news report that appears to be objective. Deciding what stories will be presented also reveals a bias. What news events don't make the news? What stories are not "fit to print"? Who decides? This work will help you become a questioning, reflective reader and will help you develop a critical framework to use when you design your own "Reading the News" project.

Next comes some practice in rereading the news. You'll examine two reports of an event and write summaries and responses, and responses to responses. Again, you'll observe some readers at work and can add your reading if you choose. Then you'll have the opportunity to compare and contrast print media representations of a news event of your choice. Guidelines, from selection to presentation, are included.

The next section focuses on reading an issue raised by a news event. You'll begin with a close analysis of two different reports of an incident that took place on a college campus. Then you are invited to role-play various points of view and finally to argue your view. You'll consider differences between expressing your opinion and arguing. Guidelines are provided for helping you prepare for a writing workshop of your first draft, and some questions are suggested for peer review.

This chapter focuses on the biases that readers bring to their reading of the news, as well as the biases of the newswriters themselves. Most of the readings focus on racial discrimination on college campuses. Racism continues in the 1990s and is, of course, not limited to college campuses. The development of your critical reading ability is both crucial to your development as a writer moving through the college curriculum and to your becoming an educated person in the world at large. How do you learn to read critically? You write. Writing is reading, and "the way to learn to read critically," explains composition theorist Ann Berthoff ("Rhetoric as Hermeneutic"), "is to learn to write."

As with all writing projects included in this text, you can vary this project. You may want to limit this project to one longer writing comparing and contrasting news presentations, for example. Or you may want to focus on reading an issue. You may want to work collaboratively as a class or in small groups with a particular set of readings related to an event or issue in the news. You may want to do all of the work included here and more. You may want to do some research on reports and responses to an event on your own campus. What I've tried to provide is a critical framework and approach as well as some readings and guidelines. I am interested in variations of this project and welcome stories of readers at work.

What's the Story?

People need to be reminded that the media tell stories.   Lewis Lapham

Newspapers don't seem to know whether they're supposed to be observers who document what happens before their eyes or analysts who connect the dots in all of what reporters see, read and hear.
Washington Post,
September 6, 1993

Lewis Lapham, who worked as a reporter for the *San Francisco Examiner* and the New York *Herald Tribune* and is now Editor of *Harper's* magazine, explains the difficulties of writing news stories: "Almost always I was writing about people whom I had never seen, sometimes furnishing them with motives and characterizations at which I could only guess . . ."*

On Saturday, September 18, 1993, three newspapers reported the "same" event. The reporters were not present at the event. Their job was to represent the event to readers.

Look how the headlines of the "same" event give different impressions:

1. *Masked Men Rob a Train in Yonkers*
   Commuters Are Unhurt in Metro-North Holdup
   The New York Times ("All the News That's Fit to Print")
2. *Gunsmoke on Railroad*
   Shades of Jesse James on Metro-North line
   Daily News (New York's Hometown Newspaper)
3. *Yonkers Train Heist Leaves Riders Reeling*
   New York Post (Founded in 1801 by Alexander Hamilton)

---

*All Lewis Lapham quotations are from "Gilding the News," *Harper's,* 1981. Copyright © 1981 by Harper's Magazine. All rights reserved. Reprinted by special permission.

Reread these headlines and compare your impressions of this event. How do your impressions of the event differ, based on these headlines? Which of the three is most informative? Why? How do these headlines differ in emphasis?

Two newspapers include similar photos of the train station and passengers but use different captions, and one frames the voice of a victim instead.

1. Photo caption (*The New York Times*): "Five men wearing ski masks held up six commuters on Thursday night when a Metro-North train stopped at the Glenwood Station in Yonkers. The robbers snatched a chair, a portable cassette-tape player, about $200 and a commuter ticket."
2. Photo caption (*Daily News*): "OLD WEST came to Metro-North's Glenwood Station in Yonkers, where five gunmen jumped on to stage a robbery."
3. Voice highlighted in *New York Post:*

> "It was like watching a movie . . . then I realized it was real."
>
> Train-Robbery Victim

The continuation of this story by *The New York Times* runs under this headline: "Metro-North Meets Wild West: Gunmen Rob Train in Yonkers" and includes a map and a second photo of a police captain talking to passengers to try to find out what happened. This word play by reporter James Barron is also highlighted:

> Riders are used to being held up in the station—but this!

How do these differences affect your reading of this event?

The use of one word instead of another in a news report makes a difference in how we read an event. It makes a difference if the robbers are described as "five men" or "five male teenagers" or a "gang" or "bandits" or "black males."

Stop now and cluster and freewrite in response to these two words: (1) *gang* and (2) *bandits*. Place the word *gang* in the center of a piece of paper and write your associations as quickly as you can, one word after another in a line, and then begin another chain of associations. Keep going. Figure 6.1 shows one writer's start. After five to eight minutes, stop and review your words and write freely what comes to your mind when you think of *gang*. Repeat the same activity with the word *bandits*. Then compare with one or two classmates what came to your mind.

Let's look a little further. How are the robbers described in each report? One reader's notes appear in the comparison frames of Figure 6.2a and b.

Consider your associations with *gang* and *bandits* in reading the descriptions of the robbers by the *Daily News* (Figure 6.2a). How does the addition of race in the description by the *New York Post* affect your reading of this news event?

Compare the description of the robbery. Notice in Figure 6.2b the differing choices of verbs to describe the robbers' entry onto the train and the different words used to describe the robbery. Also notice that *The New York Times* reports that the robbers "announced" a holdup, while the *Daily News* reports that the robbers shouted, "This is a stickup!"

Respond now, in Figure 6.3, to another quotation from Lewis Lapham's "Gilding the News." *Suggestion:* After writing, give your response to the person on your left. Write your response to that response, and exchange.

Figure 6.1

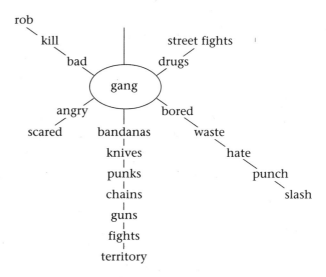

Viewing & Reviewing Activities

To characterize the reading process, Iser (1972) offers the analogy of two people looking at the night sky. The two "may both be looking at the same collection of stars, but one will see the image of a plough, and the other will make out a dipper."

> Different readers (and the same reader at different times) will see different things in the same text.*

1. Take a walk together during your class. If the weather is nice, go outdoors and walk to a place where you can view an object or scene (for example, a tree or trees, a sculpture, a building, the sky). Otherwise, go to some place in a building on campus to view something together. Look out a classroom window, if you have one!

    Write what you see. Compare your viewing with others. How are your viewings similar? How are they different? Why? What in your background and experience caused you to notice some things and not others or to form a particular impression?

> Facts can be seen only through the eyes of observers and are subject to whatever selections and distortions the observers' viewpoints impose upon them.
>
> G. A. Kelly, psychologist

> Seeing . . . is always a selective activity, a matter of *not* seeing some things in order to see others.
>
> Mina Shaughnessy, *Errors and Expectations*

> It is common knowledge that different people viewing the same scene will notice different things . . .
>
> W. I. B. Beveridge, "The Powers of Observation,"
> *The Art of Scientific Investigation*

---

*Susan V. Wall & Glynda A. Hull, "The Semantics of Error." *Writing and Response.* Edited by Chris Anson. NCTE: 1989.

2. Write down words you associate with *bias*, as you did earlier with the word *gang*. Then review your chains of associations and write quickly for five minutes about *bias*.

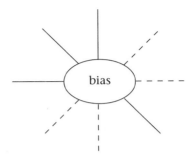

Notice how "bias" is used in these examples.

a. Mother to friend: "I think my daughter is a wonderful musician."
   Friend to mother: "Yes, though, of course, you are biased, you know."

b. Excerpt from a news article: "Youths Arrested in Bias Incident. New York (UPI)—Three Brooklyn youths Wednesday were arrested on charges of assault and civil rights violations in an attack by a gang of young men on three Jewish students. The attack left two students seriously injured. Police said the attack was triggered after one of the victims reacted to a religious slur, and said they were still considering it a bias incident."

Figure 6.2a

Category	The New York Times	Daily News	New York Post
1. Description of Robbers	"five masked men" "The witness said the five men were wearing black capes."	"Five masked gunmen" "the gang" "Five male teenagers wearing ski masks or bandannas" "the bandits"	"Five masked bandits dressed in black" "some in hockey masks, others in ski masks" "The suspects are described as black, ages 17 to 20, weighing about 170 pounds and dressed in black pants, shirts and black shoes"

Figure 6.2b

Category	The New York Times	Daily News	New York Post
1. Description Robbery	"shoved their way onto a Metro-North commuter train Thursday night and announced a holdup"	"a brazen nighttime stickup" "jumped aboard . . . . shouted, "This is a stickup!"	"the brazen heist" ["heist": slang for robbery] "organized heist" "the thieves hopped aboard" "robbers pushed"

Based on these examples, write some more about your understanding of bias. Work toward a definition. Add an example of your own. Do you think of bias as negative, positive, or neutral? Or does it vary? Keep writing, and then talk with others about what you've been writing/thinking.

3. Even if you were at an event and not relying on others to inform you, your report will still be biased.

Figure 6.3

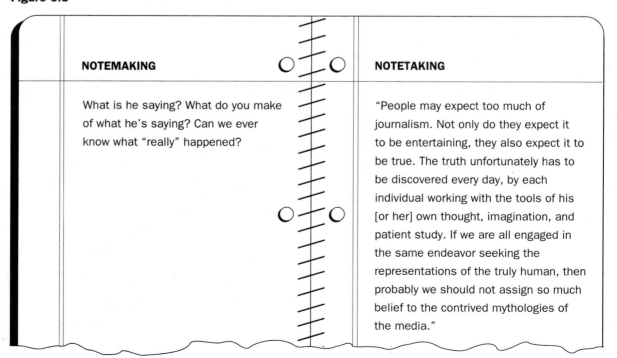

NOTEMAKING

What is he saying? What do you make of what he's saying? Can we ever know what "really" happened?

NOTETAKING

"People may expect too much of journalism. Not only do they expect it to be entertaining, they also expect it to be true. The truth unfortunately has to be discovered every day, by each individual working with the tools of his [or her] own thought, imagination, and patient study. If we are all engaged in the same endeavor seeking the representations of the truly human, then probably we should not assign so much belief to the contrived mythologies of the media."

Review a recent scene (or event) from your classroom, perhaps some argument or misunderstanding or classroom behavior that caused some discomfort or confusion. Write, briefly, of what happened. What's *your* story?

Compare your version with several others in your class. How are the stories different? Why?

After some discussion, read what educational philosopher Maxine Greene has to say (Figure 6.4). What do you understand her to say? How can you apply her explanation to your viewing of an event?

Bias of the Center! What's That?

The New York Times is a mainstream newspaper that maintains an appearance of neutrality and objectivity. Its news reports are informative and sometimes even include a photograph and a map of where the event took place so that readers feel they are getting a report of what "really happened." "People like to believe what they're told," explains Lewis Lapham, "to imagine that the implacable forces of history speak to them with a human voice." When mainstream journalists tell Jeff Cohen that "our news doesn't reflect bias of the left or right," he asks them "whether they are therefore admitting bias of center." What? "Bias of the center! What's that?" they respond. According to Cohen, "Being in the center—being a centrist—is somehow not having an ideology at all. Somehow centrism is not an 'ism' carrying with it values, beliefs, or opinions" ("The Centrist Bias of the U.S. Media" in *Extra!*). "Supposedly the media just report things as they see them. News producers—from owners to reporters—are so immersed in the dominant political culture that they may not be fully aware of how they misrepresent,

Figure 6.4

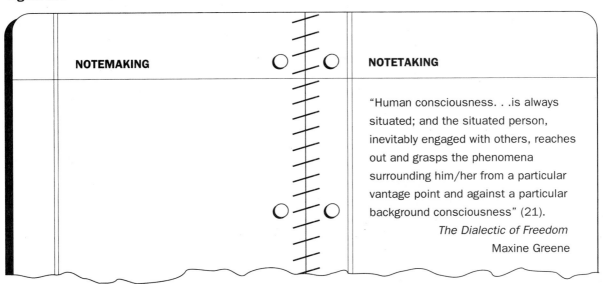

NOTEMAKING NOTETAKING

"Human consciousness. . .is always situated; and the situated person, inevitably engaged with others, reaches out and grasps the phenomena surrounding him/her from a particular vantage point and against a particular background consciousness" (21).

The Dialectic of Freedom
Maxine Greene

evade and suppress the news," explains Michael Parenti ("The News Media and Class Control" in *The Shape of This Century*).

Reader at Work

Let's look for a moment at "Reader at Work" Cynthia Tsui, who read two different news accounts of the "same" event. She opens her essay with this summary of the event.

> The surrender of Katherine Power made headlines in major newspapers on September 16, 1993. Power was involved in a robbery twenty-three years ago which resulted in the death of a police officer. After years of hiding and suffering from depression, she finally decided to turn herself in and face the consequences of her actions.

Cynthia concluded that the article in *The New York Times* ("60's Radical, Linked to a Killing, Surrenders After Hiding 23 Years") was "informative" and "straightforward." "It covered the most important facts and gave me the basic idea of what happened," Cynthia explained. The article in the *New York Post* ("The Fugitive") gave "a more sympathetic account," according to Cynthia. While it included some of the same information, it highlighted Power's story of struggle.

"Look at the two photographs in the *Post*," Cynthia pointed out. One shows her handcuffed and going to court and the other shows her in 1969. "She doesn't look like a criminal."

"Did *The New York Times* include photographs?"

"Yes, a dull one of some of her family at court and a photo of Powers. A mug shot."

"She looks harmless, innocent, even friendly in the *Post* photo, doesn't she? She could be on a Missing Persons poster."

"The *Times* says she's one of nine campus radicals on the FBI's Most Wanted List."

"Look at the word at the top of the photo of Powers in the *Times*—MURDER."

Cynthia wrote, "At first I overlooked the word *Murder* at the top of the small photo. When I noticed the word, I thought Power was a murderer when in fact she never killed anyone. She drove the getaway car that helped the actual murderer escape." Both photos exist; these two newspapers selected different ones to print in keeping with their own news representations.

I'm not going to include the two articles here. If you are interested in further details, you can look them up. The point here is that even mainstream media must select what to include and what to exclude. The selection and organization of material is a *re*-presentation, a *representation* of what happened.

To recognize that there are always multiple perspectives and multiple vantage points is to recognize that no accounting . . . can ever be finished or complete. There is always more. There is always possibility. And this is where the space opens for the pursuit of freedom.

Maxine Greene, *The Dialectic of Freedom*

Educated readers are reflective consumers of "the news":

If we read differently, we do differently—reading better, we do better.*

Jeff Cohen makes another good point. Obviously, all the news cannot be printed. *The New York Times* makes clear in its masthead that it prints "all the news that's fit to print." Decisions have to be made daily about what news events are "fit to print." I remember reading this line in Manlio Argueta's novel *One Day of Life* about war-torn El Salvador:

Almost all the houses in the area where Justino's death had been avenged were destroyed. None of this appeared in the newspapers.

Cohen's point is that "centrist propaganda finds space for certain histories and not others." Even if news accounts seem informative and balanced rather than biased, some stories are included and some are excluded, and all stories are partial or incomplete.

Gauri Viswanathan puts it this way: "Any verbal act is a representation and no analysis of reality can ever be devoid of ideological content as long as it is embedded in language" (*Masks of Conquest: Literary Study and British Rule in India*).

Rereading the News: Asian-Americans & College Admission Quotas

Comparing & Contrasting News Headlines

Compare the language in the headlines of these articles about admission policies (quotas) for Asian-Americans in prestigious universities:

"Asian-Americans Press Fight For Wider Top-College Door"
The New York Times, September 8, 1990

"Discriminatory Quotas in Colleges Confirmed"
The Asian Outlook, October/November 1990

What differing impressions do these headlines give? Why? Look at the wording. Look at the focus and who is taking action. Also, consider the newspapers in which these articles appeared. Who are the readers?

Stop now and read the two articles.

---

*James R. Kincaid, "Who Gets to Tell Their Stories?" *The New York Times Book Review,* May 3, 1992, 24–29.

Asian-Americans Press Fight
For Wider Top-College Door

Julie Johnson

Pressing an increasingly aggressive campaign of charges that the nation's top 1 universities are unfairly limiting their enrollment, Asian-Americans have begun to seek new ways to get responses to their concerns.

Organizations representing the nation's fastest-growing minority group 2 say the most prestigious universities have placed quotas on Asian-Americans admitted, even as the number of highly qualified applicants is rising.

They say the percentage of Asian-Americans accepted at the elite colleges 3 should be rising much faster than it has been because their academic qualifications are generally higher than those of other students.

Administrators at the top universities strongly deny that they discrimi- 4 nate on racial grounds in admissions, saying they are committed to shaping ethnically diverse student populations without quotas. But they say that to achieve racial, geographic and other desirable balances, some qualified students, regardless of race, have to be turned away.

Despite these denials, Asian-Americans involved in the issue say there are 5 many examples to support their assertions that they are not being admitted to the top colleges in proportion to the number that apply after graduating at the top of their high school classes with superior scores on the Scholastic Aptitude Test. The S.A.T. is the entrance examination most often considered in admissions by top colleges.

Ray Nicosia of the Educational Testing Service, which administers the 6 test, said, "Asians score by far the highest on S.A.T. math." In the 1987–88 school year, Asian-American students scored an average of 522 on the mathematics section and 408 on the verbal component of the test. By contrast, white students scored an average of 490 on the math section and 445 on the verbal component. Each section is scored from a low of 200 to a high of 800.

Documentation of actual quotas has eluded the Asian-Americans who 7 are complaining. But several universities, including Brown and Stanford, have conducted internal studies showing, the Asian-Americans suggest, that the percentages of Asian-American students accepted have remained roughly the same while the number of highly qualified applications has risen dramatically.

Frank Y. Liu, president of the Organization of Chinese Americans, said, "I 8 think it is pretty obvious that this practice of setting quotas against Asian-American students had been established."

A Slow Increase

An internal report prepared for Brown's president and trustees, covering 9 admissions over the last 10 years, shows a big increase in the number of applications from Asian-American students. In 1980, for example, 697 Asian-American students applied to Brown and 153 were accepted, a 21 percent acceptance rate. In subsequent years, the percentage of Asian-American students accepted ranged from 15 percent in 1983 to 23 percent in 1989 while the number of applications surged to a high of 1,783 this year.

Asian-American activists also point to Harvard, where the proportion of 10 Asian-Americans accepted for enrollment from 1978 to 1987 ranged from 15 percent to 11 percent. They say these are examples of the upper-limit quotas that exist for Asian-Americans at the nation's leading universities.

Eric Widmer, dean of admissions and financial aid at Brown University, 11 said: "In no sense are these quotas. But admission at any selective university tends to fall in the area of enrollment goals, which is to say we have to admit, we want to admit, a certain number of this kind of student and a certain number of that kind." The main goal, he said, is to enroll students "who will be filling all of the classrooms in all of the disciplinary areas."

But he said, "I think the Asian-American issue is founded on a justifiable 12 sense of concern."

He was unable to explain Brown's admissions figures on Asian- 13 Americans, which occurred before he took over as dean last spring, adding, "I understand the question but I can't speak to the answer particularly because I wasn't here at the time."

Some Brown officials said that one reason could be that most Asian- 14 Americans applying to Brown in the early and mid-1980's disproportionally identified biology and pre-medicine as areas of study and for reasons of academic balance all of them could not be admitted.

Progress Reported Made

But college administrators said that at Brown and some other top schools 15 Asian-Americans admissions rates have climbed in the last few years, and that this means that higher education officials are more acutely aware of racial insensitivity.

For example, Dean Widmer said that substantial progress had been made 16 to increase the numbers of Asian-Americans at Brown, and that this year their acceptance rate was higher than that for whites.

The University of California at Berkeley earlier this year announced plans 17 to substantially alter its admissions policies to correct what it called possible unintentional discrimination against Asian students.

Arriving at such selectivity takes race into account as well as a broad 18 array of factors like student participation in extracurricular activities, recommendations, essays, personal characteristics and academic performance.

Paula Bagasao, an Asian-American scholar who has studied college admissions and affirmative action programs, said that while such selectivity 19 has seemed to unfairly limit the number of Asian-American students on top campuses, rarely has it been discriminatory toward whites.

"I don't know where that happens very often that absolute numbers of 20 whites get turned away," said Ms. Bagasao, who is editing a series of magazine articles on Asian-American educational issues to be published in November by the American Association for Higher Education. She said that Asian-Americans would argue that even among those white applicants who may have been turned away from an Ivy League school, that alone does not mean they have been cast out from the nation's top universities.

"It has not pushed them down to the state schools," she said, contrasting 21 the cases of many Asian-American students who apply for admission to the best schools near their homes to allow for work or family support. In those cases if they are not accepted, the second choice may be a school of lesser prestige.

Grades Are Consistently High

Reflecting the importance the issue of possible admission quotas has gained 22 among many Asian-Americans it was one of the subjects raised with President Bush in a meeting he held in late July with 17 prominent Asian-American supporters.

With many colleges starting their fall terms this week, Asian-American 23 student organizations, including growing regional student organizations that encompass several campuses, have pledged to make sure the issue is not ignored. And Asian-Americans have established caucuses within higher-education associations while seeking to broaden their numbers on foundation boards and study commissions.

At the same time, local politicians and members of Congress with ties to 24 Asian-American groups have become more insistent in their calls for investigations into the admission practices of some of the nation's leading colleges. Congressional hearings on the issue are scheduled for late October on both the East and West Coasts.

Asian-American scholars, education officials and political leaders say 25 they are pursuing new avenues because they are frustrated by what they see as a continued discrimination against applicants whose grades and test scores are high enough to qualify them for admission in higher numbers than they are now being allowed into the nation's best universities.

Don Nakanishi, a professor of education at the University of California at 26 Los Angeles, said concern about Asian-American quotas "has clearly risen to the very top of the leadership agenda for Asian-American organizations across the country."

"This is an issue on which the two things sort of came together, the in- 27 creased demographic growth of the Asian-American college-going population and increased political strength of Asians in American electoral politics," said Professor Nakanishi, a Yale alumnus who recruits minority students for his alma mater and who is conducting a study of college admissions of Asian-American students.

And decisions to seek more direct political approaches to a decade-old 28 problem come as the Education Department concedes it is still months away from conclusions in its investigation into possible admissions bias against Asian-Americans at Harvard University and the University of California at Los Angeles.

While initial announcements about the investigations came more than a 29 year and a half ago, William L. Smith, the acting assistant secretary of education for civil rights, has said that "it has become very very clear that this is an important issue" to the Administration.

Representative Dana Rohrabacher, a freshman Republican from Califor- 30 nia who has taken on the issue of Asian-American quotas, said: "I think there is ample evidence to suggest there is a reason for us to look into the matter very carefully. There's a lot of smoke in the air."

Special to *The New York Times,* September 9, 1989. Copyright © 1989 by The New York Times Company. Reprinted by permission.

Discriminatory Quotas In Colleges Confirmed

John Kim

In 1976, there were 150,000 Asian American undergraduates in the U.S. higher education. A decade later, in the fall of 1986, there were almost three times as many—448,000.

Federal findings of discrimination against Asian Americans seeking admis- 1 sion to U.S. Universities and Colleges will be given closer scrutiny, said The Department of Education officials last month.

"We've illustrated allegations of discrimination [that] are taken very seri- 2 ously by this agency and this administration," said the department's assistant secretary for civil rights. "We anticipate expanding our compliance review activity." University of California at Los Angeles, Berkeley, and Harvard University are under investigations of setting quotas on Asian Americans.

The department's Office for Civil Rights recently released the results of a 3 30 month investigation of U.C.L.A., found that the graduate school's mathematics department gave illegal preference to whites over Asian Americans. The U.C.L.A. Chancellor, Charles E. Young, said the school would appeal the finding of discrimination.

Under Title VI of the Civil Rights Act, recipients of Federal funds cannot 4 discriminate on the basis of race, color or national origin. It is ironic, if the allegations are true, in U.C.L.A., a public institution which receives Federal funds. It is also interesting, Asian Americans choose public over private institutions. In 1986, 83 percent enrolled in public colleges and universities, compared with 77 percent of all college students.

The current investigation at U.C.L.A. found "a statistical disparity in the 5 rates of admission to the mathematics department on the basis of race, an inconsistency in how Asian American and white applicants who received the same evaluation ratings were treated, and insufficient evidence to show a nondiscriminatory basis for this pattern."

Kathryn Imahara, a lawyer for the Asian Pacific American Legal Center of 6 Los Angeles, said the results of the office's investigation "validates what

Kim

we've known to be true." She said: "You're always asking yourself: Are we being too sensitive? Are we paranoid? These things are so difficult to figure out. But it is something that the Asian community has known for years, but it is sad it is true. What we hope comes out of it is a good solid admissions policy."

Asians have faced discrimination within college communities and else- 7 where because others are "envious of the success that many Asians have had in the U.S. and are upset that their children were facing competition," said Dana Rohrabacher, a congressional Representative of California.

Mr. Rohrabacher said the findings at U.C.L.A. were "part of a whole syn- 8 drome" of discrimination against Asian Americans. He has asked the Senate Appropriations Committee to set aside $500,000 to complete the investigations at other schools by Dec. 31.

Reprinted by permission from *The Asian Outlook,* October/November, 1990.

Writing a First Response

Some college administrators claim that they must achieve "racial, geographic, and other desirable balances" and that some qualified applicants, regardless of race, have to be turned away. You have recently been admitted to college. What is your view of this "balance" policy? Do you see the point of view of these administrators? Do you agree that since the number of qualified Asian-American applicants has increased, the quotas should be lifted? Do you think this group is being discriminated against? How do you position yourself in this argument? Do you feel your race and gender played any role in your getting admitted (or not admitted) to a college?

Write a notebook entry or "First Response" to your reading of this issue. After writing your first response, read some first responses by some other students and write a little more in response to their responses.

I feel that the whole quota situation is stupid. When are we going to get over our stereotyping? Who should have the right to say someone cannot go to school because of his or her background? If someone works hard all of their lives and wants to achieve their goals, they should be able to go to the college that they want to go to, especially if they are qualified. It should not matter if the person is Asian-American, African-American, or Native-American. It should not make a difference. I see quotas as a terrible abuse of powers. Why do this? To protect the majority? Students who do the work and are willing to take on the responsibility and challenge of college should be able to carve out a future for themselves without being made to suffer because of their background.

Jeanine Perez
Latina

I do believe that Asian-Americans are being discriminated against. If you qualify, you should be accepted. On the other hand, it is not completely up to the admissions office but to standards they must meet. I think that it's all about greed and power. The people on top are intimidated by the thought of losing power to people of color.

Celines Deleon
Dominican

I actually wasn't surprised that the nation's top universities discriminated against Asian-American students. State and community colleges also discriminate against all students of color. At a community college I attended, many students of color felt that the nursing program discriminated against them. The students believed that once they took an interest in the program, the head of the department would try to direct their attention into different majors or the department would give them a hard time once they entered the nursing program. I find that when students experience racial problems within a specific college and they decide to take action on the problem, college administrators always tend to throw in students' faces that they do not discriminate on the basis of race, color, or national origin because they fear that the minority will overcome the majority in specific areas of study. So by placing quotas and limiting students of color admittance into top universities, the majority will remain ahead.

Yaminah McClendon
African-American

The issue of university quotas on Asian-American students is not news to me. Although we would like to think that everyone is equal in this country, it is not the case. There has always been discrimination against Asians and other minorities. In a place of higher learning, it is no surprise to me that Asians or any other minority groups are discriminated against. "Majority rules" is a very valid statement.

I strongly believe that the system must change. Entrance into universities should be based on qualifications. It is extremely unfair for a student who has worked so hard to get those high grades in high school only to find that they will be rejected from the college of their choice because of their race. Why can't a student be rewarded for their hard work? Entrance into a prestigious university can mean a lot to a person's future. The prestige of the university that you graduated from may very well determine if you or the person next to you will get a high-paying job.

Cynthia Tsui
Chinese-American

I cannot help but think about the stereotype of Asians as smarter than other races. Asians are trying to draw away from this stereotype, but almost every article I read about Asians is about Asians and education, how they are taking over the education of white students, how Americans resent them for being valedictorians in many high schools. People of other races think of the Asians as smart because that's how the media portrays them. I have never heard an Asian's view on blacks. I guess they relate crime and drugs to blacks, if they have never been acquainted with us.

Heather Whyte
African-American

After reading some other responses, Jeanine added: "I am not a racist; therefore, I would generally agree with the racial diversity balances. I do not feel that the quotas should be put on the minority. Instead the quotas should be put on the majority."

After adding to your response, trade your writing with someone and write back or use your response as an entry point for class discussion.

Writing a News Summary

Write a 100–150 word summary of each of the preceding articles. Summary writing is very helpful for your work across the curriculum. When you write a news summary, you do not give your response but try to follow as closely as possible the main points brought out in the article. The close and careful reading required for summarizing is very helpful when you do want to offer your reading or perspective. Like any other kind of writing, skillful summary writing requires practice.

Here are some guidelines for effective news-summary writing.

1. Reread the original text carefully. Observe carefully—study—what you are reading. Either underline the main points or cross out unimportant information (supporting details, direct quotations, unnecessary words, repetitions, and digressions).
2. Make a list of the main points on a separate piece of paper.
3. The purpose of this summary is to inform readers—that is, to report the news in brief. Your purpose is not to give your reaction or express your opinion or feelings, or to try to persuade your readers. What information should you select? What's essential? What should you leave out? Regardless of the article you're summarizing, your readers will want to

know: (a) What happened? (b) Who was involved? (c) What seemed to cause the event? and (d) What were the results? Reread the article with this list of questions in mind.

4. Write a draft in which you try to get down the main points in some kind of order. How should you arrange the information you've selected? Again, consider the purpose of a news summary.

5. Count the number of words you used to see if you stayed roughly within the word limit. You will be revising, so the word count will change. It's good, however, to have a rough idea of how much you need to cut or expand your summary.

6. A good summary is clear and concise. Reread your summary, first for word choice and then for sentence structure. Edit for one item at a time. Try out different words. If you are using a computer for writing, work with a printout. Double-space to make room for revisions. You may want to print out your summary after you've reread and revised it for various purposes (word choice and so on).

7. Read your summary aloud. Listen to how your words and sentences sound. Revise again.

8. Because you will be taking information from different parts of the article, your sentences may seem disjointed or unrelated. Again, read your summary aloud, paying attention to the way your writing sounds as a whole. Do your sentences lead logically from one to another? Do they seem disconnected at any point?

9. Rewrite your draft. Check your word count again. Can you be more concise? Do you have room to add another point?

10. Edit your "final" draft for grammar and mechanics, working with your editing list and using the editing system described in the appendix, "Guidelines for Editing Your Own Writing." (Do you need to revise your editing list? If you can now consistently control for a certain kind of error, you may want to remove it from your list. You may want to add a punctuation convention you don't automatically observe and want to remember to check on final drafts.)

Summary-Writing Workshop Activities

1. Compare your summary with two other summaries and discuss differences of presentation (language use, inclusion and exclusion, emphasis, arrangement) with the writers.

2. Perhaps select one summary from your group to submit for whole-group discussion.

3. Collaborate on a new summary after reading and talking about your individual summaries. One person can serve as the group's writer (and mediator).

Writing About Summary Writing

Take a few minutes to write about this writing experience. How did you go about writing your summary? What was your process? Was it effective? Looking back, would you make some adjustments now? Were the guidelines helpful to you? If so, what was particularly helpful? Do you have any suggestions for improving the guidelines? What advice would you give someone trying to write a news summary? What did you learn from this writing experience?

Now that you have written careful summaries of each article, take and make more notes to help you think about differences in presentation. Discuss these differences in class or write a brief summary about the differences and your observations.

A writer enters the room as a speaker might a conversation, in the hope of getting a hearing.
      Linda Brodkey

Writing a Response Letter

Read Victor Hao Li's perspective and write him a letter in response. Victor Hao Li was president of the East-West Center at Stanford University. The following analysis appeared in 1988 in *The College Board Review,* a magazine primarily for academic administrators. Imagine your response letter appearing with other letters in the next issue. In a brief opening paragraph, refer to the author and article and briefly summarize his viewpoint for readers who may have missed reading it. In this case, you would be writing for other readers. If you like, respond in a letter directly to the author.

Asian Discrimination: Fact or Fiction?

Victor Hao Li

Universities have always faced a difficult task. From a pool of qualified candidates, how can a fraction be selected for admission? In making this selection, universities must meet many criteria and deal with many constituencies. They must admit leaders and scholars, artists and athletes, alumni legacies and minority members. The process of identifying the most meritorious does not by nature lend itself to simple solutions or test score rankings. It calls for the making of judgments, and these judgments must be based on clearly articulated principles which are objectively applied. 1

In recent decades, another admissions task has been added: How can fair opportunity be given to able students whose backgrounds, for one reason or another, have adversely affected their educational achievements or aspirations? 2

The American higher education system has made tremendous progress in extending the opportunity to attend college to all groups in our society, poor as well as rich, blacks and other races as well as white. There was an earlier, shameful time when some universities discriminated against Jewish applicants. The methods used were sometimes blunt, and sometimes subtle gentlemen's agreements. Nevertheless, the result was that principles concerning the definition and value of merit were violated, often in the guise of seeking diversity or avoiding overrepresentation. 3

I especially appreciate the efforts made by many universities to increase 4 opportunities for able people from educationally disadvantaged backgrounds. In this regard, Asian applicants have posed some complex new questions for universities. Asians, though clearly a separate and minority ethnic group, do not fit into traditional categories. Indeed, a number of universities do not regard Asian-Americans as "minority" for many reasons.

What we must deal with is how to handle the large number of Asian- 5 Americans applying—and being admitted—to universities. These numbers often exceed by far the comparable proportion of Asian-Americans in the total national or regional college-age population. The success of such students is usually attributed to cultural factors that stress education, discipline, and achievement.

Asian-American communities are worried that de facto quotas or other 6 limitations on admissions have been or might be established. They want assurances that Asian-American applicants are not denied admission simply because an above-average number of such applicants may be qualified.

Universities deny that they discriminate against Asian-Americans, or that 7 they use racial quotas in any form. On the other hand, some California studies have suggested that Asian-American applicants have been accepted at a somewhat lower rate than whites. Some universities could conceivably worry that enrolling too large a concentration of Asian-Americans might harm their educational efforts by decreasing diversity, or might lead to political problems, especially in public institutions.

Questions concerning discrimination—we are speaking here, after all, 8 about discrimination and not about affirmative action—can be answered directly and readily. At the level of fundamental principle, there cannot be disagreement: No person should suffer any disadvantage because of race.

At the practical level, there should also be no controversy. In the normal 9 admissions process, applicants should be accepted on the basis of merit. Merit should have a direct and substantial bearing on academic performance and promise, although factors such as diversity of background and interests are legitimate concerns. In any case, the definition of merit and the criteria and process by which applicants are accepted should be clearly and publicly spelled out. All are entitled to know the rules of the game, and to attempt to measure performance against the stated norms.

I begin with the assumption that admissions officers are honorable and 10 conscientious people. I also recognize that selection is—and ought to be— partly subjective, as much art as science. From time to time, a valedictorian-student class president-bassoon player may be rejected for legitimate reasons. There is no doubt that mistakes will be made in some cases. But until a clear and undeniable pattern is shown, allegations of discriminatory practices are unfair.

Having said that, I do believe that some admissions officers and selection 11 processes are insensitive to Asian-American conditions and issues. I am not trying to assign fault, but simply to state a fact. Each of us is most sensitive to the familiar, and most insensitive to the unfamiliar. For large numbers of people, Asian-Americans still fall in the category of unfamiliar. The solutions to this problem are tried and true, but also take some time to implement: good will, education, training where necessary, inclusion of Asian-Americans in the admissions process, and open dialogue on all issues. I suspect that much of the criticism from Asian-American communities ultimately is aimed at insensitivity rather than discrimination.

Asian and American Communities

There is in this country a misconception—or at least, a partial conception— 12 of Asian-Americans. It causes far more serious problems than the possible discrimination in college admissions. Indeed, the misconception may lie at the heart of the insensitivity issue.

To begin with, many subgroups are labeled "Asian-Americans." These 13 persons originally come from a very large number of countries having highly distinct cultures, languages, and histories. To be sure, many from East and Southeast Asia share a Sinitic cultural heritage. Nevertheless, a Japanese is very different from a Chinese or a Vietnamese, much less an Indian or Indonesian.

Some Asian-Americans are quite well-established in American society. 14 The families of these persons may have arrived in the United States some time ago (Hawaii is celebrating in 1989 the 200th anniversary of the first Chinese immigrants); others may have come as graduate students and remained to hold good professional positions; still others may have been wealthy at the time they immigrated.

The children of such families may find that their physical appearance 15 and perhaps some cultural traits set them apart. The Nisei who were interned in World War II suffered a special disability. Others encountered discrimination, both overt and subtle, or had language and other social deficiencies. But taken as a whole, this group of young people were well-educated and were beginning good careers. They often needed extra nurturing and understanding, but that is quite different from needing affirmative action. To a significant degree, these are the persons who are pointed to as the "model minority," who exemplify the American success story, the *Time* magazine "whiz kids," or the Westinghouse science winners.

To be sure, some children of poor families or recent immigrants are also 16 high achievers. I have no doubt that the cultural factors mentioned earlier plus the hunger for survival or acceptance motivate such persons. My point is that when thinking of Asian-Americans as a group, we usually picture the high achievers from good backgrounds.

But there is an underside, a very substantial one. For many years, large 17 numbers of Asian-Americans lived in true "ghetto" circumstances. In many Chinatowns or Japantowns around the country, one could find abject poverty, abominable living conditions, little English spoken, and even less hope. These persons truly needed affirmative action programs and many other forms of assistance. But they tended to get little attention because we all were watching the "model minority" segment.

For universities, dealing with two distinctly different types of Asian- 18 Americans posed a special dilemma. If Asian-Americans were regarded as a "minority" for various affirmative action purposes, the beneficiaries undoubtedly would be the well-off group that did not need such assistance. If Asian-Americans were not regarded as a minority requiring affirmative action (because enough members of the "model minority" were part of the mainstream), then the disadvantaged would never get the opportunity to break out. And if a distinction were made between the two groups so that socio-economic (rather than ethnic) factors carried paramount weight, then complaints would likely be heard from others.

This situation was further complicated by the immigration law changes 19 of the late 1960s. Immigration quotas had previously been based on the size of a particular national origin group then in the United States. Since most of the settlers of this country came from Europe, the formal quota for almost all Asian countries was 100 persons per year. The new immigration law raised this figure to 20,000 per year, and has fundamentally changed immigration patterns in this country. Since that time, the number of immigrants from China, the Philippines, Korea, and other Asian countries has increased dramatically, and has been augmented by a large influx of refugees from Indochina. These newcomers include both "the best and the brightest" of the region and the economically and socially worst-off. In addition, huge numbers of college and graduate students have come from Asia, and many have remained in the United States after completing their studies.

How well do these newcomers do? Many excel, but again I would like to 20 draw attention to the underside. We have all read about cultural problems encountered by the Hmong people settling in Minnesota, ethnic conflict between Vietnamese and other fishermen in Louisiana, and poverty and crime among newcomers in Southern California.

Hawaii has none of these overt and festering social sores, and hence is 21 one of the better places. But even in Hawaii, the situation is alarming. About 8,000 new persons arrive there each year, mostly immigrants from China, the Philippines, and Korea, plus several hundred Indochinese refugees. Again, many excel, and we are proud of our success stories. But very many do not, or at least they have a long and difficult adjustment. For example, Hawaii's department of education found that the public schools had 9,000 persons identified as "students of limited English proficiency" (SLEP), with another 1,000 added each year.

These people must be reached by college and university admissions per- 22 sonnel. Because of their achievement and their background, these are individuals who would be model candidates for an affirmative action program. They require, I believe, a greater share of our attention and caring than do the overachievers at the top of the scale.

Mr. Li's article appeared in *The College Board Review, 32:* 149 (20–23), Fall 1988.

According to another report, Asian-Americans face widespread discrimination. Read a summary of this report by the United States Civil Rights Commission and write a response to share with students in your class.

U.S. Study Says Asian-Americans Face Widespread Discrimination

Celia W. Dugger

Asian-Americans, who make up the fastest-growing minority in the nation, face widespread discrimination in the workplace and are often victims of racially motivated harassment and violence, the Federal Civil Rights Commission said in a report made public yesterday. 1

The commission concluded that the Asian-American community, which doubled in size over the last decade to about 7.3 million people, is hobbled by less blatant but more pervasive barriers of language and culture. And, the commission concluded, immigrants who speak little or no English are frequently denied equal access to a decent education and the voting booth and treated unfairly by the police and the courts. 2

"There has been a widespread failure of government at all levels and of the nation's public schools to provide for the needs of immigrant Asian-Americans," the report stated. 3

The report, titled "Civil Rights Issues Facing Asian Americans in the 1990's," portrays an America that often stereotypes Asian-Americans as the "model minority," while neglecting the problems of poorer, less successful immigrants from Asia. 4

The commission said its report debunks the notion that Asian-Americans are treated fairly in this country. A 1991 Wall Street Journal poll found that a majority of American voters believed that Asian-Americans are not discriminated against, a finding that the commission said showed that the public is unaware of the problems confronting Asian-Americans. 5

"The report compiles evidence confirming that Asian-Americans do face widespread prejudice, discrimination and barriers to equal opportunity," the report said. 6

At a time of rising tensions between America and Japan, the report called on Presidential candidates to refrain from Japan-bashing that could inflame hatreds and encourage violence against Asian-Americans. 7

Buy America Craze

Charles Pei Wang, vice chairman of the commission and president of the New York City-based China Institute in America, said the recent craze for "Buy America" campaigns oversimplifies the reasons for the nation's competitive problems with Japan. 8

"I'd like to see us preach fair trade," he said. 9

The report, which took two years to compile, is based on reviews of court cases, bias incidents, scholarly studies, news reports and other sources. Arthur A. Fletcher, chairman of the commission, said in releasing the study yesterday at a news conference in New York that no field research was done because there were not enough staff members available to do the work. 10

The commission, a Federal fact-finding agency, is composed of eight 11 commissioners, half appointed by the President and half by Congress. It has a staff of 77, less than a third of its peak strength in the 1980's.

The report was released in New York and San Francisco, rather than in 12 Washington where the commission is based, because of the concentrations of Asian-Americans in those cities, commissioners said.

The report grew out of several conferences the commission held in 1989 13 on the civil rights concerns of Asian-Americans.

Dennis Hayashi, national director of the Japanese American Citizens 14 League, a prominent civil rights organization, said the report is "a significant first step" in combatting racial prejudice against Asian Americans.

"Last year's model minority has become this year's political scapegoat," 15 Mr. Hayashi said. "Just in the past few months we've seen a significant increase in the reports of racial harassment coming into our offices."

The commission found little reliable statistical data on hate crimes na- 16 tionally and said such violence often goes unreported, especially among Asian-Americans who distrust the police and may feel ashamed by their victimization. But it said documented cases of such incidents around the country show that racially motivated violence "occurs with disturbing frequency."

It singled out several murders, including the 1989 massacre of five Indo- 17 chinese children in an elementary school in Stockton, Calif., as well as harassment directed at Asian-Americans who move into hostile neighborhoods.

Grocery Store Boycott

The report also included a reconstruction of the year-long boycott by black 18 residents of a Korean-owned grocery store in the Flatbush section of Brooklyn. And it specifically criticized Mayor David N. Dinkins for not moving quickly enough to diffuse the tensions, saying the incident worsened the race relations in the city.

In the workplace, Asian-Americans confront discrimination in a variety 19 of guises, the report said. The most common complaint of the Asian-Americans who participated in the commission's 1989 conferences was of a "glass ceiling" that kept them from rising into management.

"Most felt that Asian-Americans are unfairly stereotyped as being unag- 20 gressive, having poor communications skills and limited English proficiency, and being too technical to become managers," the report said.

The commission said its review of national and local studies indicate that 21 the glass ceiling does exist. In records of court cases, the commission also found evidence that some employers discriminate against Asian-Americans because they speak with an accent.

The study found that there are not enough teachers who can speak the 22 many languages of the recent wave of refugee children from Asia, whom it said are "encountering more educational difficulties than earlier waves." The Asian-American community is comprised of Chinese, Filipinos, Japanese, Asian Indians, Koreans, Vietnamese, Laotians, Thais, Cambodians, Hmongs, Pakistanis and Indonesians.

Dugger

In addition, the report said there are not enough interpreters in the court 23 system, citing a 1985 case in Florida in which a Vietnamese immigrant who spoke little English stood trial for two days on murder charges. Even his own lawyer did not realize that the jail staff had brought the wrong defendant to the courtroom, since there was no interpreter.

The lack of Asian-American staff is especially pronounced in the nation's 24 police departments, the report found, where language barriers contribute to an underreporting of crime and botched criminal investigations.

Police Commissioner Lee P. Brown of New York City told Mr. Fletcher 25 yesterday that he is proposing that his department be allowed to hire Asian-Americans and other foreign-born permanent residents two years before gaining their American citizenship.

Under current New York state law, police officers must be citizens. In 26 New York City, less than 1 percent of the uniformed police are Asian-American.

Free copies of the report may be obtained by writing to the United States 27 Civil Rights Commission, Room 700, 1121 Vermont Avenue N.W., Washington, D.C. 20425.

From *The New York Times,* February 29, 1992. Copyright © 1992 by The New York Times Company. Reprinted by permission.

Readers' Dialogue

Respond in writing to someone else's response. Write back and forth and then exchange with another pair of readers and write a response to their written dialogue. Follow these exchanges of written response with small-group discussion.

Readers at Work

An event occurred. Marriott Corporation sponsored "Chinese Food Night" in the dining halls of a college campus (one of many across the country). In a Letter to the Editor of *Pipe Dream,* the primary campus newspaper, student John Choe described what he saw and how he responded.

Letters to the Editor

John Choe

Marriott's racism

To the Editor:

At Binghamton, we are all supposedly committed to "diversity." Admini- 1 strators, professors and students all talk about "diversity." It seems like every other word has "diversity" in it. One may, in fact, even be led to believe this school is not just paying lip-service to "diversity," but has a deep and truly genuine desire to be sensitive and to provide for the needs of all who are here, if . . .

If it wasn't for the concrete reality with which I am confronted and must 2 face every day. For instance, while walking to get "food" at my dining hall on Thursday night, I saw what looked like a Chinese man standing on top of the "Chinese food." It was a crepe-paper decoration of a Chinese "coolie," with slanted eyes, a "Fu Manchu" mustache, wearing a conical hat, carrying a bowl of rice and chopsticks in his hands. Marriott's food was not the only thing that was sickening that day.

Now that they have a "Chinese Food Night," why not have a "Black 3 History Month Food Night," with an "Uncle Tom" comically displayed on top of "Black Soul Food"? Why didn't they just put a big red banner up on the wall with the word "Chink," "Nigger," "Kike," or "Spic" on it? Not only was I offended by Marriott's insensitive racism but what saddened me the most was the fact that people were passing by and unconsciously acknowledging Marriott's perception of Asians.

I immediately asked them to remove these derogatory decorations but 4 they refused. Twice I asked. Twice they refused. They were not merely refusing a single individual–they were brushing aside the cultural integrity and pride that we all share in our own communities. This is a time for all cultural organizations on this campus to join together and demand the end of this type of insensitive ignorance and racism. We must demand that Marriott first explain and apologize for its callous behavior. We must also demand that Marriott stop having special "ethnic food" days, but instead incorporate these recipes into the ordinary menu. And finally, we must demand that Marriott consult the cultural unions when they plan to have "ethnic food" in the future.

Implicit in being a vendor on this campus, the Marriott Corporation has 5 an inherent responsibility to abide by the same ethical and moral standards that the administration expects from its faculty and students. Spreading racial and ethnic stereotypes across campus, with derogatory caricatures in all the on-campus dining halls, can only lead to the conclusion that Marriott has no commitment to "diversity." By allowing Marriott to get away with these racial slurs, the administration puts into question its own commitment to "diversity" and becomes an accomplice to these unbelievably insensitive acts.

Sincerely,
John Choe

In the next issue, another student responds to Choe's reading of this event—
he disagrees.

Joseph Kubler

Marriott not to blame

To the Editor:
March 17 has been a day celebrated by the Irish community for a long time. 1
St. Patrick's day has become a celebration of Irish pride . . . a day to remember

what we have overcome. On Sunday, most of us will be spending this holiday on campus eating at the nearest dining hall. Do I expect to see caricatures of the Irish, Leprechaun's with drunk "mic" written on their heads carrying jugs of whiskey? No, I expect to see the cutest of decorations put up with the best of intentions. However, I could choose to look for derogatory implications in well meant gestures.

Some members of our Asian community on campus have chosen to level 2 charges of racism against Marriott, failing to see the true issues. Marriott never intended to imply that Asian Americans were "Coolies" with "Fu Manchu's" any more than they would be implying that Irish Americans are three-foot-four and dress all in green with whiskey jugs as extension's of their arms when they put up Leprechauns. Marriott was trying to fulfill it's commitment to diversity on "Chinese Food Night" by recognizing the existence of distinct cultures within our culture.

It is our responsibility to look at the intent of people's actions and true 3 meaning behind them. If we fail to do this we create a system where people say nothing wrong, because they say nothing at all. Each culture will lose it's unique qualities because people feel more comfortable not recognizing the differences that make them special. If we choose to look for offense in everything we will only reinforce the barriers we are trying to take down.

Sincerely,
Joseph Kubler

John Choe replies to Joseph Kubler's letter to the editor.

John Choe

Racism and ignorance

Joseph Kubler's letter to the editor entitled, "Marriott not to blame," is a 1 classic example of how one can be ignorant, and at the same time, adroitly convince others of how proud one can be of that fact. Kubler's pathetic attempt to suggest that there are similarities between Irish leprechauns and Chinese "coolies" is patently absurd. Furthermore, Kubler has the audacity to use this profound piece of intellectual crap to allege that Asian Americans failed "to see the true issues" of racism and marginalization against their own community. Well, thank you Mr. PhD in Multiculturalism, for lecturing us on what we should and what we shouldn't consider offensive to our own cultural heritage. I'm sorry our behavior doesn't fit your stereotype of what it is to be Asian American.

Perhaps we should apologize for speaking up to a multi-billion dollar corporation when it twice refused to take down decorations that a customer found insensitive? Of course, Joseph "the apologist" Kubler, explains that Marriott had "the best of intentions" in ignorantly humiliating and degrading a significant cross-section of this campus. In other words, any action which hurts others is perfectly o.k. if your intentions were based on ignorance. Perhaps African Americans should apologize for rising up against the Ku Klux Klan, who lynched, raped, and mutilated them for decades?—why not—weren't those actions also based on ignorance? Rationalizing racism should no longer be one of America's favorite pastimes. As Joseph M. Mitchell, General Manager of Marriott on campus, told the Hinman College Council, "ignorance can no longer be an excuse for racism."

First of all, there is a slight difference between an Irish leprechaun and a Chinese "coolie." A leprechaun is a mythological fiction (like Santa Claus or American domestic policy) that some people still believe in (apparently Kubler believes in them since he thinks they're cute). However, "coolies" are a historical reality. These caricatures represent people who lived, worked, and died in this country. They represent a history which goes beyond the California gold rushes and the building of the trans-continental railroad (over a hundred tons of bones were returned to China). They represent an experience of being lynched and not being able to testify in a court of law; of being excluded by immigration laws such as the Chinese Exclusion Acts and various "Gentlemen's Agreements"; of being forced to attend segregated schools for "Orientals"; of being victimized by antimiscegenation laws prohibiting Asians from marrying others (these laws were later repealed only when soldiers started coming back with Asian wives); and of being denied our right as citizens of the United States and being driven into concentration camps during the Second World War. A Chinese "coolie" is not just another decoration.

It is obvious, and Mr. Mitchell wholeheartedly agrees, that using a caricature of a Chinese "coolie" as a way of selling and decorating Chinese food was entirely inappropriate. There are other symbols that people recognize as being more suitable for a celebration of Chinese New Year (such as Dragons). Kubler misses the point when he brings up the analogy of the Irish leprechaun. To many, including Kubler, this figure is an acceptable symbol of the celebration of St. Patrick's Day. Irish Americans chose by themselves to recognize this—not others. However, for many People of Color, including Asian Americans, stereotyped images have been forced upon us by the society at large—we were never given the chance to choose how we would like to be perceived. How many of you can remember the evil Asian male gangsters and exotic Asian female sex objects displayed in movies such as The Year of the Dragon? Or the wise Asian men (saying silly Confucian proverbs) used in cereal and toothpaste commercials? Just imagine the uproar if the Campus Pub decided to have an Irish Drunkard's Day, decorated with pictures of hobos.

Second, Kubler didn't even take the time to find out what our agreements with Marriott were. Marriott is currently obligated under the state contract to provide a diverse variety of food. However, because segregated and isolated "ethnic food days" had the potential for misunderstanding and insensitivity, Marriott agreed to stop them. Instead, these "ethnic" recipes will be incorporated into the regular menus and treated like any other type of "American" food. More importantly, part of the agreements (arrived at with representatives from the Black Student Union, Indian Student Organization, Hinman College Council, and the Student Association) stipulated that cultural organizations could still have ethnic food days if they requested them. Marriott also promised to consult with the cultural unions in the future.

So stop crying for America's corporate image. Marriott is a big boy now 6 and doesn't need any pampering by concerned college students. Rather than being concerned about corporations, we should be concerned about people—all people—not just those belonging to our separate little groups. Trying to understand other peoples and cultures is an integral part of one's college education. It was indeed saddening to watch people walk by the decorations during "Chinese Food Night," unconsciously accepting Marriott's perception of Asian Americans. Must we, as Asian Americans, turn to rallies and demonstrations to point out to the campus what everyone should know is hurtful and traumatic to us? Is this what it means to have a diverse campus? Or are we all just paying lip service to diversity?

In the same issue, another student responds to John Choe's original letter accusing Marriott of racism.

Scott Neufeld

In Marriott's defense

After reading John Choe's letter in the Friday, March 1 *Pipe Dream*, I felt 1 compelled to write a response in defense of Marriott, despite my usual inclination to let things slide.

At Binghamton, we have a revolution a day, and for those involved, 2 these matters are important; I certainly cannot deny that. However, as budding revolutionaries, these people have certain responsibilities that they must fulfill in order to drive their point home. Moreover, they need to examine the problem from the other side—the so-called antagonist's side. We hear the cry of racism often enough, but it is unfortunate that this word is repeatedly used instead of the more appropriate word "ignorance." And when I say ignorance, I don't necessarily mean stupid—I mean "lack of understanding."

In Marriott's defense, I would say that it wasn't at all a racist move. 3 Racism is a premeditated act designed to inflame a particular race (although "premeditated" may not apply to an ethnic slur drunkenly muttered, which is still racist). It was, quite simply, an accident. I am sorry to say that, when I think of all the motif's I've ever seen at Chinese restaurants or on Chinese take-out menus, I've seen a picture of these "coolies"—Chinese men wearing pajama-like clothing, pushing a wheelbarrow, with a thin grin beneath both a Fu-Manchu mustache, slanted eyes, and a conical hat. And, of course, he's carrying a bowl of rice and some chopsticks. Why am I sorry to say this? It bothers me to realize that, all along, I was looking at racist drawings being perpetuated by Chinese restaurants, and any images conjured by the thought of Chinese food were invariably those that I saw on the menus. Thus, Mr. Choe, if you are going to argue that Marriott created decorations designed to incite your ire, I would have to say that, in my ignorance, the decorations were appropriate.

Also, a mistake you made is that people walked by the display uncon- 4 sciously acknowledging Marriott's perception of Asians. Instead, I would argue that if nothing really struck passersby as out of the ordinary, their perception of Asians is similar to that of Marriott's. It was a decoration of a ₅ Chinese man—you took the responsibility on yourself to designate it with the racist labeling "coolie." A similar decoration of a black man would not be deemed a "nigger."

My second point is responsibility. Go ahead and speak your mind, but ₆ why bother with the little innuendoes of poor food quality ("Marriott's food was not the only thing that was sickening that day", etc.)? That strikes me as a childish lashing, designed to anger Marriott. I would think that, as a logical person, you would be satisfied with Marriott's apology—it seemed sincere enough to me, and I'm a cynic. Are you looking for reparations for mental anguish? From the sound of your letter, and how this was an "unbelievably insensitive" act, you have a distorted sense of reality. This was not unbelievably insensitive, it was merely a mistake. Hanging a red banner on the wall that says "Nigger Food" or "Kike Food" or "Spic Food" would be far more insulting than the picture of the "standardized" Chinese man, which you feel was indicative of Marriott's "brushing aside" of "cultural integrity and price"—such revolutionary jargon doesn't live with the situation, brother. When you make comparisons of racist remarks, at least make them logical. Or is Marriott the "Hitler of the 90's"?

Also in response to another of your articles, the crude cutout of the ₇ American flag was not a "bloody sin." Killing POW's is a bloody sin. What *The Binghamton Review* did was, at the very worst, tacky. Work in reality, not your radical fantasy.

Notice that the two students who defend Marriott do so on the grounds that Marriott did not intend to be racist. Neufeld defines racism as "a premeditated act designed to inflame a particular race." Do you agree with this definition? Gloria Yamato, in an essay called "Something About the Subject Makes It Hard to Name" (*Making Face, Making Soul,* ed. Gloria Anzaldúa, San Francisco, CA: Aunt Lute Foundation, 1990, 20–24), writes about various forms of racism. She would classify the Marriott incident under "unaware/unintentional" racism as opposed to "aware/blatant" or "aware/covert" racism. What do you make of the readings of this event? Was Marriott unintentionally racist in your view? Add your reading in the form of a letter to the editor.

Writing Opportunity: Comparing & Contrasting Media (Re)presentations

Defining the Task

Select two newspaper articles that reported a single news event but appeared in two different newspapers. Write about your critical reading of these two news presentations: To what extent are the two presentations alike? What do they have in common? How do the presentations differ? Cite words, phrases, and/or sentences to illustrate these differences. What did the newswriters choose to include or exclude? How is each presentation organized? Does the organization make a difference in your reading of the events described? If you read only one of these presentations, what would your understanding of the news event be, and why? Write an analysis. Your purpose is to help readers become aware of differences in news presentations and to encourage them to become questioning rather than passive recipients of "the news."

Getting Started: Browsing Through the News

Follow these suggestions for getting started.

1. Go to the library and learn what newspapers are available in the reading room. What other newspapers are available on microfilm? If you don't know how to use microfilm, now is a good time to learn. Browse through a newspaper on microfilm. You may want to go to the library with your entire class and have a reference librarian assist you.
2. Start reading, or at least browsing through, a couple of newspapers a day. Perhaps keep reading the same newspaper every day while trying out other newspapers as well.
3. Keep a "Reading the News" Writing Project notebook. Note news events of interest to you. Be sure to write down the name of the newspaper, each article's title, dates of publication, and page numbers in case you want to return to the articles later.
4. Take and make notes on articles of particular interest to you.
5. Create a project file folder. Include photocopies of some articles.

Keeping Going: Selecting a News Event

Here are some guidelines for choosing a news event to analyze:

1. When you read a news event of particular interest in one newspaper, look in other newspapers for reports of this event.
2. Don't select the first news event you come across that is represented in two newspapers, unless you are truly interested in this event and the presentations. Try not to write "from the outside"—that is, just to do the assignment. Go beyond this initial criterion (finding two news presentations of a single event). Writers (read: anyone who writes) writes better when they are interested in what they are writing about and not just performing a chore. It's awful to be in the middle of a writing project only to realize you're not really interested, so it's worthwhile to take a little more time browsing now. Select a news event you want to read critically.
3. Some cautions about selecting an event. You'll need to choose an event, not a broader issue or series of events. What is an event? Health care is an issue. An outbreak of fires in California is a problem. The struggle for power in Haiti is not a single event. You could, however, focus on one event (and two news reports) within that struggle. Discrimination is a social problem. The news release of findings from a study about Asian-Americans and college admission quotas is an event. Once you have selected an event, you may find that two news presentations of an event

are not different enough to analyze. Look at different kinds of newspapers, perhaps in the same geographic location, or in different locations if you are considering an event reported nationally or internationally. Sometimes closer (second and third) readings will bring out differences, such as a difference in focus, for example, or use of language you hadn't noticed before or inclusion of a photo and caption, but sometimes the differences are not sufficient or interesting enough to warrant a detailed analysis. Spend some time selecting a news event, and consult others about your choice so that you will have enough time for writing and rewriting.

Preparing an Analysis: Studying News-Event Presentations

After you've selected the news presentations you want to study, how can you prepare to make an in-depth analysis? To write a good critical analysis you'll need to reread both presentations several times and take and make careful notes. Try these suggestions:

1. Read both articles aloud several times, listening for differences. Make some notes. Did a particular word or phrase or sentence catch your attention? Is the omission of some fact especially apparent? What other differences did you observe?

2. If you recorded your first responses in your project notebook, look back now and compare them with your responses after rereading. Make some notes.

3. Take notes on each article (news presentation). Compare the two, perhaps using the comparison frame in Figure 6.5. It's probably also a good idea to make "first response" notes at this time for use later.

4. Based on the notes you took, write a news summary of each presentation. Your summary should be short (100–250 words, depending on the length of the article). Use the same order of presentation (the organization) as those in the original articles, but highlight the main points. Omit repetitions and minor points or minor details. What you are doing is "miniaturizing" or "condensing" the articles. This exercise will force you to read closely and will provide a foundation for your analysis. In order to think critically about what you have read, it is essential to understand the articles. Before questioning the presentations, you need to know what they're about.

5. Reread both articles again, this time making more notes. If you made notes earlier, add to these notes now. You may want to do some freewriting on one of your observations (about the use of language and its possible effects on readers, for example). Do some notemaking—some "thinking aloud"—on paper or at a computer.

6. Try giving others copies of the two articles you selected and asking them for their first impressions or readings. You may want to try your observations out on one or two other students in your class or on others outside your class. Make more notes.

7. Find out what you can about the readers (the different audiences) of these newspapers. For example, how are *The New York Times,* the *New York Post,* and *The Village Voice* (and their readers) different?

Figure 6.5

Points of Comparison	The Oracle	I.R. Committee
1. Scene (setting, situation)		
2. First Conflict		
3. Attempt at Resolution		

Writing a First Draft

1. Try beginning by working on your conclusion. You'll need to rewrite whatever you write now, but it's very helpful to have some work to rewrite or thoughts to reconsider. How do you want to leave your readers? What's the point of your analysis? What do you want to say about the comparisons you are making? While a conclusion is read last, writers usually work on a conclusion during the writing/thinking process. As you continue to work on your analysis, think about what you want to say, finally, to your readers. Perhaps you want to say something about what you learned about news reports or bias or the influence of print media on our reading. Perhaps you want to raise some questions and get your readers to think in ways they haven't before. How does the event you selected fit into a larger context? Is the event indicative of a larger social problem or issue? You may want to say something about that rather than isolating the event. Perhaps review your initial response.

How you conclude depends on the event you are writing about and what you are learning and thinking about and how you want to leave your readers. You don't simply want to conclude that the news presentations you studied are alike in some ways and different in others and therefore leave readers with different impressions. Well, you may want to conclude in this way! It's easier than thinking and rethinking through what you want to say. It sounds as though you got to the end of your back-and-forth analysis and didn't know how to conclude but what you did want to conclude was this assignment. This kind of conclusion sounds tagged on. If you aren't engaged as a writer, then will your readers be engaged? Writing a good conclusion is not easy, however, and if you have primarily written perfunctory conclusions, well, you need some critical thinking practice and also some ideas of what you might include in a conclusion for this kind of analysis.

Without rereading your notes and with your folder of notes and news clippings out of sight, try freewriting about the event and your impressions or concerns. You've done your research. Write to explore your viewpoint of these two news presentations. Sometimes the act of writing will push your thinking further toward an understanding or position. How will you position yourself in your conclusion?

Label this writing "Toward a Conclusion," and return and make notes or write further from time to time, perhaps after a first-draft workshop, for example.

2. Try rereading your notes and making a preliminary outline of points you want to make about these news presentations. Review our comparison frame (notetaking on headline differences, and so on). What do you want to include? Do you want to include every single point of comparison? Look at the notes you made about these points. What do differences show? Are the differences significant? What do you want to bring up first? What order makes sense from a reader's point of view? The order of points in your comparison frame may not be the order you want to use in your presentation. How will you illustrate your points? Quote from the news reports. Cite specific references. Before you write your first draft, work with an outline and make some notes about ideas you have for your presentation. You'll save much rewriting time if you spend time pondering now and making some notes and lists to work from when you write your first draft.

3. Summarize the event briefly for your readers who may not have the articles in front of them. Revise your summary so that it is very clear and concise but gives readers some idea of "what happened." Try in this draft beginning your introduction with a brief summary of the event. Then mention the two news reports you will examine. Provide titles, sources, dates. Place quotation marks around the titles of the articles and capitalize the important words. Use parentheses to note the source and date. Underline the name of the newspaper. (Do submit copies of the articles with your final draft so that readers, including your teacher, can read them.) Introductions are often written last after writers review what they have written. Draft an introduction now with the idea you will rewrite it later. After your summary and references, you need to guide your readers somehow into your analysis. What are they in for? Two newspapers covered the event. Okay, and how do you want to direct your readers? "While two newspapers covered this event, they . . ." Maybe try a line like this at this point. Get started, and get your readers started.

4. Consider the length of your presentation, your audience, and your purpose. Plan to write 750–1000 words. How does a consideration of length and audience affect what you select to say and how you say it? How does your purpose affect how you organize your writing? What tone should you use? How do you want to position yourself in relation to your readers?

5. Working with your tentative introduction and conclusion and notes and outline, write a first draft to read in a writing workshop or to submit for a reading. To prepare for a workshop or conference, write about what kind of help you would like. What's giving you difficulty? What questions do you have for a reader or readers?

Rewriting & Editing Your Writing

After a writing workshop or consultation, make some notes toward revision. Rewrite. Try outlining your printed revision. Review your outline of what you actually wrote. Revise your outline. Read your conclusion out loud and then your introduction. How do they relate and sound? Perhaps make some more notes. Carefully review your comparison and contrast. Reconsider your organization from the point of view of readers and in relation to your conclusion. Look back over your earlier notes and writing. Is there anything you can use now? Think further. Rewrite to the best of your ability and submit your writing for another review.

Because what you select (or do not select) to write about depends upon who you are, it could be enlightening to write about yourself as a reader of the news in comparison to other readers in your writing class. You could do so for discussion in a writing workshop or in conjunction with the submission of your final draft. How would you describe yourself as a reader of the news? What is your age? What is your student status? Where are you going to school? Where were you born? Where were you raised? Where have you lived? What is your social and cultural background? What is your gender, race, and class? What is your political orientation or bias? How does sexual orientation affect how a person reads "the news"? What else do you think is important to include in your description? How does your background affect your reading of the news event you selected?

Before you submit your final draft for presentation and evaluation, review your editing list (see the appendix, "Guidelines for Editing Your Own Writing"). What errors of convention do you keep repeating? Edit to the best of your ability. If you still don't understand a particular convention (a punctuation rule, for example), consult with someone who does. Ask someone who doesn't have difficulty with this convention to check your editing.

It's a good idea from time to time to submit a writing sample (a first draft or freewriting) to your instructor or another writing consultant for error analysis. Check the analysis for accuracy. Distinguish between a careless error and a convention you have not internalized or do not understand. Get help if you need it. Reprioritize the items on your editing list. Which error is likely to be most annoying to your readers, and which items are you still trying to learn to control? To assure success, consider only five to seven items during any session; don't try to edit for everything at once. Focus on only one item at a time by scanning your writing from the last sentence to the first for that kind of error alone. Check your editing with someone who can edit for this item. Make corrections. Revise your editing list if necessary, and make a note about your editing progress and goals. If you have gained control of errors on your list, you may want to experiment some now (with semicolon or dash usage, for example).

Reading an Issue: "The Noose Incident"

Comparing & Contrasting Media (Re)Presentations

On September 30, 1993, a community newspaper and a campus newspaper both reported a news event.

1. On the front page of the *Ithaca Times* these "teaser" headlines appeared, referred to two related articles on page 5:

> "Auburn Ouster: White Pride Marchers Are Routed by Overwhelming Counterprotest"

> "In the Noose: Racist Incident at IC"

Read the articles (briefly titled "Rejected" and "Reappearance"), which appeared together, with "Rejected" leading at top left, and "Reappearance" following, its head near the bottom of column three. A picture of the protesters was featured. Then write your "First Response" to "the noose incident." What is your understanding of this event? How is your impression biased by the inclusion and placement of the article "Rejected: Auburn Spits Out a Bitter Pill"?

2. Now read the reports of the "same" event in *The Ithacan,* "The Newspaper for the Ithaca College Community" (where the event took place). "An Appropriate Expression?" was a banner headline spanning five columns, with articles ("Criticisms" and "Art Project") in columns 1 and 5 and a photo of some of the confiscated nooses featured in the middle columns. Write your "First Response."

3. Next, make a comparison frame (as shown earlier) for notetaking and notemaking. Note differences in headlines, words, focus, and so on.

4. How is this event "read" (written) differently? How is it (re)presented in each newspaper? After reviewing your notes, write again, this time reflecting further about these two reports.

5. Discuss your reading of these "readings" of the news with other members of your class.

6. This event received national (media) attention and was even aired on a talk show. Why do you think it received so much attention? Write more. Talk more.

Auburn Ouster: *White Pride Marchers Are Routed By Overwhelming Counterprotest*

Rejected: *Auburn spits out a bitter pill*

It took over 100 police officers from six counties to protect a handful of "white supremacists" from the outrage of an overwhelming majority of demonstrators for peace and diversity in Auburn this past Saturday. A gathering of about 2,000 protesters and onlookers ejected the unwanted element, a group calling itself the USA Nationalist Party. A contingent from the Philadelphia-based neo-Nazi group had planned to deliver its message of racism in a march and rally, but its 20 or so members were prevented from even setting foot on the streets.

Prominent in the resistance effort were the National Women's Rights Organizing Coalition (NWROC), whose members are drawn from several upstate cities, and the Syracuse Peace Council.

The NWROC took up position at Auburn's City Hall, where the parade was to start. Its supporters said they were prepared to physically block the marchers. "We want people to know that the fascists will not be safe on the streets, here or anywhere else," a spokeswoman said.

The Peace Council wore colored stars and triangles on their clothing to symbolize the many groups identified by the German Nazis for extermination: yellow Stars of David for Jews, pink triangles for gay men, black triangles for gay women, red for political prisoners, brown for gypsies, and blue for the mentally or physically disabled. They formed a human chain and loudly chanted and sang.

When a few of the marchers appeared on the steps of City Hall, only a formation of police officers with batons at the ready kept them from being mobbed as the crowd surged forward, yelling slogans and waving fists in the air. There was a scuffle and some stone-throwing when the marchers finally boarded vans which took them away from the scene. Auburn Police Chief John Ecklund reports two arrests for weapons possession—a baseball bat and a knife—but no one was seriously injured.

In a letter to the *Ithaca Times,* Central New York White Pride spokesman Jack Wikoff of Aurora, New York, expressed outrage over the reception his group received in Auburn. "The police were incompetent at least and may very well have been deliberately acting to prevent us from rallying," he fumed. Wikoff claimed state troopers conducting "license checks" at city limits stopped a group of 11 Klansmen twice, delaying them "until it was too late" to join the march. He also said police failed to provide those who did try to march with adequate protection.

Asserting that White Pride "is about love of one's own people, not hatred of others," Wikoff rejected the label "supremacists." "We have no desire to enslave or exploit others," he wrote. "Our goal is to . . . create an all-White homeland in North America." He railed against counter-protesters and the mayor as "hypocrites" who denied his group their "Constitutionally protected rights of speech and assembly," and argued that "It was only our responsible decision to not go forward with the march that prevented much worse violence."

Whoever made the decision, the puniness of the militarily clad "marchers" being zipped out of town in a van with tinted windows would be laughable except for the threat of their return. "I think they are not finished here," Auburn Mayor Guy Cosentino said later that day.

As celebrating demonstrators shouted "We won! We won!" and a police sharp-shooter on a rooftop opposite City Hall folded up his gear, the street slowly cleared. One of the last to go home was Mitchell Lewicki, an Auschwitz survivor who has lived in Auburn for the last 45 years. He was wearing his striped prison jacket and he had his camp photograph folded over his breast pocket like a badge. "I was 19 when I went to Auschwitz. They took the best years of my life." Lewicki was quietly lionized as people approached him to talk and to look at his photographs: a silky-lashed boy with a dreamy smile in one, and in another, the same boy as a gaunt prisoner with dead-looking eyes. "What happened here today was good; we must not let Nazi hatred return," said Lewicki.

Wendy Skinner, Claudia Montague

In the Noose: Racist Incident at IC

Reappearance: *Ithaca College*
grapples with racist incident on campus

Meanwhile, Ithaca College officials are investigating the appearance of what looks like a racially motivated gesture on campus. According to IC spokesman

David Maley, a campus safety security officer discovered a rope in the shape of a hangman's noose tied to a tree in front of the campus center early Tuesday morning. A search of the campus turned up eight more nooses, six hanging from trees and two lying on the ground beneath trees. Five of the nooses had been dipped in tar, three in cement and one in plaster. Each noose was accompanied by a small block of wood with a name written on it, Michael Jordan, Jesus, "Malcolm" and Uncle Ben among them. One block had two names: "Tyson" and "A. Wiggins," the latter apparently referring to a former IC student who was tried and acquitted of raping a fellow student two years ago.

An unidentified male undergraduate student turned himself in Wednesday. Maley said the incident is under investigation and is being treated "very seriously." The IC Student Conduct Code prohibits conduct that "recklessly or intentionally endangers or threatens the health, safety or welfare of any person on college property," he said, and the penalty for violations can range in severity from a verbal warning to expulsion. The college did in fact expel a group of students for dressing as Ku Klux Klan members and leading another student in blackface with a rope around his neck through the campus center in the late Seventies. 2

Maley would not comment on rumors that the nooses were intended as a piece of artwork. "Students have freedom of inquiry and expression, but not to take actions that disrupt college operations," he added. "How this applies to this incident is still being determined." 3

IC President James Whalen has already issued a statement of condemnation. "This kind of action is designed to provoke fear and hatred," he asserted. "Whatever the purpose or motivation . . . what was done is completely unacceptable." 4

The college scheduled a forum to discuss the incident and the issues surrounding it for Wednesday night at 7:30 P.M. in the Emerson Suites, Maley said. 5

Claudia Montague

These articles reprinted from *The Ithaca Times*, XVI, 12, 9/30/93, by permission of the publisher.

An Appropriate Expression?

Ithacan Staff

Criticisms flare during Wednesday night forum

The students that came to the open forum on race relations Wednesday night had more on their minds than the art project of Justin Chapman '94. 1

What was to be a discussion on the racial implications of nine nooses hung around the academic quad became a heated debate between administration and students on several broader but interrelated issues: 2

• What many people said is a lack of concern the College has displayed toward previous incidents of harassment and assault. 3

Ithacan Staff

- The College's attempts to interpret this specific incident and other situations for the public by denying access to full disclosure of details. 4

- The complex process students must endure in reporting incidents of concern to the College and the perceived ineffectiveness of this "process." 5

John B. Oblak, vice president for student affairs and campus life, presided over the meeting of more than 400 members of the college community in the Emerson Suites, which lasted more than two hours. The administration became the target of student animosity, with many jeers directed at Oblak. Others questioned the absence of College President James J. Whalen. 6

The Office of Student Affairs and Campus Life called the forum to address the issues raised over the display of the nine nooses, labeled with names of various public figures, early Tuesday, Sept. 28. 7

Although interpretations varied, Oblak said the nooses were removed because "the symbol of the noose would cause very strong emotional harm" among the members of the campus community. 8

But instead of discussing the potential for harm that College officials felt existed, students strongly protested the removal of the nooses, and accused Oblak of disregarding and avoiding the issues and questions raised. 9

Whose interpretation counts?

There were many different viewpoints expressed about the art being removed before the public had a chance to form their own opinions. Because the artwork could not physically harm people, most speakers said the College overreacted. 10

"They made assumptions that it was a negative statement," said one male student. "They took away the chance for people to make their own conclusions—that is what art is for." 11

Oblak and a few people in the audience responded with concern that the community may have been emotionally damaged. "We are not opposed to people using their art to create dialogue. We were in the position of having to be aware of the use of symbols that may be perceived as a negative message," Oblak said. 12

Rita Alamshaw, a residence director, said she would have felt threatened by the nooses had she seen them on campus. "If I'd know it was art, great, but before I know it's art, my fear goes up." 13

Chapman and others argued that no one would have been physically threatened by the display. 14

Alamshaw, joined at the microphone by Chapman, told him, "My emotional and mental well-being is my physical well-being." 15

"Why now?"

Audience members questioned why a forum was called and media alerted for this seemingly harmless incident when a host of past racial and sexual harassment incidents had received little attention. 16

Students called attention to several prior incidents they felt the College had not sufficiently handled: Two Latino women racially harassed in an elevator in the Towers; the case of Mike Maison, an African-American male 17

PLATE 1
Untitled by Martin Molina, 1988. Reproduced by permission of the artist.

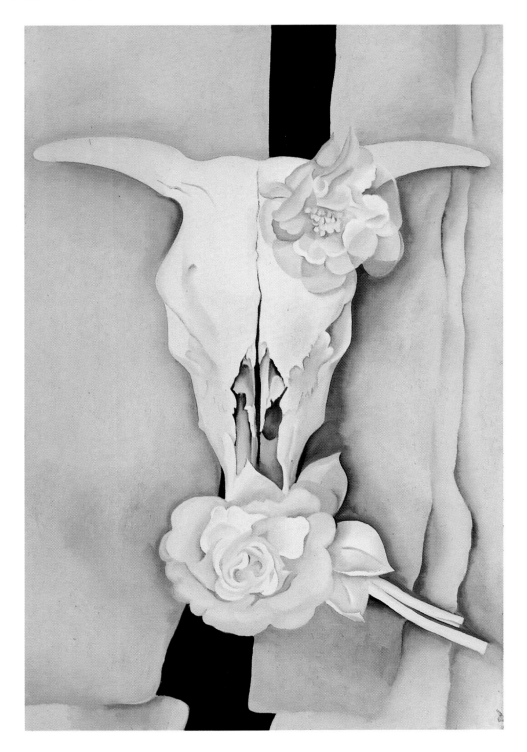

PLATE 2
Cow's Skull with Calico Roses by Georgia O'Keeffe, American, 1887–1986.

Oil on canvas, 1932, 91.2 × 61 cm, Gift of Georgia O'Keeffe, 1947.712
Photograph ©1994, The Art Institute of Chicago, All Rights Reserved.

allegedly driven from his dorm due to racial harassment and then "pissed and vomited on by a white male"; the case of music professor Einar Jeff Holm allegedly sexually harassing female students over the last decade; and the case of Andre Wiggins, a former student expelled from the College after being acquitted in court of rape charges.

"My anniversary is coming up," said one Latina woman. 18

"I was harassed last year on an IC bus. Even then it didn't make a god- 19 damn difference," she said.

"Why did I learn more through rumor about this [noose incident] and 20 people still don't know what happened to me?"

Future action

Many people believed Chapman, an African-American student who created 21 the art project, was being "hung" for his actions, while when a student of color is victimized the college turns its back.

Several students said the College should not discipline Chapman. 22

One student asked on what grounds a student would be expelled, and 23 whether the professor involved in the project would face disciplinary action as well.

Oblak, citing privacy laws, said he could not discuss student conduct or 24 personnel matters.

Chapman said after the forum that he was pleased the event took place 25 and that it went the way it did. He said he thought the ramifications of the forum would facilitate more discussion about the subject across campus.

Chapman speculated that "people would [have] been scared" if the 26 College had not taken down the artwork.

"But at least they would have made that decision on their own," he said. 27

Andrea Potochniak, Kristine Lyons, Chris Lewis and Tavon Walker contributed to this article.

Kristine Lyons, Ithacan Staff

Art project confiscated for racial overtones

An incident originally characterized by College officials as the worst racial 1 episode in years turned out to be an art student's project.

Nine pieces of rope in the shape of hangman's nooses, each dipped in ei- 2 ther tar, cement or plaster, were found in the Academic Quad early Tuesday morning, Sept. 28. Seven of the nooses were found hanging in trees and two were found on the ground under trees.

A Campus Safety officer discovered the first noose at 5:30 a.m. on the 3 south end of the Campus Center during a standard safety check.

Under each noose was a wooden block inscribed with different names: 4 "Michael Jordan," "Lonnie Granier" [sic], "Emmett Till," "Malcolm," "Malice Green," "Uncle Ben," "King 2," "Jesus," and another with "Tyson" written on one side and "A. Wiggins" on the other.

Ithacan Staff

Andrew Wiggins was an African-American student who was expelled ₅ from Ithaca College in March 1991, following his November 1991 acquittal from rape charges in Tompkins County.

During a press conference at 3:30 p.m. Tuesday, the College displayed ₆ the nooses to campus media and condemned the act.

"This kind of action is designed to provoke fear and hatred," said ₇ President James J. Whalen in a press release from the Office of Public Information. "Whatever the purpose and motivation of those making this statement, what was done is completely unacceptable. Neither racism nor threats of any kind will be tolerated at Ithaca College."

Late Tuesday afternoon the student turned himself in to the Office of ₈ Student Affairs and Campus Life, said Dave Maley, manager of public information.

College officials are considering various disciplinary actions against the ₉ art student, the worst of which is expulsion, Maley said.

A. Harry McCue, chair of the art department, referred questions to Dave ₁₀ Maley.

The student responsible for the project, Justin Chapman '94, addressed a ₁₁ crowd at a forum sponsored by the Office of Student Affairs and Campus Life, Wednesday night in the Emerson Suites.

The intent of the art project was to provoke discussion on race related is- ₁₂ sues, Chapman said.

"The intention was to spark reaction and thought on race-related issues. ₁₃ The noose is a representation of something that rendered African-Americans powerless—it is ironic that the immediate assumption was that it was a racist incident," he said.

But John B. Oblak, vice president for student affairs and campus life, said ₁₄ because of the nature of the evidence, it would not be reasonable to assume that the artwork was designed by Chapman, an African-American student.

College officials originally said they had no way of knowing the intent or ₁₅ meaning of the message, but they would be taking it very seriously. "This was done anonymously and in the dead of night," Maley said. "This is a public threat."

After learning the nooses were for an art project and the intended mes- ₁₆ sage, Nick Wharton, director of Educational Opportunity Program said, before the forum, that he was still offended and everybody would have a different interpretation.

"These symbols evoke some real things to me. This is a racist kind of ac- ₁₇ tion," Wharton said Tuesday.

Chris Lewis and Tavon Walker contributed to this article.

These articles reprinted from *The Ithacan*, September 30, 1993, by permission of the publisher.

Role-Playing: Points of View

Write briefly from the point of view of each person. Write using "I" as if you were that person in the situation described. You can try out all the roles. If you just try out one or two roles, you'll need to read through the roles to get some sense of this event.

1. You are an Ithaca College campus security officer working on the night shift. While making the rounds at 5:30 A.M. on Tuesday, September 28, you discover a rope in the shape of a hangman's noose hanging from a tree at the south side of the Campus Center. After searching the academic quad area, you discover eight additional nooses. Six were hanging from trees. Two were found on the ground under trees. Five of the nooses had also been dipped in tar, three in cement, and one in plaster. Under each of the nooses was a small block of wood, and each block had a name written on it: "Michael Jordan," "Lonnie Granier" [sic], "Emmett Till," "Malcolm," "Malice Green," "Uncle Ben," "King 2," "Jesus." One block had "A. Wiggins" on one side and "Tyson" on the other. What are your thoughts as you put this last block down and stand alone in the quadrangle looking at the nooses? What are your assumptions about this incident?

2. You are the college president. A phone call awakens you at 5:45 A.M. with news of this incident. You must respond immediately with a statement of your position for news release to the press. What do you assume motivated this incident? Only a few days earlier you read in the local paper about an attempted march in a nearby town by members of White Pride, whose goal is to create "an all-White homeland." You are aware that the local as well as the campus community will be interested in your response. (You are unaware at this point that this incident will receive national media attention.)

3. You are a first-year student at Ithaca College. You've been on campus a month and are still making adjustments. It's 6:30 A.M. You have to get up to go to your 8 o'clock writing class. Half asleep, you stagger into the dormitory bathroom. No one else is up. On a mirror under a fluorescent light you see a News Bulletin entitled "MEDIA ALERT." What's this? you wonder. Then you learn of the incident and the president's response and read these last words: "Anyone with information is asked to contact the campus safety office or hotline." Scrawled across the top is a message from your R.A.: "Floor meeting tonight!" And scrawled at the bottom: "Campus meeting to discuss this incident, Wednesday night." It is still dark outside. You feel afraid. Nooses on the quadrangle?

4. You are a senior majoring in art at Ithaca College and are African-American and male. As part of your senior-level studio art course, you were given the following assignment:

> Design a proposal for a site-specific sculpture or installation. This design should include either a model or detailed drawings depicting the sculpture and the site from different points of view. You should provide information on the method of construction and installation. It is important that you consider the site carefully and that your proposal express that consideration.

You design an art project, which includes nine pieces of rope in the shape of hangman's nooses. The nooses hung in an art room for two weeks and were seen by many people. You decide that you want to provoke discussion about racism on campus through the symbolism of these nooses. You need a more public space. At 1:30 A.M. on Tuesday, September 28, a female friend helps you put up the nooses on campus. A campus safety officer watches you. At 6 A.M. the college sends out a press release with distorted information. You hear about it and read about it. You decide to take responsibility for the nooses. "I didn't do anything wrong," you say. At the campus meeting, you get up and speak.

5. You are the president of Ithaca College again! You have just learned that the "noose incident" was an art project. Now what is your response?

6. You are a campus officer but not the one who found the nooses. You and some other officers think it's quite possible the nooses were an art project but you do not check with the art department or let any officials know of this possibility. Why not?

7. You are the director of the Educational Opportunity Program. You feel that the Ithaca College community "never had a chance to discuss the implications of guerrilla art." You also feel that in some ways the artist's "intent to discuss racism is honorable." "What do you mean?" someone asks you during a panel discussion called "Reflections on the Noose Incident."

8. You are Latina and a student at Ithaca College. When you hear about "the noose incident" and all the media attention, you wonder why your racial harassment case last year didn't receive more attention. You are sitting on a campus bus talking to a friend about your response.

9. You are an Ithaca College student reading *The Ithacan*. You read about what some members of the campus community think are key issues that need to be addressed concerning "the noose incident." Then you read two letters to the editor expressing different viewpoints. "What's your view of this issue now?" a news reporter from *The Ithacan* asks you.

The Ithacan Inquirer

Christy Ayres and Dave Slurzberg

In light of last week's incident, what are the key issues that need to be addressed?

I feel that people should take freedom of expression as a responsibility to express themselves carefully. 1

Wayne Hopkins '95, TV/R

Treat the students like adults. Talk about racism, homophobia and sexism because we should all be mature enough to discuss it. 2

Kristen Popp '94, Finance

Students deserve answers to their questions. Especially when some incidents aren't given as much attention as this one. 3

Kirsten Distel '95, Psychology

People have to learn to think beyond racist levels. The problem I have is that most people jumped to a conclusion saying that this is racist. 4

Michell Sylvester '97, Acting

Everybody needs to understand the administration can't satisfy every individual on campus. 5

David Stein '94, International Business

It's not a question of black or white, it's a question of intent. I'm interested in 6
the intent if the student has a reason to express and create a dialogue.

Gossa Tsegaye '76, TV/R Faculty

Diverse Reaction to Noose Incident

Argument was "too ambiguous"

Now that the initial outburst of controversy regarding Justin Chapman's art- 1
work has passed, I feel that it is time to start looking at the events of last
week from a more critical perspective.

My interest in art and politics compels me to use this newspaper to voice 2
my opinions, with the hope that other people interested in the same issues
will respond and take advantage of the opportunity for dialogue that these
events have opened.

The artist's intention, as stated by himself, was to provoke discussion; 3
and although the artist is not directly responsible for the quality and level of
discussion that his artwork sparks—especially when people don't have the
chance to experience the work as he intended—it is the nature and level of
the discussion that interests me (I am particularly concerned with the level
of discussion that took place at the open forum last week).

To convey a political argument, Justin decided to create a visual object, 4
and not a speech or an essay. It is indeed difficult to attempt this, to strive
for the marriage of politics and art, and it is according to his performance in
this endeavor that I would like to evaluate Justin's work.

The effectiveness of this political art project rests on the artist's ability to 5
balance his political statement with his artistic statement, and it is here that
I feel that Justin failed.

The work's aesthetics compromise the clarity of the political argument 6
and render it too ambiguous.

The reason why this happens is because, to paraphrase Barthes, the work 7
is a structure of signifieds and not a galaxy of signifiers.

The work utilizes symbols that are strong signifieds of racial oppression 8
in this country but fails to construct signifiers that would allow the viewer to
elaborate a political argument.

My critique is that the artwork presents historical facts—'nonwhite peo- 9
ple were and are systematically oppressed in this country'—but makes no
political argument about how to confront and act upon this situation.

Personally, I think this is the kind of politics that need to be developed 10
and encouraged.

What is not needed is 300 people going into a cathartic frenzy, eager to 11
participate in the humiliation of a college official who acts as a substitution
device, buying their momentary ease of conscience through such a fruitless
display of juvenile insubordination.

This behavior is what's behind the current epidemic of shallow activism 12
and political correctness, and it was the prevalent mood at the open forum
of last week.

Let's face it: asking Mr. Oblak for an explanation of all of life's injustices 13
will do us no good.

We need to start looking somewhere else for our own answers. 14

Ulises Mejias
Film '94

Art project exposed what is missed in everyday life

The recent incident on campus involving the art of Justin Chapman has 1
raised the question, "What is art, and where does it belong?"

Often, in times of controversy, I like to put things into historical perspec- 2
tive; this recent incident spurred such thought. Images of knife-toting Salon
goers in 19th century Paris whose mission it was to destroy the Works they
considered offensive immediately came to mind.

Or, when the Christians covered the genitals of nude figures in the middle- 3
ages. Let us not forget that Vincent Van Gogh died lonely and poor. His art,
largely shunned in his life, is now amongst the most costly and acclaimed in
the world.

It is often difficult to understand art within its context; it is seemingly 4
harder to understand. The interpretations of Justin's piece are numerous,
which may very well deem it a success. The revolutionaries of history have
received the most scorn, and in turn provoked new ideas and philosophies.

Art should offend, as well as delight. Since the dawn of civilization, art 5
has been a vehicle in which inner emotions have been expressed. If Justin's
piece offended you, it made you think of a great injustice in the world. It
brought forth a thought that is not present in your everyday life. That is
what art is all about. If Justin's rather "unorthodox" way of displaying the
piece is what offends you the most, consider how effective it was. The context did not let the viewer dismiss the uncomfortable message within the
realm of art.

Amongst the diverse quality of the Ithaca College community, let's also 6
be forthcoming and appreciative of the expression and freedom of the art
world. We should move forward from here, not backward.

Congratulations Justin, you are truly ahead of our time, and that is an ac- 7
complishment that countless others have sought without success.

Bethann Barresi
Art History/Anthropology '95

These articles reprinted from *The Ithacan*, October 7, 1993, by permission of the publisher.

Writing Opportunity: Arguing Your Point of View

Write an editorial for a class anthology of "Perspectives on the Noose
Incident." Use the editorials in *The Ithacan* as models for writing.

Write a brief summary of the event. Compare summaries in small groups.
Collaborate on rewriting a summary. Submit one summary from each group
and vote on which summary to use at the beginning of this anthology of
perspectives.

Perhaps an editorial board comprising of one member of each group could be formed to oversee the production (from introduction to format).

When writing your perspective, identify yourself as a reader. From what background are you reading this event? Notice how Ulises Mejias and Bethann Berresi wrote about their interests in this event. Their names led some of my students working on this project to believe that they came from different cultural backgrounds. How does cultural background affect your reading?

What is your reading of this event? What is your argument? To help you lay out your argument, study how Ulises Mejias and Bethann Barresi argue their views. What different points are they trying to make? Summarize each view in one sentence. How do they lead us to their viewpoints, and what support do they offer? Is each writer convincing? Why or why not? Are there still other ways of looking at this event or of arguing either of their points of view?

After you have written and rewritten your perspective and received comments along the way and edited your writing, consider a title for your perspective. Or, if you are making a class anthology, do you want to let an editor or editorial board give your writing a title?

Perhaps you would like to make an anthology of "Perspectives" around a different news event that raises an issue you would like to address. If the event is a recent one on your campus, you may want to submit your perspectives to a campus newspaper.

Arguing vs. Expressing Your Opinion

When I work with faculty across the curriculum, one complaint I hear about student writing, especially the writing of first-year students, is that students frequently express their opinions rather than argue and analyze. Of course, you will have opinions about whatever you read, especially if the topic is controversial. And you need to express your opinion. Your "reading" is an opinion. It is one way of reading. But how convincing is your reading? How do you argue your reading? That's another story. How do you get others to at least understand your reading? How do you convince them? It's important in building an argument to distinguish between expressions of opinion and reasons or statements you make in order to convince readers.

Here are some examples of expressions of opinion:

"I don't think he did anything wrong."

"It's wrong to punish him."

"It wouldn't be fair."

No new evidence is presented. Just more expressions of opinion.

"People are free to express themselves. No one should be denied freedom of expression."

Still an expression of opinion.

"According to the Bill of Rights (Article I), freedom of speech is a right."

OK, now you've appealed to authority. Still, you need to include reasons for your viewpoint.

Let's look now at the beginning of a computer-assisted discussion about "the noose incident." The incident was a recent occurrence. These students had just read two news reports (September 30, 1993), one in the *Ithaca Times* and the other in *The Ithacan*. They were eager to talk. They used pseudonyms and began "talking" through a computer program to other classmates on the network. Everyone could scroll through the various responses and then type a reply at any time. This excerpt comes from a transcript I printed out at the end of the discussion and made available to students for a face-to-face class discussion. When you read, separate expressions of opinion or questions that ask for opinions from evidence (reasons) and information.

Pride: The college was a little too hasty.

Mohawk: What if a white student (excuse me, *Anglo*) had put the nooses out there?

Shoe: Did the campus safety officer make the right decision in taking the nooses down?

Moose: The newspapers called it a racist incident. Was it?

Shoe: The initial reaction of the campus (the president's official statement) was that it was a racist incident done by a white student.

Mr. Greenjeans: Yeah, I think it was a racist incident.

Shoe: What if a white student had done it as an art project on his view of the persecution of the blacks? Would the students react the same?

Pride: Dear Shoe, the safety may have made the right decision in taking the nooses down. He did not know that the nooses were an art project. The question here is, did the college officials make the right decision?

Bob: I think that the artwork succeeded in getting people to be more aware of racial discrimination. I applaud Chapman for this work.

Shoe: But a lot of people do not think it is a racist incident because it was done to create dialogue about racial problems.

Caliente: I think Chapman was very clever. But I still don't like the fact that people were more concerned with this than they were about the KKK incident and the harassment of the two Latina women.

Mina: After reading the news, my first reaction was fear of my life. I don't think that when anyone sees nooses hung around the campus they would ignore the incident.

Expressing your first response or initial reading to others can help you think through your response. Try out a point of view. You don't have to use a computer network. You can do focused freewriting instead and exchange (and write back and forth if you like). Through more discussion and perhaps more reading, you may change your point of view. Once you decide on your perspective, then a different kind of work begins. You then need to explore ways of explaining and supporting your view. Everyone on the computer network was quick to give an opinion. Later in class, however, it took some time (and several drafts) to work out the reasoning behind various points of view. This is important work, not only for your schoolwork across the curriculum but also for your life beyond school. (There is life after school!)

Preparation for Writers

& don't think only inexperienced or untalented writers rewrite!
Au contraire.

Ursule Molinaro

After writing your first "get-it-out" draft, review your writing. Make a list of what you brought up: Information, explanations, reasons, opinions. Look at your statements. (My students highlighted expressions of opinion on computer-printed first drafts and then listed them.) Separate or note reasons. Look at your reasoning. Look for connections. Should you exclude anything? Did you include statements that do not help build your point of view? Do you need to include more support or to make better connections? Do you need to reorganize for your readers? Reviewing your first writing before a workshop and doing some rewriting can help you move more quickly through the rewriting process. Also, most of your classes across the curriculum will not include writing workshops. Many professors, probably most, do not ask for drafts. You are expected to go through the drafting process on your own or to seek help through a writing or tutorial center. Writing workshops will help you learn to read critically and to become a better reader of your own writing-in-progress. Writing workshops are even more useful when you come to class well prepared.

Some Questions to Guide Readers

What does the writer claim?

What reasons are given?

Are the reasons clearly stated?

How convincing are the reasons?

Does the writer use personal opinions and feelings instead of reasons? Some? Both?

Does the writer explain without giving reasons?

Is the argument valid? (Is the conclusion supported by the reasons—or are the reasons faulty/not trustworthy?)

Did the writer keep the audience in mind? Is the argument written appropriately for the intended audience? Does the writer assume too much (about the attitudes, beliefs, background of the intended audience)? Make specific references to the text where you see some problems.

Note: You may think of other questions or want to adapt (or adopt!) these. You may want to workshop one or two drafts as a whole group to develop your own critical reading skills and to establish clear criteria. What's a valid argument is a valid question, and readers need to reach some kind of agreement with the guidance of the teacher who, no matter how dialogic the classroom, will ultimately give students grades.

Defining Oneself: Ethnic Identification

Defining is a continuous process, crucial to receptive reading and persuasive writing; and it is fundamental to the critical thinking encouraged in all college courses.
Kiniry & Rose, *Critical Strategies for Academic Writing*

Ethnicity is still a complex and changing subject, which still has real political and social consequences in shaping American thinking about race relations.
Mary C. Waters, *Ethnic Options: Choosing Identities in America*

How Do We Identify Ourselves in a Diverse United States?

This writing project begins with a collaborative exploration of the Hispanic/Latino naming problem, which illustrates the larger problem of ethnic identification. You will study how the words *Hispanic* and *Latino* are defined by various sources, including the media and the people you interview. You will also do some reading that addresses problems of ethnic identification. Finally, you will explore your own ethnic identity and reflect critically on the problems of ethnic identification in the United States in the 1990s in an end-project writing, using the Hispanic/Latino naming problem as a starting point and extended example.

You can delete, substitute, or add readings or activities. I offer a framework for this project. All my students, for example, did some reading related to their own ethnic backgrounds and shared their findings or connections with the class. One student read all of Jamaica Kincaid's writing and wrote her a letter, which the student included in her final portfolio. A student from Puerto Rico read Edward Rivera's *Family Installments*. Some students read chapters in academic books. A student whose father is African-American and whose mother is Anglo-American read parts of a book called *Who is Black? One Nation's Definition,* and a Polish-American read parts of a book called *Polish Americans: Status Competition in an Ethnic Community.* A Korean-American researched recent newspaper articles about a conflict between some Koreans and African-Americans in a neighborhood in New York City. A Euro-American from upstate New York, who identified herself as "just plain American," did some reading about people who chose to identify themselves as American. She also read about media representations of women and wrote a notebook entry about how her own identity had been affected. Students gave brief oral presentations about their individual research and incorporated what they learned in their end-project essays. We also decided to read

P. M. Koch, *Between Two Worlds, Mexico,* black-and-white photograph, 9 x 6¼ inches, from the exhibit *Our Land/Ourselves,* 1992, University Art Museum, University at Albany, SUNY.

Beautiful Senoritas, a play by Dolores Prida, since she was coming to campus to give a reading. We attended her reading and interviewed her afterwards. Another group read Nicholasa Mohr's *Nilda,* which gives an eye-opening view of life in "El Barrio." There are many possibilities.

You could develop a course around this project and related readings. You can choose to work on this project to a greater or lesser extent, depending on your interest and time constraints. I worked on this project with students for about six or seven weeks in a semester-long course. It is a rich project—both engaging and rewarding. Through reflecting about your own experience and the experiences of others, you will develop a sense of authority and be able to speak and write about problems of definitions and identification as an educated person.

Collaborative Research Project: Hispanic/Latino

Prereading

Activity 1

1. Before you do any research, begin this exploration with your understanding or knowledge of these words now. How do you define them? How do you distinguish them, or do you?
2. Consider the word *Hispanic*. Take a moment now and write out your definition of the word.
3. Then compare your definition with someone else's. Copy your "dialogue" partner's definition so that you will have it for future reference and then talk about the differences and similarities.
4. Write out your definition of *Latino*.
5. Again, compare your definition with your dialogue partner's after copying it.
6. How do you and your partner identify yourselves ethnically? How does your own identification influence how you define Hispanic/Latino? In what geographic locations have you lived and how does that history inform your definitions?
7. "In the summer of 1929," Nicholas Callaway wrote in his afterward to *Georgia O'Keeffe: One Hundred Flowers* (NY: Knopf, 1989), "O'Keeffe made a trip to New Mexico, and though she completed several great paintings of flowers there, it was the desert landscape that entranced her. Her first paintings of bones, which symbolized the desert for her, date from 1930, and were combined with flowers. She shipped back East a big wooden barrel full of bones and animal skulls, their crevices stuffed with the calico flowers which Hispanic people of the Southwest used to ornament graves." (See Plate 2, "Cow's Skull with Calico Roses, opposite p. 173.) Who would you assume these "Hispanic people of the Southwest" to be? How is this word being used here? Would *Latino* also be appropriate?
8. Finally, write a brief summary of your discussion about these terms. Were your definitions similar? If they were different, how did they differ? How do you account for similarities and/or differences? What did you learn?

Activity 2

1. What's the story of these words? Look up the definitions and histories of *Hispanic* and *Latino* in the *Oxford English Dictionary* (O.E.D.). Consult

Figure 7.1

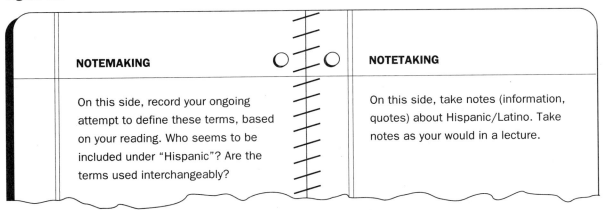

NOTEMAKING

On this side, record your ongoing attempt to define these terms, based on your reading. Who seems to be included under "Hispanic"? Are the terms used interchangeably?

NOTETAKING

On this side, take notes (information, quotes) about Hispanic/Latino. Take notes as your would in a lecture.

other sources as well. What other sources could help you with this problem of definition? Write what you learned about these words from your library research.

2. Write about what you make of this quotation taken from *Critical Strategies for Academic Writing* (Kiniry & Rose):

> Dictionaries can't be trusted. They are useful tools for helping us work out meanings; and they can be particularly helpful in showing how the meanings of a word may vary and how those meanings may change over time. But the real burden of defining will fall on you—on your powers of inference as a reader and your powers of management as a writer.

3. Try paraphrasing this quotation in one sentence. How would you summarize it?

4. Can you think of an instance when confusion or some problem resulted when someone used a word in a way different from that which you were familiar?

5. Can you think of a situation in which the way a word is defined is crucial?

6. When you come across a word you don't understand, do you consult a dictionary? If so, how helpful is a dictionary definition? If not, how do you arrive at a meaning?

7. Can you think of some words or terms you had difficulty defining in courses you have taken in different disciplines?

Definitions are flexible. They can expand, contract, or shift in emphasis, all according to the uses to which they are put. They are also powerful . . . . Definitions help to shape what we see and don't see.

Kiniry & Rose,
Critical Strategies for Academic Writing

Reading Newspaper Articles

Read several newspaper articles specifically for their usage of *Hispanic* and/or *Latino*. You may want to include additional articles or substitute or delete some. You may want to look at some articles from newspapers in different parts of the country, for example. You should read a variety of articles, however, so that you can study the usage of these words in the print media and make some observations.

Take and make notes specifically for the purpose of understanding the usage of Hispanic and Latino (Figure 7.1).

Figure 7.2

Hispanic/Latino Research Project	Researcher:
Author:	
Article Title:	
Source:	
Date of publication:	
Edition: **Section:** **Page:**	

Notemaking	Notetaking

Reader's Dialogue

You can make copies of the form included here (Figure 7.2) if you like. On the back of your notes or on a separate page, I suggest that you write your First Response or reaction to each article after a quick first reading and then reread and take and make notes.

Articles

- "Study Discovers That 'Latinos' Are Not All the Same"
  Francisco Garcia Azuero
- "Study: Hispanics Lag in Wealth"
  Associated Press
- "Hispanic Women Can Do More Than Wash Corporate Glass Ceilings"
  Myriam Marquez
- "Rising Segregation Found for Hispanic Students"
  Karen DeWitt
- "Census Shows Profound Change in Racial Makeup of the Nation"
  Felicity Barringer
- "Study Points to Increase in Tolerance of Ethnicity"
  Tamar Lewin

See also articles in the "Enrollment Issues in Education" section of the "Becoming Educated" Writing Project (Chapter 5).

Study Discovers That "Latinos" Are Not All the Same

Francisco Garcia Azuero

I remember feeling white when I first arrived in this country 22 years ago. 1
Born in Colombia with light skin, I was called "blanco" or white, by paisanos with darker skin.

But I also remember the surprise to find out that here my ethnic origin 2
had been changed. Now I was "Latino" or "Hispanic." I was suddenly given a nationality I didn't know anything about. I was even more surprised to find that there were other "Latinos" or "Hispanics" in college who were definitely Native-American or black.

That new nationality was the source of many heated debates in our col- 3
lege cafeteria. It puzzled us to be all lumped under one name when we were obviously so different.

But now, a recent study discovered what we as young college students 4
from Spanish-speaking countries knew all along. That we are not all the same.

That's right. Finally, those marketing geniuses from New York who 5
lumped all of us in one block so they could more easily sell us things we don't need have seen the light. We are white, or black, or Native-American, or any available skin color, hair texture or social class as you may find among people anywhere in the world.

The recently completed study also showed that people from Spanish 6
speaking countries have similar values to other Americans, such as individu-alism, patriotism and distrust of government.

In the oddly titled Latino National Political Survey, 2,800 people from 7
Cuba, Mexico and Puerto Rico were interviewed. In their answers they said they don't see themselves as Latino or Hispanic.

The great majority of them, or about 90 percent, declined to be identi- 8
fied as such. Instead, about 80 percent preferred to be grouped with others from their country of origin. About 10 percent saw themselves simply as Americans.

The survey was recently presented to the American Political Science 9
Association as [it] is one of the first of its kind developed nationally.

There were many marked differences [among] the three groups. 10

About 40 percent of Cubans and Mexicans, for instance, agreed that the 11
individual is responsible for providing their basic necessities for life. On the other hand, 37 percent of the Mexicans and 31 percent of the Cubans said the government should create jobs. Puerto Ricans want the government to play a stronger role in all areas of life.

Cubans expressed more patriotism than Mexicans and Puerto Ricans. 12
The Cubans also said they trusted the government much more than the other two groups.

The three groups showed a high level of intolerance for different political 13
beliefs. Not surprisingly, Cubans mentioned communism as the group they dislike most. Mexicans and Puerto Ricans most disliked the Ku Klux Klan.

Azuero

More than 20 percent of Mexicans and Puerto Ricans said they disliked ho- 14
mosexuals most.

While the majority of Cubans and Mexicans expressed similar beliefs, 15
Puerto Ricans expressed the widest variety of opinions and beliefs in most
issues.

The study may show that indeed we are a mixed bunch. 16

But many of us already know that. 17

I remember a conversation with my 30-year-old sister who migrated from 18
Colombia three years ago.

She was filling out a U.S. Census questionnaire and had marked "His- 19
panic" for her ethnic group.

"I was born white and I will die white," she protested. "But I can try to
tell them that until I'm blue in the face and they'll never understand."

Francisco Garcia Azuero writes for the International Media Syndicate and reports for the
Miami Herald. Reprinted by permisson of the author.

Encuesta descubre que los latinos no son todos iguales

Francisco García Azuero

Yo me acuerdo que sentía que era blanco al llegar a este país hace 22 años. 1
Nací en Colombia con piel clara. Mis paisanos más oscuritos me llamaban
"el blanco."

Pero también me acuerdo de la sorpresa que sentí al descubrir que 2
aquí mi origen étnico había cambiado. Ahora era "Latino" o "Hispano."
Súbitamente me habían dado una nacionalidad de la cual yo poco sabía. Me
sorprendí aún más al notar que otros "Latinos" o "Hispanos" en la universi-
dad donde estudiaba eran obviamente negros o nativoamericanos.

Esa nueva nacionalidad fue fuente de muchas airadas discusiones en la 3
cafetería. Nos confundía este hecho de vernos agrupados bajo un solo nom-
bre cuando bien sabíamos que eramos tan diferentes.

Pero ahora una encuesta recientemente publicada ha descubierto lo que 4
nosotros como jovenes estudiantes ya sabíamos. Que no somos todos iguales.

Finalmente, esos genios de mercado en New York, quienes nos habían 5
agrupado bajo una sola etiqueta para poder vendernos con más facilidad las
cosas que no necesitabamos, han visto la luz. Nosotros somos blancos, o negros, o nativoamericanos, de todo color de piel y textura de cabello, como se
pueda hallar en el resto del mundo.

El estudio mostró también que tenemos valores similares a los del resto 6
de los americanos, tales como el individualismo, el patriotismo o la descon-
fianza al gobierno.

En el estudio, titulado "Latino National Political Survey," 2,800 personas 7
de Cuba, México, y Puerto Rico fueron entrevistadas. En sus respuestas dijeron que no se ven como latinos o hispanos.

La gran mayoria, o casi 90 por ciento, no quisieron ser identificados 8
como tales. En cambio, el 80 por ciento prefirió ser agrupado por pais de ori-

gen. Cerca del 10 por ciento se vieron como latinos o hispanos. El resto dijo que eran americanos.

La encuesta es una de las primeras que se realizan nacionalmente y muestra las diferencias entre los tres grupos. 9

Cerca del 40 por ciento de los cubanos y los mexicanos, por ejemplo, acordaron que el individuo era principalmente responsable por ganarse la vida. Por el contrario, el 37 por ciento de los mexicanos y el 31 por ciento de los cubanos opinaron que el gobierno debía crear empleos para la gente. Los puertorriqueños dijeron que el gobierno debía ser más activo en la vida del pueblo. 10

Los cubanos demostraron ser más patrióticos que los mexicanos y los puertorriqueños. Los cubanos también dijeron tener más confianza en el gobierno que los otros dos grupos. 11

Los tres grupos demostraron un alto nivel de intolerancia contra ideas políticas diferentes. Como era de esperarse, el comunismo era la ideología menos popular entre los cubanos. El Ku Klux Klan es el grupo menos popular entre los mexicanos y los puertorriqueños. Más del 20 por ciento de los mexicanos y los puertorriqueños dijeron no gustar los homosexuales. 12

Mientras que la mayoría de los cubanos y mexicanos expresaron valores similares, los puertorriqueños expresaron la mayor variedad de opiniones en muchos asuntos. 13

El estudio puede que demuestre que nosotros seamos un grupo bien revuelto. 14

Pero muchos de nosotros ya lo sabíamos. 15

Yo me acuerdo de una conversación que tuve con mi hermana de 30 años de edad, quen se vino de Colombia hace tres años. 16

Ella llenaba el formulario del censo y había marcado "Hispanic" como su grupo étnico. 17

"Yo nací blanca y yo me moriré blanca," protestó ella. "Pero yo puedo hablar hasta el día del juicio final y ellos nunca lo van a entender." 18

Francisco García Azuero reporta para el *Miami Herald* en Miami, Florida. [Reprinted from the Austin (Texas) *La Prensa,* November 1, 1991, by special permission of Francisco García Azuero.]

Study: Hispanics Lag in Wealth; 1980s Left Sharp Economic Divisions Among Latinos

Associated Press

WASHINGTON — Eight years of prosperity lifted Hispanics to new heights of wealth and education, the government said Thursday. But they were also more likely than other Americans to be poor, undereducated laborers. 1

A Census Bureau study drew a sharp contrast between the extremes of Hispanic economic success and failure. It showed Hispanics shared in the economic boom that dominated the 1980s. But their slice of prosperity was smaller than the rest of the country's. 2

Associated Press

Hispanic buying power increased by 70 percent from the start of the 3
boom in 1982 until its end in 1990, nearly three times the increase for other
Americans.

"There obviously has been some improvement," said Sonia Perez, senior 4
policy analyst with the National Council of La Raza in Washington. "But
when you see the increases in poverty and unemployment, it is really difficult to say we are doing better."

The Census Bureau study compared ethnic Hispanics with non- 5
Hispanics.

The study listed facts that showed the rapid rise in Hispanic financial 6
clout left many people behind:

• Hispanics were twice as likely as other Americans to be poor. Hispanic 7
children were three times as likely to live in poverty.

• One in three Hispanic men worked as a laborer, helper, machine opera- 8
tor or similar job, compared with one in five among other men.

• Only half of Hispanics had four years of high school. Three-fourths of 9
other Americans had reached that level of education.

Perez said a lack of education kept some Hispanics from getting their full 10
share of prosperity. Because they are less educated, they get lower-paying
jobs. They're more likely to be laid off and therefore more likely to be poor,
she said.

The diversity of the findings shows "that Hispanics are not one homoge- 11
neous glob," said Jesus Garcia, the Census Bureau demographer who, with
Patricia Montgomery, wrote the report. "We have people that are very
wealthy, and I think people that are not doing as well. I think Hispanics mirror America in general."

The Census Bureau also found: 12

• In 1990, one in seven Hispanic households had $50,000 or more in in- 13
come. Eight year earlier, only one in nine had that much money.

• One in six Hispanics was unemployed in 1982. By 1990, that number 14
had shrunk to one in 10.

• A Hispanic's chances of going to college improved in the 1980s. One in 15
10 had four years of college education in 1990.

Reprinted from the Austin (Texas) *American-Statesman,* November 8, 1991. Used by permission of the Associated Press.

Hispanic Women Can Do More Than Wash Corporate Glass Ceiling

Myriam Marquez

A Puerto Rican friend of mine couldn't believe what she was watching. There 1
on Univision, the largest Spanish-language TV station in the United States,
was actress Debbie Reynolds, giving her best advice for Hispanic women trying to get ahead: Get a job cleaning house.

"That is a field that I think is very open today. I'm always fascinated why 2 more people don't go into it," said Reynolds, in her usually perky, if decidedly condescending, tone. Then she went on to note that she sympathized with Latin women because "it's hard when you have 14 or 15 children." In between these two stereotypical remarks, she pointed out that "a very good friend of mine is Ricardo Montalban."

The brouhaha over the Reynolds interview was so great that even some 3 of the major TV networks followed up. Last week, she dutifully apologized. Gee, thanks.

Fact is, the majority of Hispanic women in this country are working in 4 jobs that require more skills than housekeeping. And while housekeeping is a perfectly fine job done by millions of women—of every color, creed and ethnic origin—it is by no means a job that most people "aspire to."

Not withstanding the corporate "glass ceiling" that still needs to be broken at the top ranks of most corporations, American women are moving up in the work force, and Hispanic women are no different. Yet the perception of what type of work Hispanic women are qualified to do seems to still play to the worst stereotyping, and that blocks their upward mobility.

According to a March 1988 study by the Census Bureau, 41 percent of 6 Hispanic women employed outside the home work in technical, sales and administrative support occupations. They are sales clerks, cashiers, computer operators, typists, secretaries, receptionists, bookkeepers, teacher aides. And 16 percent of working Hispanic women are in the highest-paying managerial and professional ranks, compared with 25 percent of all American women in that category.

Yet it was the 21 percent employed in service jobs like housekeeping that 7 Reynolds thought to bring up as the role model for Hispanic women. Interestingly, 17 percent of all American women work in service occupations, so Hispanic women are not that overwhelmingly represented in this category.

There also are differences among Hispanic subgroups, partly because of 8 the nature of their migration to the States—whether they come from rural or urban backgrounds, for instance. About 22 percent of women of Mexican origin work in service jobs, while 13 percent are at the professional/managerial level. By contrast, 15 percent of Puerto Rican women and 13 percent of Cuban women work in service jobs—far fewer than the 20.5 percent of Puerto Rican women and 27.3 of percent Cuban women who are in the professional/managerial category.

"With such a culturally diversified group as the Hispanics, noma are unclear, and stereotyping would be inappropriate," Maria Aristigueta, who teaches public administration at the University of Central Florida, wrote recently on the issue of Hispanic women in the work force. "The migration of Hispanic women to American will vary not only in culture and race, but also in levels of education and training."

For Hispanic women trying to get to upper management, Aristigueta 10 adds: "The question becomes, 'How comfortable are your superiors with you personally?' rather than, 'How competent are you?' Gender, color of skin and degree of foreign accent may all come into play in reaching beyond the glass ceiling."

Marquez

The real issue is: As the U.S. work force continues to become more diverse, 11 will companies break free of stereotyping and recognize Hispanic women for all they can do? Or will they relegate us to washing the glass ceiling?

Marquez is an editorial page columnist for *The Orlando* (Florida) *Sentinel*. Reprinted by permission from *The Orlando Sentinel*, November 10, 1991.

Rising Segregation Is Found for Hispanic Students

Karen De Witt
Special to *The New York Times*

Segregation of Hispanic students in the nation's public schools has grown 1 over the last two decades while gains in desegregation among blacks in the South have remained largely stable, a study released today has found.

"Hispanics in California and Texas are more segregated than blacks in 2 Alabama or Mississippi in terms of educational experiences," said Dr. Gary Orfield, an author of "Status of School Desegregation: The Next Generation." The study, which analyzed 20 years of school enrollment data collected by the Department of Education's Office of Civil Rights, was sponsored by the National School Boards Association.

New York, New Jersey, Texas and California, Dr. Orfield said, were the 3 states where Hispanic segregation was most intense. Among the reasons for the growing segregation of Hispanic children, who in the last 20 years have come to account for 10 percent of the nation's students, he said, were that they were increasing rapidly in number and were concentrated in some areas. Fifty-seven percent of the nation's Hispanic residents in California and Texas.

"Hispanic segregation has been steadily increasing," he said. "It is more 4 serious for Puerto Ricans than for Mexican-Americans, but it is growing for Mexican-Americans as well."

He said that in 1988 and 1989, 10 percent more Hispanic students than 5 black students attended schools where whites were a minority. "Since 1970," he said, "the percent of whites in the school of the typical Hispanic student has fallen by 12 percent, while the level has remained relatively stable for blacks."

School districts in inner cities have grown increasingly segregated be- 6 cause of demographic changes like white flights to the suburbs and an over-all decline in the number of white students, Dr. Orfield said, but he added that a pattern of segregated schools was also occurring when minorities moved to the suburbs.

"We can't think of the suburbs as white any more," said Dr. Orfield, a 7 professor of education and social policy at Harvard University and a leading expert on school desegregation. "The country is becoming more racially diverse. And the most rapidly changing school districts are suburban."

Dr. Orfield said the study showed that Federal desegregation efforts had 8 produced more integrated schools in the 38 years since the Supreme Court found that segregated schools were inherently unequal and that places where desegregation efforts were mandatory had the most stable, long-term success with integration. He said such efforts had turned the schools of the South, once the most segregated in the country, into the most integrated.

He also said that after the 1970's the Federal Government had relaxed 9 its efforts to enforce school desegregation, but that despite that relaxation, "there was no significant reversal of integration of blacks in schools in the 1980's."

But Dr. Orfield said that he believed that the stability of school integra- 10 tion might be undermined by moves by the Federal courts to return desegregation responsibilities to local school boards.

The report also addressed the status of Asian students, concentrated in 11 California, and the most rapidly growing group of students in the nation's schools.

"There's now half again as many Asians as blacks in the state of Cali- 12 fornia," Dr. Orfield said. "They're not segregated significantly. They tend to be very well integrated in schools, and that's one of the things we should think about when we think about the remarkable mobility that they've achieved into the mainstream of American society."

Dr. Orfield said that because the United States was becoming a multira- 13 cial society, the enactment of a new Federal program was necessary to maintain school integration.

He also recommended a major study of the effects of segregated schools 14 on Hispanic students, a comprehensive program that considered housing patterns in an effort to support stable suburban school integration and a major upgrading of Federal statistics on the racial makeup of schools.

From *The New York Times,* January 9, 1992. Copyright © 1992 by The New York Times Company. Reprinted by permission.

Reviewing Activity

Stop now and review your notes and summarize your findings. What did you observe about the usage of *Hispanic* and *Latino* in the articles you read? Review your first attempt at defining these words. Would you revise your definitions? Do you want to raise any questions at this point?

Suggested Collaborative Activity

In class, pass your informal report to the person on your left and write a brief response to the one you receive. Then talk with your neighbors. Perhaps follow this dialogue with a whole-class discussion. Near the end of class or after class, make more notes based on your discussion.

From *The New York Times*. Copyright © 1994 by The New York Times Company. Reprinted by permission.

Summarizing

Read both of the following articles and summarize one after rereading. (Perhaps divide your class in two.) See guidelines for "Writing a News Summary" on pages 250–51.

1. Write a 100-word summary of "Census Shows Profound Change in Racial Makeup of the Nation" for a "News in Brief" section of a newspaper. As much as possible, use exact wording from the article. You may want to paraphrase in order to be more concise, and you may also want to add some transitions. Select "key points" and some specifics for illustration. Keep the same order of presentation. Do not write your reaction to this article or offer your own illustrations in your summary. Your purpose here is to write a condensed version of this news presentation.

2. Write a 100-word summary of "Study Points to Increase in Tolerance of Ethnicity." What is the overall finding of this study? How was the study conducted? What will you select to say about the pollster's ranking (and perceptions) of ethnic groups? Who conducted this study and for what purpose? Who sponsored this study? Do you plan to include this information in your summary? Why or why not?

Census Shows Profound Change in Racial Makeup of the Nation; Shift Toward Minorities Since 1980 Is Sharpest for the 20th Century

Felicity Barringer

The racial complexion of the American population changed more dramati- 1 cally in the past decade than at any time in the 20th century, with nearly one in every four Americans having African, Asian, Hispanic or American Indian ancestry. In 1980, one in five Americans had such minority backgrounds.

In the field of population statistics, where change sometimes seems 2 glacially slow, the speed at which the country's racial mix was altered in the 1980's was breathtaking, Census Bureau figures show. The rate of increase in the minority population was nearly twice as fast as in the 1970's. And much of the surge was among those of Hispanic ancestry, an increase of 7.7 million people or 56 percent, over 1980.

"About half the Hispanic increase is due to immigration," said Jorge del 3 Pinal, the bureau's chief of ethnic and Hispanic statistics. "But there would have been a tremendous growth even in the absence of any immigration." The increase was also a result of high birth rates among Hispanic people, the legalization of many new Hispanic citizens and the counting of illegal residents.

Whites Are 80.3 Percent

With the wave of immigration from Latin America, and separate influxes 4 from the Philippines, China, India and Southeast Asia, the total number of minority residents rose to 61 million to 62 million. The exact figure will not be known until the people who identified themselves as "other race" are statistically allocated among the four categories recognized for census purposes: white, black, Asian or Native American.

Whites now make up 80.3 percent of the nation's resident population. 5 This group includes the vast majority of Hispanic residents, who can be of any race.

Whites of European or Middle Eastern background comprise slightly less 6 than 76 percent of the resident population of 248.7 million people.

'Incredibly Poetic Fact'

"This is the dawning of the first universal nation," said Ben J. Wattenberg, 7 an author and demographer. "It's going to cause some turmoil, but on balance it's an incredibly poetic fact."

In recent years, he said, more than 4 in 5 legal immigrants to the United 8 States have had non-European backgrounds. That proportion will decline under the most recent immigration law, Mr. Wattenberg said, but of the

700,000 immigrants allowed in annually, about 3 of every 4 are likely to be from countries outside Europe or Canada. These estimates do not take account of the effect of illegal immigration.

The predominant racial group still traces it roots to Europe. "If you believe that the descendant of an English lord and a descendant of a Polish shtetl are part of the same group, then that group is going to continue in the majority for a long time to come," said Mr. Wattenberg. "Still, there's a big difference between a 90 percent majority, a 70 percent majority or a 55 percent majority." 9

The dimensions of the change became clear this weekend as the Census 10 Bureau made public the racial breakdowns for Alaska, the last of the 50 states to receive a statistical portrait derived from the 1990 census. The racial and ethnic totals from each state are needed by state legislatures to redraw Congressional and legislative district boundaries.

But the new totals may give ammunition to some urban officials who 11 charge that many blacks were missed in the census. While the 1990 count found more Hispanics, Asians and American Indians than population experts had expected, the numbers for blacks lagged behind the estimates.

According to the census data, the resident population of the United 12 States breaks down this way:
- 30.0 million blacks, an increase of 13.2 percent since 1980. 13
- 7.3 million Asians, an increase of 107.8 percent. 14
- 2.0 million American Indians, an increase of 37.9 percent. 15
- 22.4 million Hispanic people, an increase of 53 percent. 16
- 9.8 million people who classified themselves as "other race," an in- 17 crease of 45.1 percent from 1980. In earlier censuses, the vast majority of the "other race" group were eventually incorporated into the white category.

Blacks, the largest minority, are about 12 percent of the population. 18 Hispanic people are about 9 percent, Asians about 3 percent and American Indians about 0.8 percent.

The resident population of the United States does not include more than 19 900,000 military personnel and other Federal employees overseas on April 1, 1990. There are no racial and ethnic statistics for this group, which is included in the nation's total population count of 249.6 million.

Whites Edge Toward Minority

In some states, like New Mexico and California, the population of whites 20 who are not of Hispanic descent dwindled so dramatically that the once-dominant group could become a minority by the year 2000.

The change in California, the nation's fastest-growing state, was most 21 striking. In 1980, two-thirds of Californians were whites from European backgrounds. In 1990, the figure was 57 percent, meaning that nearly 13 million of the 29.8 million Californians are from minority backgrounds. California's population included about 35 percent of the nation's total Hispanic population and 39 percent of the Asians in the United States.

In New Mexico, where the first European settlers were 16th century 22 Spaniards, whites without Hispanic backgrounds account for just 50 percent in the new census.

The dramatic changes were evident elsewhere in the Sun Belt. The Texas 23 minority population increased to 39 percent, or more than 6.6 million people, including 4.3 million Hispanic residents. Florida's minority population rose to 27 percent, or 3.5 million people.

In New York, minority residents make up about 31 percent of the population, up from 25 percent in 1980. In New Jersey, the minority population 24 rose to 26 percent from 21 percent. In Connecticut, minority people now make up 16 percent of the population, as against 12 percent in 1980.

Northern New England and the Upper Midwest remain the whitest areas 25 of the county, with 98 percent of the populations in Maine and Vermont and 97 percent in New Hampshire consisting of whites from non-Hispanic backgrounds. The populations of Iowa, Minnesota, Wisconsin, Idaho, North Dakota, South Dakota, Montana, Wyoming, Utah, Oregon and Kentucky are also all more than 90 percent white.

The majority of the nation's Asian-Americans live in the West, but there 26 has been a rapid increase in the Asian populations of New York and Texas. There are now more Asian-Americans in New York (694,000) than in Hawaii (685,000).

American Indian populations were concentrated in Oklahoma, Alaska, 27 the Southwest and the Rocky Mountain states.

The people who assigned themselves to the "other race" category on census forms will be assigned to recognized categories by statistical means. 28 Census officials say most of these are of Hispanic origin, but their cultures have established different racial categories since so many are of mixed Spanish, Indian and black descent. Faced with the unfamiliar census categories, they are likely to check "other."

If 90 percent of these people are eventually assigned to the "white" column, the number of whites, including Hispanics, will be about 209 million. 29 In the 1980 census, more than 95 percent of people in the "other" category were eventually classified as "white." Just 3 percent of the "other race" category was eventually transferred to the "black" column.

The assignment of blacks, and discrepancies between the census figures 30 and earlier estimates, are likely to fuel the debate between local officials and the Census Bureau.

For the final census figures to equal the estimates, the total for blacks, 31 now 650,000 below the estimates, would have to include more than 5 percent of the "other race" people. The 1990 estimate of blacks was 30.6 million; the current census total is slightly less than 30 million.

Census officials acknowledge the gap between the estimates and the actual count for blacks, but they caution that estimates, based on records of 32 births, deaths and legal immigration, plus estimates of illegal immigration, are not necessarily more accurate than the count. "It's possible that the estimates are off. There's nothing sacred about the estimates," said Mr. del Pinal of the Census Bureau.

Throughout the 1990 census, urban leaders, led by Mayor David Dinkins 33 of New York, have argued that current methods guarantee an undercount of urban poor people, depriving the cities of political power and Federal aid.

From *The New York Times,* March 11, 1991. Copyright © 1991 by The New York Times Company. Reprinted by permission.

Study Points to Increase
In Tolerance of Ethnicity

Tamar Lewin

Tolerance of ethnicity seems to be rising and anti-Semitism dropping, ac- 1
cording to a study of polls conducted over several years by seven national
polling organizations in which people were asked to describe or rank different ethnic groups. The study was made public yesterday.

The new analysis of existing polling data, sponsored by the American 2
Jewish Committee, provides intriguing glimpses of the images, social standing and conflicts that different ethnic groups are generally perceived to
have. One section of the report is based on a poll in which respondents were
asked to rank the social standing of 58 ethnic groups.

European groups generally monopolized the top of the ladder, and 3
within the European groups their perceived status mostly followed the order
of immigration, with those groups that arrived in this country first, like the
British and Protestants, assigned the highest standing.

Non-Europeans at Bottom

The Germans, Irish and Scandinavians, who immigrated in the mid-19th 4
century, came next, followed by Italians, Greeks, Poles, Russians and Jews,
who came to America later.

Most people assigned the bottom rungs of the ladder to non-Europeans, 5
including a fictitious ethnic group, "Wisians."

"We were trying to see if people were being too compliant with us, and 6
the good news is that 61 percent didn't rank the Wisians," said Tom W. Smith,
author of the American Jewish Committee report and director of the General
Social Survey, the largest and longest-term project supported by the National
Science Foundation's Sociology program. "My explanation for the low ranking is that people probably thought that if they were foreign-sounding, and
they'd never heard of them, they couldn't be doing too well."

Strong Gains by 3 Groups

The ratings of almost every group drifted up slightly from 1964 to 1989, the 7
American Jewish Committee analysis found, but the groups whose social
standings were perceived to have improved most significantly were the
Japanese, Chinese and blacks.

Despite the improvement, blacks, who were identified as Negroes in the 8
1989 poll so the wording would be comparable to that of the 1964 survey,
were still perceived as having low social standing, akin to American Indians
and Mexicans.

In 1989, the Japanese were thought to rank about the same as French 9
Canadians and Jews, while the Chinese stood between Spanish Americans
and Hungarians.

The study found that anti-Jewish attitudes are at historic lows, by most 10
indicators. Jews were even perceived in the 1990 General Social Survey, an

in-person poll of 1,372 representative adults nationwide, as leading whites in general, Southern whites, Asian-Americans, Hispanic-Americans and blacks in terms of who was regarded as harder working, richer, less prone to violence, more self-supporting and more intelligent.

The only characteristic on which Jews were not top-rated was patriotism, 11 on which whites and Southern whites were perceived more favorably, followed by Jews and blacks, and then Asian- and Hispanic-Americans.

The study also analyzed data from several polls about groups were 12 thought to have too much power in the Unites States.

In The 1990 General Social Survey, 25 percent of the respondents said 13 whites had too much power, as against 21 percent who said Jews had too much power. Among the other groups, 14 percent thought blacks had too much power, 6 percent said Asian-Americans did and 5 percent said Hispanic-Americans did.

Conversely, when asked which groups should have more power, 47 per- 14 cent said blacks, 46 percent said Hispanic-Americans, 37 percent Asian-Americans, 15 percent said Southern whites, 13 percent said Jews and 6 percent said whites.

Possible Source of Concern

One source of possible concern about anti-Semitism, the study found, was 15 that those who thought Jews were richer than whites in general were almost twice as likely to say that Jews had too much influence as those who thought the two groups were equally wealthy.

And while the images of Jews as rich, smart and hard-working were gen- 16 erally positive, Mr. Smith said those very images might someday lead to renewed anti-Semitism.

"While these evaluations are positive on their face, they identify Jews as 17 a possible target of envy and resentment," the study said.

Still, the American Jewish Committee said the report should come as a 18 relief to American Jews who fear a possible increase in anti-Semitism.

"With the recent events involving David Duke, Crown Heights and 19 Leonard Jeffries, the anxiety level of American Jews has risen," said David Singer, director of information at the American Jewish Committee. "The study is an important grounding in reality."

Perceptions of tension between different ethnic groups were measured in 20 a May 1990 telephone poll of 3,004 representative adults, conducted by Princeton Survey Research Associates.

"The major conflict that was perceived was the black-white conflict," 21 Mr. Smith said. "Others, like tensions between blacks and Jews, or Hispanics or Asians, just didn't come anywhere near that level."

Indeed, 56 percent of those polled said blacks disliked whites, and 53 22 percent said whites did not like blacks. Only 10 percent said blacks were disliked by Asians-Americans and 11 percent said blacks were disliked by Jews.

From *The New York Times,* January 8, 1992. Copyright © 1992 by The New York Times Company. Reprinted by permission.

Writing a News Summary

1. Reread the original text carefully. Observe carefully—study—what you are reading. Either underline the main points or cross out unimportant information (supporting details, direct quotations, unnecessary words, repetitions, and digressions).
2. Make a list of the main points on a separate piece of paper.
3. The purpose of this summary is to inform readers—that is, to report the news in brief. Your purpose is not to give your reaction or express your opinion or feelings, or to try to persuade your readers. What information should you select? What's essential? What should you leave out? Regardless of the article you're summarizing, your readers will want to know: (a) What happened? (b) Who was involved? (c) What seemed to cause the event? and (d) What were the results? Reread the article with this list of questions in mind.
4. Write a draft in which you try to get down the main points in some kind of order. How should you arrange the information you've selected? Again, consider the purpose of a news summary.
5. Count the number of words you used to see if you stayed roughly within the word limit. You will be revising, so the word count will change. It's good, however, to have a rough idea of how much you need to cut or expand your summary.
6. A good summary is clear and concise. Reread your summary, first for word choice and then for sentence structure. Edit for one item at a time. Try out different words. If you are using a computer for writing, work with a printout. Double-space to make room for revisions. You may want to print out your summary after you've reread and revised it for various purposes (word choice and so on).
7. Read your summary aloud. Listen to how your words and sentences sound. Revise again.
8. Because you will be taking information from different parts of the article, your sentences may seem disjointed or unrelated. Again, read your summary aloud, paying attention to the way your writing sounds as a whole. Do your sentences lead logically from one to another? Do they seem disconnected at any point?
9. Rewrite your draft. Check your word count again. Can you be more concise? Do you have room to add another point?
10. Edit your "final" draft for grammar and mechanics, working with your editing list and using the editing system described in the appendix, "Guidelines for Editing Your Own Writing." (Do you need to revise your editing list? If you can now consistently control for a certain kind of error, you may want to remove it from your list. You may want to add a punctuation convention you don't automatically observe and want to remember to check on final drafts.)

Summary-Writing Workshop Activities

1. Compare your summary with two other summaries and discuss differences of presentation (language use, inclusion and exclusion, emphasis, arrangement) with the writers.

2. Perhaps select one summary from your group to submit for whole-group discussion.
3. Collaborate on a new summary after reading and talking about your individual summaries. One person can serve as the group's writer (and mediator).

Writing About Summary Writing

Take a few minutes to write about this writing experience. How did you go about writing your summary? What was your process? Was it effective? Looking back, would you make some adjustments now? Were the guidelines helpful to you? If so, what was particularly helpful? Do you have any suggestions for improving the guidelines? What advice would you give someone trying to write a news summary? What did you learn from this writing experience?

Writers at Work

"When I wrote the first draft of my summary, I felt it to be more of a reaction—a critique. I was not really summarizing the pollster's findings. Also, I felt I was being targeted, so I felt the need to react rather than report," wrote one graduate student trying out this project in a course on teaching writing.

Listen to what other graduate students say about summary writing.

Ginger Woolever: "I had a very difficult time summarizing the article in so few words. Summaries are never easy to write, but when they are on topics of such a delicate nature, like ethnicity, they become even more problematic. It is so easy to omit a word or two for the sake of brevity, but the writer must be careful that this omission does not offend or anger. There is also a question of objectivity and if the writer can ever be truly faithful to that which she is summarizing."

Roxanne Shank: "How did I go about writing this summary? I don't usually think about how I write, so this will take a bit of thought.

"First, of course, I read the article to get an overall idea of its content. Then I reread it, taking notes and looking for specific points of information. Reviewing my notes, I selected those that revealed the findings of the study rather than the biases and/or opinions extrapolated from it.

"Having been active in journalism in high school, back in the dark ages 20-odd years ago, I know the style required for such a summary as would be used in a 'News in Brief' piece. I sat down at the computer and began to write. Checking the word count occasionally for adherence to the 100-word guidelines, I added and deleted information, based on its importance to the overall thrust of the original article.

"I tend to revise as I go along, a process Professor Gay refers to as 'percolating.' I've always done it in some form or other, often writing directly into the typewriter and throwing away a lot of sheets! Even when I did that, though, I would mentally compose a paragraph, or at least an entire sentence, from my notes, before setting it down on paper. The word processor makes this operation infinitely easier, since it eliminates the need to retype salvageable material when a portion is discarded. It also means that my notes may be in a much less polished form than before the electronic age infiltrated my home. I made most of my revisions the first time around. Later revisions I did make were a result of rereading the summary the next day, at which time I realized that I had omitted an important aspect, that of identifying the source of the study."

Listen now to these students talking about their Draft 1 summary-writing workshop experiences.

"Each member of our group presented quite different interpretations. After reading to one another, we discussed the differences in our approaches to summary. We also agreed that there was a need to define what 'summary' meant. We did not agree on a definition. How could you possibly write a summary without including a bias?"

"We all had different ideas about what should be included. Some things I had not included in my summary I decided to include after hearing them in another summary."

"After listening to other summaries, my ideas of a summary changed."

"Our group agreed that no matter how each one of us tried to write an objective summary, it would fall short of the task. Even by choosing certain ideas or quotes from the text, the reader shows subjectivity."

I Am Joaquín: *Yo Soy Joaquín*

Rodolfo Gonzales

"I AM JOAQUÍN!"
La Raza!
Méjicano!
Español!
Latino!
Hispano!
Chicano!
or whatever I call myself
I look the same
I feel the same
I cry
and
sing the same.
I am the masses of my people and
I refuse to be absorbed.

Excerpt from epic poem published as book of the same title by Bantam Books, 1967 (98, 100). Reprinted by special permission of Rodolfo Gonzales.

Rodolfo "Corky" Gonzales, the son of a migrant worker, has been involved for a long time in the civil and human rights struggle for Mexican-

Americans and is founder of the first all-Chicano school in the United States. Joaquín Murrieta was a miner who worked in California from 1849 to 1851. According to Gonzales, in a guide to references in his poem:

> After Anglo miners raped and killed his [Joaquín's] wife Rosita, drove him from his gold claim, and then whipped him in public on a false horse-stealing charge, Murrieta vowed revenge. He became the leader of a large band of desperadoes, conducting a vendetta marked by daring robberies and narrow escapes. He became a legendary figure, *el bandido terrible,* the "Robin Hood of El Dorado." The California government offered a reward of $5,000 for him, dead or alive, and—because his last name was not well known—California became unsafe for anyone whose name happened to be Joaquín.
>
> Whatever the derivation of the word "Chicano . . ." to apply it to one's self is a political act. It is an act of cultural identification with one's Mexican-Spanish-Indio heritage. One who seeks to become assimilated in the Anglo-American society would not use "Chicano."
>
> Carlotta Cardenas, 1977

The Carlotta Cardenas quotation, along with "I am Joaquín!," was part of "Chicano Art: Resistance and Affirmation," An Interpretive Exhibition of the Chicano Art Movement 1965–1985, San Antonio Museum of Art, May 28–August 1, 1993.

Untitled

liz jiménez-fernández

liz jiménez-fernández is a graduate student at Binghamton University, State University of New York. This poem was originally published in Colors, *a literary journal at Hamilton College, where she was an undergraduate.*

red
white
brown
olive
yellow
tan
black
colors in the spectrum of life
each distinct
and yet
when the skin is sliced
one color remains . . .
BLOOD RED.

Reprinted by permission of liz jiménez-fernández.

latina love

Lissette Norman

Lissette Norman, a former basic-writing student, wrote this poem in an advanced writing class her senior year as part of a collection of writing she entitled searching for drums.

olle latina   1
yeah you sista!
say it
come on say it
say it with your true accent
the one you brushed up so well
aqui en los junited estates
why is it so hard
are those words too big for your mouth

it's time you return to who you are for   2
you have been every other race
except your own
looking for one that fits you
ashamed to speak in your given tongue
you have allowed for others to put your people down
acting like it didn't bother you
like you didn't care

how can i trust you   3
who denies su madre
vende patria

i mean look   4
look at the riquesa running through your
platano arroz abichuela sancocho mondongo veins
and listen
listen to the merengue salsa mambo
so dependent on your every movement
coño, we are a people full of life
a people full of color
tenemos ese saborrr
una cultura so rich
con la sangre caliente
so no lo niegue
because it's people like you
que mata la raza latina
it's people like you
who kills our race

but hey . . .   5
maybe you didn't know yourself
how beautiful we are
maybe no one ever taught you
that the latin race es algo tan lindo
maybe . . . maybe no one ever showed you that
being latina was something to be proud of
maybe . . .
yeah . . .
say it
say it however you want to say it:

yo soy latina   6
Yo soy latina
YO SOY LATINA!

Words strain,
Crack and sometimes break, under the burden,
Under the tension, slip, slide, perish,
Decay with imprecision, will not stay in place,
Will not stay still.

T. S. Eliot, *Four Quartets*

Ethnographic Interviewing

Interview five to ten people about their definitions of *Hispanic/Latino*. Vary age, ethnicity, gender, class, occupation. Use a notebook for your field notes.

Taking Field Notes

Who's doing the defining? Note some information about the person you are interviewing (age, ethnic identification, and so on). Include in your notes some exact quotations.

Consider these questions as you prepare for an interview.

1. With what ethnic group or groups does the interviewee identify?
2. Does the person seem knowledgeable about the problems of ethnic identification? (Does it appear to you that this person has thought about these distinctions before?)
3. To what degree would you say this person is interested in the problems of ethnic identification (especially Hispanic/Latino)? Would you say this person is concerned?
4. How does the interviewee distinguish Hispanic/Latino? Does the person use these words interchangeably? Did the interviewee respond immediately with definitions or have to ponder first?

Read and discuss the following excerpt from *The Ethnographic Interview* by James Spradley to help you prepare for this experience. Create your own

Figure 7.3

Ethnographic Interview Record _____

Project: Hispanic/Latino _____

Interviewer: _____

Date of interview: _____

Informant (name or person interviewed): _____

Informant's occupation or student status: _____

Informant's gender: _____ **Approximate age:** _____

Informant's ethnic identification: _____

Exact quotations

Summary

Comments

---

interview guide. Attach responses to the interview record. (See suggested format in Figure 7.3.) After completing all your interviews, write a paragraph about what you learned from this interview process.

The Ethnographic Interview

James Spradley

James Spradley is a cultural anthropologist who has helped clarify the nature of ethnography (the study of culture and cultural diversity). In his book Participant Observation _(1980) he makes explicit some basic concepts and skills needed for doing ethnography._ The Ethnographic Interview _(1979), from which this selection is taken, provides guidelines for students to do ethnography without years of_ *training. "Ethnography," Spradley explains in this Preface, "offers all of us the chance to step outside our narrow cultural backgrounds, to set aside our socially inherited ethnocentrism." Ethnography is "more than a tool for anthropologists." It is "a pathway into understanding the cultural differences that make us what we are as human beings." Here Spradley provides a sequence of steps for conducting a successful ethnographic interview that will lead to a rich description and, one hopes, greater understanding.*

Ethnographers work together with informants to produce a cultural description. This relationship is complex . . . The success of doing ethnography depends, to a great extent, on understanding the nature of this relationship. I use the term *informant* in a very specific way, not to be confused with concepts like subject, respondent, friend, or actor. In this chapter I want to clarify the concept and role of informant. 1

According to *Webster's New Collegiate Dictionary,* an informant is "a native 2 speaker engaged to repeat words, phrases, and sentences in his own language or dialect as a model for imitation and a source of information." Although derived primarily from linguistics, this definition will serve as a starting point for our discussion. Informants are first and foremost *native speakers,* a fact made clear in the last chapter. Informants are engaged by the ethnographer to speak *in their own language or dialect.* Informants provide a *model for the ethnographer to imitate;* the ethnographer hopes to learn to use the native language in the way informants do. Finally, informants are *a source of information;* literally, they become teachers for the ethnographer.

Most people act as informants at one time or another without realizing 3 it. We offer information to others in response to questions about our everyday lives. "What kind of family did you come from?" "What do you do at school?" "What kinds of problems do you have working as a cocktail waitress?" "You collect comic books? That sounds interesting: what does it involve?" Such questions place us in the role of informant.

An ethnographer seeks out ordinary people with ordinary knowledge 4 and builds on their common experience. Slowly, through a series of interviews, by repeated explanations, and through the use of special questions, ordinary people become excellent informants. Everyone, in the course of their daily activities, has acquired knowledge that appears specialized to others. A shaman know how to perform magic rituals; a housewife can prepare a holiday meal; a sportsman is an expert in fishing for lake trout; a physician knows her way around a large hospital and can perform open heart surgery; a tramp has acquired strategies for making it; a boy can maneuver with skill on a skate board. Knowledge about everyday life is a common property of the human species. So is the ability to communicate that knowledge in a native language. This ability makes it possible for almost anyone to act as an informant.

Interviewing informants depends on a cluster of interpersonal skills. 5 These include: asking questions, listening instead of talking, taking a passive rather than an assertive role, expressing verbal interest in the other person, and showing interest by eye contact and other nonverbal means. Some people have acquired these skills to a greater degree than others; some learn them more quickly than others. I recall one novice ethnographer who felt insecure about interviewing an urban planner. During the interviews she kept thinking about the next question she should ask and often looked down at a list she had prepared. Each time she lost eye contact with her informant, he interpreted it as lack of interest. She seldom nodded her head or encouraged her informant with such statements as, "That's really interesting," or "I never realized urban planners did so much!" Although she continued the interviews, rapport developed slowly because she lacked this specific skill of showing interest.

Activities

1. Make a list of potential informants (or cultural scenes). (A beginning ethnographer seeking a scene to study should list 40 to 50 possibilities.) 6
2. Identify five or six of the most likely informants (or cultural scenes). 7
3. Compare this list of potential informants on the five minimal requirements for a good informant. Place the selections in rank order. 8

Examing the Ethnographic Interview

When we examine the ethnographic interview as a speech event, we see that it shares many features with the friendly conversation. In fact, skilled ethnographers often gather most of their data through participant observation and many casual, friendly conversations. They may interview people without their awareness, merely carrying on a friendly conversation while introducing a few ethnographic questions. 9

It is best to think of ethnographic interviews as a series of friendly conversations into which the researcher slowly introduces new elements to assist informants to respond as informants. Exclusive use of these new *ethnographic elements,* or introducing them too quickly, will make interviews become like a formal interrogation. Rapport will evaporate, and informants may discontinue their cooperation. At any time during an interview it is possible to shift back to a friendly conversation. A few minutes of easygoing talk interspersed here and there throughout the interview will pay enormous dividends in rapport. 10

The three most important ethnographic elements are its *explicit purpose, ethnographic explanations,* and *ethnographic questions.* 11

1. *Explicit purpose.* When an ethnographer and informant meet together for an interview, both realize that the talking is supposed to go somewhere. The informant only has a hazy idea about this purpose; the ethnographer must make it clear. Each time they meet it is necessary to remind the informant where the interview is to go. Because ethnographic interviews involve purpose and direction, they will tend to be more formal than friendly conversations. Without being authoritarian, the ethnographer gradually takes more control of the talking, directing it in those channels that lead to discovering the cultural knowledge of the informant. 12
2. *Ethnographic explanations.* From the first encounter until the last interview, the ethnographer must repeatedly offer explanations to the informant. While learning an informant's culture, the informant also learns 13

something—to become a teacher. Explanations facilitate this process. There are five types of explanations used repeatedly.

a. *Project explanations.* These include the most general statements about what the project is all about. The ethnographer must translate the goal of doing ethnography and eliciting an informant's cultural knowledge into terms the informant will understand. "I am interested in your occupation. I'd like to talk to you about what beauticians do." Later one might be more specific: "I want to know how beauticians talk about what they do, how they see their work, their customers, themselves. I want to study beauticians from your point of view." 14

b. *Recording explanations.* These include all statements about writing things down and reasons for tape recording the interviews. "I'd like to write some of this down," or "I'd like to tape record our interview so I can go over it later; would that be OK?" 15

c. *Native language explanations.* Since the goal of ethnography is to describe a culture in its own terms, the ethnographer seeks to encourage informants to speak in the same way they would talk to others *in their cultural scene.* These explanations remind informants *not* to use their translation competence. They take several forms and must be repeated frequently throughout the entire project. A typical native language explanation might be, "If you were talking to a customer, what would you say?" 16

d. *Interview explanations.* Slowly, over the weeks of interviewing, most informants become expert at providing the ethnographer with cultural information. One can then depart more and more from the friendly conversation model until finally it is possible to ask informants to perform tasks such as drawing a map or sorting terms written on cards. At those times it becomes necessary to offer an explanation for the type of interview that will take place. "Today I'd like to ask you some different kinds of questions. I've written some terms on cards and I'd like to have you tell me which ones are alike or different. After that we can do the same for other terms." This kind of interview explanation helps informants know what to expect and to accept a greater formality in the interview. 17

e. *Question explanations.* The ethnographer's main tools for discovering another person's cultural knowledge is the ethnographic question. Since there are many different kinds, it is important to explain them as they are used. "I want to ask you a different type of question," may suffice in some cases. At other times it is necessary to provide a more detailed explanation of what is going on. 18

3. *Ethnographic questions.* Throughout this book I have identified more than thirty kinds of ethnographic questions (Appendix A). They will be introduced by stages; it is not necessary to learn all of them at once. The design of this book allows a person to master one form of ethnographic question and make it a part of their interviews; then the next form will be presented and explained. For now, I only want to identify the three main types and explain their function. 19

a. *Descriptive questions.* This type enables a person to collect an ongoing 20 sample of an informant's language. Descriptive questions are the easiest to ask and they are used in all interviews. Here's an example: "Could you tell me what you do at the office?" or "Could you describe the conference you attended?"

b. *Structural questions.* These questions enable the ethnographer to dis- 21 cover information about *domains,* the basic units in an informant's cultural knowledge. They allow us to find out *how* informants have organized their knowledge. Examples of structural questions are: "What are all the different kinds of fish you caught on vacation?" and "What are all the stages in getting transferred in your company?" Structural questions are often repeated, so that if an informant identified six types of activities, the ethnographer might ask, "Can you think of any other kind of activities you would do as a beautician?"

c. *Contrast questions.* The ethnographer wants to find out what an infor- 22 mant *means* by the various terms used in his native language. Later I will discuss how meaning emerges from the contrasts implicit in any language. Contrast questions enable the ethnographer to discover the dimensions of meaning which informants employ to distinguish the objects and events in their world. A typical contrast question would be, "What's the difference between a *bass* and a *northern pike?*"

The Verbatim Principle

The ethnographer must *make a verbatim record of what people say.* This obvi- 23 ous principle of getting things down word for word is frequently violated. Whether recording things people say in natural contexts or in more formal ethnographic interviews, the investigator's tendency to translate continues to operate. When I began research with tramps I did not realize the importance of the verbatim principle. I freely summarized, restated, and condensed what informants said without realizing it.

Consider the following example: (a) Informant's actual statement: "I 24 made the bucket in Seattle one time for pooling; I asked a guy how much he was holding on a jug and he turned out to be a ragpicker and he pinched me." (b) Field notes entry: "I talked to Joe about his experience of being arrested on skid row when he wasn't drunk." At the time, this condensed entry appeared sufficient; I certainly did not feel it was a distortion of what Joe said. I didn't fully understand all his words but I thought I knew roughly what they meant. However, this entry lost some of the most important clues to the informant's culture. These clues came from such folk terms as *pooling* (a complex routine for contributing to a fund for purchasing something), *the bucket* (city jail), *ragpicker* (a certain kind of policeman), and *pinched* (arrested). Joe's phrases were leads to further questions; my summary was not. As my research progressed, I became aware that the words informants spoke held a key to their culture and so I began to make a verbatim record.

It may seem wiser, under the pressure of an interview situation, or in 25 some natural context, to make a quick and more complete summary rather than a partial verbatim record. Such is not the case. In the previous example it would have been more valuable to make a partial, but verbatim, record such as the following:

"made the bucket"   26

"holding on a jug"   27

"a ragpicker . . . pinched me"   28

These scattered phrases could then have been used to generate ethnographic questions; the summary could not.   29

Both *native terms* and *observer terms* will find their way into the field notes. The important thing is to carefully distinguish them. The native terms must be recorded verbatim. Failure to take these first steps along the path of discovering the inner meaning of another culture will lead to a false confidence that we have found out what the natives know. We may never even realize that our picture is seriously distorted and incomplete.   30

The best way to make a verbatim record during interviews is to use a tape recorder. It is especially valuable to tape record the first two or three interviews in order to quickly acquire a larger sample of informant statements. However, tape recorders are not always advisable, especially during the first few interviews when rapport is beginning to develop. The use of a tape recorder may threaten and inhibit informants. Each ethnographer must decide on the basis of the willingness of informants and their feelings about using a tape recorder. When interviewing tramps, I often did not use a tape recorder because it aroused suspicion. When I interviewed cocktail waitresses, I always used a recorder with the full cooperation of waitress-informants. Here are some general rules for making a decision: 31

1. Always take a small tape recorder in case the opportunity arises to use it. One ethnographer decided not to tape record his first interview with an encyclopedia saleswoman. But when he started the interview, she asked, "Don't you want to tape record this?" If he had brought a tape recorder, he could have easily brought it out and started the tape.   32

2. Go slowly on introducing a tape recorder immediately. Often the first interview is likely to be a time to get acquainted, a time to develop rapport and trust. Informants will not know what kind of questions to expect. With an enthusiastic and eager informant, it is possible to ask casually, "How would you feel about tape recording this interview?" If the informant shows any hesitation, one might want to say, "Well, maybe it would be best to wait, perhaps later when we get into things." Sometimes it is necessary to wait until the second or third interview or even discard the idea entirely. It is possible to do good ethnography without a tape recorder; it is not possible to do good ethnography without rapport with key informants.   33

3. Watch for opportunities to tape record even a small part of an interview. After talking for half an hour, it might be appropriate to say, "This is so interesting and I'm learning so much, I wonder if you would mind if I tape recorded some of this. I can turn it off any time you want." Most informants will be more than willing to oblige.   34

Whether or not the ethnographer tape records interviews, it is still nec- 35
essary to take notes during each interview. Sometimes tape recorders do not
work; often some information from the interview is needed before it can be
transcribed. Let's look more closely at how to take field notes.

Kinds of Field Notes

There are several different kinds of field notes that will make up an ethno- 36
graphic record. Each investigator will develop a unique way to organize a file
and field notebook. The following suggested format reflects the organization
I have found most useful.

The Condensed Account

All notes taken during actual interviews or field observations represent a 37
condensed version of what actually occurred. It is not humanly possible to
write down everything that goes on or everything that informants say.
Condensed accounts often include phrases, single words, and unconnected
sentences. Consider the experience of one ethnographer who decided to interview a policeman. After making contact, her informant wanted her to
ride in the squad car for a four-hour shift. However, it would be impossible
to record in the car. In the squad car, she began to make notes of things that
occurred, the places they drove, calls that came over the radio, and many of
the phrases and terms used by her informant. During the four hours she
recorded several pages of *condensed notes* in her notebook. She left the first
interview with a feeling that she had only recorded a fraction of what she
had experienced. Still, this condensed account was of enormous value because it had been recorded on the spot.

It is advisable to make a condensed account during every interview. Even
while tape recording, it is good to write down phrases and words used by
your informants. The real value of a condensed account comes when it is expanded after completing the interview or field observation.

The Expanded Account

The second type of field notes represents an expansion of the condensed 38
version. As soon as possible after each field session the ethnographer should
fill in details and recall things that were not recorded on the spot. The key
words and phrases jotted down can serve as useful reminders to create the
expanded account. When expanding, different speakers must be identified
and verbatim statements included.

Much of my research among skid row men took place at the alcoholism 39
treatment center where I mingled informally with informants while they
worked, ate meals, played cards, and sat around talking. Occasionally, I jotted down condensed notes on small cards carried in my pocket. After several
hours of listening and watching, I would slip away to a private office and
expand my notes with as many details as I could remember. Like most
ethnographers, I discovered my ability to recall events and conversations in-

creased rapidly through the discipline of creating expanded accounts from condensed ones.

Tape-recorded interviews, when fully transcribed, represent one of the most complete expanded accounts. Despite the tedious and time-consuming nature of the work, making a full transcription becomes invaluable for conducting the series of ethnographic interviews discussed in this book. However, some investigators transcribe only parts of an interview or listen to the tape to create an expanded account, marking all verbatim phrases and words. Short of a complete transcription, an "index" of the tape can aid in locating relevant topics for later transcription. 40

Field Work Journal

In addition to field notes that come directly from observing and interviewing (the condensed account and expanded account), ethnographers should always keep a journal. Like a diary, this journal will contain a record of experiences, ideas, fears, mistakes, confusions, breakthroughs, and problems that arise during field work. A journal represents the personal side of field work; it includes reactions to informants and the feelings you sense from others. 41

Each journal entry should be dated. Rereading at a later time shows how quickly you forget what occurred during the first days and weeks of field work. Months later, when the ethnographer begins to write up the study, the journal becomes an important source of data. Doing ethnography differs from many other kinds of research in that *the ethnographer* becomes a major research instrument. Making an introspective record of field work enables a person to take into account personal biases and feelings, to understand their influence on the research. 42

Analysis and Interpretation

The fourth type of field notes provides a link between the ethnographic record and the final written ethnography. Here is the place to record analyses of cultural meanings, interpretations and insights into the culture studied. Most of the tasks in the remaining steps involve detailed analysis and can be recorded in this category of field notes. 43

Analysis and interpretation notes often represent a kind of brainstorming. Ideas may come from past reading, from some particular theoretical perspective, from some comment made by an informant. It is important to think of these field notes as a place to "think on paper" about the culture under consideration. 44

Activities

1. Set up a field-work notebook or file with sections for   45
   a. condensed accounts
   b. expanded accounts
   c. journal
   d. analysis and interpretation

Spradley

2. Begin making an ethnographic record with entries in each section for field work completed to date. 46
3. Contact an informant and arrange for the first ethnographic interview. 47

From *The Ethnographic Interview* by James P. Spradley, copyright © 1979 by Holt, Rinehart and Winston, Inc. Reprinted by permission of the publisher.

Writers at Work

Excerpts from Interviews

I interviewed nine people of different ages, races, and backgrounds. However, I only selected five I thought were more insightful for me to better understand the meanings of these terms. Some felt insulted when classified as Hispanic . . .

Bernadette Rotolo
First-year undergraduate

. . . . .

From interviews by Elizabeth Kim, a first-year undergraduate:

I feel that we should be called *Latinos* because we are not in the hands of Spain anymore (J.E., Dominican, age 21).

To me, the word *Hispanic* is a sexist term. It literally means "the Son of Spain." At least the word *Latino* is not sexist: *Latino, Latina* (M. R.-L. Anglo-Portuguese).

If you ask me what my ethnicity is, I'll say "I'm black," but if you ask me what my nationality is, I'll tell you "I'm Jamaican." I use the word *Hispanic* because I can't tell whether they are from Latin America or not. It's like [my] calling you *Asian.* If I didn't know where you were from, it's not fair for me to call you *Chinese* when you are not Chinese, you are Korean. It should be like [using] the word[s] *Asian,* . . . *Chinese, Korean, Japanese* (R.N., Jamaican, age 18).

. . . . .

Howard Woodhouse, also a first-year undergraduate, explains his interview process:

I asked my interviewees questions about how they felt about the terms. I interviewed three girls and two guys. All were of different age and school status. I basically asked them how they felt about the two terms, which one did they feel is the better term. The results of the interview showed me that *Hispanic* is a political term initiated by the government; *Latino* is based on culture and heritage of people from dominant Spanish-speaking countries.

Howard focuses here on one interview:

One interviewee (V.H., female, black-Latina, age 21, college junior) stated that she didn't want to choose an identity because she is culturally aware of other ethnic groups including her own—Panamanian. (I feel the same way about myself. Because I too have a heritage of different cultures.) V.H. calls herself *black* because when people look at her they see "a strong black woman." Also because her ancestors are from Africa. She states, "To be a Latina is to compose a culture, a heritage, and not just a language." She said that before the word Latina/o came about, she considered herself a black-Panamanian. She doesn't want to choose an identity, but for now she'll be a black-Latina.

. . . . .

Here are excerpts from interviews by Robert Marzec, who is a first-year graduate student:

Marybeth: "I am American first—not because of pride—just because that was where I was born. I am of Italian descent—but don't think of this ethnically. It's hard to think of myself ethnically—because of my background. I've never been excluded—subjected—because I'm white. My father's Italian, but not my mother. I consider my father only half-Italian—even though both his parents were born in Italy—but he was born here. So that would make him only half-Italian, right? I feel privileged not because I'm better in some way—but society makes you—because society makes the majority."

Lara: "Well, I'm white. I don't ID myself as white—but I am—you can't ignore that—you can't ignore race, no matter what group you're in. I consider myself German-American."

John: "Yes. It's something you can't ignore. All of us are raced. All of us are gendered. You can't ignore the fact that others have race—the concept of white becomes invisible. Certainly whites are more able to ignore their race—but that's dangerous.

John (when asked about Hispanic/Latino): "I don't know. I assume *Hispanic* means of Spanish descent. And *Latino* is indirectly Spanish—South America."

Lara: "Whites refer to any South American as *Hispanic.* But I think it also carries the idea of 'colonized by the Spanish.' Yes, people of South America colonized."

John: "My stepfather's mother is from Puerto Rico but he was born and raised in New York City. He calls himself Hispanic—I don't think he'd care to re-label himself as Latino. He's bilingual. He went to a party, a kind of Latino party once—they took ethnic dishes—and some of the people there chided him about his accent. They said it wasn't really Spanish and called it 'New Yorican' (yor-ee-kan)—a kind of bastard dialect of English-Spanish and New York City accent. And it's an actual term—they didn't make it up. But I prefer to use *Latino,* with its variation of *Latina,* because it allows women to make a claim for sisterhood. I think, though, that most would prefer to identify themselves according to country of origin."

Virgilio Bravo, a first-year undergraduate, age 18, from Chile and a member of the Latin American Student Union, told Lisette Andrades in an interview that he would rather be identified as Chilean. *"Hispanic,"* he said, "is a predominantly Anglo-European term that has been used to characterize us and classify us. *Latino* characterizes all Spanish-speaking countries as one—and they are not the same. They have different histories. You can't call the Native Americans in South America and Central America *Latinos* because they have Indian dialects and speak Spanish."

Aaron: "I'm mixed. First side, English/Anglo, the other Russian/Jew. I used to think of myself as White Male, but now I'm not so sure. I have started to think of Judaism as more than a religion—ethnically, racially. Yes, the problem of identity disturbs me deeply. The problem is, I don't know if Jews are "white" or not. I don't know whether I'm a Jew or not. There's the problem of Orthodox Jews—some feel some way—others feel certain features . . . Hispanic. Yes, I know. Historically, for anyone who spoke Spanish. Colonizers are Hispanic in Mexico—from the continent, from Europe. And *Latino,* a much newer term—Latin South American. The word has less of a cloaking power. It tries to take in nation and it is also gender-specific. But I don't call someone something they don't want to be called."

Angela: "Ethnicity poses a big problem for me. I'm all Italian—but that doesn't solve anything. I'm half-Sicilian. So that means part of me is from the mainland and the other part from the island. And a lot of Italians don't consider Sicilians to be true Italian. And *white,* I can't use that term without historicizing. . . . Yes, *Latino* is the preferred term right now. You shouldn't refer to people as *Hispanic.* That was a construct of the white male majority and has little to do with the people categorized by that label."

· · · · ·

A physician (L.V., Italian-American, male, age 50) whose patients are mostly Puerto Rican told interviewer Toby Venier (a first-year graduate student) that he "prefers to identify people by their country of origin rather than putting them all under one term—Hispanic or Latino." However, he said that he sometimes uses *Hispanic* because the media uses this word. He recalled one patient who "almost hit the ceiling" when asked if she were Puerto Rican. (She was Cuban.)

· · · · ·

S.E.: "I am an American white female from upstate New York. I very rarely use the term *Latino.* However, I think this was the term used in my Cultural Identities course when we talked about Nicholasa Mohr, Sandra Cisneros, and Gloria Anzaldúa. *Hispanic* is the word I tend to use." [P. Gay: At the time of this writing, I received an announcement that

Nicholasa Mohr would be coming to my campus. The title of her talk: "Growing up Latina in the USA: A Writer's Perspective."]

. . . . .

Excerpt from an interview report by Sherita Greene, first-year undergraduate:

> When Dolores Prida, a New York–based playwright, was asked how she would like to be classified, she responded: "I really don't care what I'm called. But I consider myself to be a Cuban-Rican New Yorker because I was born of a Cuban father, a Puerto Rican mother and I now live in New York. Yet if I had to choose, I would prefer to be called *Latina* because *Hispanic* doesn't include many groups."

Many people like to classify themselves by the countries from which they came. One of the problems with that is it is not one of the terms included on those forms which asks you to state an identity. Hispanic, African-American, Caucasian, Asian, and "Other" are the only categories listed. Therefore, Ms. Prida would have to classify herself in the "Other" category, which would later be turned into white.

. . . . .

Excerpt from an interview report by Bernadette Rotolo, first-year undergraduate:

> The term *Latino,* as I discovered, is used as an encompassing term including people from around the world. Contrary to this, *Hispanic* is solely used to identify people in the United States. Kathy Blackmer (personal communication, April 6, 1992), a graduate sociology student, argues that "there is a political reason why these terms came about." It was a way in which the Truman administration categorized people entering the country for census purposes in the 1950s. According to Blackmer, the term *Latino* excludes people from Spain and focuses on the people residing in Latin America and South America. Furthermore, she explains, *Hispanic* is a generic name classifying all Spanish-speaking people and occurs in general usage, unlike *Latino.*

. . . . .

Finally, here are two complete interview write-ups. Elizabeth Berliner, graduate student and teacher of basic writing, chose to use a combination of summary and quotations from the actual interview.

> Thomas M. was born and raised in Germany, and is currently a visiting doctoral student in chemistry at Binghamton University. He identifies himself as German, claiming that all of his ancestors can be traced through Germany. When I first asked him to take part in this interview he declined, claiming that in German they do not have the words *Latino/a* or *Hispanic* and so he was unable to answer the questions. However, I continued the conversation and found some quite interesting information regarding the different ways that ethnicity can be named.

E: What do they call people from Latin America in Germany?

T: Latina—yeah—I guess it's the same word. But actually people most often trace people to their country of origin. So I would probably choose *Latino/a* because of the connotation of Latin America. What does *Hispanic* mean?

I explained a little of what I have learned in other interviews—that some people associate the word Hispanic with the history of Spanish domination in the Latin American region and for this reason reject the word. Tom jumped in and said, yes, that is what it conveyed to him also. I continued by posing some hypothetical situations to Tom regarding choices he might make if he stayed in the U.S.

E: If you applied for citizenship in the U.S.—if you decided you wanted to stay here, marry, etc., and you wanted to be a citizen—how might you refer to yourself then?

T: Probably German-American. I could never consider myself American, solely American.

E: How about if you had children here. The U.S. would consider them to be American if born on our soil. What would you consider them to be?

T: German. In my eyes they would be German. Maybe German-American.

I then asked what he checks on forms here in the United States when he needs to complete them. He responded *white* and when I asked if *Caucasian* meant the same to him, he responded with a surprised "No. In German, *Caucasian* solely refers to people from the region of the Caucasus Mountains"—so we quickly grabbed a dictionary and indeed the first three meanings refer to the mountain range, only the last recognizing the wider-spread use of the word *Caucasian* to specify "white" people.

Tom also spoke about the use of the word *kraut* (from sauerkraut) as a slur against Germans. Though he says it does not bother him (nothing bothers this guy, believe me) he knows other Germans who are greatly offended by the term.

Comments

Look ahead and read the material from the ethnographic interview of Figure 7.4 (pp. 320–21). I'm fascinated with the difference between the way people identify themselves publicly and how they identify themselves privately. I've found that the two are rarely the same. José's response became almost humorous in the light of his fiancee's remark. He didn't even realize that he identified himself differently for different people. Though he will classify himself as *Hispanic,* he doesn't seem really to identify with the term. To himself, he is Dominican.

His comments about everyone being "ethnic," and ethnicity as something you don't just pick up one day, seemed to me to be extremely enlightening. I mentioned to him that one person I interviewed didn't consider herself ethnic in any way and he just laughed and said that was an impossibility. He thinks [I believe] that if you aren't a "purebred" person your specific ethnicity may be more difficult to identify, but it is nonetheless there. It is there, but more complex and intermingled. Ethnicity is not something we choose one day, he says, we learn it all of our lives. I really liked this perception of his.

What came through most strongly was that he was tired of people trying to identify themselves just for the sake of it or because it was the politically correct thing to do. He seems very secure with his own identity (probably because he grew up in a predominantly "Hispanic" country) and thinks that the most important thing about people is their individuality, not what group they belong to. He wants to be José. I have to agree in many ways. This is the ideal. I do find this whole ethnic-identity question often separates people more than it brings them together. I think we can dwell too much on it. At the same time, there are those who just can't seem to see beyond someone else's race. If we don't address the issue of ethnicity and open minds regarding it, how will things ever change?

Legal Alien

Pat Mora

Bi-lingual, Bi-cultural,
able to slip from "How's life?"
to *"Me 'stan volviendo loca,"*
able to sit in a paneled office
drafting memos in smooth English,
able to order in fluent Spanish
at a Mexican restaurant,
American but hyphenated,
viewed by Anglos as perhaps exotic,
perhaps inferior, definitely different,
viewed by Mexicans as alien,
(their eyes say, "You may speak
Spanish but you're not like me")
an American to Mexicans
a Mexican to Americans
a handy token
sliding back and forth
between the fringes of both worlds
by smiling
by masking the discomfort
of being pre-judged
Bi-laterally.

Reprinted with permission from the publisher of *Chants* (Houston: Arte Publico Press–University of Houston, 1985).

Figure 7.4

Ethnographic Interview Record

Interviewer: Suzanne Hart, Graduate Student

Date: 30 September, 1992

Informant: José Polanco

Occupation: Graduate Student

Gender: Male

Age: 33

Exact Quotations

HART: Could you tell me what the word *ethnic* means to you? How would you define it?

POLANCO: [very long pause] That's a very good question and kind of tough to answer. I guess immediately I think minority, but when I think deeper than that it's the cultural, social background—the way they're brought up. I don't think anyone is more "ethnic" than anyone else. I feel pretty strongly about that. We've all come from somewhere and been shaped by something. No one group has a corner on the market.

HART: If you were asked to ethnically identify yourself, what would you say?

POLANCO: I'd say *Hispanic.*

HART: I'm just curious, is that the way you honestly identify yourself personally, or is it how you do it publicly? Is there a difference between the public and private for you?

POLANCO: No, I don't really think so. I guess I think of myself as Hispanic. [His fiancee has overheard this part of the conversation. She is not Hispanic. She bursts out at this point, "I've never once heard you call yourself Hispanic, you always say you're Domini-can!"] OK, well, I guess I do say I'm Dominican when someone asks. I kind of assume from looking at me they know I'm Hispanic so I wouldn't be telling them anything new by saying I'm Hispanic. To my friends, I say I'm Dominican, but on forms and applications and stuff I say I'm Hispanic.

HART: On forms, do you ever check the "Other" box instead of Hispanic?

Figure 7.4 continued

POLANCO: Yes, I guess I do sometimes, but I never write anything in. Not all forms have Hispanic on them either.

HART: Has your ethnicity been something you've thought about a lot, or that you've had a hard time coming to terms with?

POLANCO: No. Identifying myself that way hasn't been a big deal to me. Maybe it's because I actually grew up in the Dominican Republic and not here, and it wasn't such a big question mark there. I know who I am, and that's what's been important to me.

HART: Do you think that we should even think ethnically? Do you think that we should try to identify ourselves in this way?

POLANCO: No. No, I don't. It's not something that just suddenly occurs. You learn your ethnicity all of your life. You don't suddenly, one day, have to categorically say I'm this, or I'm that. At Brown [University] as an undergrad it was a big issue. I think it caused more problems and divisions because people were so intense about saying they were this or that.

HART: José, what does the word *Hispanic* mean to you?

POLANCO: People who speak Spanish. I think it's almost entirely a linguistic word. It's people who speak Spanish in the United States.

HART: How about *Latino*?

POLANCO: It's Hispanic people (Spanish speakers) from Central and South America and the Caribbean. I don't think of it as people living in the United States. I guess because it's actually a Spanish word.

HART: What images do these words call to your mind?

POLANCO: I guess I have to say they make me think of the inner city, bad conditions, lots of kids, poor, uneducated. Those are the stereotypes. I think *Latino* is just a more respectable or "politically correct" way of saying the exact same thing.

HART: I want to go backwards a minute here. You said this whole issue was a "hot" topic at Brown. Did it become a big issue for you, then?

POLANCO: Well, yeah. I did have to think about it a lot as an undergrad. I took classes that discussed it and stuff and others [Hispanics] made me think about it. Mostly, though, I know who I am. I don't worry what others think. I think when we draw too much of a line, we can't see ourselves as real people anymore. I become José the Hispanic, not José the person, and that's all anyone can see.

Documented/Undocumented

Guillermo Gómez-Peña

Guillermo Gómez-Peña is a visual artist living in Santa Monica, California. This essay appeared in The Graywolf Annual Five: Multi-Cultural Literacy— Opening the American Mind, *published by Graywolf Press, 1988. It appeared originally in the* L.A. Weekly. *Read now about Gómez-Peña's problems with ethnic identification. Take and make notes as you continue to work on this problem.*

I live smack in the fissure between two worlds, in the infected wound: half a 1 block from the end of Western Civilization and four miles from the start of the Mexican-American border, the northernmost point of Latin America. In my fractured reality, but a reality nonetheless, there cohabit two histories, languages, cosmologies, artistic traditions, and political systems which are drastically counterposed. Many "deterritorialized" Latin American artists in Europe and the U.S. have opted for "internationalism" (a cultural identity based upon the "most advanced" of the ideas originating out of New York or Paris). I, on the other hand, opt for "borderness" and assume my role: My generation, the *chilangos* [slang term for a Mexico City native], who came to "el norte" fleeing the imminent ecological and social catastrophe of Mexico City, gradually integrated itself into otherness, in search of that other Mexico grafted onto the entrails of the et cetera . . . became Chicano-ized. We de-Mexicanized ourselves to Mexi-understand ourselves, some without wanting to, others on purpose. And one day, the border became our house, laboratory, and ministry of culture (or counterculture).

Today, eight years after my departure [from Mexico], when they ask me 2 for my nationality or ethnic identity, I can't respond with one word, since my "identity" now possesses multiple repertories: I am Mexican but I am also Chicano and Latin American. At the border they call me *chilango* or *mexiquillo;* in Mexico City it's *pocho* or *norteño;* and in Europe it's *sudaca.* The Anglos call me "Hispanic" or "Latino," and the Germans have, on more than one occasion, confused me with Turks or Italians. My wife Emilia is Anglo-Italian, but speaks Spanish with an Argentine accent, and together we walk amid the rubble of the Tower of Babel of our American post-modernity.

The recapitulation of my personal and collective topography has become 3 my cultural obsession since I arrived in the United States. I look for the traces of my generation, whose distance stretches not only from Mexico City to California, but also from the past to the future, from pre-Columbian America to high technology and from Spanish to English, passing through "Spanglish."

As a result of this process I have become a cultural topographer, border- 4 crosser, and hunter of myths. And it doesn't matter where I find myself, in Califas or Mexico City, in Barcelona or West Berlin; I always have the sensation that I belong to the same species: the migrant tribe of fiery pupils.

My work, like that of many border artists, comes from two distinct tradi- 5 tions, and because of this has dual, or on occasion multiple, referential codes. One strain comes from Mexican popular culture, the Latin American literary "boom," and the Mexico City counterculture of the '70s . . . the other comes directly from fluxus (a late-'60s international art movement that explored alternative means of production and distribution), concrete poetry, conceptual art, and performance art. These two traditions converge in my border experience and they fuse together.

In my intellectual formation, Carlos Fuentes, Gabriel García Márquez, 6 Oscar Chávez, Felipe Ehrenberg, José Agustin, and Enrique Cisneros were as important as Burroughs, Foucault, Fassbinder, Lacan, Vito Aconci, and Joseph Beuys.

My "artistic space" is the intersection where the new Mexican urban po- 7 etry and the colloquial Anglo poetry meet; the intermediate stage somewhere between Mexican street theater and multimedia performance; the silence that snaps in between the *corrido* and punk; the wall that divides "*neográfica*" (a 1970s Mexico City art movement involved in the production of low-budget art and graphics) and graffiti; the highway that joins Mexico City and Los Angeles; and the mysterious thread of thought and action that puts pan-Latin Americanism in touch with the Chicano movement, and both of these in touch with other international vanguards.

I am a child of crisis and cultural syncretism, half hippie and half punk. 8 My generation grew up watching movies about cowboys and science fiction, listening to *cumbias* and tunes from the Moody Blues, constructing altars and filming in Super-8, reading the *Corno Emplumado* and *Artforum*, traveling to Tepoztlán and San Francisco, creating and de-creating myths. We went to Cuba in search of political illumination, to Spain to visit the crazy grandmother and to the U.S. in search of the instantaneous musico-sexual Paradise. We found nothing. Our dreams wound up getting caught in the webs of the border.

Our generation belongs to the world's biggest floating population: the 9 weary travelers, the dislocated, those of us who left because we didn't fit anymore, those of us who still haven't arrived because we don't know where to arrive at, or because we can't go back anymore.

Our deepest generational emotion is that of loss, which comes from our 10 having left. Our loss is total and occurs at multiple levels: loss of our country (culture and national rituals) and our class (the "illustrious" middle class and upper middle). Progressive loss of language and literary culture in our native tongue (those of us who live in non-Spanish-speaking countries); loss of ideological meta-horizons (the repression against and division of the left) and of metaphysical certainty.

In exchange, what we won was a vision of a more experimental culture, 11 that is to say, a multi-focal and tolerant one. Going beyond nationalisms, we established cultural alliances with other places, and we won a true political conscience (declassicization and consequent politicization) as well as new options in social, sexual, spiritual, and aesthetic behavior.

Our artistic product presents hybrid realities and colliding visions within 12 coalition. We practice the epistemology of multiplicity and a border semiotics. We share certain thematic interests, like the continual clash with cultural otherness, the crisis of identity, or, better said, access to trans- or multiculturalism, and the destruction of borders therefrom; the creation of alternative cartographies, a ferocious critique of the dominant culture of both countries, and lastly, a proposal for new creative languages.

We witness the borderization of the world, by-product of the "deterrito- 13 rialization" of vast human sectors. The borders either expand or are shot full of holes. Cultures and languages mutually invade one another. The South rises and melts, while the North descends dangerously with its economic and military pincers. The East moves west and vice-versa. Europe and North America daily receive uncontainable migrations of human beings, a majority of whom are being displaced involuntarily. This phenomenon is the result of multiple factors: regional wars, unemployment, overpopulation, and especially in the enormous disparity in North/South relations.

The demographic facts are staggering: The Middle East and Black Africa 14 are already in Europe, and Latin America's heart now beats in the U.S. New York and Paris increasingly resemble Mexico City and São Paulo. Cities like Tijuana and Los Angeles, once socio-urban aberrations, are becoming models of a new hybrid culture, full of uncertainty and vitality. And border youth—the fearsome "cholo-punks," children of the chasm that is opening between the "first" and the "third" worlds—become the indisputable heirs to a new *mestizaje* (the fusion of the Amerindian and European races).

In this context, concepts like "high culture," "ethnic purity," "cultural 15 identity," "beauty," and "fine arts" are absurdities and anachronisms. Like it or not, we are attending the funeral of modernity and the birth of a new culture.

In 1988, the unigeneric and monocultural vision of the world is insuffi- 16 cient. Syncretism, interdisciplinarianism, and multi-ethnicity are sine qua nons of contemporary art. And the artist or intellectual who doesn't comprehend this will be banished and his or her work will not form part of the great cultural debates of the continent.

Art is conceptual territory where everything is possible, and by the same 17 token there do not exist certainties nor limitations within it. In 1988, all the creative possibilities have been explored, and therefore they are all within our reach.

Thanks to the discoveries and advancements of many artists over the last 18 fifteen years, the concept of *metier* is so wide and the parameters of art so flexible that they include practically every imaginable alternative: art as political negotiation (Felipe Ehrenberg—Mexico, as social reform (Joseph Beuys—Germany), as an instrument of multicultural organization (Judy Baca—Los Angeles), or as alternative communication (*Post Arte*—Mexico, and Kit Galloway & Sherri Rabinowitz—USA). Others conceive art as a strategy of intervention aimed at mass media, or as citizen-diplomacy, social chronicle, a popular semiotics, or personal anthropology.

In 1988, our artistic options in terms of the medium, methodology, sys- 19 tem of communication, and channels of distribution for our ideas and images are greater and more diverse than ever. Not understanding and practicing this freedom implies operating outside of history, or, worse yet, blindly accepting the restrictions imposed by cultural bureaucracies.

Our experience as Latino border artists and intellectuals in the U.S. fluc- 20 tuates between legality and illegality, between partial citizenship and full.

For the Anglo community we are simply "an ethnic minority," a subculture, that is to say, some kind of pre-industrial tribe with a good consumerist appetite. For the art world, we are practitioners of distant languages that, in the best of cases, are perceived as exotic.

In general, we are perceived through the folkloric prisms of Hollywood, 21 fad literature and publicity; or through the ideological filters of mass media. For the average Anglo, we are nothing but "images," "symbols," "metaphors." We lack ontological existence and anthropological concreteness. We are perceived indistinctly as magic creatures with shamanistic powers, happy bohemians with pretechnological sensibilities, or as romantic revolutionaries born in a Cuban poster from the '70s. All this without mentioning the more ordinary myths, which link us with drugs, supersexuality, gratuitous violence, and terrorism, myths that serve to justify racism and disguise the fear of cultural otherness.

These mechanisms of mythification generate semantic interference and 22 obstruct true intercultural dialogue. To make border art implies to reveal and subvert said mechanisms.

The term *Hispanic,* coined by techno-marketing experts and by the de- 23 signers of political campaigns, homogenizes our cultural diversity (Chicanos, Cubans, and Puerto Ricans become indistinguishable), avoids our indigenous cultural heritage and links us directly with Spain. Worse yet, it possesses connotations of upward mobility and political obedience.

The terms *Third World culture, ethnic art,* and *minority art* are openly eth- 24 nocentric and necessarily imply an axiological vision of the world at the service of Anglo-European culture. Confronted with them, one can't avoid asking the following questions: Besides possessing more money and arms, is it that the "First World" is qualitatively better in any other way than our "underdeveloped" countries? That the Anglos themselves aren't also an "ethnic group," one of the most violent and antisocial tribes on this planet? That the five hundred million Latin American *mestizos* that inhabit the Americas are a "minority"?

Between Chicanos, Mexicans, and Anglos there is a heritage of relations 25 poisoned by distrust and resentment. For this reason, my cultural work (especially in the camps of performance art and journalism) has concentrated itself upon the destruction of the myths and the stereotypes that each group has invented to rationalize the other two.

With the dismantling of this mythology, I look, if not to create an in- 26 stantaneous space for intercultural communication, at least to contribute to the creation of the groundwork and theoretical principles for a future dialogue that is capable of transcending the profound historical resentments that exist between the communities on either side of the border.

Within the framework of the false amnesty of the Immigration Reform 27 and Control Act and the growing influence of the North American ultra-right, which seeks to close (militarize) the border because of supposed motives of "national security," the collaboration among Chicano, Mexican, and Anglo artists has become indispensable.

Anglo artists can contribute their technical ability, their comprehension 28 of the new mediums of expression and information (video and audio), and their altruist/internationalist tendencies. In turn, Latinos (whether Mexican,

Gómez-Peña

Chicano, Caribbean, Central or South American) can contribute the originality of their cultural models, their spiritual strength, and their political understanding of the world.

Together, we can collaborate in surprising cultural projects but without forgetting that *both should retain control of the product,* from the planning stages up through to distribution. If this doesn't occur, then intercultural collaboration isn't authentic. We shouldn't confuse true collaboration with political paternalism, cultural vampirism, voyeurism, economic opportunism, and demagogic multiculturalism.   29

We should clear up this matter once and for all: 30

We (Latinos in the United States) don't want to be a mere ingredient of the melting pot. What we want is to participate actively in a humanistic, pluralistic and politicized dialogue, continuous and not sporadic, and that this occur between equals that enjoy the same power of negotiation.   31

For this "immediate space" to open, first there has to be a pact of mutual cultural understanding and acceptance, and it is precisely in this that the border artist can contribute. In this very delicate historical moment, Mexican artists and intellectuals as well as Chicanos and Anglos should try to "recontextualize" ourselves, that is to say, search for a "common cultural territory," and within it put into practice new models of communication and association.   32

Translated by Rubén Martínez. Reprinted by special permission of Guillermo Gómez-Peña.

Some Questions for Rereading

1. "When they ask me for my nationality or ethnic identity, I can't respond with one word . . . ," wrote Gómez-Peña. What problem does he have with identifying himself ethnically? And what do you understand him to mean when he says he opted for "borderness"?
2. Use the following questions to guide more notetaking and notemaking on the use of *Hispanic* and *Latino:*
   a. How do Anglos identify Gómez-Peña?
   b. How does he identify himself?
   c. How does he view the term *Hispanic*?
   d. How does he define *Latino*?
3. How does Gómez-Peña define his purpose as an artist?

Writers at Work

Notetaking and Notemaking: Documented & Undocumented

The term *Hispanic,* coined by techno-marketing experts and by the designers of political campaigns, homogenizes our cultural diversity (Chicanos, Cubans, and Puerto Ricans become indistinguishable), avoids our indigenous cultural heritage and links us directly with Spain. Worse yet, it possesses connotations of upward mobility and political obedience.

Gómez-Peña

Sherita Greene: "I found this [passage] to be very interesting because it states a legitimate reason why Spanish-speaking people, who are not born in Spain, do not wish to be classified as 'Hispanic.' Every Spanish-speaking country has its own cultural identity which should be kept distinguishable from others. They should each be recognized separately because they have achieved different goals and they are on different levels of development. It is unfair to change the classificatory term to a culture just to suit 'techno-marketing experts,' as Peña puts it:"

Our deepest generational emotion is that of loss, which comes from our having left. Our loss is total and occurs at multiple levels: loss of our country (culture and national rituals) and our class (the "illustrious" middle class and upper middle). Progressive loss of language and literary culture in our native tongue.

Lisette Andrades: "Why is it that Mexicans seem to be the first group to lose their culture once they migrate to the U.S.? It was mentioned in the article titled "Generational Chasm Leads to Cultural Turmoil for Young Mexicans in U.S." by reporter Robert Suro (*The New York Times,* January 20, 1992) that Mexicans face many problems trying to handle both cultures once they have migrated. Also that adapting to a new culture is 'one of the biggest and most unpredictable factors for Mexican teenagers.' Also their language is lost as well. The Mexicans stop speaking Spanish at their homes, even to their parents. English becomes their language now. But your language is what identifies you, it's part of your culture. I think it's sad when you think about it."

In exchange, what we won was a vision of a more experimental culture, that is to say, a multi-focal and tolerant one.

Lisette: "I can see how they have won the experience of a different culture. That's good, but they have also assimilated into this other culture where they have forgotten their own. I don't agree with that. I think it's great to learn about other cultures because you become more knowledgeable that way, but I also feel you shouldn't forget who you are, or where you came from no matter where you're at, even if it's just to fit in. I don't think that's cool at all."

Read this editorial, which appeared on the Op-Ed page of *The New York Times.* It directly addresses this naming problem. Then read some responses and write your own Letter to the Editor.

Latino, Sí. Hispanic, No.

Earl Shorris

When the King of Spain was asked last year what name he used for those people in the U.S. who were related to him by language, he is reported to have said, with regal certainty, "Hispanic." 1

Ricardo Gutiérrez, a salesman from the east side of Los Angeles, faced with the same question, answered with equal certainty, "Latino." 2

Although Mr. Gutiérrez would seem to have superior knowledge of cultural issues in the U.S., many people and institutions, including the Census Bureau, side with the King. I am not one of them. 3

Of course, there are those who think that the King and the salesman are wrong. They oppose the use of any single word to describe all of the King's linguistic relatives—a lawyer whose family came from Puerto Rico, a waiter who emigrated from Spain, a Quiché Indian farmworker from Guatemala, a poet from the Dominican Republic and a taxi driver from Columbia. 4

They raise a serious issue. The use of a single word to name a group including people as disparate as Mexicans and Cubans conflates the cultures. And whatever conflates cultures destroys them. Nevertheless, there will have to be a name, for political power in a democratic society requires numbers, and only by agglomeration does the group become large enough to have an important voice in national politics. Agreement on one encompassing name is therefore vital. And possible, for any set that can be defined can be named. Which brings up another problem. 5

The group cannot be defined racially, because it includes people whose ancestors came from Asia to settle in the Western Hemisphere thousands of years ago, as well as people from Europe, the Iberian Peninsula and Africa. Religion won't do either. The group comprises Roman Catholics, many Protestant denominations, Jews and people who still have deep connections to Mixtec, Nahua and other native American religious rites and beliefs. 6

Economically, the group ranges from the chairman of the Coca-Cola Company to undocumented farmworkers who sleep in burrows dug into the ground in the hills east of Oceanside, Calif. 7

Nothing is left to define the linguistic relatives of the King but the language itself. There must be some connection to the Spanish language, if not in use, then in memory. If the language was not acquired from Roman soldiers who landed in Spain 2,000 years ago, then it was acquired from Spanish soldiers who landed in the Western Hemisphere 500 years ago. 8

During preparations for the 1980 U.S. Census, several names for the group were discussed. Latino won out, according to people who took part in the discussions, but at the last minute someone said it was too close to Ladino, an ancient language of Spain, now spoken by only a few Spanish Jews. Hispanic was chosen instead. 9

Since then, Hispanic and Latino have taken on political, social and even geographic meaning. Latino is used in California. In Florida, Hispanic is preferred by Cubans no matter what political, social or educational views they hold. Hispanic is used more often than Latino in Texas but neither word is used much; Mexican, Mexican-American and Chicano dominate there. Chicago, which has a mixture of people from the Caribbean and the mainland, has adopted Latino. In New York City, both names are used, depending largely on one's politics. 10

Hispanic belongs to those in power; it is the choice of establishments, exiles, social climbers and kings. Latino has been adopted by almost everyone else. Latino and Hispanic are the left and the right, commoner and king of names. Democrats are generally Latinos, Republicans are Hispanics. Many 11

Anglos, people who oppose bilingual education and those who support English-only laws prefer Hispanic, which is an English word meaning "pertaining to ancient Spain."

But neither politics nor economics should determine the choice of a 12 name. Language defines the group, provides it with history and home; language should also determine its name—Latino. The vowels of Latino are a serenade, Hispanic ends like broken glass. Latino/Latina has gender, which is Spanish, as against Hispanic, which follows English rules. Perhaps the course of democracy and assimilation dictates that someday this linguistic connection to culture must die, but there is no hurry, we need not be assassins now.

Earl Shorris is author of Latinos: A Biography of the People.
From *The New York Times*, October 28, 1992. Copyright © 1992 by The New York Times Company. Reprinted by permission.

Latino? Hispanic? Quechua? No, American

The New York Times **Editorials/Letters**
Wednesday, November 18, 1992

To the Editor:

"Latino, Sí. Hispanic, No." (Op-Ed, Oct. 28) by Earl Shorris is a fine ex- 1 ample of the creation of artificial groups of people so that they can be counted and controlled politically.

I have a friend who was born in Peru. She is a naturalized United States 2 citizen. Her first language was Quechua. Her second language was Italian. Her third language was Spanish. Her fourth language was English, and now she is studying Yiddish.

I am an amateur historian, and I have been able to trace her genealogy 3 back to before 1460. She is a descendant of an Inca prince, a former president of Argentina and a Spanish conquistador who left Spain to avoid the Inquisition. One branch of her family went to Galicia from Portugal in 1460. Later there was a marriage to a young Basque woman.

So to me, my friend is not Latino or Hispanic. She is a Portuguese, 4 Galician, Basque, Spanish, Quechua, Argentine, Peruvian, Jewish 100 percent American.

But ask her where her family came from, and she says, "If you go back far 5 enough my family came from the Garden of Eden, so I guess that makes me Edish."

Bob Krebs
Mount Vernon, N.Y.
Oct. 29, 1992

Take Your Pick

To the Editor:

Earl Shorris (Op-Ed, Oct. 28) argues that the term Latino is better than 1 Hispanic because "Latino/Latina has gender, which is Spanish, as against

Guadalupe

Hispanic, which follows English rules." If the original language determines the name of a group, we must stop using all English names for ethnic groups such as Chinese-Americans, Haitian-Americans and Japanese-Americans.

Hispanics use that term in its English form only when speaking English. Otherwise they say Hispano or Latino, both of which are consistent with the spoken language. 2

Mr. Shorris confirms that Hispanic is the preferred usage in Florida and Texas, and that both terms are used in New York. He should know both terms were used long before the Census Bureau picked up Hispanic for demographic statistical purposes. 3

Despite wide usage of the term, Mr. Shorris asserts that "Hispanic belongs to those in power." That is a contradiction, unless he is stating that power (whatever he means by it) is held only by Hispanics (or Latinos) in Florida, Texas and New York. 4

He asserts also: "The use of a single word to name a group including people as disparate as Mexicans and Cubans conflates the cultures. And whatever conflates the cultures destroys them." 5

Nevertheless he rushes headlong to advocate the name Latino as a substitute for Hispanic because, in his words, Hispanic does not sound "like a serenade." This sounds stereotypical and maybe even a little offensive. 6

A better argument would be that Latino is a more inclusive term: my Brazilian and Haitian friends refer to themselves as Latino, although certainly not Hispanic. Thus, although all Hispanics are Latinos, not all Latinos are Hispanic. 7

Indeed, Italians and French may call themselves Latinos, probably with more justification than hundreds of thousands of Latinos in the United States who hardly speak Spanish or any other Latin-based language, and who are further removed from their Latin roots than their parents or grandparents. 8

I suggest that both terms are acceptable because millions of people use them in self-reference and as a badge of pride. Thus, both terms reflect a sense of identity with Spanish or Latin roots. Yet, neither term is accurate because they both exclude the indigenous population of Latin America, as well as Africans, Asians and countless other non-Latin European populations. If Hispanic is an imposed official term, so is Latino, since it was the French who imposed that name on the southern continent of our hemisphere. 9

So, take your pick. But implying political connotations to our choices is doing a disservice to our need for unity and socioeconomic empowerment. Implying that one term is elitist and the other is correct is an elitist assumption. Remember, there are Hispanic as well as non-Hispanic Latinos in our nations. All are victims of an imposed colonial system that sets each against all. Let us stop bickering about these two externally imposed terms and let's get on with education, achievement and cultural growth. 10

Héctor Vélez Guadalupe
Associate Prof. of Sociology
Ithaca College
Ithaca, N.Y., Oct. 29, 1992

Who Is Left Out

To the Editor:

Earl Shorris (Op-Ed, Oct. 28) displays the power of language to communicate and obfuscate. The terms Latino and Hispanic refer to peoples who for almost half a millennium have been called something else: mestizo, mulatto, ladino. Paradoxically, there are no Hispanics or Latinos in Latin America; in no country but this do census or social practices acknowledge such ethnicities. 1

In the United States, the terms have served to deflect the impact of racism and, subtly, to insure its survival. Since the 1944 "Caucasian Resolution" in Texas, which declared Mexican-Americans white in a rigidly segregated society, Anglo-Americans have attempted to fit newcomers from the south into an existing racial scheme. The use of cultural terms with vague Mediterranean affinities suits this purpose at present. 2

Sadly, 500 years after the landing of Columbus, such terms serve to obliterate the indigenous and African elements that have formed the majority of the peoples of the Caribbean and of Mesoamerica. 3

I. K. Sundiata
Chmn., African and Afro-American Studies
Brandeis University
Waltham, Mass., Nov. 6, 1992

To live in the Borderlands means you

Gloria Anzaldúa

To live in the Borderlands means you 1
 are neither *hispana india negra española*
 ni gabacha, eres mestiza, mulata, *half-breed*
 caught in the crossfire between camps
 while carrying all five races on your back
 not knowing which side to turn to, run from;
To live in the Borderlands means knowing 2
 that the *india* in you, betrayed for 500 years,
 is no longer speaking to you,
 that *mexicanas* call you *rajetas,*
 that denying the Anglo inside you
 is as bad as having denied the Indian or Black;
Cuando vives en la frontera 3
 people walk through you, the wind steals your voice,
 you're a *burra, buey,* scapegoat,
 forerunner of a new race,
 half and half—both woman and man, neither—
 a new gender;

Figure 7.5

Binghamton Review,
Summer 1992

From the Editor: "We see political correctness and the new left as the greatest threat to free speech and academic freedom on the American campus today. We are dedicated to promoting traditional American values and to providing a forum to challenge this entrenched leftist orthodoxy."

This cartoon was furnished to the *Binghamton Review* by USIC Educational Foundation, 220 National Press Bldg., Washington, D.C. 20045.

> To live in the Borderlands means to
>   put *chile* in the borscht,
>   eat whole wheat *tortillas,*
>   speak Tex-Mex with a Brooklyn accent;
>   be stopped by *la migrala* at the border checkpoints;
> Living in the Borderlands means you fight hard to
>   resist the gold elixer beckoning from the bottle,
>   the pull of the gun barrel,
>   the rope crushing the hollow of your throat;
> In the Borderlands
>   you are the battleground
>   where enemies are kin to each other;
>   you are at home, a stranger,
>   the border disputes have been settled
>   the volley of shots have shattered the truce
>   you are wounded, lost in action
>   dead, fighting back;

4

5

6

To live in the Borderlands means
    the mill with the razor white teeth wants to shred off
    your olive-red skin, crush out the kernel, your heart
    pound you pinch you roll you out
    smelling like white bread but dead;
To survive the Borderlands
    you must live *sin fronteras*
    be a crossroads.

---

gabacha—a Chicano term for a white woman
rajetas—literally, "split," that is, having betrayed your word
burra—donkey
buey—oxen
sin fronteras—without borders

From *Borderlands/La Frontera: The New Mestiza,* copyright © 1987 by Gloria Anzaldúa.
Reprinted with permission from Aunt Lute Books, San Francisco (415) 826-1300.

Writing/Reading Opportunity

Telling Your Own Ethnic Identification Story

"And what is your ethnic background?"

Write about your own ethnic background and how you identify yourself ethnically and perhaps how others identify you. Write at first quickly and in one sitting. You can return to your story later and develop it more fully if you like. This first writing will be used as a starting point for dialogue with other members of your writing community.

Exchange stories, based on what you wrote, with your dialogue partner or partners. Listen to accounts by your classmates. How would you describe the ethnic makeup of your class? What did you learn from listening to these accounts?

As you continue reading and talking with others, return to your own ethnic identification story and questions and concerns or reflections. You can "log in" entries, citing the date if you like, or do another freewriting or two. This writing will help you pause and record your ongoing thinking. Also, when you stop and write informally like this, sometimes more and more thoughts or recollections come to mind, thus enriching what you finally have to say. You may also want to share these reflections with your class or one or two other writers. You may want to write more after you read "Cultural Baggage"—a lighter look at ethnic identification that appeared in a column called "Hers" in *The New York Times Magazine*—and some other accounts by students who worked on this project. Your written reflections will be an important resource when you work on your end-project essay.

Cultural Baggage

Barbara Ehrenreich

An acquaintance was telling me about the joys of rediscovering her ethnic 1
and religious heritage. "I know exactly what my ancestors were doing 2,000
years ago," she said, eyes gleaming with enthusiasm, "and *I can do the same
things now.*" Then she leaned forward and inquired politely, "And what is
your ethnic background, if I may ask?"

"None," I said, that being the first word in line to get out of my mouth. 2
Well, not "none," I backtracked. Scottish, English, Irish—that was something, I supposed. Too much Irish to qualify as a WASP; too much of the
hated English to warrant a "Kiss Me, I'm Irish" button; plus there are a number of dead ends in the family tree due to adoptions, missing records, failing
memories and the like. I was blushing by this time. Did "none" mean I was
rejecting my heritage out of Anglo-Celtic self-hate? Or was I revealing a hidden ethnic chauvinism in which the Britannically derived serve as a kind of
neutral standard compared with the ethnic "others"?

Throughout the 60's and 70's, I watched one group after another— 3
African-Americans, Latinos, Native Americans—stand up and proudly re-
claim their roots while I just sank back ever deeper into my seat. All this excitement over ethnicity stemmed, I uneasily sensed, from a past in which
their ancestors had been trampled upon by *my* ancestors, or at least by people who looked very much like them. In addition, it had begun to seem almost un-American not to have some sort of hyphen at hand, linking one to
more venerable times and locales.

But the truth is, I was raised with none. We'd eaten ethnic foods in my 4
childhood home, but these were all borrowed, like the pasties, or Cornish
meat pies, my father had picked up from his fellow miners in Butte, Mont. If
my mother had one rule, it was militant ecumenism in all matters of food
and experience. "Try new things," she would say, meaning anything from
sweetbreads to clams, with an emphasis on the "new."

As a child, I briefly nourished a craving for tradition and roots. I im- 5
mersed myself in the works of Sir Walter Scott. I pretended to believe that
the bagpipe was a musical instrument. I was fascinated to learn from a
grandmother that we were descended from certain Highland clans and
longed for a pleated skirt in one of their distinctive tartans.

But in "Ivanhoe," it was the dark-eyed "Jewess" Rebecca I identified with, 6
not the flaxen-haired bimbo Rowena. As for clans: Why not call them
"tribes," those bands of half-clad peasants and warriors whose idea of cuisine was stuffed sheep gut washed down with whisky? And then there was
the sting of Disraeli's remark—which I came across in my early teens—to
the effect that his ancestors had been leading orderly, literate lives when my
ancestors were still rampaging through the Highlands daubing themselves
with blue paint.

Motherhood put the screws on me, ethnicity-wise. I had hoped that by 7
marrying a man of Eastern European-Jewish ancestry I would acquire for my

descendants the ethnic genes that my own forebears so sadly lacked. At one point, I even subjected the children to a seder of my own design, including a little talk about the flight from Egypt and its relevance to modern social issues. But the kids insisted on buttering their matzohs and snickering through my talk. "Give me a break, Mom," the older one said. "You don't even believe in God."

After the tiny pagans had been put to bed, I sat down to brood over 8 Elijah's wine. What had I been thinking? The kids knew that their Jewish grandparents were secular folks who didn't hold seders themselves. And if ethnicity eluded me, how could I expect it to take root in my children, who are not only Scottish-English-Irish, but Hungarian-Polish-Russian to boot?

But, then, on the fumes of Manischewitz, a great insight took form in my 9 mind. It was true, as the kids said, that I didn't "believe in God." But this could be taken as something very different from an accusation—a reminder of a genuine heritage. My parents had not believed in God either, nor had my grandparents or any other progenitors going back to the great-great level. They had become disillusioned with Christianity generations ago— just as, on the in-law side, my children's other ancestors had shaken off their Orthodox Judaism. This insight did not exactly furnish me with an "identity," but it was at least something to work with: we are the kind of people, I realized—whatever our distant ancestors' religions—who do *not* believe, who do not carry on traditions, who do not do things just because someone has done them before.

The epiphany went on: I recalled that my mother never introduced a 10 procedure for cooking or cleaning by telling me, "Grandma did it this way." What did Grandma know, living in the days before vacuum cleaners and disposable toilet mops? In my parents' general view, new things were better than old, and the very fact that some ritual had been performed in the past was a good reason for abandoning it now. Because what was the past, as our forebears knew it? Nothing but poverty, superstition and grief. "Think for yourself," Dad used to say. "Always ask why."

In fact, this may have been the ideal cultural heritage for my particular 11 ethnic strain—bounced as it was from the Highlands of Scotland across the sea, out to the Rockies, down into the mines and finally spewed out into high-tech, suburban America. What better philosophy, for a race of migrants, than "Think for yourself"? What better maxim, for a people whose whole world was rudely inverted every 30 years or so, than "Try new things"?

The more tradition-minded, the newly enthusiastic celebrants of Purim 12 and Kwanzaa and Solstice, may see little point to survival if the survivors carry no cultural freight—religion, for example, or ethnic tradition. To which I would say that skepticism, curiosity and wide-eyed ecumenical tolerance are also worthy elements of the human tradition and are at least as old as such notions as "Serbian" or "Croatian," "Scottish" or "Jewish." I make no claims for my personal line of progenitors except that they remained loyal to the values that may have induced all of our ancestors, long, long ago, to climb down from the trees and make their way into the open plains.

A few weeks ago, I cleared my throat and asked the children, now mostly 13 grown and fearsomely smart, whether they felt any stirrings of ethnic or religious identity, etc., which might have been, ahem, insufficiently nourished at home. "None," they said, adding firmly, "and the world would be a better place if nobody else did, either." My chest swelled with pride, as would my mother's, to know that the race of "none" marches on.

From *The New York Times,* April 5, 1992. Copyright © 1992 by The New York Times Company. Reprinted by permission.

No one today is purely one thing. Labels like Indian, or woman, or Muslim, or American are no more than starting points, which if followed into actual experience for only a moment are quickly left behind. . . . Just as human beings make their own history, they also make their cultures and ethnic identities.

Edward Said

Writers at Work

Excerpts from Ethnic Identification Stories

I am a white female who was born into a middle-class American household in upstate New York in the early fifties. Both of my parents were born in America. My mother's parents, also born in America, were a mixture of Irish, Scotch, and Dutch. None of this cultural heritage is part of my daily life. My father's parents were born in Austria-Hungary. But because my parents did not settle in the local Slovakian neighborhood where my father grew up and did not remain in the Slovakian church, I find that most of this cultural heritage has been lost to me. Holidays, weddings, and funerals are the only occasions for my assimilation into the Slovakian traditions of baking, dancing, and egg decorating. So I really consider myself simply an American. Yet with all the examining of ethnic terminology that we have been doing, I'm not really even sure I know exactly what this means!

Suzanne Erle

When I am asked about my ethnic identity I inevitably end up telling lies. I'm not intentionally devious; I just respond differently depending on the context, because I don't have a stable ethnic identity. My father's family is German/ English, ancestry-wise, but they are small-town, upper-middle class Methodists who have been in the United States for generations. They have no connection to the old country.

However, I never met anyone from my father's family until I was about eleven, and I see them very seldom. My sisters and I are much closer to our mother's Italian/Irish/Scotch/French middle-class Catholic family. Although my grandfather's family came from Italy around 1915, he was born here, and did not raise his children to be "Italian-Americans," but just Americans.

To complicate matters, I am adopted, so even if my family were not just generic white people, I couldn't completely align myself with my family's ancestry except socially. Even more confusing, I was born in Japan, and even though I do not remember the country or speak the language, I feel an affinity and identification. Also, I am a Japanese citizen. You can see how I could easily look like a compulsive liar, since I tell people that my family is Italian/Irish, but my father is German/English, and yes, I am Japanese.

You would think it would be untangle-able if I could take some time to explain the full situation to people, but it's not, because when I finish they always ask "So what are *you*?" To this I have no answer. I have no idea what gene pool I sprang from, and it's kind of annoying in this age where everyone has ethnic pride. When I was a little child this was never an issue; I was just the same thing my parents were. The first time I had my eyes opened was when the new lunch-lady asked the recess-lady who the little "Oriental" girl was. I wanted to know too, since everybody in our class was white. Turns out it was me. I wondered how she knew, but once I got older and moved into more urbane circles, people would ask unsolicited if I were Chinese, or Native American—or as one woman, trying to get me to fill in a box for my ethnic identification, said: "Are you Amer- um, Eur- uh . . . would you be half Asian, dear?" I sat on the urge to tell her that I'd send her a postcard when I figured it out.

Patti Weaver

I identify myself ethnically as "American." The dictionary definition of *ethnic* reads "of or pertaining to a race or people." I identify with the people of America, America's traditions, American culture, and the values of American society. There is no other group of people or country that I identify with so closely. Just because ethnically I don't identify with a foreign country, doesn't mean I lack an ethnic identity. My ethnic identity is simply American. I'm able to track part of my heritage back more than 250 years in the United States. I think that once one's familiar ancestry is within the United States for so long there is some extent (if not a very large extent) of intercultural mixing. There's also a development and adaptation of American tradition that takes place. Now, this society called America has a culture all of its own, which is the one I identify with, and is the one that is continually being developed and added to every year.

Kristine Olsen

Seated before a plate of parsley, horseradish, and apples chopped with nuts to look like mortar, the boy with the gentile hair asked:

"Why is this night different from all other nights?"

Because we recline, because we dip our food in salt water, because we are gathered as a family finally here in one place.

The oldest uncle, Nathan, whose beard grew independently wise, whose eyes opened half closed, as if remembering a yesterday in which despite his pain God felt more close—he told us about his boyhood: how his father left one night, disappearing towards the city, ocean, port; how his mother (our grandma's mother) followed with her children after, hidden beneath bales of hay which left their ghetto after the sun had dried it enough for the cattle to feed on in the months to come.

These are the fondest memories of my ethnic identity, a family of stories told over bitter herbs and flat tasteless bread. A family that gathers to thank God for not forgetting them, for not passing absently over them this year.

But I, the boy with the blue eyes and the gentile hair, no longer feel that presence. I no longer feel a god's hand above the pressure of hay piled above me. Serving matzoh balls to my Catholic girlfriend's family on Easter Sunday, I felt a separate shade of blood define itself within me.

I am also my father's son. I am the boy at the Thanksgiving table. I am the boy eating from a Christmas turkey and an Easter ham. The old warmth, the old surety, the old identity is blending, fading into something else. For the first time, I painted Easter eggs this spring. I laughed and smiled and looked confused, but I dipped these eggs, like we once dipped our herbs in salt water, and I forgot the beards of my mother's family as they grew whiter and wiser. This new culture may not warm me, but it surrounds me.

Jonathan Winslow

The part of my heritage that I am the most familiar with is my Finnish background. My mother is pure Finn, both of my maternal grandparents were first-generation Americans whose parents entered the United States through Ellis Island in the 1920s.

I do not know much more about that branch of my family. My grandparents do speak Finnish, but they do not follow any particular customs or ceremonies from the old country. The biggest reason for this is that my grandparents are recovering alcoholics who drank heavily from the late thirties to 1965. As a result, they did not have much time to pass down any family traditions to my mother, who spent most of her childhood in various foster families.

My mother's maternal grandmother, who spoke only Finnish, spent a lot of time with my mother when she was a child. Until my mother was five, she spoke more Finnish than English because of her grandmother's influence. However, when my mother entered school and the teachers complained about her poor English, she was forbidden to speak Finnish. Today my mother can only speak a few words in Finnish.

The greatest influence Greatgrandma had on mother was in the kitchen. My mother has several recipes left to her by her grandmother. One of these, a recipe for bula, or Finnish coffee bread, has put my mother in great demand in the large Finnish community around Spencer and Van Etten. People offer my mother considerable sums of money for loaves of this bread made from Greatgrandmother's recipe. People who remember say that the only person who baked bula better than my mother was her grandmother.

My father's side of the family is less interesting and is much harder to trace. The name Woolever is German, though how the family got to this country from Germany is quite a mystery. I do know that my grandfather's grandfather moved into Lockwood, New York before the turn of this century because he was following the railroad. There is a small cemetery tucked away in the hills of Lockwood that contains quite a few Woolever headstones, some of which date back to the late 1800s.

My grandmother's family is even more of a mystery. We have had success only in tracing her lineage back to her father. We assume that her maiden name of Arnold is English, but we do not know for sure.

Ginger Woolever

In this poem, jiménez-fernández discusses her own identity crisis as a Latina with a white complexion. She read this poem at an event on the Binghamton University campus of the State University of New York, where she is a graduate student. Excerpts from her poem are included here.

Face Value

i am not a slim kid.
in fact,
i am somewhere between chunky and fat
some tease, some teased a lot
who cares?
i never wanted to be on the cover of *Vogue*,
anyway.

i am a blue-eyed daughter
of Dominican parents
i don't fit "the look,"
so i don't belong.
who really belongs in this world?

i am an American
with the last names Jiménez-Fernández
it isn't Smith or Jones
i don't mind
afterall, isn't this the melting pot?
....

all of these are labels,
classifications, WE as society created
for reference, for communication.
so for these reasons—
i am a
misplaced,
overweight,
genetically mutated,
Dominican,
American,
intelligent,
aggressive, woman.

sounds drastic?
welcome to reality—

that's what we do
everytime we refer
to this group or that group,
this person or that person
to praise or condemn them
for complying with our visions of acceptance
or
defying our conception of unison.

words are necessary for communication—
i don't argue that . . .
but even as I am an
overweight,
Latina,
Dominican,
American,
aggressive,
intelligent,
woman,
shouldn't you
first and foremost
approach me and respect me
for what i am . . .
a human being?

liz jiménez-fernández

It is hard for me to identify myself ethnically. I hate labeling myself, especially when there are so many other people who impose their own labels on me regardless of what I tell them.

When people ask that ever popular question, "What are you?" I always answer, "I'm just a black woman trying to survive." I'm sure you can imagine the variety of responses that I receive. I am not trying to escape the question at all. That is exactly how I feel I must respond to the question of ethnicity. I guess I could say something about being Jamaican because that is where my grandmother, and her mother before her, were born and raised. I could probably also say something about Panama because that is where my grandfather and my mother were born. But my mother went back to Jamaica, so what does that mean? I guess I could even say something about the United States because I was born and raised here, but I choose not to.

When people ask me about my ethnicity I also translate that into, "What culture do you most identify with?" No offense, but I certainly do *not* identify with this thing called "American" culture. I hate apple pie and I don't even remember the words to the Star Spangled Banner, much less the Pledge of Allegiance. Yeah, I wear Levi's and I shop at the Gap, but that's about as far as it goes. The strongest cultural influences in my family have been Caribbean, African-American, and ultimately African. These include everything from music and books to speech patterns and spiritual beliefs.

Despite these particularly strong cultural influences, I refuse to take on the label "Afro-Caribbean." That label says nothing at all about my experience, the history of my family, or the culture of my people worldwide. To minimalize my existence to one of those funky little labels on a census form or college application is insulting. I do not wish to participate in a game of taxonomy that was never meant for my benefit.

For me to say that I am just a black woman trying to survive is to accurately tell my story, both figuratively and literally. It tells my mother's story. It tells my grandmother's story. In my opinion, it also sums up in a few words the story of my people in this country as well as all over the world. Just ask Eleanor Bumpers' daughter, Rodney King's mother, or any woman in Somalia. I identify with a culture and a people that have literally been trying to survive *despite* the "powers that be." My constant struggle to remain on this campus is proof of that, but that is another story.

My people have been scattered all over the world, and with them is all of the struggle and experience that I embrace as part of my culture. I, therefore, identify with all that I know and all that I will learn about my people.

Deborah Cowell

I am an African-American. My ancestors were brought from Africa to the southern states of the United States against their will. Decades later, my parents were born into a world of segregation and misconception. From Georgia and North Carolina they fled at young ages to New York City in hopes of better lives—lives that included children and good jobs.

My brother and I were born in Brooklyn. All of us now reside in Queens. We were brought up by southern values and traditions, which we shall always cherish.

I have always heard people of my race being called many different types of names from nigger, to negro, to black, and now African-American. I haven't always considered myself to be African-American. *Black* was the term I used. Yet after evaluating the term *African-American,* I now realize that this term is suitable for my ethnicity. Even though I agree with the new classificatory term, African-American, many people of my race wouldn't because they originated from other countries and would like to be identified with that country.

I am contented with the fact that the government is trying to upgrade the commonly used ethnic terms (black and white) to sound more professional and non-derogatory like African-American, Caucasian, Hispanic, Asian and "other" for those not included in the previous categories. With all the controversy involved in ethnic identification, the terms just might change again to please the concensus of the people.

Sherita Greene

I was born in South Korea and came to the United States in 1985. It's been seven years since I left my country. When I came here it was all different. Different environment, different kind of people and, most of all, different culture.

I consider myself an Asian-American/Korean. But sometimes, I don't even like to be called an "Asian." I mean, I know I'm Asian and everyone could tell that I'm Asian, so why do people have to ask me whether I'm Asian or not. The word *Asian* groups everyone in the same category and I don't think that everyone is same. For example, Chinese and Koreans are not the same. We speak different languages, have different cultures and traditions. When someone sees an Asian walking by, he/she would say that's a Chinese person without even knowing who it really is. I myself hate to be called Chinese even though I have nothing against Chinese people. I hated it because of the fact that I'm not Chinese. I just want to be called as what I am: Korean and not Chinese.

I never even heard of the word *racism* until about six years ago. We first went to Florida when we came to the United States. People over there treated our family very nicely. I guess one of the reasons is because of the fact that they rarely see Asians in their neighborhood.

I remember the time when I first entered elementary school down in Florida. It was great! They treated me like I was someone special. They came up to me and started talking to me and tried to teach me English. One thing that surprised me was the first day at school. It was around noontime when everyone got up and started lining up by the door. I didn't know what was going on so I got up and stood by the door with them. Then we started walking out the door. When we got out of the classroom, I saw many other people walking towards the same building as we were. I was totally lost at that point. As soon as I entered the building, I saw many people having their lunch and having fun with their friends. It surprised me a lot because in Korea, we don't have cafeteria. We eat in our classroom and have to bring our own food to school.

A year after that, we moved to New York state, Rockland County. I entered middle school as a seventh grader. It was totally different from what I had experienced in Florida. People looked at me as if I were from a different planet or something. They would talk behind my back and won't even say hello to me when they would see me walking by. There is one thing that I thought was a racist act when I was eating lunch with one of my friends who was Chinese. When we were halfway through our lunch, I felt something wet on my back. It was a piece of food that someone from across the cafeteria threw. When I turned around to see who it was, they were laughing at me. I didn't say or do anything about it because I didn't know much English. But they kept throwing food at me. So next day I went to my guidance and told him what happened and he was very understanding. And the same day those girls came up to me and said sorry. They said sorry only because my counselor had said something to them. This was not the only thing I thought was a racist act. There were many others but I'm not going to go into any details or even mention them. Because as I write this, I get angrier and angrier just by thinking about the past.

After living in this Rockland County for almost two years, I realized that this country was not what I thought it was. I always thought that this country was a perfect country where everyone gets treated equally. I guess I was wrong. Especially for people like us: immigrants from other countries, who get treated as if we are not a human.

My family moved around a lot. My parents tried so hard to find a better place to live for my brother and me. The last stop is where we are currently living. We now live in Queens where it's not so homogeneous. You can always find someone different, from different countries. Well, anyway, I entered junior high school and it felt like home because there were a lot of

Koreans who went to the school where I was registered. Many Koreans who went to that school had just come to the United States, just like me. I began to interact with Koreans more than with any other race. I guess part of the reason why I started hanging out with Koreans was because of what I had experienced in the other school.

It felt good hanging out with Koreans but somehow after awhile I didn't feel like I belong with them. I mean, most of my friends were those who just came to this country and I had lived in this country longer than they did. So, I knew more about this country's culture than any other of my friends. At that time I was more Americanized than they were, so we didn't get along. We had lot of conflicts because they wanted things done in Korean ways and I wanted things done in American ways. This was in junior high school.

But once we went to high school, I began to interact more with those Koreans who lived in this country longer than I was and the friends from junior high interact more with those who just came to this country. The group that I was in and the group that my old friends were in didn't get along very well. I started to dress more like Korean-Americans and tried to forget my own culture, to really fit into the group I was in. I was naive and stupid then.

I wanted to be like Americans. At some point, I wished that I was American and not Korean. I saw my American friends with parents who are liberal and understanding; I wished that my parents were like that. But now I realize how stupid I was then. Because if it wasn't for my parents, I wouldn't be here right now. Especially, if it wasn't for my mom. My mom works so hard and tries her best to provide me and my brother the best.

Since my dad left, our family went through a lot. My mom is working as a cashier, earning only $300/week. It hurts me to see my mom coming home after her work. She works eleven hours a day and six days a week.

Now, I'm in college. I'm old enough to know what's wrong from right. My mother's dream is to see me as a pharmacist working in my own pharmacy. She always told me that I should be a pharmacist if I want to have comfortable life. I heard the same speech over and over since I was in elementary school. Maybe that's why I don't know what I want to be, but to become a pharmacist. She never gave me a chance to think about it. But somehow I don't regret that. I'm transferring to a pharmacy school, because I feel that becoming a pharmacist is nothing compared to what my mom went through. At least this way I could pay her back as a appreciation of her sacrifice.

Being an immigrant living in this country is not easy. It feels like you are living in two different worlds. Unless you find the way to balance the two different cultures, you'll live in a world within a world.

Elizabeth Kim

Gone With the Unum

RUSSELL BAKER

Russell Baker, whose autobiographical writing appears in the "Recollections & Reflections" Writing Project, writes a column called "Observer" for The New York Times. *One of these columns, "School as Spin Control," appears in the "Becoming Educated" Writing Project and is followed by letters of response from students.*

I have always been an "E Pluribus Unum" person myself, but the future does not look bright for an "E Pluribus Unum" America. The melting pot in which the Pluribus were to be combined into the Unum was not the success its advertisers had promised. 1

Well, what ever is? It is the destiny of Americans to be oversold by slogans. They know it instinctively, which is why advertising is far more to blame than Richard Nixon and Lyndon Johnson combined for the cynicism in which we now wallow. 2

What is new these days is the passion with which we now pursue our tribal identities. 3

A generation ago the sociologists Nathan Glazer and Patrick Moynihan (since gone to the Senate) created a stir by pointing out that we had been oversold on America as melting pot. The one people that was supposed to emerge from the many stirred into the pot simply refused to come forth, they observed. 4

Anyone who had grown up in working-class America already knew all this. If you ran with Italian kids and got caught alone among Irish kids, you knew loosened teeth or blackened eye, and possibly both, might ensue. Persons of African ancestry were isolated in remote neighborhoods and rarely encountered. 5

My home was dominated by a woman born of a marriage between Ireland and Cuba. In that age with its unbuttoned indifference to ethnic delicacy, her husband lovingly teased her by saying, "The only thing dumber than a dumb Swede is a smart Irishman." 6

Since she ruled the domain, she could tolerate and even laugh at the cruelty of failed-melting-pot humor, but no one ever mentioned her Cuban blood. In fact her Irish mother had been read out of the family for marrying a Cuban. 7

You grew up knowing instinctively that the melting pot was an inferior vessel, but at the same time you were encouraged to believe that it ought to work, that it must work for America to succeed (whatever that meant), and that in time it eventually would work. Every schoolchild was taught at least enough Latin to know what "E Pluribus Unum" meant: "From many, one people." 8

How this will all play out is beyond my crystal ball's vision, but the game 9
is already far afoot, and we old "E Pluribus Unum" people ought to be flex-
ing our own tribal muscles on the possibility that it's going to be all Pluribus
and no Unum for a long time to come.

My own tribe, I noticed while browsing in the press the other day, is 10
being called "Caucasian." This is absurd. The Caucasus is a region between
the Caspian and Black Seas and contains Russians, Georgians, Azerbaijanis
and Armenians.

The etiquette of the new ethnic sensitivity entitles each of us to decide 11
what we want to be called, and it's hard to believe that many in my tribe
want to face the coming struggle carrying the banner for the Caucasus, especially since Americans of Armenian, Georgian, Azerbaijani and Russian
blood might sensibly object that we are ethnically impure.

"Caucasian" has long been a fussy, stuffy way of saying "a whitey." Cops 12
with literary aspirations have used it for years. It's one of those nice-Nelly
terms that throttle our ability to discuss the race problem without hypocrisy.
Is it important to make clear that the perpetrator was not black, African-
American, Negro, Afro-American, a person of color, Hispanic, Latino, Chicano or Asian-American? If so, announce that he was Caucasian.

The tribal dignity of all whiteys is demeaned by the embrace of this silly 13
term. Choosing a name that will honor us as we have a right to be honored
is not for me to do. It will require a committee. "Whiteys," incidentally, will
not do, as we vary in color from glorious purple to mausoleum gray.

The Hispanic solution, calling us "Anglos," is pretty, but almost as wrong 14
as "Caucasian." It will also offend Celtics among us who despise England.
The Jewish "goyim," while picturesque—and who doesn't like being picturesque?—is equally applicable to everybody not Jewish.

The New York acronym "Wasp"—white Anglo-Saxon Protestant—is pleas- 15
ant ("Wasps of America, unite before your stingers are plucked!") but offensive to white Anglo-Saxon Catholics, white Anglo-Saxon agnostics, white
Gallic Protestants, white Central European anarchists and millions more.

O Unum, what misery we courted when we forsook thee for Pluribus. 16

From *The New York Times*, May 3, 1994. Copyright © 1994 by The New York Times Company. Reprinted by permission.

Write a letter to the editor (150–200 words) in response to "Gone with the
Unum." You could distribute the letters in class, using them to promote additional discussion. An alternative, if you have access to a computer network, is
to engage in electronic dialogue and then use the printout as a basis for face-
to-face discussion. Writing letters using E-mail is still another possibility.

End-Project Writing

Explore the problem of ethnic identification in the 1990s in the United
States, using the Hispanic/Latino naming problem as an extended example.
Write an essay about what you learned from this research process about the
words *Hispanic* and *Latino* and the problem of ethnic identification.

Our definitions . . . do much to influence what we subsequently see. That's a good reason for questioning and then requestioning our definitions, for considering the contexts in which we create them and the purposes we ask them to serve.

Kiniry & Rose,
*Critical Strategies
for Academic Writing*

Include usage of these words in the reading you did. Cite specific sentences or passages to illustrate how these words are being used and to help readers understand your reading or the conclusions you've drawn. What have you observed or noticed about the usage of these words? What led you to draw certain conclusions?

Include research based on interviews. What did you learn? How did those you interviewed help you understand the usage of Hispanic/Latino or the problem of ethnic identification?

Include some description of your own ethnic background and whether ethnic identification has presented a problem. If you have read or listened to accounts of ethnic backgrounds and/or identification problems by your classmates, include some commentary if you like.

You can draw on newspaper articles and other readings describing changes in ethnic groups or changing perceptions. You can also draw on reflections by Gómez-Peña in his essay on ethnic identity. And you can incorporate reflections from other works you have read on your own or as a class.

End your essay with some commentary on the problem or a discussion of what you learned, or raise questions or concerns.

Cite specific references (newspaper articles, personal interviews, essays, stories) in your essay and provide a list of references at the end.

Introductions & Conclusions

Lisette Andrades had difficulty writing an introduction. I suggested she work with the body of her essay first and report her findings. Many writers write their introductions last, I explained, and most writers revise their introductions after finishing writing what they want to say. Sometimes the act of writing pushes their thinking still further.

An introduction helps a reader get started but often is not where the writer begins.

Lisette began a draft by discussing definitions she had read and stating her confusion, and then went on to report what she learned from interviews. Later she reread what she wrote and tried this beginning.

I believe there will always be problems concerning ethnic identification as long as this country stays diverse. There are so many problems when it comes to race. Many people forget who they are once they immigrate to another country. They begin to deny their ethnic background and become assimilated into the American ways. Some people just don't know how to identify themselves once they have migrated. The usage of the words *Hispanic* and *Latino* is a good illustration of this problem.

"Can I begin an introduction by being personal or do I have to be more formal?" Elizabeth Kim asked. She decided to give an account of her introduction to these words and this naming problem.

"Is Tony Spanish?" I asked. "You mean, is Tony Latino?" Joe replied with an offended tone of voice. "Yeah, that's what I meant, Latino," I answered back, not knowing the difference. Coming from Korea, it never occurred to me the difference between the words. I heard the word *Hispanic* before but *Latino* I never heard until I came to college. I have learned that among the Hispanic/Latino group naming is a big issue.

Later in her essay, she discusses her own problems with ethnic identification, especially by others who often assume she is Chinese.

Wlodek Dzwonczyk, who came to the United States from Poland, concluded his essay this way.

The USA is a multinational country where there are many problems due to the abundance of nationalities and different ethnic groups. In order to keep track of the changes that occur in the structure of the American society, it is impossible not to use labels that are imposed by the government. The problem regarding ethnic identity in the USA is not a problem of how a person views himself or herself but how that person is perceived by others.

Writing & Editing Workshops

Set up several writing workshops according to the needs of students in your class. What kind of workshops would be most helpful to you?

After a first-draft workshop for focus and development, perhaps set up a workshop on introductions and conclusions. Another workshop could be devoted to integrating sources and another to editing for a style guide and another to grammatical and mechanical errors that you have recorded in your "Editing Projects" notebook. What patterns of error have you noted? Do you know how to edit for these errors or problems? Practice editing throughout your course, working in class with other students and your teacher and also in conference. If you need more help and have a writing or tutorial center, set up a tutorial and get tutoring, one way or another, and on a regular basis if you need ongoing one-to-one help.

Suggestions for Further Reading

Agueros, Jack. 1993. *Dominoes and Other Stories from the Puerto Rican*. Curbstone Press.

Brady, Vivian. 1992. "Black Hispanics: The Ties That Bind." From *Race, Class and Gender in the United States: An Integrated Study*. ed. Paula Rothenberg (183–85). New York: St. Martin's Press.

Cofer, Judith Ortiz. 1993. "The Myth of the Latin Woman: I Just Met a Girl Named Maria." From *The Latin Deli*. University of Georgia Press, 1993.

Conciatore, Jacqueline, & Rodriguez, Roberto. 1992. "Blacks and Hispanics: A Fragile Alliance." From *Race, Class and Gender in the United States: An Integrated Study,* ed. Paula Rothenberg (185–89). New York: St. Martin's Press.

"Ethnography and the English Classroom." 1983. *The English Record.* New York State English Council. *34, 4.*

Hess, Beth; Markham, Elizabeth; & Stein, Peter. 1992. "Racial and Ethnic Minorities: An Overview." From *Race, Class and Gender in the United States: An Integrated Study*, ed. Paula Rothenberg (145–55). New York: St. Martin's Press. (See also earlier version in 1988 edition.)

Jen, Gish. 1991. *Typical American.* Boston: Houghton Mifflin–S. Lawrence.

Novak, Michael. 1973. "How American Are You If Your Grandparents Came from Serbia in 1888?" From *The Rediscovery of Ethnicity,* ed. Sallie McFague. New York: Harper & Row.

Reed, Ishmael. March–April 1989. "What's American about America?" *Utne Reader.*

Santiago, Esmeralda. 1993. *When I Was Puerto Rican.* Reading, MA: Addison-Wesley.

Santiago, Robert. 1989. "Black and Latino." *Essence.* Also in *Common Ground: Reading & Writing about America's Cultures.* Laurie Kirszner and Stephen Mandell. New York: St. Martin's Press, 1994 (385–87).

Verburg, Carol J. 1994. *Ourselves Among Others: Cross-Cultural Readings for Writers.* New York: St. Martin's Press.

Waters, Mary C. 1990. "Influences on Ancestry Choice" (Chapter 3), Appendix A (1980 Census Ancestry Options), Appendix B (Interview Questions)," *Ethnic Options: Choosing Identities in America.* Berkeley: U. of California Press.

Zaitchik, Joseph; Roberts, William; & Zaitchik, Holly. 1994. *Face to Face: Readings on Confrontation and Accommodation in America.* Boston: Houghton Mifflin.

Note: See also Suggestions for Further Reading, "Recollections & Reflections" (Mohr, Rivera, and others).

Appendix: Guidelines for Editing Your Own Writing

The Role of Punctuation: Reading Without Interference

Try reading the following passage from John McPhee's *Oranges* (1966) with the punctuation removed:

> The custom of drinking orange juice with breakfast is not very widespread taking the world as a whole and it is thought by many peoples to be a distinctly American habit but many Danes drink it regularly with breakfast and so do Hondurans Filipinos Jamaicans and the wealthier citizens of Trinidad and Tobago the day is started with orange juice in the Columbian Andes and to some extent in Kuwait Bolivians don't touch it at breakfast time but they drink it steadily for the rest of the day the "play lunch" or morning tea that Australian children carry with them to school is usually an orange peeled spirally halfway down with the peel replaced around the fruit the child unwinds the peel and holds the orange as if it were an ice-cream cone people in Nepal almost never peel oranges preferring to eat them in cut quarters the way American athletes do. (p. 3)

It's difficult (though not impossible) to read without punctuation to mark the pauses and stops, isn't it? With a little patience, such run-together sentences can be understood. You go forward and then have to backtrack some, a distracting movement that takes away from meaning, and you have to pay more attention to sentence formation. As a writer, you want your readers to keep up with you and pay attention to what you have to say. If readers keep getting off the track of your sentences, then their concentration is broken. If there is too much grammatical/mechanical interference—too much "noise"—your readers may give up. If readers reread your writing, you want them to do so because what you have to say bears rereading and rethinking, not because of some grammatical/mechanical problems.

If you want to succeed in writing across the curriculum and if you want to go public with your writing and reach many readers, then you need to know certain grammatical/mechanical conventions or agreements. Later, in some writing situations, you may choose to adhere to these conventions, and in other situations you may choose to ignore them. In her novel *Positions with White Roses* (1983), Ursule Molinaro intentionally uses space rather than commas to punctuate a phrase within a sentence: "His speech had sounded noticeably slurrier   at least to him   when he'd finally broken their silence & asked her about the postcard." She continues with a fragment of a

Drawing by Maslin; © 1987 the New Yorker Magazine, Inc. Reprinted by permission.

"Sorry, but I'm going to have to issue you a summons for reckless grammar and driving without an apostrophe."

sentence: "Which had been made from a photograph, taken in her presence by a friend who had a summer house on the Jersey shore: she'd told him." Molinaro knows the conventions of punctuation and sentence structure but chooses to break the rules for stylistic effect. Whether you adhere to conventions or not should be a choice, not an accident.

The Role of Editing in Writing

Listen to what two students have to say about grammar and mechanics:

> I think I need to read a handbook, do a complete review. I never learned the rules. That's my problem. I don't know grammar. I'm lousy at punctuation. I make all these mistakes when I write. I know I can't write. I have to be more careful so I don't make mistakes.

> ~~resistent~~ resistant I can't remember how to spell that word. I always get this word wrong. I need to start using a spelling checker. Then I wouldn't have to keep stopping. Does a comma go here or not? Let's see now. I forgot what I was saying.

Keep Editing in Its Place

It is important that you write frequently without worrying about grammar and mechanics so that you develop fluency and so that an editing consultant can see what kinds of errors surface when you are just writing along. The conventions or rules you haven't yet internalized and thus need to learn or review will become evident once a consultant takes a look at your "automatic" writing. When you are writing in your notebook or working on an early draft of a writing project, do not try to write ideas down and edit at the same time. Editing at this point in your writing process will disrupt your thinking and inhibit the flow of words. Keep editing in its place—at the end of writing and just before you are ready to make public the product of your thinking.

Learn to Control Your Internal Editor

Your "internal editor" (a critical voice or voices) may try to intrude when you are writing to learn what you think or know or feel. Listen to the descriptions by some developing writers of their internal editors:

"My internal editor has a split personality. One [personality] will politely point out my errors and help me along. The other one is impatient and very quick to tell me to write anything down, forget all the errors, and be done with it."

"My internal editor is like a board of authors I have read. They all sit on a committee and expect only Pulitzer Prize–winning writing."

"Punctuation is my main internal editor. Deciding whether a comma or semicolon or colon should be used in a sentence usually stops my thought."

"My internal editor consists of a lot of questions. 'Is this correctly worded? Is this correctly punctuated? Are these thoughts and words relevant to what you're trying to communicate?'"

If your internal editor's voice is persistent, have a dialogue with this critic and have it out with the intruder. Write down what your internal editor is telling you and respond to it. Talk back to the editor. Then continue writing freely. It's important to learn to turn critical (counterproductive) voices on and off and be able to tell your critic to "BUG OFF!" You could make this dialogue an entry in a notebook about yourself as a developing writer, or you could file it away for reference for when you write about your writing progress.

Practice Editing Regularly

It's also important to practice editing regularly. Even though editing should be put off until the end of your writing process, you'll then have only a limited amount of time to edit and submit your final draft for publication. You'll need to practice editing regularly so that when it's time to edit and publish your writing, you'll be ready. You can both participate regularly in in-class editing workshops and practice on your own, checking your success with an editing consultant who could be another student, a tutor, or a teacher.

Getting Started Editing

Take an Editing-Approach Inventory

To identify your approach to editing, respond to the following questions:

1. Do you usually edit your writing (check it for grammatical and mechanical correctness)?
2. If you do, how do you go about editing? Do you use
   _____ a. the edit-as-you-write method,
   _____ b. the I'd-better-check-it-over-before-I-turn-it-in method, or
   _____ c. some other method?

Briefly describe (in writing) your approach to editing. Then meet with two other editors in your class, perhaps those who are already in a writing-project group with you. Compare your approaches to editing. Read or talk about what you wrote.

Use Your Speaking & Listening Ability to Help You Edit Your Writing

How will you know what to edit when it is time to edit your writing? You already know more than you think you know about grammatical and mechanical conventions. You learned to speak in sentences before you ever went to school and began the formal study of writing. And you could recognize where one sentence ended and another began even before you could utter them. It's likely, however, that your speaking ability is more developed than your writing ability. In fact, you can use your speaking and listening ability to help you edit your writing; try the following activity to see how.

Self-Editing Activity

Try reading aloud to yourself (or to another writer) a sample of writing you wrote without worrying about spelling, punctuation, or other mechanical or grammatical conventions. Listen to your "voice" in your writing; listen to how your writing sounds. Stop and make any changes that will help you read your writing better. Perhaps you'll want to add or delete a comma here, or change a word there, or rewrite a sentence that didn't sound quite right to you. Then reread your self-edited writing to hear whether it sounds better to you. Can you now read your writing better?

Critically Read Writing by Others to Help You Develop as a Writer & Editor

Although you probably don't often pay conscious attention when you read to the marking of sentences, the agreement of subjects and verbs, the use of the apostrophe, and so on, with a little effort you can see and understand and learn more about writing than you might think. Read the following excerpts and consider the questions that come after them.

In this excerpt, from *An American Childhood* (1987), Annie Dillard recollects her childhood growing up in Pittsburgh in the 1950s. One of the places she roamed was Frick Park, 380 acres of woods in residential Pittsburgh.

My father forbade me to go to Frick Park. He said bums lived there under bridges; they had been hanging around unnoticed since the Depression. My father was away all day; my mother said I could go to Frick Park if I never mentioned it.

I roamed Frick Park for many years. Our family moved from house to house, but we never moved so far I couldn't walk to Frick Park. I watched the men and women lawn bowling—so careful the player, so dull the game. After I got a bird book I found, in the deep woods, a downy woodpecker working a tree trunk; the woodpecker looked like a jackhammer man banging Edgerton Avenue to bits. I saw sparrows, robins, cardinals, juncos, chipmunks, squirrels, and—always disappointingly, emerging from their magnificent ruckus in the leaves—pedigreed dachshunds, which a woman across the street bred.

I never met anyone in the woods except the woman who walked her shiny dachshunds there, but I was cautious, and hoped I was braving danger. If a bum came after me I would disarm him with courtesy ("Good afternoon"). I would sneak him good food from home; we would bake potatoes together under his bridge; he would introduce me to his fellow bums; we would all feed the squirrels.

How do you see Frick Park through the youthful Dillard's eyes? Reread this piece (preferably aloud); listen to the rhythm and observe her use of punctuation. How does she use the semicolon? Why does she place a comma before "but"? Why does she set off "in the deep woods" with commas? Try reading the first half of that sentence without the commas. Why does she use dashes? Why doesn't she use more commas?

For the second excerpt, read (again) the passage that opens John McPhee's book *Oranges,* which really is about oranges and orange juice. You first read this passage at the beginning of this chapter, but with most of the punctuation removed. The story goes that McPhee started writing an article but encountered so much irresistible information that he found he had written a book.

The custom of drinking orange juice with breakfast is not very widespread, taking the world as a whole, and it is thought by many peoples to be a distinctly American habit. But many Danes drink it regularly with breakfast, and so do Hondurans, Filipinos, Jamaicans, and the wealthier citizens of Trinidad and Tobago. The day is started with orange juice in the Colombian Andes, and, to some extent, in Kuwait. Bolivians don't touch it at breakfast time, but they drink it steadily for the rest of the day. The "play lunch," or morning tea, that Australian children carry with them to school is usually an orange, peeled spirally halfway down, with the peel replaced around the fruit. The child unwinds the peel and holds the orange as if it were an ice-cream cone. People in Nepal almost never peel oranges, preferring to eat them in cut quarters, the way American athletes do.

How does McPhee's use of punctuation aid you as a reader? Why does he set off "taking the world as a whole" and "or morning tea"? Why does he place a comma before "but"? And so on.

Look at a passage from reading related to the writing project you are currently working on. Perhaps copy a passage and study the sentence structure and use of punctuation. Your teacher could also dictate some sentences from reading you are doing for class and then you could check your punctuation with the author's.

Developing an Editing System

Submit a Writing Sample to an Editing Consultant

Make a sample of your writing available to a teacher or tutor for a diagnosis of your editing needs. Collect a variety of writing samples (drafts, notebook entries, essay tests, writing in other courses) for further diagnosis and editing practice.

Have an Editing Consultation

Get help with editing your writing. Although you can get started editing your own writing by reading aloud what you wrote and using your voice and ear as a guide, you'll need some help identifying and grouping errors and exploring possible causes. Do you keep writing "to," for example, instead of "too" because you are confused about the usage, or do you know the difference but have gotten into the habit of writing one for the other? Do you place a comma between some sentences because the ideas are related and you want to bring them together for the reader, or because you don't know how to use the semicolon or the dash or other ways to combine ideas to get your meaning across? Do you always place commas between sentences, or just sometimes? If sometimes, when and why? Even though replacing a comma with a period between sentences will correct the problem, are you ready to learn other options and perhaps make a better choice for your readers? Sometimes a grammatically incorrect sentence (or an incomplete sentence) stems from a problem with writing and thinking—you haven't thought through what you want to say and, in this case, you need to rethink and rewrite an entire passage rather than mechanically correct a single sentence. A consultant (teacher or tutor) can help you get started thinking about editing your writing.

Keep an Editing Notebook

Take Notes

1. Document your errors, using the right side of your notebook.
2. Record your errors by category (subject-verb agreement, for example).
3. Label each kind of error on a separate page in your notebook. Allow several pages for frequent errors.
4. Record examples of each error from your own writing. Write out the full sentence.
5. Then write out corrections. If you need help, consult your writing instructor, a tutor, a handbook, or members of your writing group who do

not have the same problem and can help you. If you have written an ungrammatical, incomplete, or confusing sentence, you may not be able to make the sentence work simply by applying rules of grammar or punctuation. You may need to rewrite this and the surrounding sentences. If you are confused, ask for a consultation.

Make Notes

Make notes on the left side of your notebook opposite the errors you documented. Explore possible causes of each kind of error. You may have reasons that can be helpful to a teacher-tutor working with you.

Did you not know a particular rule or convention? Ricardo, for example, often confused plural and possessive forms:

Incorrect: Everybodies ear would start to hurt.

Correct: Everybody's ears would start to hurt.

Incorrect: I like people who find the most odd way's of making money.

Correct: I like people who find the oddest ways of making money. (Or, I like people who find the most odd ways of making money.)

(Other corrections were made here, but only one kind of error was the focus at the time.) Ricardo needed to study the formation and usage of plurals and possessives and to practice editing his own writing for this kind of error.

Are you incorrectly following some rule, or is your understanding of some rule faulty? What is your reasoning behind each error? In another writing sample, Ricardo was describing his first day of school at P.S. 92 in New York City. He had just arrived from Jamaica and spoke English with a heavy accent. He felt out of place. The children all stared at him, waiting for him to speak. Hardly anyone could understand him. His writing included these two problem sentences:

"As the day went on I refused to speak I was very quiet."

"After school while I was waiting for my mother on the steps. Randy and his friend came over to me and started picking on me."

Ricardo had begun to learn how to stop run-on sentences and combine sentences, but he was hesitant. In a consultation, he spoke about his notion of sentence length. He didn't think "I was very quiet" could be a sentence; he thought it was too short. And he didn't write "After school, while I was waiting for my mother on the steps, Randy and his friend came over to me and started picking on me" because he thought that would be too long for a sentence. So he stopped after "steps" when he should have paused (used a comma).

Make notes to help you with your editing (see sample entry of Figure A-1). Note grammar rules or misconceptions (about sentence length, for example).

Each time you record an error, review previous examples and, on the notemaking side, write about this error. Is this error new to you? Is it an error

Figure A.1   Sample Editing Notebook Entry: Comma Splices

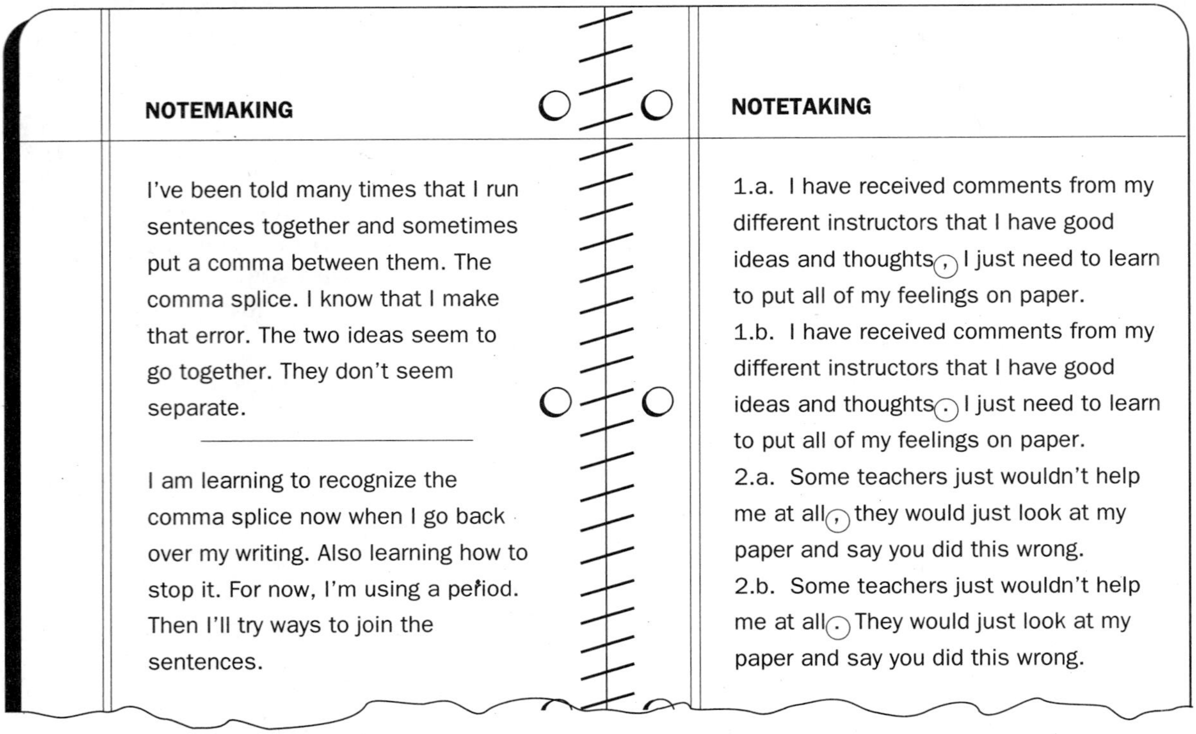

NOTEMAKING

I've been told many times that I run sentences together and sometimes put a comma between them. The comma splice. I know that I make that error. The two ideas seem to go together. They don't seem separate.

I am learning to recognize the comma splice now when I go back over my writing. Also learning how to stop it. For now, I'm using a period. Then I'll try ways to join the sentences.

NOTETAKING

1.a. I have received comments from my different instructors that I have good ideas and thoughts⌒ I just need to learn to put all of my feelings on paper.

1.b. I have received comments from my different instructors that I have good ideas and thoughts⌒ I just need to learn to put all of my feelings on paper.

2.a. Some teachers just wouldn't help me at all⌒ they would just look at my paper and say you did this wrong.

2.b. Some teachers just wouldn't help me at all⌒ They would just look at my paper and say you did this wrong.

you make frequently? Have you been told about this error before? What are you unclear about? How are you addressing this error? Keep returning to make notes about your understanding and progress. Practice editing for this error. Are you recording this error less often in your notebook? Understanding will not automatically eliminate your habit of making this error. You can control an error, however, through systematic editing over time.

Make an Editing List

Begin to make an editing list with the help of a teacher-tutor consultant. Base your list on categories listed in your notebook. You'll probably need help prioritizing your errors. Which one do you want to focus on first? Which one is most annoying to your readers?

Place your editing list in a section of your notebook and review it from time to time to see if it needs to be revised. Psychologists say that we can concentrate on five to seven items at a time. It would be unwise to try to edit for all kinds of errors. Your chances of being successful would be low. If, however, your concentrate on editing for a few items at a time, your chances of editing successfully will improve.

Some items can be removed from your list when you have gained control and find you are not recording a particular error. Then other items can be added. Also, different kinds of errors sometimes appear in different kinds of writing. When practicing editing or when editing a final draft, refer to your latest editing list and edit for one kind of error at a time, working with your notes.

Editor at Work: Ricardo Sewell

Read the following writing sample (an unedited notebook entry) submitted by one writer.

Train Story 1

When I use to take the A train to school their was a homeless man that I use to see every day. He was very strange. Just his appearance made people stare. Looking at him I would break out laughing. He had on gold and silver antenna. His glasses had little lights around the rims that was blinking off and on. He also had aluminum foil wrap around his legs and body he wore all black with gold painted sneakers. He had a multicolored Sax-a-phone. He walk in the train car and make an announcement. He would scream out loud that he was from outer space and he was sent here to terrorize us with his music. And if we didn't give him money he will play his music. Every one will start laughing and he would say you making me mad than he would play his sax. The music was'n really terrorizing. It was hurting my ears I wanted to give him money so he could leave the car. Everybodies ear would start to hurt and everyone would pull out their money and give it to him. His music really worked because people were giving him so he can leave the train car. I admire him because he got what he wanted the money. I like people who find the most odd way's of making money.

Ricardo

Based on the sample of writing Ricardo submitted, his teacher-consultant made this editing list:

1. run-on sentences
2. +ed (past-tense marker)
3. plurals vs. possessives
4. spelling
5. subject-verb agreement (was, were)

This editing list is not complete; Ricardo made five or six other kinds of errors in his writing sample. The list is only a starting point that includes the more prominent errors. When Ricardo looked at his list in class, he did not understand what all the items meant. Through editing consultations in and outside of class and in editing workshops, he learned to identify the kinds of errors he made and the persistent patterns of his errors, to work with an editing list, and to control for these kinds of errors. Other samples of his writing were reviewed subsequently, and his editing list was revised periodically.

Practice Editing

Edit for one kind of error at a time; then return to your editing list to identify and control for another kind of error.

Why edit for only one kind of error at a time? Why not edit for two or three items or everything at once? Concentrating on one kind of error will increase your chances of editing successfully. If you are editing for one kind of error (subject-verb agreement, for example) and notice another kind of error (a spelling error, perhaps), acknowledge the error. Underline the error or make a check mark by it; return to it later to correct it, and also see if the error is on your editing list. If it isn't, add it then.

Keep editing for one specific kind of error. Do not edit for commas in general, for example; edit for a specific comma rule. If there is more than one way to correct an error, consider your options and choose the most effective one. You can actually work very quickly when you scan for only one kind of error at a time. Think of yourself as a computer objectively searching for a single kind of error. Don't scatter your attention and try to edit for several items at once; editing for a single kind of error will increase your chances of editing successfully.

Edit from your last sentence to your first sentence. Why read your sentences in reverse order? When you are learning to edit your own writing and are just developing a system for editing, reading from the last sentence to your first helps you detach yourself momentarily from your writing and read objectively for a particular kind of error. Cover the rest of your sentences with a sheet of paper and focus your attention on one sentence at a time; look for a single problem with grammar, mechanics, or usage. Edit sentence by sentence until you get to the first sentence in the writing. If you find that a sentence is unclear, stop and put the sentence back in context by rereading several of the surrounding sentences. Perhaps the sentence (or several sentences) needs to be rewritten.

If you are using a computer, you can edit "on screen," using the blinking cursor as a guide, but you should also make a printout and edit it. Frequently it's easier to catch errors on printed copy. At least doublecheck all the "on-screen" editing you do.

Check Your Editing with Another Editor

Have another editor check your success as an editor of your own writing. When you have finished editing, label the kinds of errors you were trying to control so that another editor can check the editing you did. Ask the editor to put a check mark next to any line in which there may be an editing error. Discuss your editing. If the editor is uncertain about any particular rule or convention, ask for a consultation from your teacher or another consultant.

Make notes about your overall progress and put them after your current editing list. Note what you practiced editing, the date, your success, and any confusion you had. If you made an editing error, log in the error and your correction of it. Keep an individual record of errors, and also make notes. Be sure to include the date. You can use this record to help you decide what to include in your editing list and also for reference when editing.

Review your editing list. Do you need to keep all the items on the list, or can some of them be removed? Do you need to add any? Should you change the order?

Get into the Habit of Editing

After you have successfully edited several times for a particular kind of error (run-on sentences, for example), do not assume that you will never write run-on sentences again. Practice editing for this error from time to time, for it takes time and effort to break undesirable habits. With repeated editing practice, errors will disappear, only to reappear (perhaps) when you are writing under pressure. Keep in practice; maintaining the good editing habits you form will help you communicate accurately with your readers.

Assess Your Editing Progress

To monitor the improvement in your editing skills, answer the following questions:

1. How successful have you been in your editing efforts?
2. If you were not 100 percent successful, why not? Did you just gloss over any errors, or are there still some rules or conventions you do not understand? Clear up any confusion by checking with an editing consultant.
3. How much, and in what way, has your editing ability improved?
4. Have you consistently recorded your progress in your editing notebook?

Setting Up Editing Workshops

& of course it's useful to know the basic rules of grammar & spelling before you break them. Any rule that is broken must be a conscious defiance.

Ursule Molinaro

Just as you break the class into writing workshop groups, you can also break into editing workshop groups. You can begin in a workshop by identifying errors and making an editing list. Then you can practice editing, using the list you made.

If you have problems with sentence structure, what kinds of problems do you have? If you are running sentences together or joining them with a comma (which is not conventional in Standard English), then practice editing for that kind of error. How can you correct the error? What are your options? Which option is most effective, considering what you want to communicate and how you want your writing to sound?

You may want to review sentence coordination and subordination and related punctuation conventions as a class, and then practice editing. This basic review and whole-group work can help you think about sentence relationships, effectiveness, and correctness, and will also help you learn a system for editing that you can apply to your own writing. Your instructor could conduct whole- or small-group editing activities, including the review of certain conventions. A list of perhaps ten "problem" sentences could be compiled that are related to the conventions you are reviewing and written by students in your class. If the writer is present, the writer could select a preference.

Editing can then be individualized. Everyone may need to learn to edit for subject-verb agreement, for example, but only a few may need to edit for "-ed" endings on the past tense of regular verbs. Perhaps you write unconventional sentences, sentences that do not make sense to most readers and cannot be fixed simply by adding a word or a mark of punctuation. Such sentences may need to be rewritten because what you had in mind does not match what appeared on the page. Talking with others in an editing workshop group can help you express what you want to say. Then you can rewrite, and try out, a new sentence or passage on your writing group.

Bring your editing list to an editing workshop. Work in a group of three—perhaps the same group of people who are in your writing group. Edit your writing for one or more kinds of errors and exchange edited writing with group members. Check each other's editing. If you are unsure, ask for an editing consultation. (Perhaps a consultant can move from one group to another, or certain class members may be designated consultants for certain kinds of errors or problems.) At the end of each workshop, remember to make notes in your editing notebook about your success and what you still need to work on.

Whole-group and small-group editing workshops, as well as individual editing consultations in and out of class, can be held throughout the term. Once you have something you want to communicate, once you have some writing you care to present, editing your own writing is surprisingly easy (if you work systematically) and very rewarding. You'll develop confidence in your ability to edit and will become less dependent on others.